The ARRL
General Class
License Manual
For Ham Radio

NEW! Eighth Edition

All You Need to Pass Your General Class Exam!

By **Ward Silver NØAX**

Contributing Editor: Mark Wilson, K1RO

Production Staff: **Jodi Morin, KA1JPA,** Assistant Production Supervisor, Layout
Michelle Bloom, WB1ENT, Production Supervisor, Layout
Maty Weinberg, KB1EIB, Editorial Assistant
David Pingree, N1NAS, Senior Technical Illustrator
Sue Fagan, KB1OKW, Graphic Design Supervisor, Cover Design

ARRL The national association for **AMATEUR RADIO®**
225 Main Street, Newington, CT 06111-1494
www.arrl.org

Upper left cover photo by: Don Decker, KAØGWS
Center cover photo by: Bob Inderbitzen, NQ1R

This book may be used for General class license exams given beginning July 1, 2015. *QST* and the ARRL website (**www.arrl.org**) will have news about any rules changes affecting the General class license or any of the material in this book.

We strive to produce books without errors. Sometimes mistakes do occur, however. When we become aware of problems in our books (other than obvious typographical errors), we post corrections on the ARRL website. If you think you have found an error, please check **www.arrl. org/general-class-license-manual** for corrections. If you don't find a correction there, please let us know by sending an e-mail to **pubsfdbk@arrl.org**.

The ARRL General Class License Manual **ON THE WEB**

www.arrl.org/general-class-license-manual

Visit *The ARRL General Class License Manual* home on the web for additional resources.

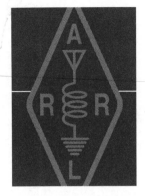

Contents

Foreword

Welcome to the eighth edition of the ARRL's *General Class License Manual*, the premier guide to passing the General class Amateur Radio examination. You will have a lot of company as you begin to communicate across the country and around the world on the HF bands. Nearly one quarter of all amateurs hold a General class license as of early 2015 and half of all hams have General class or higher HF privileges.

If your interests include public service, adding General privileges increases your capabilities dramatically! You can experiment with the many new digital modes being invented and used by hams, begin working toward achieving operating awards and explore all the interesting opportunities of radio on the HF bands. You won't regret upgrading from Technician to General as you will get a lot more out of using your new privileges than the amount of study required to pass the test.

Once you have upgraded to General class, you can participate in the largest of all amateur volunteer examiner (VE) programs and become certified by the ARRL VEC. General class licensees can "give back" by volunteering as a VE for Technician class license exams. You can learn more about providing this valuable and appreciated service at **www.arrl.org/become-an-arrl-ve**.

In order to help you make good use of your new privileges, the ARRL *General Class License Manual* does more than just help you memorize the answers in the question pool. Each topic is addressed in sufficient detail to help you learn the "why" behind the rules, the "what" of basic electronics, and the "how" of amateur operating practices. There are drawings, photographs, and tables to guide you in your studies. If you would like a more concise study guide, the ARRL *General Class Q & A* is a companion to this book, presenting each question and a short explanation of the correction answer. The pair is a powerful one-two punch to help you pass the exam.

Even the best study material can't address all of the things you'll encounter as a General, so the book's companion website (**www.arrl.org/general-class-license-manual**) provides supplemental information and links to resources that go beyond the exam questions. This book and the website also list a number of other useful references that you'll find especially helpful in translating your new privileges into on-the-air operating.

Whatever your preference in Amateur Radio, there are books and supplies in the ARRL's "Radio Amateurs Library" that support almost any amateur operating practice. Contact the Publication Sales Office at ARRL Headquarters to request the latest publications catalog or to place and order. (You can reach us by phone — 860-594-0200; by fax — 860-594-0303 and by email via **pubsales@arrl.org**. The complete publications catalog is on-line, too, at the ARRL's home page: **www.arrl.org**. Look for the "Products" window, browse the latest news about Amateur Radio, and tap into the wealth of services provided by the ARRL to amateurs.

Thanks for making the decision to upgrade — we hope to hear you using your new General class privileges and enjoying more of the many opportunities Amateur Radio has to offer. Good luck!

David Sumner, K1ZZ
Chief Executive Officer
Newington, Connecticut
March 2015

ARRL Membership Benefits

QST Monthly Magazine

QST covers new trends and the latest technology, fiction, humor, news, club activities, rules and regulations, special events, and much more. Here is some of what you will find every month:

- Informative product reviews of the newest radios and accessories
- A monthly conventions and hamfest calendar
- A public service column that keeps you up to date on the public service efforts hams are providing around the country and shows you how you can join in this satisfying aspect of our hobby
- Eclectic Technology, a monthly column that covers emerging Amateur Radio and commercial technology
- A broad spectrum of articles in every issue ranging from challenging topics to straightforward, easy-to-understand projects

ARRL members also get preferred subscription rates for QEX, the ARRL Forum for Communications Experimenters.

Members-Only Web Services

- **QST Digital Edition**
  All ARRL members can access the online digital edition of QST. Enjoy enhanced content, convenient access and a more interactive experience. Apps for Apple and Android devices are also available.

- **QST Archive and Periodicals Search**
  Browse ARRL's extensive online QST archive. A searchable index for QEX and NCJ is also available.

- **Free E-Newsletters**
  Subscribe to a variety of ARRL e-newsletters and e-mail announcements: ham radio news, radio clubs, public service, contesting and more!

- **Product Review Archive**
  Search for, and download, QST Product Reviews published from 1980 to present.

- **E-Mail Forwarding Service**
  E-mail sent to your **arrl.net** address will be forwarded to any e-mail account you specify.

- **Customized ARRL.org home page**
  Customize your home page to see local ham radio events, clubs and news.

- **ARRL Member Directory**
  Connect with other ARRL members via a searchable online Member Directory. Share profiles, photos and more with members who have similar interests.

Technical Information Service (TIS)

Get answers on a variety of technical and operating topics through ARRL's Technical Information Service. Our experts can help you overcome hurdles and answer all your questions.

Member Benefit Programs and Discounts

- **ARRL "Special Risk" Ham Radio Equipment Insurance Plan**
  Insurance is available to protect you from loss or damage to your station, antennas and mobile equipment by lightning, theft, accident, fire, flood, tornado, and other national disasters.

- **Liberty Mutual® Auto and Home Insurance**
  ARRL members may qualify for special group discounts on home and auto insurance.

- **The ARRL Visa Signature® Card**
  Show your ham radio pride with the ARRL Visa credit card. You earn great rewards and every purchase supports ARRL programs and services.

Outgoing QSL Service

Let us be your mail carrier and handle your overseas QSLing chores. The savings you accumulate through this service alone can pay your membership dues many times over.

Continuing Education/Publications

Find classes to help you prepare to pass your license exam or upgrade your license, learn more about Amateur Radio activities, or train for emergency communications or public service. ARRL also offers hundreds of books, CDs and videos on the technical, operating, and licensing facets of Amateur Radio.

Regulatory Information Branch

Reach out to our Regulatory Information Branch for information on FCC and regulatory questions; problems with antenna, tower and zoning restrictions; and reciprocal licensing procedures.

ARRL as an Advocate

ARRL supports legislation in Washington, D.C. that preserves and protects access to existing Amateur Radio frequencies as a natural resource for the enjoyment of all hams. Members contribute to the efforts to preserve our privileges.

ARRL
The national association for
AMATEUR RADIO®

Join ARRL and experience the BEST of Ham Radio!

ARRL Membership Benefits and Services:

- *QST* magazine — your monthly source of news, easy-to-read product reviews, rules and regulations, special events and more. Enjoy the digital edition of *QST* and apps for Apple and Android devices.

- Technical Information Service — access to problem-solving experts!

- Members-only Web services — find information fast, anytime!

- And much more

Join Today and Select a Free Gift!

ARRL The national association for **AMATEUR RADIO®**

What is Amateur Radio?

Perhaps you've picked up this book in the library or from a bookstore shelf and are wondering what Amateur Radio is all about. You may have encountered a "ham" performing public service or maybe you have a friend or relative who is a ham. Read on for a short explanation.

Amateur Radio or "ham radio" has been part of wireless technology since the very beginning. Amateur experimenters — known affectionately as hams — were operating right along with Marconi in the early part of the 20th century. They have helped advance the state-of-the-art in radio, television, digital communication and dozens of other wireless services since then, right up to the present day. There are more than 700,000 amateurs in the United States and several million more around the world!

Formally, Amateur Radio in the United States is an official communications service, administered by the Federal Communications Commission or FCC. Amateur Radio is intended to foster electronics and radio experimentation, provide emergency backup communication, encourage private citizens to train and practice operating, and even spread the goodwill of person-to-person contact over the airwaves.

BOB STARKENBURG, W4TTX

BOB GAULT, KD4NEC

Direction-finding or "DF-ing" is a popular outdoor activity that combines Amateur Radio and orienting. This Tennessee club made it a club project to build inexpensive DF-ing antennas.

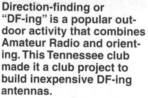

Field Day is an opportunity for individual hams and clubs to exercise their emergency communications skills while operating from portable stations. The Raleigh (NC) Amateur Radio Society, W4DW, set up eight stations that operated around the clock.

Who is a Ham and What Do Hams Do?

Anyone can be a ham — there are no age limits or physical requirements that prevent anyone from passing their license exam and getting on the air. Kids as young as five years old have passed the basic exam and there are many hams out there over the age of 100.

Once you get on the air and start meeting other hams you'll find a wide range of capabilities and interests. Of course, there are many technically skilled hams who work as engineers, scientists or technicians. But there are just as many who do not have a deep technical background. You're just as likely to encounter writers, public safety personnel, students, farmers, truck drivers — anyone with an interest in personal communications over the radio.

The activities of Amateur Radio are incredibly varied. Amateurs who hold the Technician class license — the first license for hams in the US — communicate primarily with local and regional amateurs using relay stations called repeaters. Known as "Techs," many sharpen their skills of operating mobile and portable stations, often joining emergency communications teams. Some choose to focus on the burgeoning wireless data networks assembled and used by hams around the world. Techs can make use of the growing number of Amateur Radio satellites, built and launched by hams along with the commercial "birds." Technicians transmit their own television signals, push the limits of radio wave propagation through the atmosphere and experiment with microwaves. Hams hold most of the world records for long-distance communication on microwave frequencies, in fact!

By upgrading their license to General class, Technicians gain additional operating privileges to use signals that travel worldwide to make direct contacts with foreign hams. No Internet, phone systems or data networks are required. It's just you, your radio, and the ionosphere — the upper layers of the Earth's atmosphere!

Hams use many types of signals to communicate. Along with voice signals similar to AM and FM broadcast stations, hams send digital data across radio links. Their innovations are making significant contributions to this important technology. And, yes, Morse code is alive and well on the "ham bands" with many thousands of practitioners of "the code" on the air every day. All of these different types of signals are part of today's Amateur Radio — voice, data, video, Morse — whatever you prefer.

A common element for amateurs is that all of their operation is noncommercial, especially for volunteers who provide emergency communications. Hams pursue the hobby purely for personal enjoyment and to advance their skills, taking satisfaction from providing valuable services to their fellow citizens. This is especially valuable after natural disasters such as hurricanes and earthquakes when commercial systems are knocked out for a while. Amateur operators rush in to provide backup communications until the regular systems are restored. All this is available to you with a little study and a simple exam!

Public service is an important aspect of the amateur service. In support of the Oklahoma City Memorial Marathon, more than 75 amateurs provided communications for the event. Brian Teters, AE5MT (front), Andrew Wolfe, KE5YBC, and Richard Sharp, KE5NCR (back) worked together to coordinate the runner pick-up vehicles.

COURTESY BILL VANDERHEIDE, N7OU

Making contacts with exotic locations — called "DXing" — has always been a thrilling part of Amateur Radio. It's even more fun to travel to such a spot as Bill Vanderheide, N7OU, did on his adventure to the Pacific island of Tokelau, operating as ZK3OU.

Want to Find Out More?

If you'd like to find out more about Amateur Radio in general, there is lots of information available on the Internet. A good place to start is on the American Radio Relay League's (ARRL)

Amateur Radio is unique in that hams are encouraged to build and use their own equipment. This sensing unit for the output power of a transmitter or amplifier, built by Ed Toal, N9MW, is a good example of useful "home-brewing" widespread in ham radio.

ham radio introduction web page at **www. arrl.org/new-to-ham-radio**. Books such as *Ham Radio for Dummies* and *Getting Started With Ham Radio* will help you "fill in the blanks" as you learn more.

Along with books and web pages, there is no better way to learn about ham radio than to meet your local amateur operators. It is quite likely that no matter where you live in the United States, there is a ham radio club in your area, even several! The ARRL provides a club lookup service at **www.arrl.org/ find-a-club** where you can find a club just by entering your Zip code or state. Carrying on the tradition of mutual assistance, many clubs make helping newcomers to ham radio a part of their charter.

If this sounds like hams are confident that you'll find their activities interesting, you're right! Amateur Radio is much more than just talking on a radio, as you'll find out. It's an opportunity to dive into the fascinating world of radio communications, electronics, and computers as deeply as you wish. Welcome!

When to Expect New Books

A Question Pool Committee (QPC) consisting of representatives from the various Volunteer Examiner Coordinators (VECs) prepares the license question pools. The QPC establishes a schedule for revising and implementing new Question Pools. The current Question Pool revision schedule is as follows:

Question Pool	Current Study Guides	Valid Through
Technician (Element 2)	The ARRL Ham Radio License Manual, 3rd Edition ARRL's Tech Q&A, 6th Edition	June 30, 2018
General (Element 3)	The ARRL General Class License Manual, 8th edition ARRL's General Q&A, 5th Edition	June 30, 2019
Amateur Extra (Element 4)	The ARRL Extra Class License Manual, 10th Edition ARRL's Extra Q&A, 3rd Edition	June 30, 2016

As new question pools are released, ARRL will produce new study materials before the effective date of the new Pools. Until then, the current Question Pools will remain in use, and current ARRL study materials, including this book, will help you prepare for your exam.

As the new Question Pool schedules are confirmed, the information will be published in QST and on the ARRL website at **www.arrl.org**.

Online Review and Practice Exams

Use this book with the *ARRL Exam Review for Ham Radio* to review material you are learning chapter-by-chapter. Take randomly generated practice exams using questions from the actual examination question pool. You won't have any surprises on exam day! Go to **www.arrl.org/examreview**.

About the ARRL

The seed for Amateur Radio was planted in the 1890s, when Guglielmo Marconi began his experiments in wireless telegraphy. Soon he was joined by dozens, then hundreds, of others who were enthusiastic about sending and receiving messages through the air—some with a commercial interest, but others solely out of a love for this new communications medium. The United States government began licensing Amateur Radio operators in 1912.

By 1914, there were thousands of Amateur Radio operators—hams—in the United States. Hiram Percy Maxim, a leading Hartford, Connecticut inventor and industrialist, saw the need for an organization to band together this fledgling group of radio experimenters. In May 1914 he founded the American Radio Relay League (ARRL) to meet that need.

Today ARRL, with more than 166,000 members, is the largest organization of radio amateurs in the United States. The ARRL is a not-for-profit organization that:
• promotes interest in Amateur Radio communications and experimentation
• represents US radio amateurs in legislative matters, and
• maintains fraternalism and a high standard of conduct among Amateur Radio operators.

At ARRL headquarters in the Hartford suburb of Newington, the staff helps serve the needs of members. ARRL is also International Secretariat for the International Amateur Radio Union, which is made up of similar societies in 150 countries around the world.

ARRL publishes the monthly journal *QST*, as well as newsletters and many publications covering all aspects of Amateur Radio. Its headquarters station, W1AW, transmits bulletins of interest to radio amateurs and Morse code practice sessions. The ARRL also coordinates an extensive field organization, which includes volunteers who provide technical information and other support services for radio amateurs as well as communications for public-service activities. In addition, ARRL represents US amateurs with the Federal Communications Commission and other government agencies in the US and abroad.

Membership in ARRL means much more than receiving *QST* each month. In addition to the services already described, ARRL offers membership services on a personal level, such as the Technical Information Service—where members can get answers by phone, email or the ARRL website, to all their technical and operating questions.

Full ARRL membership (available only to licensed radio amateurs) gives you a voice in how the affairs of the organization are governed. ARRL policy is set by a Board of Directors (one from each of 15 Divisions). Each year, one-third of the ARRL Board of Directors stands for election by the full members they represent. The day-to-day operation of ARRL HQ is managed by an Executive Vice President and his staff.

No matter what aspect of Amateur Radio attracts you, ARRL membership is relevant and important. There would be no Amateur Radio as we know it today were it not for the ARRL. We would be happy to welcome you as a member! (An Amateur Radio license is not required for Associate Membership.) For more information about ARRL and answers to any questions you may have about Amateur Radio, write or call:

ARRL—The national association for Amateur Radio
225 Main Street
Newington CT 06111-1494
Voice: 860-594-0200
Fax: 860-594-0259
E-mail: **hq@arrl.org**
Internet: **www.arrl.org**

Prospective new amateurs call (toll-free):
800-32-NEW HAM (800-326-3942)
You can also contact us via e-mail at **newham@arrl.org**
or check out the ARRL website at **www.arrl.org**

Chapter 1

Introduction

In this chapter, you'll learn about:
- **Expanded privileges enjoyed by Generals**
- **Reasons to upgrade from Technician**
- **Requirements and study materials for the General exam**
- **How to prepare for your exam**
- **How to find an exam session**
- **Where to find more resources**

Welcome to *The ARRL General Class License Manual*! Earning your General class license opens up the full Amateur Radio experience — the excitement and challenge of traditional shortwave operation along with the VHF+ and limited HF privileges enjoyed by Technician class licensees. You'll gain access to the broadest and most capable set of communication privileges available to private citizens. Only Amateur Extra licensees have more.

This study guide will not only teach you the answers to the General class exam questions, but will also provide explanations and supporting information. That way, you'll find it easier to learn the basic principles involved. That knowledge helps you remember what you've learned. The book is full of useful facts and figures, so you'll want to keep it handy after you pass the test and are using your new privileges.

1.1 The General Class License and Amateur Radio

Most of this book's readers will have already earned their Technician class license. Some may have been a ham for quite a while and others may be new to the hobby. In either case, you're to be commended for making the effort to upgrade. We'll try to make it easy to pass your exam by teaching you the fundamentals and rationale behind each question and answer.

REASONS TO UPGRADE

If you're browsing through this book, trying to decide whether to upgrade, here are a few good reasons:

● *More frequencies.* The General class licensee has access to lot more space in which to enjoy Amateur Radio! See **Figure 1.1** for details of all of the frequencies available to General licensees.

Rusty Epps, W6OAT, mentors Rodna Presley, KJ6GVQ, at the Palo Alto Amateur Radio Association, W6ARA, Field Day operation. Field Day is the largest event in Amateur Radio as thousands of North American hams practice the skill of operating from portable stations. [James W. Brown, K9YC, photo]

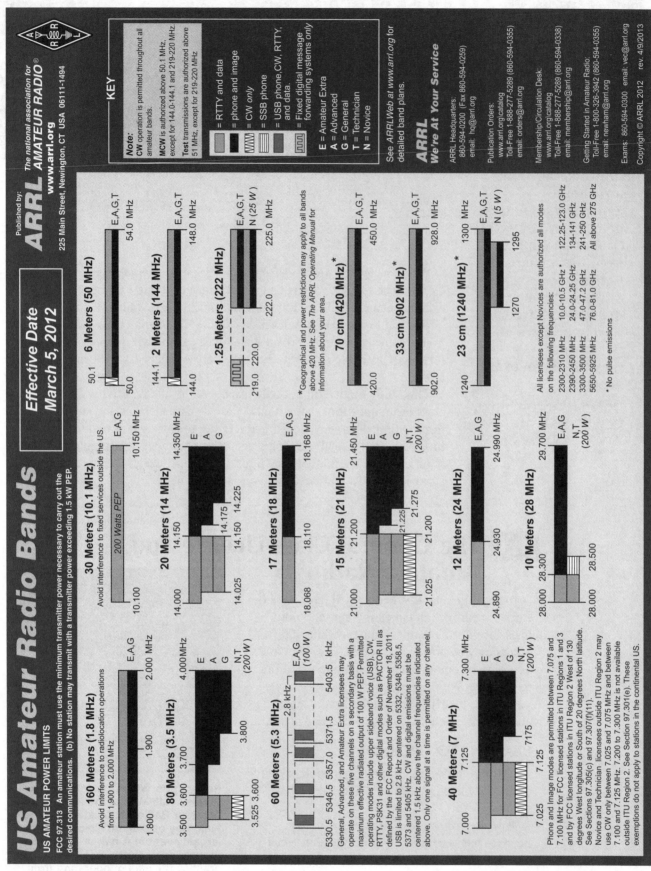

Figure 1.1 — Amateur operating privileges.

Dr Carol Milazzo, KP4MD, operated in the 2014 ARRL January VHF Contest using software-defined radios (SDR) and transverters. She entered the Single-Operator, 3-Band category, making contacts on 50, 144, and 432 MHz. [Dr Carol Milazzo, KP4MD, photo]

- *More communications options.* Those new frequencies give you many more ways to make contacts on new modes and with new groups of hams. Your new skills are also valuable to your club or public service team.
- *New technical opportunities.* With your new privileges come new ways of assembling and operating a station. The effects of the ionosphere and solar conditions will become second nature to you. Your improved technical understanding of how radio works will make you a more knowledgeable and skilled operator.
- *More fun.* Take part in ragchewing (conversational contacts) with new acquaintances worldwide. Join the chase of DXing (searching for distant stations) and contesting or *radiosport* (on-the-air competitions) which attract more hams every year.

Not only does upgrading grant you more privileges, but your experiences will be much broader. You'll enjoy the hobby in ways that give you a whole new view of ham radio. The extra privileges are well worth your effort!

GENERAL CLASS OVERVIEW

There are three classes of license being granted today: Technician, General and Amateur Extra. Each grants the licensee more and more privileges, meaning access to frequencies and modes. **Table 1.1** shows the elements for each of the amateur licenses as of early 2015.

As shown in **Table 1.2**, to qualify for a General class license, you must have passed Elements 2 (Technician) and 3 (General). If you hold a Technician license, you are credited with Element 2, so you don't have to take it again. If you currently hold a Technician license issued before March 21,

Table 1.1
Amateur License Class Examinations

License Class	Element Required	Number of Questions
Technician	2 (Written)	35 (passing is 26 correct)
General	3 (Written)	35 (passing is 26 correct)
Amateur Extra	4 (Written)	50 (passing is 38 correct)

Table 1.2
Exam Elements Needed to Qualify for a General Class License

Current License*	Exam Requirements	Study Materials
None or Novice	Technician (Element 2)	The ARRL Ham Radio License Manual and/or ARRL's Tech Q&A
	General (Element 3)	The ARRL General Class License Manual and/or ARRL's General Q&A
Technician (issued on or after March 21, 1987)**	General (Element 3)	The ARRL General Class License Manual and/or ARRL's General Q&A

*Individuals who were previously licensed as a General, Advanced, or Extra Class may receive credit for those exam elements by presenting documentation of having been licensed and then passing Element 2 (Technician).
**Individuals who qualified for the Technician license before March 21, 1987, will be able to upgrade to General class by providing documentary proof to a Volunteer Examiner Coordinator, paying an application fee and completing NCVEC Quick Form 605. No additional exam is required.

Mobile operation provides an opportunity for combining travel adventures with some ham radio fun. Gene Chapline, K5YFL, participates in the FJ Summit annual back-country off-road event, shown here on a road through Corkscrew Gulch in the San Juan Mountains. [Josie Chapline, K5JTC, photo]

Morse code operating is alive and well on the amateur bands. Combining skill and efficiency, Morse or "CW" is a favorite mode for many hams. The WB9Z multioperator team (L-R) of Jerry, KE9I; Don K9NR; Val, NV9L; Mike, K9XZ; and Carl, K9CS; enjoys entering the ARRL 160 Meter Contest which is an all-Morse event. [Jerry Rosalius, WB9Z, photo]

1987, you can upgrade to General simply by going to a test session with proof of being licensed before that date.

If you were previously licensed as a General, Advanced, or Extra but your license expired, you can still receive credits for those elements you passed before. Present documentation of your previous license (a copy of the license or a *Callbook* copy, for example) and pass the Element 2 exam (Technician) to receive the necessary credits. Welcome back!

The 35 question multiple-choice test for Element 3 is more comprehensive than the Element 2 Technician exam because you'll be granted wider privileges. As we mentioned before, the General class licensee gains access to nearly all amateur frequencies. There are no bands on which a General class ham can't transmit! As a more experienced ham, your wider knowledge will allow you to experiment with, modify and build equipment and antennas to improve your communications abilities.

Want More Information?

Looking for more information about General class instruction in your area? Are you ready to take the General class exam? Do you need a list of ham radio clubs, instructors or examiners in your local area? The following web pages are very helpful in finding the local resources you need to successfully pass your General exam:

✔ **www.arrl.org/general-class-license-manual** — the website that supports this book

✔ **www.arrl.org/find-a-club** — a search page to find ARRL-Affiliated clubs

✔ **www.arrl.org/find-an-amateur-radio-license-exam-session** — the ARRL/VEC exam session search page

✔ **www.arrl.org/technical-information-service** — the ARRL's Technical Information Service is an excellent resource

✔ **www.ac6v.com** — a website that compiles links to hundreds of ham radio web pages

On any of the popular social media services such as YouTube, Facebook, Google Groups, or Yahoogroups, search for "ham radio" or "amateur radio" to find dozens of helpful resources.

MORSE CODE

Although you no longer need to learn Morse code for any license exam, Morse code or "CW" has been part of the rich amateur tradition for 100 years and many hams still use it extensively. If you are interested in learning Morse code, the ARRL has a complete set of resources listed on its web page at **www.arrl.org/learning-morse-code**.

Computer software and on-the-air *code practice* sessions are available for personal training and practice. Organizations such as FISTS (**www.fists.org**) — an operator's style of sending is referred to as his or her "fist" — help hams learn Morse code and will even help you find a "code buddy" to share the learning with you.

1.2 How to Use this Book

To earn a General class Amateur Radio license, you must pass (or receive credit for) FCC Elements 2 (Technician class) and 3 (General class). This book is designed to help you prepare for and pass the Element 3 written exam. If you do not already have a Technician license, you will need some additional study materials for the Element 2 (Technician) exam.

The Element 3 exam consists of 35 questions about Amateur Radio rules, theory and practice, as well as some basic electronics. A passing grade is 74%, so you must answer 26 of the 35 questions correctly.

The General Class License Manual begins with chapters on the operating practices you'll encounter on the HF bands and the applicable rules and regulations. The following chapters delve into radio technology — Circuits and Components, Radio Signals and Equipment, Digital Modes, Antennas, and Propagation. Radio and electrical safety is covered in its own chapter. At the back of the book you'll find a large Glossary of radio terminology. It is followed by the Question Pool, which includes the complete set of exam questions and answers.

Each section may begin with a short review of related material from the Technician exam and has practical examples and information you can use for reference later. As you learn about each topic, the set of exam questions covered in that section is listed so that you can immediately review what you learned. Turn to the Question Pool and confirm that you can answer those questions before moving on.

The ARRL also maintains a special web page for General class students at **www.arrl.org/general-class-license-manual**. Organized in the same manner as this text, you can go to the web page and find helpful supplements and clarifications to the material in the book. The useful and interesting online references listed there put you one click away from related and useful information.

If you are taking a licensing class, help your instructors by letting them know about areas in which you need help. They want you to learn as thoroughly and quickly as possible, so don't hold back with your questions. Similarly, if you find the material particularly clear or helpful, tell them that, too, so it can be used in the next class!

Rita Haberman, NH6RH, recently operated from Nairobi, Kenya (5Z4) with Peter Vekinis, KH6VP, on a vacation-style all-solar QRP (low-power) expedition. They used a simple wire antenna and a 20 W solar panel to power the station. [Peter Vekinis, KH6VP, photo]

WHAT WE ASSUME ABOUT YOU

You don't have to be a technical guru or an expert operator to upgrade to General class! As you progress through the

David Johnston, KD8BQN, provided communications support during Colorado wildfires. Hams organize and practice emergency communications operation all year long as part of their commitment to provide public service. [Robert Strieby, WØPT, photo]

material, you'll build on the basic science of radio and electricity that you mastered for Technician. No advanced mathematics is introduced and for help with math an online tutorial information is available at **www.arrl.org/general-class-license-manual**. As with the Technician license, mastering rules and regulations will require learning some new words and remembering a few numbers. You should have a basic calculator, which you'll also be allowed to use during the license exam.

Advanced Students

If you have some background in radio, perhaps as a technician or trained operator, you may be able to short-circuit some of the sections. To find out, turn to the list of review questions in the text that show the exam questions for each topic. Turn to the Question Pool and if you can answer the questions correctly, move to the next topic in the text. It's common for technically minded students to focus on the rules and regulations while students with an operating background tend to need the technical material more. Whichever you may be, be sure that you can answer the questions because any question could certainly be on the test!

Self-Study or Classroom Students

The ARRL General Class License Manual can be used either by an individual student studying on his or her own, or as part of a licensing class taught by an instructor. If you're part of a class, the instructor will guide you through the book, section by section. The solo student can move at any pace and in any convenient order. You'll find that studying with a friend makes learning the material more fun as you help each other over the rough spots.

Taking part in the 2014 European Radio-sport Team Championship are the bronze medal team from Estonia — ES1XQ, ES5HTA, ES6AXS — and onlookers LY2EN and LY5AT from Lithuania. Sponsored by Youngsters On The Air (YOTA), the event was held in Finland with 75 young operators from 15 European countries. [Martti Laine, OH2BH, photo]

Don't hesitate to ask for help! Your instructor can provide information on anything you find difficult. Classroom students may find asking their fellow students to be helpful. If you're studying on your own, there are resources for you, too! If you can't find the answer in the book or at the website, email your question to the ARRL's New Ham Desk, **newham@arrl.org**. The ARRL's experts will answer directly or connect you with another ham who can answer your questions.

USING THE QUESTION POOL

As you complete each topic, be sure to review each of the exam questions highlighted in the text. This will tell you which areas need a little more study time. When you understand the answer to each of the questions, move on. Resist the temptation to just memorize the answers. Doing so leaves you without the real understanding that will make your new General class privileges enjoyable and useful. *The General Class License Manual* covers every one of the exam questions, so you can be sure you're ready at exam time.

When using the Question Pool, cover or fold over the answers at the edge of the page to be sure you really do understand the question. Each question also includes a cross-reference back to the section of the book that covers that topic. If you don't completely understand the question or answer, please go back and review that section. The ARRL's condensed study guide, *ARRL's General Q&A*, also provides short explanations for each one of the exam questions.

ONLINE PRACTICE EXAMS

When you feel like you're nearly ready for the actual exam you see if you are prepared by using ARRL's online General class practice exams. This web-based service uses the question pool to construct an exam with the same number and variety of questions that you'll encounter on exam day. You can practice taking the test over and over again in complete privacy.

These exams are quite realistic and you get quick feedback about the questions you missed. When you find yourself passing the online exams by a comfortable margin, you'll be ready for the real thing!

To find out more about ARRL's online practice exams, visit the *General Class License Manual* web page (**www.arrl.org/general-class-license-manual**) and follow the links. If you choose to use third-party software or websites to practice for the exam, be sure that the questions are from the correct question pool. The current question pool is in effect from July 1, 2015 through June 30, 2019.

Books to Help You Learn

As you study the material on the licensing exam, you will have lots of other questions about the how and why of Amateur Radio. The following references, available from your local bookstore or the ARRL (**www.arrl.org/shop**) will help "fill in the blanks" and give you a broader picture of the hobby:

✔ *Ham Radio for Dummies, 2nd edition* by Ward Silver, NØAX. Written for new Technician and General class licensees, this book supplements the information in study guides with an informal, friendly approach to the hobby.

✔ *ARRL Operating Manual.* With in-depth chapters on the most popular ham radio activities, this is your guide to nets, award programs, DXing and more. It even includes a healthy set of reference tables and maps.

✔ *Understanding Basic Electronics* by Walter Banzhaf, WB1ANE. Students who want more technical background about electronics should take a look at this book. It covers the fundamentals of electricity and electronics that are the foundation of all radio.

✔ *Basic Radio* by Joel Hallas, W1ZR. Students who want more technical background about radio theory should take a look at this book. It covers the key building blocks of receivers, transmitters, antennas and propagation.

✔ *ARRL Handbook.* This is the grandfather of all Amateur Radio references and belongs on the bookshelf of all hams. Almost any topic you can think of in Amateur Radio technology is represented here.

✔ *ARRL Antenna Book.* After the radio itself, all radio depends on antennas. This book provides information on every common type of amateur antenna, feed lines and related topics, and practical construction tips and techniques.

Volunteer examiners will try to make Exam Day as painless as possible. They grade the tests at the end of the exam session, so you'll know right away how you did. After you pass the exam, you will be issued a Certificate of Successful Completion (CSCE) and can start using your General privileges right away. Just use the identifier "slash AG" after your call sign until your upgrade appears in the FCC online database, or your new license shows up in the mail. [Joe Counsil, KØOG, photo]

FOR INSTRUCTORS

The ARRL has created supporting material for instructors such as an *Instructor's Manual*, graphics files, handouts, and a detailed topics list. Check **www.arrl.org/resources-for-license-instruction** for support materials.

CONVENTIONS AND RESOURCES

Throughout your studies keep a sharp eye out for words in *italics*. These words are important so be sure you understand them. Many are included in the extensive Glossary in the back of the book. Another thing to look for are the addresses or URLs for web resources in **bold**, such as **www.arrl.org/general-class-license-manual**. By browsing these web pages while you're studying, you will accelerate and broaden your understanding.

Throughout the book, there are many short sidebars that cover special material on the subject you're studying. These sidebars may just tell an interesting story or they might tackle a subject that needs its own space in the book.

1.3 The Upgrade Trail

As you begin your studies remember that you've already overcome the biggest hurdle of all — taking and passing your first license exam! The questions may be more challenging for the General class exam, but you already know all about the testing procedure and the basics of ham radio. You can approach the process of upgrading with confidence!

FOCUS ON HF AND ADVANCED MODES

The General class exam mostly deals with the new types of operating you'll encounter on the HF bands. You'll also be expected to understand more about the modes you're already familiar with from operating as a Technician. We'll cover more advanced modes and signals, too. The goal is to help you "fill in the blanks" in your ham radio knowledge. Here are some examples of topics that you'll be studying:

- Operating effectively on HF
- Digital modes such as PSK31, PACTOR, WINMOR, and the WSJT family
- Solar effects on HF propagation
- Test instruments such as the oscilloscope
- Practical electronic circuits
- More types of antennas

Not every ham uses every mode and frequency, of course. By learning about this wider range of ideas, it helps hams to make better choices for regular operating. You will

Special event stations attract a lot of attention on the air. For example, Edgardo Garcia, NP4EG, manager of the 2014 Puerto Rico Section Convention, activated KP4PR from the convention floor.

become aware of just how wide and deep ham radio really is. Better yet, the introduction of these new ideas may just get you interested in giving them a try!

TESTING PROCESS

When you're ready, you'll need to find a test session. If you're in a licensing class, the instructor will help you find and register for a session. Otherwise, you can find a test session by using the ARRL's web page for finding exams, **www.arrl.org/find-an-amateur-radio-license-exam-session**. If you can register for the test session in advance, do so. Other sessions, such as those at hamfests or conventions, are available to anyone that shows up or to *walk-ins*. You may have to wait for an available space though, so go early!

As for all amateur exams, the General class exam is administered by Volunteer Examiners (VEs). All VEs are certified by a Volunteer Examiner Coordinator (VEC) such as the ARRL/VEC. This organization trains and certifies VEs and processes the FCC paperwork for their test sessions.

Bring your current license *original* and a photocopy (to send with the application). You'll need two forms of identification including at least one photo ID, such as a driver's license, passport or employer's identity card. Know your Social Security Number (SSN). You can bring pencils or pens, blank scratch paper and a calculator, but any kind of computer or online device is prohibited.

Once you're signed in, you'll need to fill out a copy of the National Conference of Volunteer Examiner Coordinator's (NCVEC) Quick Form 605 (see **Figure 1.2**). This is an application for a new or upgraded license. It is used only at test sessions and for a VEC to process a license renewal or a license change. *Do not* use an NCVEC Quick Form 605 for any kind of application directly to the FCC — it will be rejected. Use a regular FCC Form 605 (**Figure 1.3**) for direct FCC applications. After filling out the form, pay the current test fee and get ready.

THE EXAM

The General test takes from 30 minutes to an hour. You will be given a question booklet and an answer sheet. Be sure to read the instructions, fill in all the necessary information and sign your name wherever it's required. Check to be sure your booklet has all the questions and be sure to mark the answer in the correct space for each question.

You don't have to answer the questions in order — skip the hard ones and go back to them. If you read the answers carefully, you'll probably find that you can eliminate one or more "distracters." Of the remaining answers, only one will be the best. If you can't decide which is the correct answer, go ahead and make your best guess. There is no additional penalty for an incorrect guess. When you're done, go back and check your answers and double-check your arithmetic — there's no rush!

Once you've answered all 35 questions, the Volunteer Examiners (VEs) will grade and verify your test results. Assuming you've passed (congratulations!) you'll fill out a *Certificate of Successful Completion of Examination* (CSCE). The exam organizers will submit your results to the FCC while you keep the CSCE as evidence that you've passed your General test.

If you are licensed and already have a call sign, you can begin using your new privileges immediately. When you give your call sign, append "/AG" (on CW or digital modes) or

NCVEC QUICK-FORM 605 APPLICATION FOR
AMATEUR OPERATOR/PRIMARY STATION LICENSE

SECTION 1 - TO BE COMPLETED BY APPLICANT

PRINT LAST NAME	SUFFIX (Jr., Sr.)	FIRST NAME	INITIAL	STATION CALL SIGN (IF ANY)
Grimaldi		Amanda	E	KB1KJC

MAILING ADDRESS (Number and Street or P.O. Box)
225 Main St.

SOCIAL SECURITY NUMBER (SSN) or (FRN) FCC FEDERAL REGISTRATION NUMBER
0005189337

CITY	STATE CODE	ZIP CODE (5 or 9 Numbers)
Newington	CT	06111

E-MAIL ADDRESS (OPTIONAL)

DAYTIME TELEPHONE NUMBER (Include Area Code) OPTIONAL
860-594-0200

FAX NUMBER (Include Area Code) OPTIONAL

ENTITY NAME (IF CLUB, MILITARY RECREATION, RACES)

Type of Applicant: ☒ Individual ☐ Amateur Club ☐ Military Recreation ☐ RACES (Modify Only)

CLUB, MILITARY RECREATION, OR RACES CALL SIGN

SIGNATURE OF RESPONSIBLE CLUB OFFICIAL (not trustee)

I HEREBY APPLY FOR (Make an X in the appropriate box(es))

☐ **EXAMINATION** for a **new** license grant

☒ **EXAMINATION** for **upgrade** of my license class

☐ **CHANGE** my **name** on my license to my new name

Former Name: _____
(Last name) (Suffix)   (First name)   (MI)

☐ **CHANGE** my mailing address to **above** address

☐ **CHANGE** my station **call sign** systematically

Applicant's Initials: _____

☐ **RENEWAL** of my license grant.

Do you have another license application on file with the FCC which has not been acted upon?	PURPOSE OF OTHER APPLICATION	PENDING FILE NUMBER (FOR VEC USE ONLY)

I certify that:
- I waive any claim to the use of any particular frequency regardless of prior use by license or otherwise;
- All statements and attachments are true, complete and correct to the best of my knowledge and belief and are made in good faith;
- I am not a representative of a foreign government;
- I am not subject to a denial of Federal benefits pursuant to Section 5301of the Anti-Drug Abuse Act of 1988, 21 U.S.C. § 862;
- The construction of my station will NOT be an action which is likely to have a significant environmental effect (See 47 CFR Sections 1.1301-1.1319 and Section 97.13(a));
- I have read and WILL COMPLY with Section 97.13(c) of the Commission's Rules regarding RADIOFREQUENCY (RF) RADIATION SAFETY and the amateur service section of OST/OET Bulletin Number 65.

Signature of applicant (Do not print, type, or stamp. Must match applicant's name above.) (Clubs: 2 different individuals must sign)

X *A. Grimaldi*   Date Signed: 01 / 23 / 15

SECTION 2 - TO BE COMPLETED BY ALL ADMINISTERING VEs

Applicant is qualified for operator license class:

☐ **NO NEW LICENSE OR UPGRADE WAS EARNED**

☐ **TECHNICIAN**   Element 2

☒ **GENERAL**   Elements 2 and 3

☐ **AMATEUR EXTRA**   Elements 2, 3 and 4

DATE OF EXAMINATION SESSION
01-23-2015

EXAMINATION SESSION LOCATION
Newington CT

VEC ORGANIZATION
ARRL

VEC RECEIPT DATE

I CERTIFY THAT I HAVE COMPLIED WITH THE ADMINISTERING VE REQUIRMENTS IN PART 97 OF THE COMMISSION'S RULES AND WITH THE INSTRUCTIONS PROVIDED BY THE COORDINATING VEC AND THE FCC.

	VEs STATION CALL SIGN	VEs SIGNATURE (Must match name)	DATE SIGNED
1st VEs NAME (Print First, MI, Last, Suffix) Maria Somma	AB1FM	*Maria Somma*	01-23-2015
2nd VEs NAME (Print First, MI, Last, Suffix) PERRY T GREEN	WY1O	*Perry Green*	01-23-2015
3rd VEs NAME (Print First, MI, Last, Suffix) Penny Harts	N1NAG	*Penny Harts*	01-23-2015

DO NOT SEND THIS FORM TO FCC – THIS IS NOT AN FCC FORM.
IF THIS FORM IS SENT TO FCC, FCC WILL RETURN IT TO YOU WITHOUT ACTION.

NCVEC FORM 605 - February 2007
FOR VE/VEC USE ONLY - Page 1

Figure 1.2 — This sample NCVEC Quick Form 605 shows how your form will look after you have completed your upgrade to General.

FCC 605
Main Form

Quick-Form Application for Authorization in the Ship, Aircraft, Amateur, Restricted and Commercial Operator, and General Mobile Radio Services

Approved by OMB
3060 - 0850

See instructions for
public burden estimate

1) Radio Service Code:	HA

Application Purpose (Select only one) (**MD**)

2) **NE** – New	**RO** – Renewal Only	**WD** – Withdrawal of Application
MD – Modification	**RM** – Renewal / Modification	**DU** – Duplicate License
AM – Amendment	**CA** – Cancellation of License	**AU** – Administrative Update

3)	Does this filing request STA (Special Temporary Authorization)? If 'Y', attach the required exhibit as described in the instructions.	(N) <u>Y</u>es <u>N</u>o
4)	If this request is for an Amendment or Withdrawal of Application, enter the file number of the pending application currently on file with the FCC.	File Number
5)	If this request is for a Modification, Renewal Only, Renewal / Modification, Cancellation of License, Duplicate License, or Administrative Update, enter the call sign (serial number for Commercial Operator) of the existing FCC license. If this is a request for consolidation of DO & DM Operator Licenses, enter serial number of DO. Also, if filing for a ship exemption, you must provide call sign.	Call Sign/Serial # KB1KJC
6)	If this request is for a New, Amendment, Renewal Only, or Renewal Modification, enter the requested expiration date of the authorization (this item is optional).	MM DD
7)	Does this filing request a Waiver of the Commission's Rules? If 'Y', attach the required showing as described in the instructions.	(N) <u>Y</u>es <u>N</u>o
8)	Are attachments (other than associated schedules) being filed with this application?	(N) <u>Y</u>es <u>N</u>o

Applicant/Licensee Information

9) FCC Registration Number (FRN): 0001234567

10) Applicant/Licensee legal entity type: (Select One)

☒ Individual ☐ Corporation ☐ Unincorporated Association ☐ Trust ☐ Government Entity
☐ Consortium ☐ General Partnership ☐ Limited Liability Company ☐ Limited Liability Partnership
☐ Limited Partnership ☐ Other (Description of Legal Entity) _____

11) First Name (if individual): MARIA	MI:	Last Name: SOMMA	Suffix:

12) Entity Name (if other than individual):

13) If the Licensee name is being updated, is the update a result from the sale (or transfer of control) of the license(s) to another party and for which proper Commission approval has not been received or proper notification not provided?   (   ) <u>Y</u>es <u>N</u>o

14) Attention To:

15) P.O. Box:	And/Or	16) Street Address: 225 MAIN ST.

17) City: NEWINGTON	18) State: CT	19) Zip Code/Postal Code: 06111	20) Country:

21) Telephone Number: 860-594-0200	22) FAX Number:

23) E-Mail Address:

Ship Applicants/Licensees Only

24) Enter new name of vessel:_____

Aircraft Applicants/Licensees Only

25) Enter the new FAA Registration Number (the N-number):_____
   NOTE: Do not enter the leading "N".

FCC 605 – Main Form
April 2014 - Page 1

Figure 1.3 Front — Portions of FCC Form 605 showing the sections you would complete for a modification of your license, such as a change of address.

Fee Status

26) Is the Applicant/Licensee exempt from FCC application fees?	(*N*) Yes	No
27) Is the Applicant/Licensee exempt from FCC regulatory fees?	(*N*) Yes	No

General Certification Statements

1) The Applicant/Licensee waives any claim to the use of any particular frequency or of the electromagnetic spectrum as against the regulatory power of the United States because of the previous use of the same, whether by license or otherwise, and requests an authorization in accordance with this application.

2) The Applicant/Licensee certifies that all statements made in this application and in the exhibits, attachments, or documents incorporated by reference are material, are part of this application, and are true, complete, correct, and made in good faith.

3) Neither the Applicant/Licensee nor any member thereof is a foreign government or a representative thereof.

4) The Applicant/Licensee certifies that neither the Applicant/Licensee nor any other party to the application is subject to a denial of Federal benefits pursuant to Section 5301 of the Anti-Drug Abuse Act of 1988, 21 U.S.C. § 862, because of a conviction for possession or distribution of a controlled substance. **This certification does not apply to applications filed in services exempted under Section 1.2002(c) of the rules, 47 CFR § 1.2002(c).** See Section 1.2002(b) of the rules, 47 CFR § 1.2002(b), for the definition of "party to the application" as used in this certification.

5) Amateur or GMRS Applicant/Licensee certifies that the construction of the station would NOT be an action which is likely to have a significant environmental effect (see the Commission's Rules 47 CFR Sections 1.1301-1.1319 and Section 97.13(a) rules (available at web site http://wireless.fcc.gov/rules.html).

6) Amateur Applicant/Licensee certifies that they have READ and WILL COMPLY WITH Section 97.13(c) of the Commission's Rules (available at web site http://wireless.fcc.gov/rules.html) regarding RADIOFREQUENCY (RF) RADIATION SAFETY and the amateur service section of OST/OET Bulletin Number 65 (available at web site http://www.fcc.gov/oet/info/documents/bulletins/).

Certification Statements For GMRS Applicants/Licensees

1) Applicant/Licensee certifies that he or she is claiming eligibility under Rule Section 95.5 of the Commission's Rules.

2) Applicant/Licensee certifies that he or she is at least 18 years of age.

3) Applicant/Licensee certifies that he or she will comply with the requirement that use of frequencies 462.650, 467.650, 462.700 and 467.700 MHz is not permitted near the Canadian border North of Line A and East of Line C. These frequencies are used throughout Canada and harmful interference is anticipated.

4) Non-Individual Applicants/Licensees certify that they have NOT changed frequency or channel pairs, type of emission, antenna height, location of fixed transmitters, number of mobile units, area of mobile operation, or increase in power.

Certification Statements for Ship Applicants/Licensees (Including Ship Exemptions)

1) Applicant/Licensee certifies that they are the owner or operator of the vessel, a subsidiary communications corporation of the owner or operator of the vessel, a state or local government subdivision, or an agency of the US Government subject to Section 301 of the Communications Act.

2) This application is filed with the understanding that any action by the Commission thereon shall be limited to the voyage(s) described herein, and that apart from the provisions of the specific law from which the Applicant/Licensee requests an exemption, the vessel is in full compliance with all applicable statues, international agreements and regulations.

Signature

28) Typed or Printed Name of Party Authorized to Sign

First Name: MARIA	MI:	Last Name: SOMMA	Suffix:

29) Title:

Signature: *Maria Somma*	30) Date: 07-01-2015

Failure to Sign This Application May Result in Dismissal Of The Application And Forfeiture Of Any Fees Paid

WILLFUL FALSE STATEMENTS MADE ON THIS FORM OR ANY ATTACHMENTS ARE PUNISHABLE BY FINE AND/OR IMPRISONMENT (U.S. Code, Title 18, Section 1001) AND / OR REVOCATION OF ANY STATION LICENSE OR CONSTRUCTION PERMIT (U.S. Code, Title 47, Section 312(a)(1)), AND / OR FORFEITURE (U.S. Code, Title 47, Section 503).

FCC 605 – Main Form
April 2014 - Page 2

Figure 1.3 Back — Portions of FCC Form 605 showing the sections you would complete for a modification of your license, such as a change of address.

Do you like to build electronic kits? There are plenty of kits available such as this 50 W amplifier that covers the 160 through 6 meter bands. [Phil Salas, AD5X, photo]

"slash AG" (on phone). As soon as your name and call sign appear in the FCC's database of licensees, typically a week to 10 days later, you can stop adding the suffix. The CSCE is good for 365 days in case there's a delay or problem with license processing or you decide to upgrade to Amateur Extra before receiving your paper license.

If you don't pass, don't be discouraged! You might be able to take another version of the test right then and there if the session organizers can accommodate you. Even if you decide to try again later, you now know just how the test session feels — you'll be more relaxed and ready next time. The bands are full of hams who took their General test more than once before passing. You'll be in good company!

FCC AND ARRL/VEC LICENSING RESOURCES

After you pass your exam, the examiners will file all of the necessary paperwork so that your license will be granted by the Federal Communications Commission (FCC). Soon you will be able see your new call sign in the FCC's database via the ARRL's website and later you'll receive a paper license by mail.

When you passed your Technician exam, you may have applied for your FCC Federal Registration Number (FRN). This allows you to access the information for any FCC licenses you may have and to request modifications to them. These functions are available via the FCC's Universal Licensing System website (**wireless.fcc.gov/uls**) and complete instructions for using the site are available at **www.arrl.org/universal-licensing-system**.

Hams design many types of equipment, including this professional-quality audio distribution system designed and built by William Ellis, KF7PB.

Hams enjoy exchanging colorful and informative QSL cards to confirm contacts. QSL cards are often used to apply for operating achievement awards such as Worked All States (WAS) or the DX Century Club (DXCC).

The ARRL/VEC can also process license renewals and modifications for you as described at **www.arrl.org/call-sign-renewals-or-changes**.

TIME TO GET STARTED

By following these instructions and carefully studying the material in this book, soon you'll be joining the rest of the General and Amateur Extra licensees on the HF bands. Each of us at the ARRL Headquarters and every ARRL member look forward to the day when you join the fun. 73 (best regards) and good luck!

Table 1.3

General Class (Element 3) Syllabus

SUBELEMENT G1 — COMMISSION'S RULES
[5 Exam Questions — 5 Groups]
G1A — General Class control operator frequency privileges; primary and secondary allocations
G1B — Antenna structure limitations; good engineering and good amateur practice; beacon operation; prohibited transmissions; retransmitting radio signals
G1C — Transmitter power regulations; data emission standards
G1D — Volunteer Examiners and Volunteer Examiner Coordinators; temporary identification
G1E — Control categories; repeater regulations; harmful interference; third party rules; ITU regions; automatically controlled digital station

SUBELEMENT G2 — OPERATING PROCEDURES
[5 Exam Questions — 5 Groups]
G2A — Phone operating procedures; USB/LSB conventions; procedural signals; breaking into a contact; VOX operation
G2B — Operating courtesy; band plans; emergencies, including drills and emergency communications
G2C — CW operating procedures and procedural signals; Q signals and common abbreviations; full break in
G2D — Amateur Auxiliary; minimizing interference; HF operations
G2E — Digital operating; procedures, procedural signals and common abbreviations

SUBELEMENT G3 — RADIO WAVE PROPAGATION
[3 Exam Questions — 3 Groups]
G3A — Sunspots and solar radiation; ionospheric disturbances; propagation forecasting and indices
G3B — Maximum Usable Frequency; Lowest Usable Frequency; propagation
G3C — Ionospheric layers; critical angle and frequency; HF scatter; Near-Vertical Incidence Skywave

SUBELEMENT G4 — AMATEUR RADIO PRACTICES
[5 Exam Questions — 5 Groups]
G4A — Station Operation and set up
G4B — Test and monitoring equipment; two-tone test
G4C — Interference with consumer electronics; grounding; DSP
G4D — Speech processors; S meters; sideband operation near band edges
G4E — HF mobile radio installations; emergency and battery powered operation

SUBELEMENT G5 — ELECTRICAL PRINCIPLES
[3 Exam Questions — 3 Groups]
G5A — Reactance; inductance; capacitance; impedance; impedance matching
G5B — The Decibel; current and voltage dividers; electrical power calculations; sine wave root-mean-square (RMS) values; PEP calculations
G5C — Resistors, capacitors, and inductors in series and parallel; transformers

SUBELEMENT G6 — CIRCUIT COMPONENTS
[2 Exam Questions — 2 Groups]
G6A — Resistors; Capacitors; Inductors; Rectifiers; solid state diodes and transistors; vacuum tubes; batteries
G6B — Analog and digital integrated circuits (ICs); microprocessors; memory; I/O devices; microwave ICs (MMICs); display devices

SUBELEMENT G7 — PRACTICAL CIRCUITS
[3 Exam Questions — 3 Groups]
G7A — Power supplies; and schematic symbols
G7B — Digital circuits; amplifiers and oscillators
G7C — Receivers and transmitters; filters, oscillators

[continued on next page]

SUBELEMENT G8 — SIGNALS AND EMISSIONS
[3 Exam Questions — 3 Groups]

G8A — Carriers and modulation; AM; FM; single sideband; modulation envelope; digital modulation; over modulation

G8B — Frequency mixing; multiplication; bandwidths of various modes; deviation

G8C — Digital emission modes

SUBELEMENT G9 — ANTENNAS AND FEEDLINES
[4 Exam Questions — 4 Groups]

G9A — Antenna feed lines; characteristic impedance, and attenuation; SWR calculation, measurement and effects; matching networks

G9B — Basic antennas

G9C — Directional antennas

G9D — Specialized antennas

SUBELEMENT G0 — ELECTRICAL AND RF SAFETY
[2 Exam Questions — 2 Groups]

G0A — RF safety principles, rules and guidelines; routine station evaluation

G0B — Safety in the ham shack; electrical shock and treatment, safety grounding, fusing, interlocks, wiring, antenna and tower safety

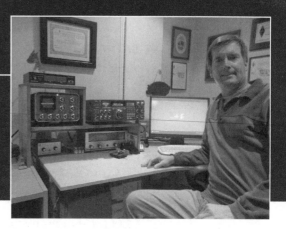

Chapter 2

Procedures and Practices

In this chapter, you'll learn about:
- **Basic HF operating procedures**
- **Common HF practices and modes**
- **Receiving and transmitting on HF**
- **Digital operating on HF**
- **Emergency communications**
- **ARES and RACES organizations**
- **Distress calls**

Technician licensees focus their studies and develop operating skills for techniques used on the VHF and higher bands. The most popular mode of operation on these bands is FM voice repeaters with evenly spaced channels and local or regional contacts. On HF, however, operating is similar to that of the so-called "weak signal" modes on the lower portions of the VHF and UHF bands. Simplex SSB, CW, and digital modes are by far the most commonly used. As a Technician, you may have some HF experience on 10 meters or the 80, 40, and 15 meter CW bands. The General license opens up many more frequencies, modes and activities.

Before proceeding, don't forget to add **www.arrl.org/general-class-license-manual** to your Internet browser's list of bookmarked web pages for easy reference. That page contains supplemental information and on-line resources you may find helpful during your studies.

2.1 HF Operating Techniques

BASIC OPERATING

To begin with, HF operation is not channelized at all, except for the small 60 meter band that consists of five specific channels for operation with USB (upper sideband voice), CW and certain digital modes. Channel designations are not used, although *calling frequencies* are common along with regular meeting frequencies for nets and special operations. On the HF amateur bands, "channel" only means "current frequency," not "assigned frequency."

As a result, HF equipment is designed for continuous tuning. The control used for continuous frequency adjustment is called a *VFO* for *variable frequency oscillator*. This is usually the largest knob on an HF transceiver (**Figure 2.1**), replacing the channel select control on a VHF/UHF FM rig. The VFO tunes the radio (both receiver and transmitter) in small steps, usually less than 100 Hz. The minimum frequency change is called *step size* or *step rate*. (Memory channels are also used on HF, but they are not the primary way frequencies are selected.)

Aside from nets and schedules, random contacts are the norm on HF as hams tune across the bands looking for someone calling CQ or an ongoing QSO that sounds interesting. While calling CQ is rare on

Figure 2.1 — The VFO control is usually front-and-center on a transceiver. It allows continuous frequency adjustments in small steps for smoothly tuning in signals.

VHF/UHF FM channels, that is how most contacts are initiated on HF. When calling CQ, a station from literally anywhere could respond to your call.

To call CQ on phone, you would say "CQ CQ CQ, this is [your call repeated three times using phonetics]" and then repeat that sequence two or three times. On CW, "this is" is replaced by the abbreviation "DE" and of course no phonetics are used. Many stations say "from" rather than "this is" on phone. "DE" is usually used on digital modes too, although some stations may use "from." You may have to repeat your CQ several times before you get an answer. Calling variations include:
- CQ DX (DX meaning "distant stations" — usually outside the CQing station's country) [G2A11]
- CQ for stations operating in a contest or from a special event
- CQ for stations from a certain area

Joining an ongoing QSO or *breaking in* is also common. On phone the customary procedure is to say just your call sign during a pause in the conversation. [G2A08] On CW or digital modes, send "BK" (break). Your transmission must be short to be received as stations switch from receive to transmit, called "turning it over." If you are heard and the stations in the ongoing QSO want to accept stations breaking in, they will stand by and ask "the breaking station" to go ahead or some similar remark. Identify yourself with your call sign and ask if you may join the contact.

At first you'll find HF practices somewhat different from what you're used to on VHF and UHF FM phone. Nevertheless, you'll quickly learn the basics!

GOOD PRACTICES

Almost everything you know about operating courtesy and good practices from VHF and UHF operating can be applied to HF operating. There are some differences in terminology, of course, but the main difference comes from the new environment of VFO-based operating.

Selecting a Frequency

Choosing a frequency to use is the most important step. Use that choice to make a good first impression! The process is greatly simplified by tuning around the band and finding some other station calling CQ or engaged in a QSO. You can answer or break in as described above. If you're unsure of yourself, listen for other stations answering or calling and emulate successful and friendly practices.

If you want to call CQ yourself — and why shouldn't you? — start by selecting an appropriate band. If you're interested in short-range, regional contacts, maybe 80 or 40 meters would be a good choice. Longer range contacts are easiest on the higher-frequency bands of 30 through 10 meters, depending on solar conditions. Don't use a long-distance band for short-range contacts since your signal will be heard over a much wider range than you are using. This needlessly occupies precious radio spectrum space.

What if a nearby ham calls you on a long-distance band? The best thing to do is to change bands and move to a frequency more suitable for short distance contacts — even to a VHF or UHF repeater! (There is an extensive discussion of signal propagation in Chapter 8 where you can find out more about the properties of the different bands.)

Now that you've decided on which band to use, what's next? As a General, you should check the FCC Part 97 frequency and mode restrictions to be sure you're within the privileges allocated to Generals. Charts showing frequency privileges for the various license classes can be downloaded from **www.arrl.org/graphical-frequency-allocations**. Once that's done, check to be sure your QSO will follow the recommendations of the *band plan*, which we'll discuss later in this chapter. [G2B07]

Table 2.1

Recommended Signal Separation

CW	150 – 500 Hz
SSB	2.5 – 3 kHz
RTTY	250 – 500 Hz
PSK31	150 – 500 Hz

Within the appropriate frequency limits, tune around looking for a clear frequency. On a repeater, you simply have to wait until any ongoing QSOs are over before making your call. On HF, however, a perfectly clear channel is a rarity. There will always be some noise present and the signals of other stations may occasionally be heard. Your goal is to find a frequency on which your transmissions minimize interference to adjacent stations and vice versa. **Table 2.1** shows the recommended station-to-station spacings for different modes under normal conditions. [G2B04, G2B05]

If the band is very busy, such as on the weekends when many more hams may be active in contests, chasing DX, or just making QSOs, you will find fewer open frequencies and experience more incidental interference. Learning how to make contacts under such circumstances is part of being a good operator!

Whose Frequency Is It?

The answer is "Nobody's frequency!" As a Technician licensee, you may be used to having channels dedicated to a particular purpose or group but that's not how things work on HF! Channelized operation works on VHF and UHF because of the regional nature of propagation on those bands. This is not good practice on HF because of long-distance skywave propagation. For example, on 75 meter phone even modest stations can routinely cover a range of hundreds of miles and QRP operation around the world is common on the higher bands. While it's convenient to make one frequency a meeting place, don't expect it to be available all the time. Either tune to a nearby frequency that's clear — your group will find each other — or have an alternate operating plan when the band is congested. Frequency flexibility is one of the Amateur Service's greatest assets, take advantage of it!

After finding an apparently clear frequency, check for any other station that might be using it. Just as with a VHF simplex contact, you might not be able to hear both stations taking part in a QSO. On phone, the customary technique is to ask "Is the frequency in use? This is [your call]" once or twice before starting your CQ. On CW and the digital modes, "QRL? DE [your call]" does the trick. It means "Is this frequency in use?" or "Are you busy?" [G2B06, G2C04] If a station is listening, they'll usually say, "Yes, it is" or send "C" or "R" or make some other transmission that lets you know the frequency is occupied. Move to a new frequency and try again.

If you're engaged in a QSO and a station calls to request the use of a frequency for a scheduled activity, try to accommodate their need and move your contact to a new frequency. After all, we are a variable frequency service! All parties must remember that no group or amateur has priority access to any frequency except in the case of emergency communications. Be flexible, taking advantage of Amateur Radio's unique ability to use any frequency within its allocations. [G2B01]

In summary, choosing a frequency is very simple:

- Be sure the frequency is authorized to General class licensees
- Follow the band plan under normal circumstances
- Listen to the frequency to avoid interfering with ongoing communications

It's just that easy! [G1B08]

Nets and Schedules

Many on-the-air activities are scheduled in advance, such as person-to-person contacts between friends or family members ("skeds") and regularly scheduled nets. For scheduled contacts and events to go smoothly, flexibility is required from two sides.

If you're the one scheduling the activity, avoid the calling frequencies and popular band areas. Use the ARRL Net Search and Contest Corral calendars to avoid congestion (see the sidebar, "Radio Calendars"). Always have a "Plan B," such as an alternate time or frequency for your contact. For example, if you are a net control station and find the net's chosen frequency to be occupied, find a clear frequency nearby and run the net there or change to your backup frequency.

Band Plans

The FCC's regulations dividing the amateur bands help stations using compatible modes stay together. There are additional divisions of the band, however, created by amateurs themselves and strictly voluntary. These are called *band plans*. You are probably familiar with them from the VHF and UHF bands where repeaters are grouped together in one section of the band. Other modes and activities, such as satellites or amateur television, have their own segments. The ARRL maintains a set of band plans for 160 meters through the microwaves at **www.arrl.org/band-plan**. The band plans for HF may be found in The Considerate Operator's Frequency Guide at the end of this chapter.

Band plans go beyond what the FCC requires and were created in the interests of efficient operating. Many features of band plans evolved over the years while others were created deliberately to address a particular need. In either case, the FCC considers the band plans "good practice" and expects amateurs to follow them voluntarily when possible and practical.

A typical band plan for the 20 meter band is shown in **Table 2.2**. This set of recommendations does not overrule the FCC license class and mode rules — not at all! Instead, it works *within* the FCC rules to reduce interference and frustration. For example, listing the international beacon frequency of 14.100 MHz alerts all stations to the beacon's presence and helps them avoid unintentionally interfering with stations that use the beacons to assess long-distance propagation.

The band plans often list frequencies associated with the mode or style of operating you intend to use. Sometimes a range of frequencies is designated; in other cases a single frequency is shown. Other stations using that mode are much more likely to be operating around that frequency than on other frequencies. That's what band plans are for — education and guidance.

Table 2.2
Typical HF Band Plan (20 Meters)

Frequency (MHz)	Mode or Use
14.070 – 14.095	RTTY/Data
14.07015	PSK31 calling frequency
14.095 – 14.0995	Automatically controlled data stations
14.100	IBP/NCDXF beacons
14.1005 – 14.112	Automatically controlled data stations
14.230	SSTV
14.233	D-SSTV
14.236	Digital voice
14.285	QRP SSB calling frequency
14.286	AM calling frequency

Windows on the World

Outside the United States, particularly in ITU Regions 1 and 3, amateur allocations on the 160 and 80 meter bands may be very limited or shared with government and commercial stations. Even though this is becoming less common, a *DX window* designates the part of a band where the amateurs with restricted privileges can be found. This allows the restricted amateurs to make better use of their limited privileges. Where a DX window is specified in a US band plan or contest rules, contact between stations in the 48 contiguous United States and Canada are discouraged. [G2B08]

Band plans are voluntary, but they are also flexible. A band plan is not a regulation; it is a guideline. Like special events in your town, there will be circumstances in which conditions or the number of stations on the band overwhelm the usual customs. For example, a major contest or DXpedition can result in thousands of stations on a band at once, making it very difficult to follow a plan describing normal conditions. These situations are just temporary, however, and things return to normal in a short time.

Housekeeping and Operating Support

Part of keeping an orderly and efficient station is maintaining a *log*, a record of your station's activities. A typical log contains the time, date, and frequency or band of each contact; the contacted station's call sign; and information about the contact such as signal reports, names, and equipment used. [G2D09] The FCC does not require a formal log, but most amateurs keep a log because it helps them verify contacts in the future and remember items of interest, such as personal, technical, and operating information. (Requirements for written record keeping are discussed in Chapter 3.) Many amateurs collect awards and that requires keeping data about contacts you have made. Your log is the most convenient way to keep track. A log also establishes the identity of the control operator at any date and time in case it is questioned by the FCC or others. [G2D08] **Figure 2.2** shows typical log entries. Computer logging makes it easy to find and sort QSO information.

A log is also needed to support *QSLing*, the practice of exchanging cards or electronic

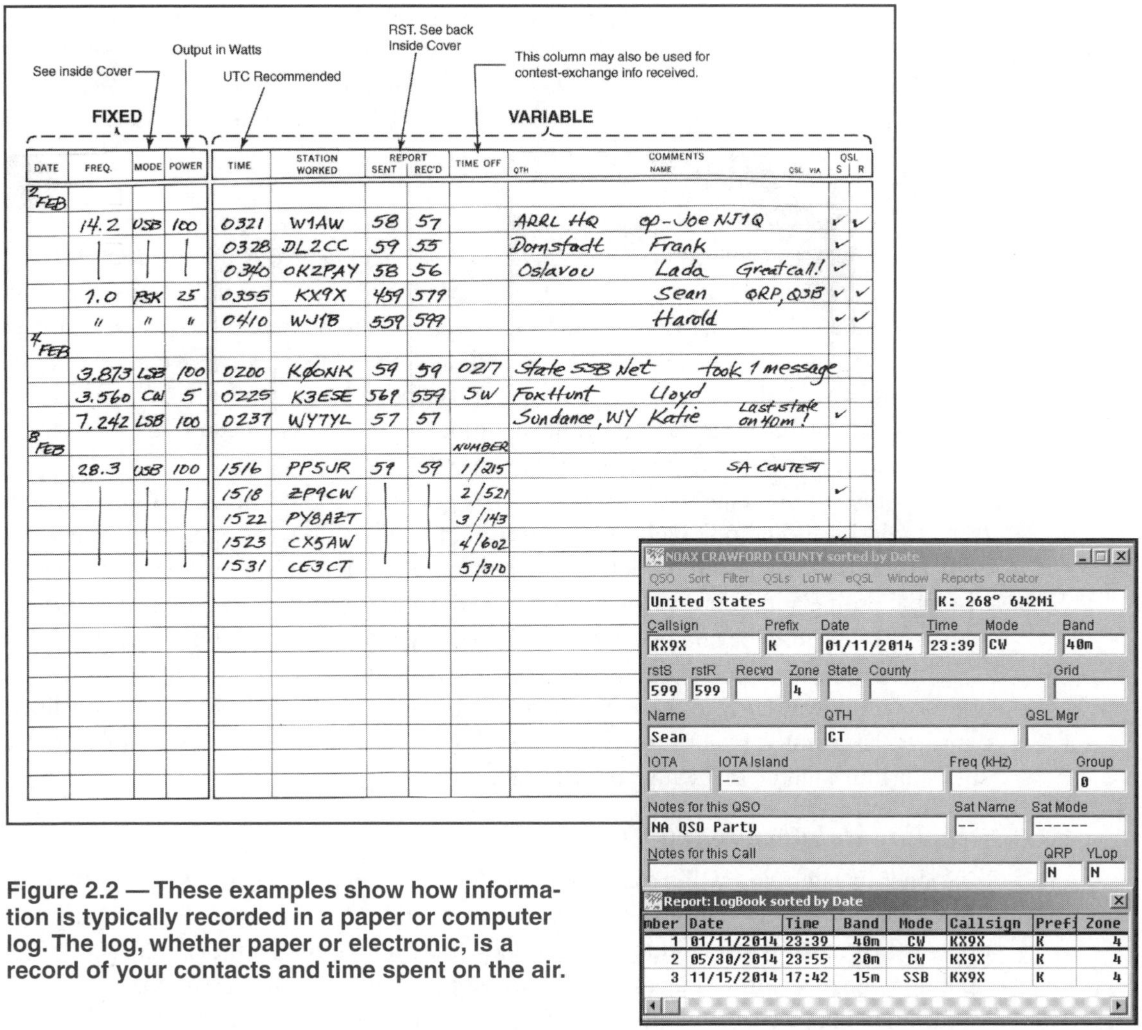

Figure 2.2 — These examples show how information is typically recorded in a paper or computer log. The log, whether paper or electronic, is a record of your contacts and time spent on the air.

records to confirm a contact. (QSL stands for "I acknowledge receipt.") Collecting interesting and colorful *QSL cards* from around the world is very popular among HF operators.

MANAGING INTERFERENCE

Amateur Radio's HF frequencies are not channelized and there are very many amateurs. *Voila*! Interference! Interference occurs not only from crowding, but also from propagation and personal choice. Regardless of its source, every amateur needs to be skilled at dealing with interference. This section talks about dealing with interference from other amateur signals but not interference from signals generated by consumer electronics or atmospheric noise.

Types of Interference

Most interference caused by signals from other hams is incidental and not terribly disruptive. Once you've gained some experience, it's easy to copy a desired signal through a little bit of QRM (interference) from a nearby signal. You may experience (or even cause!) accidental interference when another station begins transmitting on or very near a frequency that you're using. Like collisions between shopping carts at the store, these incidents are easily managed.

There are two types of interference, however, that are not so easily managed. The first is *harmful interference*, defined by the FCC in §97.3(a)(23) as "Interference which…seriously degrades, obstructs or repeatedly interrupts a radiocommunication service operating in accordance with the Radio Regulations." Harmful interference is not always illegal, but needs to be resolved for all parties to be able to continue communicating. The second and more pernicious type of interference is *malicious, deliberate* or *willful interference* and it is specifically forbidden by the FCC rules [§97.101(d)]. Sad to say that it does happen on the amateur bands, but it is uncommon.

Avoiding Interference

The best way to avoid interference is to be smart and use your knowledge of the amateur service to your advantage, starting with reasonable expectations. Learn what bands are crowded and when. Learn the characteristics of each band with respect to propagation and noise. Know how to use your station and understand its weaknesses and strengths. Check published calendars so that you are not surprised by major operating events. Armed with this information, you'll have a much better idea of what to expect and a much higher chance of having a good experience on the air.

Next, hone your frequency selection skills. There are many sources of good propagation predictions to help you choose an optimum band or time for operating. Band plans and calling frequencies are widely published on the web and in print. Net frequencies are available online and in directories. With a few minutes of research, you can avoid many sources of interference and operate on a frequency well-suited for your intended purpose.

While on the air, operate so as to maximize the enjoyment of other operators. Use an appropriate power level to the job at hand. Avoid long-distance bands for short-distance contacts. Especially, make sure your transmitted signal is "clean," meaning free of excessive spurious signals that cause interference.

Reacting to Interference

Sooner or later, you will experience interference. What is the appropriate way to react? Start by keeping your options open and being flexible. No one has a claim to any frequency — it's often simplest to change frequency to avoid an interfering signal. Know how to operate your receiver to reject interference from nearby and strong signals.

During a contact, you should expect signal propagation to change as the Earth rotates which changes the way sunlight illuminates the ionosphere. Propagation may improve or degrade to your target area and you may begin to hear other stations on the same frequency — and they may begin to hear you! Changing the heading of a directional antenna or switching to a different antenna may reduce signals to and from the newly heard region. If possible, changing to another frequency is an effective and courteous response. [G2B03]

Plan ahead by always having a backup or alternate operating plan in place. This is particularly important for scheduled contacts and nets. Everyone involved should know what to do in case the primary frequency is occupied or propagation is poor. The time to create these procedures is in advance, not at contact time!

Above all, keep a cool head! Sometimes harmful interference leads to deliberate interference when emotions get the better of us. Don't let a sorehead get into your head! Even though it may be vexing, don't react to a jammer or someone creating deliberate interference as that just encourages them. Sometimes it's just best to turn the power switch OFF and find something else to do. Encourage your fellow amateurs to follow these simple guidelines and everyone will benefit.

MODES

Amateurs use many different modes of communication — more than any other service, licensed or unlicensed. The invention, use, and management of different modes are good examples of Amateur Radio fulfilling its mission to advance the state of the radio art. (That's a key part of the "basis and purpose" of Amateur Radio as set forth in Part 97 of the FCC regulations.) This section presents some of the conventions associated with each mode and compares them.

CW

Morse code, called "CW" for *continuous wave*, is found in the lower ranges of each HF band because FCC rules prohibit phone and data signals there. It's often forgotten that CW can be transmitted anywhere on the HF bands, including the portion allocated to phone operation! Nevertheless, most CW operators tend to operate in the segments of the band reserved for CW and data. CW is generated simply by turning a transmitter on and off in the pattern of Morse code. Because all of a CW signal's power is concentrated into one frequency, an operator can detect or "copy" CW over long distances at much lower power than more complex signals carrying speech or data. This makes CW a favorite mode of low-power enthusiasts ("QRPers") and hams who want to get the most out of simple stations.

AM and SSB Phone

On the HF bands, single sideband (SSB) is by far the most common voice mode or phone signal. [G2A05] First introduced in the 1950s, SSB displaced AM as the preferred HF voice modulation method. SSB uses less spectrum space than AM — a properly-adjusted SSB signal occupies about 3 kHz and an AM signal 6 kHz. In contrast to an AM signal, SSB signals do not contain a carrier and "extra" sideband so all of the power is allocated to the speech information, increasing efficiency. [G2A06, G2A07] The result is that under equal conditions an SSB signal will have a greater range than an AM signal.

Even with those disadvantages, AM has a role to play on the amateur bands. AM transmitters tend to give a "warmer" sound to the speaker's voice and tuning is less critical than on SSB. AM calling frequencies can be found on many band plans, and a sizeable group of AM and antique radio enthusiasts are active every day.

SSB is the more popular mode, but which of the two sidebands is used? Because of technical considerations in early SSB radio design, amateur convention is to use upper sideband (USB) on frequencies above 9 MHz (20 through 10 meter bands) and lower

A new type of phone signal is appearing on the HF bands — digital phone! The operator's voice is converted to and from a stream of digital information by a modem or sound card, just like computer-generated digital signals. The modem or sound card then connects to a regular SSB transceiver's microphone input and speaker or headphone output. The digital phone transmissions have comparable fidelity to regular SSB signals but are less affected by fading and there is less noise in the recovered voice signal. This type of phone transmission is likely to become more popular as the technique is refined.

sideband (LSB) elsewhere except on 60 meters. On VHF and UHF, the upper sideband is used. [G2A01 to G2A04, G2A09]

FM, in general, is not used on HF because the higher noise levels and wide bandwidth of the mode do not result in good signal-to-noise performance. But FM repeaters can be found on the higher frequencies of 10 meters (above 29 MHz) where cross-continent and DX contacts can be made when the band is open!

Digital Modes

You may have used packet radio on VHF or UHF to exchange digital data. There are plenty of digital signals on HF, as well. The oldest and still one of the most popular is *radioteletype* or *RTTY*. (Most hams pronounce it as "ritty.") Effective at low power levels, the modes PSK31 and JT65 or JT9 have also become very popular for low-speed contacts between individuals. PACTOR or WINMOR are used for semi-automatic and automatic data communications. On HF, SSB radios are used to send and receive the digital signals, which are transmitted as audio tones. There are many more digital modes used on HF than on VHF. (Chapter 6 explores digital modes, protocols, and operating practices in detail.)

Image Modes

Image mode transmissions on HF encode pictures and graphics as tones. The tones are then reconstructed at the receiver to display the image on a computer screen or other display device. Image modes are permitted wherever phone transmissions are allowed, except on 60 meters.

Amateurs commonly use slow-scan television (SSTV). Images are transmitted and received using SSB equipment following the same sideband conventions as for SSB phone.

Table 2.3
Mode Comparison

Mode	Bandwidth	Examples	Data Rate	Notes
CW	Up to 150 Hz		Up to 60 WPM	
AM	6 kHz			Can be higher fidelity than SSB
SSB	3 kHz			
Narrow Bandwidth HF Digital	Up to 500 Hz	RTTY, PSK31 JT65 or JT9	Up to 100 WPM	Keyboard-to-keyboard
Wide Bandwidth HF Digital	Up to 2.3 kHz	PACTOR, WINMOR	Up to 1200 baud	Keyboard-to-keyboard and file transfer
VHF/UHF Digital	Up to 100 kHz	Packet, D-STAR		Max bandwidth varies by band
Narrow Bandwidth Image	3 kHz max on HF	SSTV		
Video (full motion)	6 MHz max	NTSC, HDTV		UHF and microwave only

SSTV sends a video image or *frame* over a voice channel. Each frame takes several seconds, thus the name "slow scan." Computers and sound cards have greatly simplified the use of image modes and software for SSTV operation is readily available.

Fast-scan amateur television (ATV), which allows full motion video, is restricted to the 70 cm and higher bands due to its wide bandwidth.

Mode Comparison

Table 2.3 lists common modes and compares their basic characteristics. You'll learn about the details of these modes in Chapters 5 and 6. This table is intended to summarize the overview you've just read.

Before you go on, study test questions G1B08, G2A01 through G2A09, G2A11, G2B01, G2B03 through G2B08, G2C04, G2D08 and G2D09. Review this section if you have difficulty.

HF RECEIVING

On VHF, FM receivers have three basic controls: frequency (or channel), squelch, and volume. SSB/CW receivers have many more adjustments such as those shown in **Figure 2.3** because they are designed for non-channelized, continuous-tuning operation. They must be able to receive desired signals in the presence of noise and interference from adjacent channels. Squelch is generally not used on amateur SSB and CW because of the higher noise levels on HF.

Selectivity, the ability to discriminate between closely-spaced signals, is more important on HF than *sensitivity*, the ability to detect a signal. This is because atmospheric noise, referred to as *QRN*, is much higher on the HF bands than on VHF and UHF. QRN is caused by storms or other natural atmospheric processes, and by man-made sources such as sparks generated by motors and power lines. *Preamplifiers* are rarely required except on higher HF bands such as 15 through 10 meters. [G2C10]

❥ On HF, signals close to the noise level often need to be received in the presence of stronger signals on adjacent or nearby frequencies. Those signals may be 10 to 100 million times more powerful (70 to 80 dB) than the weaker signal!

HF receivers use sharp filters to reject the unwanted signals. Discrete or standalone filters are made using quartz crystals or mechanical assemblies. Radios also use digital signal processing (DSP) software to perform the filtering and some radios use a combination of discrete and DSP filters. A typical receiver has at least one filter with response and bandwidth tailored for SSB reception, another for CW and a third for AM or FM.

Because HF operation is not channelized, you'll also encounter signals close enough in frequency to be audible as low- or high-pitched speech fragments or CW tones. This is the interference referred to as *QRM*. Along with the main VFO tuning control, HF receivers offer the ability to shift the receive frequency without changing the transmit frequency to fine-tune desired signals and avoid or minimize QRM. This is called *receiver incremental tuning* or *RIT*. Some transceivers also offer the ability to shift the *transmit* frequency without changing the receiver — *transmitter incremental tuning* or *XIT*. A steady tone from a station tuning up or a broadcast carrier can be rejected by a *notch filter*

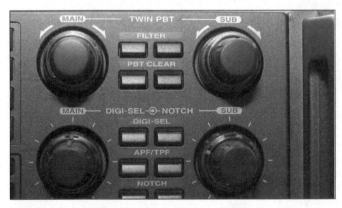

Figure 2.3 — HF transceivers have a variety of controls to help minimize interference on crowded bands.

that removes a narrow range of signal frequencies from the channel.

To avoid interference-like effects from *overload* or *intermodulation* (signals mixing together and creating unwanted byproducts), a receiver's gain should be set so that it is just sensitive enough for the job. Features such as noise blankers and preamplifiers can make a receiver easy to overload and should only be used when necessary. Receiver technology is discussed in more detail in Chapter 5.

HF TRANSMITTING

This section discusses methods of using an HF transmitter. The details of adjusting a transmitter are covered in Chapter 5.

Phone

On HF phone, there are several ways to put your transceiver into transmit (called "keying" the transmitter) when you want to talk. If you're used to an FM mobile or handheld radio, you'll find *push-to-talk* (*PTT*) works just the same as on VHF and UHF. PTT is best when operating in noisy environments. HF operators sometimes use a footswitch rather than the PTT button on a microphone to key the transmitter during busy operating periods.

HF operators also frequently use *voice-operated transmit*, most often referred to as simply *VOX*. A special circuit in the transmitter uses audio from the microphone input to turn on the transmitter when the operator is speaking. VOX allows hands-free operation, which is more convenient for long periods of operation. [G2A10] Mobile operators use VOX to keep both hands on the steering wheel! (Note: It is unsafe to wear headphones while driving and illegal in many areas.)

There are three basic controls for the VOX circuit.
• VOX Gain — sets the sensitivity of the VOX circuit to your speech
• VOX Delay — sets the length of time the transmitter remains keyed after you stop speaking
• Anti-VOX — prevents speaker or headphone audio from activating the VOX circuit

Each of these will be thoroughly described by your radio's operating manual and a typical set of manual VOX adjustments is shown in **Figure 2.4**. (Many transceivers use software menus to adjust VOX operation.) Get to know the individual controls so that you can adjust the VOX circuit properly at any time.

VOX can also be used for CW and digital transmissions. For CW, closing the external key activates the VOX circuit as for voice. VOX Gain and Anti-VOX have no effect when using CW. For digital transmissions, the audio output from a modem or sound card activates the VOX system just as a voice does. All three VOX controls have the same function in digital and voice operation.

Phone Procedures and Abbreviations

You've already learned about the procedural signals "CQ" and "Break." From operating on VHF and UHF, you know when to use "Over" and "Clear." HF phone operation uses all of those signals and a few more. HF operators also make heavy use

Figure 2.4 — VOX controls — Gain, Anti-VOX (called Anti-Trip on this transceiver) and Delay. Because they aren't often adjusted, many rigs place manual Gain and Anti-VOX controls out of the way. They are menu items if controlled by software. Delay is adjusted most often and is usually made the easiest to access. Some radios even have separate Delay controls for CW and phone.

Signal Reporting

One of the first items of information exchanged between stations at the beginning of a contact is the signal report. This lets each station know how well their signal is being received so that they can adjust procedures accordingly. There's no need to repeat everything twice if you're loud and in the clear!

The most common signal reporting system is the RST (Readability, Strength, Tone) numeric system. Readability is reported on a scale of 1 to 5 with 5 being the best. Strength and Tone are both reported on a 1 to 9 scale. (Tone is only exchanged for CW and digital mode contacts.) A strength of 9 roughly corresponds to an S9 reading on a receiver. Tone values of less than 9 indicate some kind of transmitter problem. C added after an RST indicates an unstable signal or "chirp" — a short change in frequency at the beginning of each dot or dash. [G2C07] Some digital stations are adopting the RSQ system (**www.rsq-info.net**) that substitutes signal quality for tone and redefines R and S in terms more applicable to digital signals.

of the standard phonetics listed on the *General Class License Manual* web page, **www.arrl.org/general-class-license-manual**. Don't forget to give your call sign every 10 minutes and at the end of the contact.

You will also hear many operators using Q-signals on phone, even though they were really intended for use on CW. Their meaning is so widely understood, for example QRM and QRN that you met in the previous section, that it is hard to resist using them. A good reason to use Q-signals on phone is when you are in contact with an operator who does not speak the same language. That is why Q-signals were developed so many years ago.

In any case, avoid the use of "10 codes" such as "10-4" since those are long obsolete and no longer used even by most police and fire departments. Professional radio users have decided it's better to use plain speech for clarity and understanding. If you're going to change frequency or close down the station, say just so.

CW

Morse contacts are far more common on HF than above 30 MHz. The code segments of open bands are busy with signals and sometimes filled to overflowing! Morse is alive and well on the ham bands. If you decide to learn "the code," you will add a powerful radio tool to your rapidly growing collection.

Most CW operators begin with a *straight key*, but soon graduate to the use of an electronic *keyer* for easier sending at higher speeds. A keyer, shown in **Figure 2.5**, automatically generates Morse elements — the dits and dahs — with a microprocessor or digital logic circuit. [G4A10] The operator uses a *paddle* to tell the keyer which to generate. Some radios have keyers built-in.

Morse speed for on-air contacts ranges from 5 to 10 WPM to the majority of day-to-day contacts at speeds between 15 and 30 WPM. Contest signals are faster but contesters will slow down if asked when there aren't faster operators calling. Slower signals tend to be found at the high end of the CW and data band segments. To get started with Morse, try the CW calling frequencies for QRP operation (see **www.qrparci.org**) and FISTS (**www.fists.org**).

There are two choices as to how to set up a transceiver to switch between sending and receiving when using Morse. If you use the VOX circuit as described in the previous section on phone operating, the rig will switch back to receive after the VOX delay period expires. This is *semi break-in* operation. VOX delay can be set to a very short

Figure 2.5 — An electronic keyer generates precisely formed and spaced dits and dahs under the control of a paddle. This combination makes it easy to send code at speeds over 15 words per minute with much less effort.

time to drop out between words or long enough that the transmitter stays on the whole time you're sending.

Under some circumstances, it is more convenient to be able to hear what is going on between the Morse characters and elements. You might want to do this when the station you're in contact with has to interrupt your transmissions or if interference is present. Most modern radios include a *full break-in* option in which the radio switches between transmit and receive in just a few milliseconds. When using full break-in, the operator can hear incoming signals between all transmitted code characters and elements. [G2C01] Full break-in is also referred to as *QSK*, the Q-signal for break-in operation.

CW and Digital Mode Prosigns and Abbreviations

Just as with text messaging, it is a lot of work to spell out the full text of all words and phrases, so telegraphers developed an extensive set of abbreviations and procedural signals called *prosigns*. Prosigns are two letters sent together as a single character as indicated by an overbar. For example, the prosign $\overline{AR}$ (didahdidahdit) is used to indicate "End of Message." [G2C08]

Abbreviations are used to shorten common words, for example "AND" becomes "ES," "GOING" becomes "GG" and "WEATHER" becomes "WX" in Morse code. This saves a lot of time and energy! Long lists of abbreviations and prosigns are available online at **www.arrl.org/general-class-license-manual**. Digital operation follows many of the same conventions, using the same prosigns and abbreviations.

As mentioned before, calling CQ on CW follows the same form as on phone. "DE" is an abbreviation used in place of "from" and the procedural signal K replaces "over":

CQ CQ CQ DE W1AW W1AW W1AW K

A response to a CQ looks like this:

W1AW DE WB8IMY WB8IMY K

There's no need to send the CQing station's call more than once unless there is interference or the signal is weak. When signals are strong and clear, operators responding to a CQ may send their own call only once or twice.

Respond to a CQ at the speed of the calling station. [G2C05] If you are uncomfortable receiving at that speed, send the Q-signal "QRS" ("send slower") before the final K. If you want to go faster, "QRQ" means "send faster." [G2C02]

Remember to adjust your transmitting frequency so that your signal is "zero beat" with the other signal so that you will be on the same frequency. This means the two signals produce the same audio tone in a receiver. Check your radio's operating manual for instructions on how to zero beat another signal. [G2C06]

Once you are in contact with another station, the prosign $\overline{KN}$ is used instead of K to prevent other stations from breaking in during the contact. It means, "Only the station with whom I am in contact should respond." [G2C03] When asked if you are ready to receive information, "QRV" means "I am ready to copy." After receiving the message, "QSL" means "I acknowledge receipt." [G2C09, G2C11]

When it's time to end the QSO, the prosign $\overline{SK}$ is used to let any listener know that the contact is completed:

WB8IMY DE W1AW $\overline{SK}$

If you are going off the air, add CL for "closing station." As always, be sure to give your call sign every ten minutes and at the end of the contact.

Before you go on, study test questions G2A10, G2C01 through G2C03, G2C05 through G2C11, and G4A10. Review this section if you have difficulty.

2.2 Emergency Operation

Providing service to your community is a significant factor in the decision of many people to become hams and more importantly, to stay hams. Recent events around the world clearly demonstrate that Amateur Radio is needed and emergency communications is an important part of our operation, just as much as technical experimentation and operator knowledge.

Amateurs should be familiar with emergency rules and procedures so that they can contribute effectively when normal communications are unavailable. Even if you are not affected by the emergency or disaster directly, you may receive emergency communications from an amateur who is. Emergency communications in any form take priority over *all* other types of amateur communication. Regardless of what else is happening on a frequency, all other operators must stand by and wait for the emergency communications to occur. You should be prepared to respond effectively.

As you know from your Technician exam studies, you may not assist organizations such as the news media in acquiring or disseminating information. The only exception is made by rule §97.113(b) that states "... communications directly related to the immediate safety of human life or the protection of property may be provided by amateur stations to broadcasters for dissemination to the public where no other means of communication is reasonably available...." [G1B04] **Table 2.4** lists the FCC rules pertaining to emergency communications.

ARES and RACES

Amateurs have organized themselves in order to respond effectively to emergencies. There are two primary organizations for this purpose: the *Amateur Radio Emergency Service* (ARES®) and the *Radio Amateur Civil Emergency Service* (RACES). ARES is sponsored by the ARRL and RACES is sponsored by government agencies. The missions of ARES and RACES are similar and may overlap in many areas, but RACES has different rules from ordinary amateur operation.

ARES is organized and managed by members of the ARRL's Field Organization (**www. arrl.org/field-organization**). The mission of ARES is to provide communications assistance to local and regional government and relief agencies. Served agencies include organizations such as the American Red Cross, Salvation Army and National Weather Service. ARES may also assist local and regional emergency management agencies or even the Federal Emergency Management Agency (FEMA) if normal communications systems fail.

Membership in ARES is open to any licensed amateur, whether an ARRL member or not, although League membership is required to hold an official appointment. ARES teams are led by Emergency Coordinators (ECs) at the local level. District Emergency Coordinators (DECs) lead the local teams in a larger area (such as a county), and ARES leadership for the entire ARRL Section is handled by the Section Emergency Coordinator (SEC). The SEC reports to the ARRL Section Manager.

RACES is a specific part of the Amateur Service governed by FCC rule §97.407 to provide communications for civil defense purposes during local, regional, or national civil emergencies (**www.arrl.org/chapter-4-ares-and-races**). Although RACES is sponsored by the Federal Emergency Management Agency (FEMA), it is usually administered by local, county and state emergency management agencies.

To participate in RACES and operate as a RACES station, you must register with a local civil defense organization. Only FCC-licensed amateurs may be the control operators of RACES stations [§97.407(a)]. [G2B09] RACES stations may communicate only with other RACES stations and certain government stations. All RACES communications must

Table 2.4
FCC Emergency Communications Rules

§97.401 Operation during a disaster.
A station in, or within 92.6 km (50 nautical miles) of, Alaska may transmit emissions J3E and R3E on the channel at 5.1675 MHz (assigned frequency 5.1689 MHz) for emergency communications. The channel must be shared with stations licensed in the Alaska-Private Fixed Service. The transmitter power must not exceed 150 W PEP. A station in, or within 92.6 km of, Alaska may transmit communications for tests and training drills necessary to ensure the establishment, operation, and maintenance of emergency communication systems.

§97.403 Safety of life and protection of property.
No provision of these rules prevents the use by an amateur station of any means of radiocommunication at its disposal to provide essential communication needs in connection with the immediate safety of human life and immediate protection of property when normal communication systems are not available.

§97.405 Station in distress.
(a) No provision of these rules prevents the use by an amateur station in distress of any means at its disposal to attract attention, make known its condition and location, and obtain assistance.
(b) No provision of these rules prevents the use by a station, in the exceptional circumstances described in paragraph (a), of any means of radiocommunications at its disposal to assist a station in distress.

§97.407 Radio amateur civil emergency service.
(a) No station may transmit in RACES unless it is an FCC-licensed primary, club, or military recreation station and it is certified by a civil defense organization as registered with that organization, or it is an FCC-licensed RACES station. No person may be the control operator of a RACES station, or may be the control operator of an amateur station transmitting in RACES unless that person holds a FCC-issued amateur operator license and is certified by a civil defense organization as enrolled in that organization.
(b) The frequency bands and segments and emissions authorized to the control operator are available to stations transmitting communications in RACES on a shared basis with the amateur service. In the event of an emergency which necessitates invoking the President's War Emergency Powers under the provisions of section 706 of the Communications Act of 1934, as amended, 47 U.S.C. 606, RACES stations and amateur stations participating in RACES may only transmit on the frequency segments authorized pursuant to part 214 of this chapter.

be carried out under the direction of a civil defense organization. FCC rules provide for RACES members to conduct regular training and drills so that they can provide orderly and efficient communications for the civil defense organizations they serve [§97.407(c), (d), (e)]. Furthermore, the FCC is empowered to restrict the operating frequencies of RACES stations if the War Emergency Powers have been activated [§97.407(b)]. [G2B10]

Distress Calls

Because amateurs operate from so many locations and on so many frequencies, distress calls are sometimes received by amateurs. It's important that each amateur know what to do if a distress call is received or how to make a distress call.

What would you do if you heard a call for help? Your responsibility is to react to the call for help and do your best to obtain assistance for the station in distress.

(c) A RACES station may only communicate with:

(1) Another RACES station;

(2) An amateur station registered with a civil defense organization;

(3) A United States Government station authorized by the responsible agency to communicate with RACES stations;

(4) A station in a service regulated by the FCC whenever such communication is authorized by the FCC.

(d) An amateur station registered with a civil defense organization may only communicate with:

(1) A RACES station licensed to the civil defense organization with which the amateur station is registered;

(2) The following stations upon authorization of the responsible civil defense official for the organization with which the amateur station is registered:

(i) A RACES station licensed to another civil defense organization;

(ii) An amateur station registered with the same or another civil defense organization;

(iii) A United States Government station authorized by the responsible agency to communicate with RACES stations; and

(iv) A station in a service regulated by the FCC whenever such communication is authorized by the FCC.

(e) All communications transmitted in RACES must be specifically authorized by the civil defense organization for the area served. Only civil defense communications of the following types may be transmitted:

(1) Messages concerning impending or actual conditions jeopardizing the public safety, or affecting the national defense or security during periods of local, regional, or national civil emergencies;

(2) Messages directly concerning the immediate safety of life of individuals, the immediate protection of property, maintenance of law and order, alleviation of human suffering and need, and the combating of armed attack or sabotage;

(3) Messages directly concerning the accumulation and dissemination of public information or instructions to the civilian population essential to the activities of the civil defense organization or other authorized governmental or relief agencies; and

(4) Communications for RACES training drills and tests necessary to ensure the establishment and maintenance of orderly and efficient operation of the RACES as ordered by the responsible civil defense organizations served. Such drills and tests may not exceed a total time of 1 hour per week. With the approval of the chief officer for emergency planning the applicable State, Commonwealth, District or territory, however, such tests and drills may be conducted for a period not to exceed 72 hours no more than twice in any calendar year.

First, immediately suspend your existing contact, if any. Then:

1) Immediately acknowledge to the station calling for help that you hear them.

2) Stand by to receive the location of the emergency and the nature of the assistance required.

3) Relay the information to the proper authorities and stay on frequency for further information or until help arrives. [G2B02]

If you are the station making the distress call:

1) On a voice mode, say "Mayday Mayday Mayday" or on CW or a digital mode send "SOS SOS SOS" followed by "any station come in please." (Mayday should not be confused with the Pan-Pan urgency call)

2) Identify the transmission with your call sign.

3) State your location with enough detail to be located and the nature of the situation.

4) Describe the type of assistance required and give any other pertinent information.

Figure 2.6 — In time of emergency, when normal communications are disrupted, Amateur Radio Emergency Service volunteers set up portable stations to assist emergency management agencies and relief organizations.

FCC rule §97.405 allows a station in distress and requesting emergency help to use *any* means of radio communication at their disposal to attract attention and request help. *Any* frequency on which you think you will be heard, any mode, any power level necessary — even those outside your normal privileges — may be used as long as the emergency exists. [G2B11, G2B12] Even unidentified transmissions outside of amateur bands, such as to allow direction finding, are permitted if required to provide the necessary communications. Similarly, if you hear a distress call, the same permission to respond by any means necessary applies to you.

Before you go on, study test questions G1B04, G2B02, G2B09 to G2B12. Review this section if you have difficulty.

The Considerate Operator's Frequency Guide

The following frequencies are generally recognized for certain modes or activities (all frequencies are in MHz) during normal conditions. These are not regulations and occasionally a high level of activity, such as during a period of emergency response, DXpedition or contest, may result in stations operating outside these frequency ranges.

Nothing in the rules recognizes a net's, group's or any individual's special privilege to any specific frequency. Section 97.101(b) of the Rules states that "Each station licensee and each control operator must cooperate in selecting transmitting channels and in making the most effective use of the amateur service frequencies. No frequency will be assigned for the exclusive use of any station." No one "owns" a frequency.

It's good practice — and plain old common sense — for any operator, regardless of mode, to check to see if the frequency is in use prior to engaging operation. If you are there first, other operators should make an effort to protect you from interference to the extent possible, given that 100% interference-free operation is an unrealistic expectation in today's congested bands.

Frequencies	Modes/Activities
1.800-2.000	CW
1.800-1.810	Digital Modes
1.810	QRP CW calling frequency
1.843-2.000	SSB, SSTV and other wideband modes
1.910	SSB QRP calling frequency
1.995-2.000	Experimental
1.999-2.000	Beacons
3.500-3.510	CW DX window
3.560	QRP CW calling frequency
3.570-3.600	RTTY/Data
3.585-3.600	Automatically controlled data stations
3.590	RTTY/Data DX
3.790-3.800	DX window
3.845	SSTV
3.885	AM calling frequency
3.985	QRP SSB calling frequency
7.030	QRP CW calling frequency
7.040	RTTY/Data DX
7.070-7.125	RTTY/Data
7.100-7.105	Automatically controlled data stations
7.171	SSTV
7.173	D-SSTV
7.285	QRP SSB calling frequency
7.290	AM calling frequency
10.130-10.140	RTTY/Data
10.140-10.150	Automatically controlled data stations
14.060	QRP CW calling frequency
14.070-14.095	RTTY/Data
14.095-14.0995	Automatically controlled data stations
14.100	IBP/NCDXF beacons
14.1005-14.112	Automatically controlled data stations
14.230	SSTV

Frequencies	Modes/Activities
14.233	D-SSTV
14.236	Digital Voice
14.285	QRP SSB calling frequency
14.286	AM calling frequency
18.100-18.105	RTTY/Data
18.105-18.110	Automatically controlled data stations
18.110	IBP/NCDXF beacons
18.162.5	Digital Voice
21.060	QRP CW calling frequency
21.070-21.110	RTTY/Data
21.090-21.100	Automatically controlled data stations
21.150	IBP/NCDXF beacons
21.340	SSTV
21.385	QRP SSB calling frequency
24.920-24.925	RTTY/Data
24.925-24.930	Automatically controlled data stations
24.930	IBP/NCDXF beacons
28.060	QRP CW calling frequency
28.070-28.120	RTTY/Data
28.120-28.189	Automatically controlled data stations
28.190-28.225	Beacons
28.200	IBP/NCDXF beacons
28.385	QRP SSB calling frequency
28.680	SSTV
29.000-29.200	AM
29.300-29.510	Satellite downlinks
29.520-29.580	Repeater inputs
29.600	FM simplex
29.620-29.680	Repeater outputs

ARRL band plans for frequencies above 28.300 MHz are shown in *The ARRL Repeater Directory* and on **www.arrl.org**.

Chapter 3
Rules and Regulations

In this chapter, you'll learn about:
- International operating rules
- The ITU, FCC and FAA
- Rules for exams and examiners
- Frequency privileges
- Managing interference issues
- Third-party rules
- Technical rules and standards
- Good amateur practices

As a General class licensee, your frequency privileges expand dramatically from those of the Technician class. You'll be operating on a whole new set of HF bands and probably using new modes. Along with different propagation and procedures, there are also new regulations and frequency limits that apply. We'll build on the rules and regulations you learned to pass your Technician exam.

The exact text of the FCC Part 97 regulations won't be reproduced in this book in most cases. You can quickly access the exact wording of any rule through the ARRL's website (**www.arrl.org**) by entering the rule number, such as "97.301" in the search function window. For a complete copy of Part 97, see **www.arrl.org/part-97-amateur-radio**.

You are encouraged to access the regulations discussed in the book, not only to help remember them, but to gain experience in reading the regulations governing the Amateur Service. This will help when you refer to them with questions after you've received your General class license. More information on rules and regulations can be found through the resources at **www.arrl.org/general-class-license-manual**.

3.1 Regulatory Bodies

On the HF bands, signals routinely travel long distances and cross international borders with ease. That makes the international rules and regulations much more than an academic exercise! The rules for the amateur service vary around the world, sometimes dramatically. Let's start by asking the question, who's in charge here?

INTERNATIONAL TELECOMMUNICATION UNION (ITU)

The International Telecommunication Union or ITU is the organization responsible for all international radio regulations. Individual nations agree by treaty to abide by those regulations. Each country decides how to administer and implement those regulations and may even add additional regulations, as long as they do not conflict with the ITU regulations.

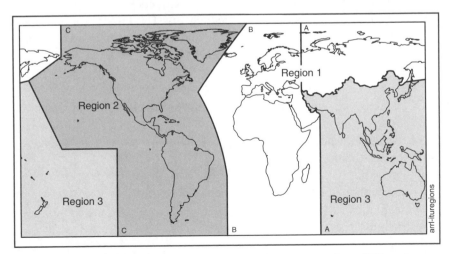

Figure 3.1 — This map shows the world divided into the three ITU regions.

The ITU has created three administrative areas, called *regions*. Each region has its own set of frequency *allocations* or divisions of the radio spectrum. **Figure 3.1** shows the three ITU regions. The continental United States, Alaska, Hawaii and most US territories and possessions are in Region 2. Certain US-administered Pacific islands (American Samoa, the Northern Mariana Islands, Guam and Wake Island) are in Region 3.

ITU regions have their greatest effect on amateurs in frequency allocations around the world. For example, the 75 meter allocation varies from 50 kHz in Region 1 to 250 kHz in Region 2. (Individual country allocations vary even more.) In Region 2, General Class licensees have access to 7.175-7.300 MHz. Section 97.301 contains a complete listing of frequency allocations by region. Parts (a) and (d) of that section contain the Region 2 frequency allocations that apply to General class amateurs operating from the US. [G1A14]

FCC STRUCTURE AND AUTHORITY

The Federal Communications Commission (FCC) is the agency in the United States charged with writing and administering the rules for US amateurs. FCC regulations apply to any amateur (US or foreign) operating where the FCC has jurisdiction. Outside the 50 states, that includes all US possessions and territories, as well as operation from US-flagged vessels operating in international waters.

Frequency sharing arrangements on the different bands are controlled by §97.303. Rule 97.305(f)(11) applies to US amateurs using phone in the Pacific and Caribbean. US amateurs operating abroad are required to abide by the appropriate regional frequency limits, subject to their host government's regulations.

Amateur Auxiliary

The Amateur Service prides itself on being largely *self-policing* so that amateurs follow FCC regulations with as little government monitoring and supervision as possible. The ARRL's Official Observer program (**www.arrl.org/official-observer-1**) was created to provide feedback to amateurs on operating practices and signal quality. In 1982, an additional step was taken when the *Amateur Auxiliary* was formally created so that amateurs could assist the FCC. These volunteers monitor the amateur frequency bands for rule violations and intruders not licensed to use amateur frequencies. The mission of both the ARRL's Official Observers and the Amateur Auxiliary is to encourage amateur self-regulation and compliance with the FCC rules. [G2D01, G1D02]

FAA RULES

Along with the FCC, there is one other federal agency that has jurisdiction in amateur affairs and that is the *Federal Aviation Administration* or *FAA*. Amateurs who want to construct an antenna structure more than 200 feet high must notify the FAA and register the tower with the FCC to avoid unknowingly creating hazards to aircraft. Additional restrictions apply if the antenna is within about 4 miles of a public use airport or heliport. [G1B01]

Before you go on, study test questions G1A14, G1B01, and G2D01 to G2D03. Review this section if you have difficulty.

3.2 Amateur Licensing Rules

As a Technician class licensee, you've already experienced a unique aspect of the Amateur Service — the volunteer-administered licensing program. Along with being largely self-policing, amateurs and amateur organizations keep licensing and examination services widely available in a time of shrinking government services. After you receive your General class license, you'll be able to fully participate in this program. This section covers the regulations that govern the volunteer licensing program and the individuals who make it a success.

LICENSE ELEMENTS

You passed Element 2 to get your Technician license. To reach General class, you must now pass Element 3. This is the General class written exam with 35 multiple-choice questions. The Amateur Extra exam is Element 4. There is no Element 1; that was the 5 WPM Morse code exam which is no longer required for any license class.

EXAMINER RULES

The volunteer licensing program is administered by *Volunteer Examiner Coordinators* (VECs). VECs are organizations that have entered into an agreement with the FCC to coordinate amateur license examinations. The ARRL is the largest VEC (**www.arrl.org/volunteer-examiners**), but there are 13 other VECs. You can find them on the National Conference of Volunteer Examiner Coordinators' website (**www.ncvec.org**).

To become *accredited* by the ARRL VEC program, you must meet the FCC's requirements (see the sidebar, "So You Want to be a VE?") and must pass a short multiple-choice test based on the *Volunteer Examiner's Manual*. Becoming accredited costs nothing and you can then administer amateur license exams. You don't have to be a US citizen to be accredited as a VE as long as you hold a General class or higher US amateur license and meet all the criteria. [G1D05, G1D07, G1D08]

EXAMINATION RULES

No matter what licensing elements are available in the exam session, the rules are the same. Every exam session must be coordinated by one of the VECs and administered under the observation of three primary VEs accredited by that VEC. (Other VEs may assist,

Table 3.1
Allowed License Exams by VE License Class

VE License Class	Allowed Examinations
General	Technician (Element 2)
Advanced	General (Element 3) Technician (Element 2)
Amateur Extra	Amateur Extra (Element 4) General (Element 3) Technician (Element 2)

but at least three VEs from the coordinating VEC must be present.) The three primary VEs must hold the necessary license class shown in **Table 3.1** to give the exam elements. For example, at least three General Class VEs must observe the test session to administer Technician Class exams. [G1D04]

The VEs are in charge of administering all parts of the exam session. The three primary VEs (if there are more than three) must observe all aspects of the exam session. Observation can be conducted via video from off-site so the primary VEs need not be physically present if other VEs are available to administer the exam process. VEs grade all exams and are responsible for determining the correct answers. There are other requirements, all spelled out in §97.509.

Not all license exams can be administered by any VE. As a General class licensee, you are only allowed to administer the Element 2 Technician class exam. Table 3.1 shows which exams can be administered by VEs holding the various license classes. [G1D02]

Once the exams are completed, the VEs must also supply the necessary paperwork. Each successful applicant is given a *Certificate of Successful Completion of Examination* (CSCE) showing what elements the examinee has passed. (**Figure 3.2** shows a filled out CSCE.) The CSCE is good for 365 days and can be presented at any other exam session as evidence of having obtained credit for specific elements. [G1D09] Use the CSCE until your new license arrives from the FCC. An NCVEC Quick-Form 605 (shown in **Figure 3.3**) must also be filled out for each candidate who successfully acquires or upgrades their amateur license class.

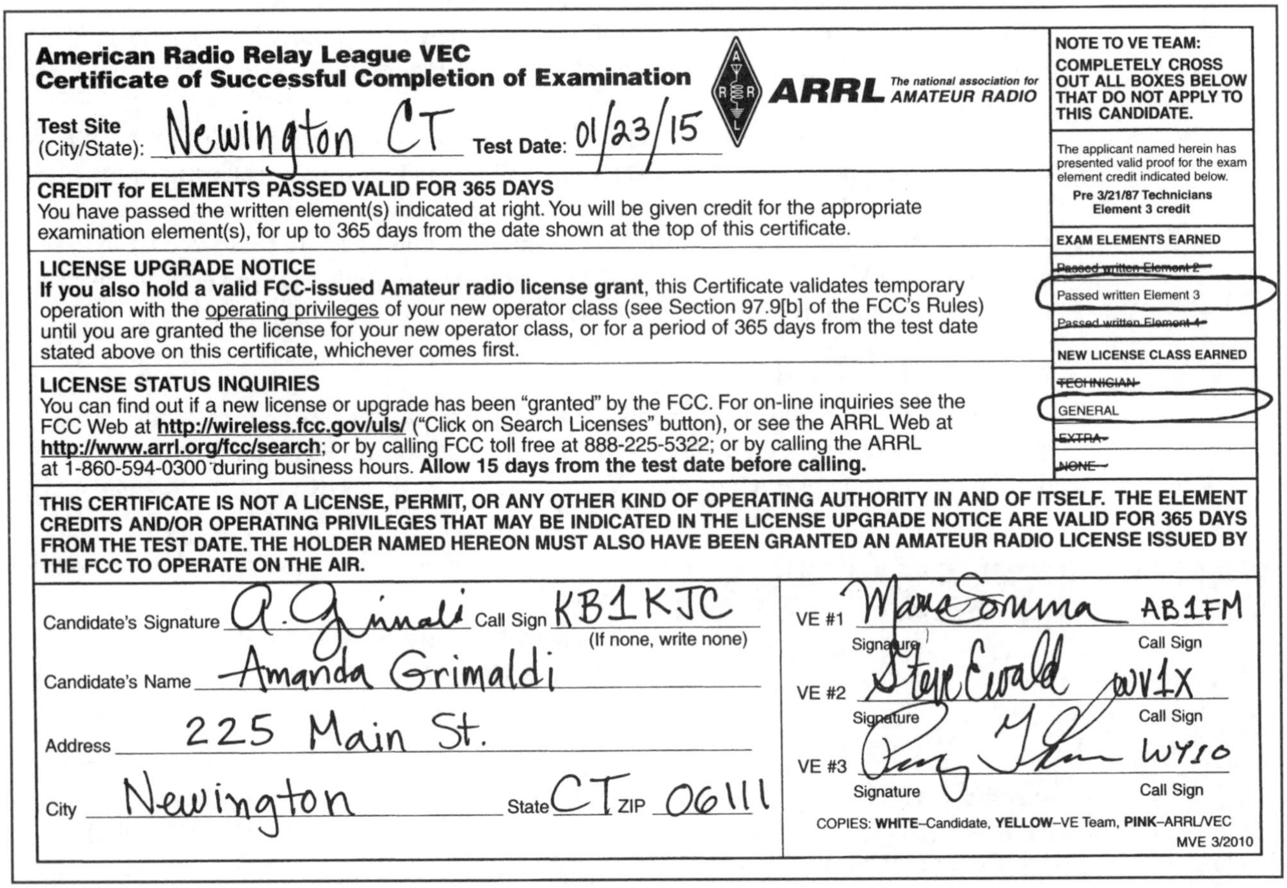

American Radio Relay League VEC
Certificate of Successful Completion of Examination

ARRL The national association for AMATEUR RADIO

Test Site (City/State): Newington CT **Test Date:** 01/23/15

NOTE TO VE TEAM: COMPLETELY CROSS OUT ALL BOXES BELOW THAT DO NOT APPLY TO THIS CANDIDATE.

The applicant named herein has presented valid proof for the exam element credit indicated below. **Pre 3/21/87 Technicians Element 3 credit**

CREDIT for ELEMENTS PASSED VALID FOR 365 DAYS
You have passed the written element(s) indicated at right. You will be given credit for the appropriate examination element(s), for up to 365 days from the date shown at the top of this certificate.

EXAM ELEMENTS EARNED
~~Passed written Element 2~~
Passed written Element 3
~~Passed written Element 4~~

LICENSE UPGRADE NOTICE
If you also hold a valid FCC-issued Amateur radio license grant, this Certificate validates temporary operation with the operating privileges of your new operator class (see Section 97.9[b] of the FCC's Rules) until you are granted the license for your new operator class, or for a period of 365 days from the test date stated above on this certificate, whichever comes first.

NEW LICENSE CLASS EARNED
~~TECHNICIAN~~
GENERAL
~~EXTRA~~
~~NONE~~

LICENSE STATUS INQUIRIES
You can find out if a new license or upgrade has been "granted" by the FCC. For on-line inquiries see the FCC Web at **http://wireless.fcc.gov/uls/** ("Click on Search Licenses" button), or see the ARRL Web at **http://www.arrl.org/fcc/search**; or by calling FCC toll free at 888-225-5322; or by calling the ARRL at 1-860-594-0300 during business hours. **Allow 15 days from the test date before calling.**

THIS CERTIFICATE IS NOT A LICENSE, PERMIT, OR ANY OTHER KIND OF OPERATING AUTHORITY IN AND OF ITSELF. THE ELEMENT CREDITS AND/OR OPERATING PRIVILEGES THAT MAY BE INDICATED IN THE LICENSE UPGRADE NOTICE ARE VALID FOR 365 DAYS FROM THE TEST DATE. THE HOLDER NAMED HEREON MUST ALSO HAVE BEEN GRANTED AN AMATEUR RADIO LICENSE ISSUED BY THE FCC TO OPERATE ON THE AIR.

Candidate's Signature A. Grimaldi Call Sign KB1KJC (If none, write none)
Candidate's Name Amanda Grimaldi
Address 225 Main St.
City Newington State CT ZIP 06111

VE #1 Signature Maria Somma Call Sign AB1FM
VE #2 Signature Steve Ewald Call Sign WV1X
VE #3 Signature Perry Green Call Sign WY1O

COPIES: **WHITE**–Candidate, **YELLOW**–VE Team, **PINK**–ARRL/VEC
MVE 3/2010

Figure 3.2 — The CSCE (Certificate of Successful Completion of Examination) is your test session receipt that serves as proof that you have completed one or more exam elements. It can be used at other test sessions for 365 days.

NCVEC QUICK-FORM 605 APPLICATION FOR
AMATEUR OPERATOR/PRIMARY STATION LICENSE

SECTION 1 - TO BE COMPLETED BY APPLICANT

PRINT LAST NAME	SUFFIX (Jr., Sr.)	FIRST NAME	INITIAL	STATION CALL SIGN (IF ANY)
Grimaldi		Amanda	E	KB1KJC

MAILING ADDRESS (Number and Street or P.O. Box)
225 Main St.

SOCIAL SECURITY NUMBER (SSN) or (FRN) FCC FEDERAL REGISTRATION NUMBER
0005189337

CITY	STATE CODE	ZIP CODE (5 or 9 Numbers)	E-MAIL ADDRESS (OPTIONAL)
Newington	CT	06111	

DAYTIME TELEPHONE NUMBER (Include Area Code) OPTIONAL	FAX NUMBER (Include Area Code) OPTIONAL	ENTITY NAME (IF CLUB, MILITARY RECREATION, RACES)
860-594-0200		

Type of Applicant: ☒ Individual ☐ Amateur Club ☐ Military Recreation ☐ RACES (Modify Only)

CLUB, MILITARY RECREATION, OR RACES CALL SIGN

SIGNATURE OF RESPONSIBLE CLUB OFFICIAL (not trustee)

I HEREBY APPLY FOR (Make an X in the appropriate box(es))

☐ **EXAMINATION** for a **new** license grant

☒ **EXAMINATION** for **upgrade** of my license class

☐ **CHANGE** my **name** on my license to my new name

Former Name: _____
(Last name) (Suffix) (First name) (MI)

☐ **CHANGE** my mailing address to **above** address

☐ **CHANGE** my station **call sign** systematically

Applicant's Initials: _____

☐ **RENEWAL** of my license grant.

Do you have another license application on file with the FCC which has not been acted upon?	PURPOSE OF OTHER APPLICATION	PENDING FILE NUMBER (FOR VEC USE ONLY)

I certify that:
* I waive any claim to the use of any particular frequency regardless of prior use by license or otherwise;
* All statements and attachments are true, complete and correct to the best of my knowledge and belief and are made in good faith;
* I am not a representative of a foreign government;
* I am not subject to a denial of Federal benefits pursuant to Section 5301of the Anti-Drug Abuse Act of 1988, 21 U.S.C. § 862;
* The construction of my station will NOT be an action which is likely to have a significant environmental effect (See 47 CFR Sections 1.1301-1.1319 and Section 97.13(a));
* I have read and WILL COMPLY with Section 97.13(c) of the Commission's Rules regarding RADIOFREQUENCY (RF) RADIATION SAFETY and the amateur service section of OST/OET Bulletin Number 65.

Signature of applicant (Do not print, type, or stamp. Must match applicant's name above.) (Clubs: 2 different individuals must sign)

X _A. Grimaldi_   Date Signed: 01 | 23 | 15

SECTION 2 - TO BE COMPLETED BY ALL ADMINISTERING VEs

Applicant is qualified for operator license class:

☐ **NO NEW LICENSE OR UPGRADE WAS EARNED**

☐ **TECHNICIAN** — Element 2

☒ **GENERAL** — Elements 2 and 3

☐ **AMATEUR EXTRA** — Elements 2, 3 and 4

DATE OF EXAMINATION SESSION
01-23-2015

EXAMINATION SESSION LOCATION
Newington CT

VEC ORGANIZATION
ARRL

VEC RECEIPT DATE

I CERTIFY THAT I HAVE COMPLIED WITH THE ADMINISTERING VE REQUIRMENTS IN PART 97 OF THE COMMISSION'S RULES AND WITH THE INSTRUCTIONS PROVIDED BY THE COORDINATING VEC AND THE FCC.

1st VEs NAME (Print First, MI, Last, Suffix)	VEs STATION CALL SIGN	VEs SIGNATURE (Must match name)	DATE SIGNED
Maria Somma	AB1FM	Maria Somma	01-23-2015
2nd VEs NAME (Print First, MI, Last, Suffix) PERRY T GREEN	WY1O	Perry Green	01-23-2015
3rd VEs NAME (Print First, MI, Last, Suffix) Penny Harts	N1NAG	Penny Harts	01-23-2015

DO NOT SEND THIS FORM TO FCC – THIS IS NOT AN FCC FORM.
IF THIS FORM IS SENT TO FCC, FCC WILL RETURN IT TO YOU WITHOUT ACTION.

NCVEC FORM 605 - February 2007
FOR VE/VEC USE ONLY - Page 1

Figure 3.3 — This sample NCVEC Quick Form 605 shows how your form will look after you have completed your upgrade to General.

After the exam session, the VEs send the paperwork to their VEC. There it is reviewed and information is sent on to the FCC so that licenses and upgrades can be issued.

IDENTIFICATION REQUIREMENTS

As soon as you receive a CSCE showing that you've achieved General class, you can start using *all* of your new privileges right away. [G1D03] As long as you already have a call sign in the FCC database, you don't have to wait for the FCC to update your license class! You must, however, add an *indicator* to your call sign whenever you operate outside Technician privileges. This tells a listener that you are operating legally. On phone, say your call sign followed by "temporary AG" or "slash AG." On CW or digital modes, add "/AG" to your call sign. [G1D06] (If you pass the General class exam before your initial call sign is added to the FCC database, congratulations on the quick work but you'll have to wait for your call sign to be assigned before you can operate.) As soon as your license class is updated in the FCC database, you can stop adding the indicator.

One new wrinkle to operating on HF is that you may be able to practice your foreign language skills with amateurs in other countries! This is an excellent use of Amateur Radio. The only restriction on speaking foreign languages on the air is that you are required to identify your station in English or by using the English language alphabet. [G1E09]

> *Before you go on, study test questions G1D01 through G1D11 and G1E09. Review this section if you have difficulty.*

3.3 Control Operator Privileges

Along with all of your new privileges comes the responsibility to operate within them. This section covers the basic requirements that a General class licensee must satisfy on the air. Some, such as the prohibition against broadcasting, you'll find familiar from your Technician class studies. Others, such as third-party rules, are new and may take a little study to understand clearly. Nevertheless, since you have already passed the Technician exam, you already know how radio "works" — that will make understanding easier!

Table 3.2
Summary of Amateur HF Bands

Wavelength (meters)	Frequency (MHz)
160	1.800 – 2.00
80 and 75	3.500 – 3.600 and 3.600 – 4.000
60	5.3305, 5.3465, 5.3570, 5.3715, and 5.4035 (USB carrier frequency – see note)
40	7.000 – 7.300
30	10.100 – 10.150
20	14.000 – 14.350
17	18.068 – 18.168
15	21.000 – 21.450
12	24.890 – 24.990
10	28.000 – 29.700

Note – on 60 meters, CW and digital emissions must be centered 1.5 kHz above the carrier frequencies indicated above. Only one signal at a time is permitted on any channel.

FREQUENCY PRIVILEGES

While General class licensees gain access to all those new frequencies on HF, you are also expected to know what those frequencies are. Relax — it's not necessary to have every individual band segment memorized! The way most General licensees operate is to have a frequency chart at the operating position, such as the one shown in **Figure 3.4**. (For reference and study, download your own copy of the chart from **www.arrl.org/graphical-frequency-allocations**.) When you tune the bands, check the chart to be sure you're within the proper band segment before transmitting. Of course, you're allowed to *listen* anywhere and are encouraged to do so.

You should learn the basic frequency limits of each band as shown in **Table 3.2**. This is easier than you might think because most of the amateur HF bands are harmonically related. For example, it's easy to remember the sequence "1.8 - 3.5 - 7 - 14 - 21 - 28 MHz" because the frequencies are close to being multiples of each other. These are the "traditional" HF amateur bands. You can convert the frequencies to wavelength as 300 / f (frequency in MHz) to get "160 - 80 - 40 - 20 - 15 - 10." (For example, 300 / 21 = 14.3. The conversion isn't exact — it's just a handy approximation.) Practice those two sequences and you're more than halfway home! [G1A05 and G1A07 to G1A10]

Other HF bands have been made available to amateurs since 1980: the "WARC" bands

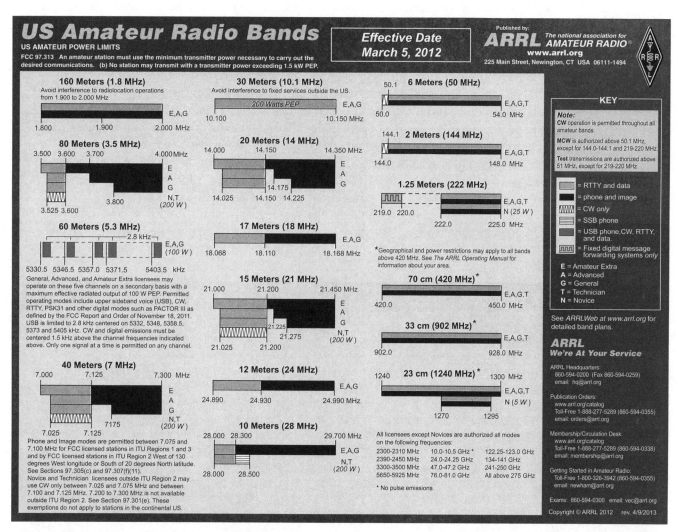

Figure 3.4 — Current Amateur Allocations Guide.

and 60 meters. (WARC stands for World Administrative Radio Conference.) At the 1979 WARC, amateurs were granted allocations at 30, 17 and 12 meters (10, 18, and 24 MHz). Amateurs also gained access to five fixed-frequency channels on 60 meters (5 MHz) in 2003.

General class license privileges extend across all of these frequency bands but not completely. As the frequency chart shows, for all bands where Generals have only partial access, their privileges for each mode are located at the top of the band where that mode is permitted. [G1A11] For example, on 40 meters Generals are only restricted from using CW, RTTY, and data at the lowest frequencies of 7000 – 7025 kHz. On 40 meter phone, General privileges begin at 7175 kHz and extend to the top of the band at 7300 kHz. On 75 meters, it's 3800 – 4000 kHz. [G1A06] Generals have all amateur privileges on the 160, 60, 30, 17, 12, and 10 meter bands. [G1A01] Note that on HF, repeaters are only authorized on the 10 meter band between 29.5 and 29.7 MHz.

There are two HF bands that have special regulations. The 60 meter band privileges permit channelized operation on USB, CW and certain digital modes *only* with a power limit of 100 W ERP (see the Technical Rules and Standards section later in this chapter for details). The 30 meter band privileges permit only CW, RTTY, and data signals with a power limit of 200 W PEP. [G1A02, G1A03, G1A04] The 60 meter and 30 meter bands are also *secondary amateur allocations*, meaning that stations in the *primary services* have priority and must be avoided. If you are operating in a secondary amateur allocation and a station in the primary service begins transmitting, you must stop transmitting and move to a clear frequency. [G1A12, G1A13]

Beacons

Beacon transmissions are very useful on the HF bands, just as they are on VHF and UHF. Beacons are used for observation of propagation and reception, as well as for other related activities. [G1B03] They alert operators to band openings that might otherwise be missed and provide a source of on-air signals for amateurs to calibrate and adjust their equipment. The sidebar "A System of DX Beacons" describes a worldwide system of beacons operating in a coordinated manner on several bands. Many individuals operate beacons on the 10 meter (28 MHz) band. The *General Class License Manual* website provides links to beacon directories in the Propagation section.

Perhaps you would like to put up your own beacon station. The rules, contained in §97.203, are quite simple. The most important are that there must be no more than one

A System of DX Beacons

Contacting stations around the world is one of the pleasures largely unique to the HF amateur bands, but how can an individual tell if the bands are open and to where? To be sure, there are terrific propagation prediction programs, but nothing substitutes for real on-the-air reception. The Northern California DX Foundation (NCDXF — **www.ncdxf.org**) in cooperation with the International Amateur Radio Union (IARU) operates and maintains a system of beacons operating on 14.100, 18.110, 21.150, 24.930 and 28.200 MHz. Special licenses were obtained from the FCC for the beacons operating below 28 MHz. There are 18 beacons distributed around the world on every continent except Antarctica. The beacons all take turns transmitting on each of the five frequencies at different power levels so that the listener can gauge propagation in that direction. Take a listen and see what you can hear!

There is also a system of automated receiving stations called the Reverse Beacon Network (RBN — **www.reversebeacon.net**) that performs a similar function in reverse. These stations, which are also distributed worldwide, decode CW and RTTY signals and post signal reports for them. The combination of the NCDXF and RBN systems gives amateurs unprecedented levels of information about worldwide HF propagation!

Special Circumstances

Amateurs are required to take special steps to mitigate interference in the following circumstances [G1E04]:

✔ When operating within one mile of an FCC Monitoring Station

✔ When transmitting spread spectrum emissions

✔ When using a band where the amateur service is secondary

FCC Monitoring Stations require an environment free of strong or spurious signals that can interfere with their receivers. The location of monitoring stations can be determined from a regional FCC office. Spread spectrum (SS) transmissions, because of their nature, have the potential to interfere with fixed frequency stations, so SS users should be sure their transmissions will not cause interference. And remember that Amateur Radio is not the primary service on 60 and 30 meters. On those bands, we are a secondary service and must not interfere with primary users.

beacon signal in the same band from a single location and beacons are limited to 100 W PEP output. The FCC rule also lists the frequency ranges in which beacon operation is permitted. [G1B02, G1B10]

Repeater Coordination

To minimize repeater-to-repeater interference, *regional repeater coordinators* or *frequency coordinators* have been established. These volunteer frequency coordinators are a good example of the self-organizing nature of Amateur Radio. They derive their authority voluntarily from the amateurs in the areas they serve. The ARRL is not a frequency coordinator, nor does the ARRL "certify" coordinators. Anyone planning on installing a repeater should check with the local frequency coordinator prior to such installation. A listing of frequency coordinators can be found on the National Frequency Coordinator's Council website, **nfcc.us**.

Not all repeater owners choose to participate in the coordination process. If interference occurs between a *noncoordinated* and a *coordinated* repeater systems, though, the licensee of the noncoordinated repeater has the primary responsibility of resolving the interference. The FCC has made it quite clear that they expect amateurs to use and respect the local frequency coordination process as a matter of "good amateur practice." [G1E06]

THIRD-PARTY TRAFFIC

Amateur Radio is often used to send messages on behalf of someone who is not an amateur. This is called *third-party communication*. Because Amateur Radio can bypass the normal Internet, telephone, and postal systems, particularly over the long-distance HF bands, many foreign governments have a legitimate interest in limiting this loss of revenue.

The FCC recognizes that third-party communication is part of the ham radio mission, specifically to train operators and to provide an effective emergency communications resource. Handling messages, also called "passing traffic," is part of both normal and emergency communications. As a result, third-party communications may be exchanged between any two amateur stations operating under FCC rules with the constraint that the communications must be noncommercial and of a personal, unimportant nature or be messages relating to emergencies or disaster relief. [G1E05] Aside from third-party communications discussed below, it is permitted for US amateurs to communicate with amateur stations in countries outside the areas administered by the Federal Communications Commission *unless* the country's administration has notified the ITU that it objects to such communications. [G2D05]

Definitions and Rules

Let's start by defining third-party communications. Any time that you send or receive information via ham radio on behalf of any unlicensed person or organization, even if the person is right there in the station with you — that's third-party communications. Here are some clarifying points:

- The entity on whose behalf the message is sent is the "third party" and the control operators who make the radio contact are the first and second parties.
- A licensed ham generates third-party traffic by communicating a message to or from someone who is not a licensed amateur.
- A licensed amateur capable of being a control operator at either station is not considered a third party regardless of whether he or she is at the station. A message from one ham to another ham is not third-party communications, whether directly transmitted or relayed by other stations.
- The third party need not be present in either station. A message can be taken to a ham station or a ham can transmit speech from a third-party's telephone call over ham radio (this is called a *phone patch*).
- The communications transmitted on behalf of the third party need not be written. Spoken words, data or images can all be third-party communications, as can messages or files transmitted via digital modes.
- The third party may participate in transmitting or receiving the message at either station. An unlicensed person in your station engages in third-party communications when they speak into the microphone, send Morse code, or type on a keyboard. Letting an unlicensed friend make a contact under your supervision is third-party communications, even if the contact is short and for demonstration or training purposes, such as during a contest or special event.
- An organization, such as a church or school, can also be a third party.
- Third-party traffic may never be exchanged on behalf of someone whose amateur license has been suspended or revoked and not reinstated. [G1E01]

International Considerations

When signals cross national borders, the rules change. International third-party communications are prohibited unless the country in question specifically allows third-party communications to and from US hams. [G1E07, G1E08] **Table 3.3** shows which countries have third-party agreements with the United States. If the other country isn't on this list, third-party communication to or from that country is not permitted. This is important to remember because hams like to be helpful and can inadvertently violate third-party rules if not careful.

If you contact a DX station who then asks you to pass a message to his family, doing so would be third-party communications. Check to be sure the DX station's country has a third-party agreement with the US before accepting the message.

Making a contact to allow a visiting student to talk to his family in South America is third-party communications even if both the student and the family are present at the stations involved. Be sure there is a third-party agreement in place.

PROHIBITED AND RESTRICTED COMMUNICATIONS

The FCC has allowed amateurs a lot of room to operate, so to speak, giving hams a free hand to transmit what they like. There are a few general prohibitions. For example, transmitting a false distress signal is absolutely prohibited under all circumstances, as is obscene or indecent speech. Some other prohibitions have special exceptions, however.

You're already aware that transmitting music is prohibited, even music that is just part of the background noise in your station or your vehicle. (Turn down the broadcast audio when you're on the air!) Is it ever permitted? Only when it is an incidental part of a manned space craft transmission. Incidental means that you're listening to an International Space Station transmission and retransmitting it for other amateurs to hear, which is permitted. If music happens to be part of the audio, it's okay for it to be included in the retransmission. [G1B05]

Table 3.3

Third-Party Traffic Agreements List

Occasionally, DX stations may ask you to pass a third-party message to a friend or relative in the States. This is all right as long as the US has signed an official third-party traffic agreement with that particular country, or the third party is a licensed amateur. The traffic must be noncommercial and of a personal, unimportant nature. During an emergency, the US State Department will often work out a special temporary agreement with the country involved. But in normal times, never handle traffic without first making sure it is legally permitted.

US amateurs may handle third-party traffic with:

V2	Antigua/Barbuda	C5	Gambia, The	OA-OC	Peru
LO-LW	Argentina	9G	Ghana	DU-DZ	Philippines
VK	Australia	J3	Grenada	VR6	Pitcairn Island*
V3	Belize	TG	Guatemala	V4	St. Kitts/Nevis
CP	Bolivia	8R	Guyana	J6	St. Lucia
E7	Bosnia-Herzegovina	HH	Haiti	J8	St. Vincent and
PP-PY	Brazil	HQ-HR	Honduras		the Grenadines
VE, VO, VY	Canada	4X, 4Z	Israel	9L	Sierra Leone
CA-CE	Chile	6Y	Jamaica	ZR-ZU	South Africa
HJ-HK	Colombia	JY	Jordan	3DA	Swaziland
D6	Comoros (Federal	EL	Liberia	9Y-9Z	Trinidad/Tobago
	Islamic Republic of)	V7	Marshall Islands	TA-TC	Turkey
TI, TE	Costa Rica	XA-XI	Mexico	GB	United Kingdom
CM, CO	Cuba	V6	Micronesia,	CV-CX	Uruguay
HI	Dominican Republic		Federated States of	YV-YY	Venezuela
J7	Dominica	YN	Nicaragua	4U1ITU	ITU - Geneva
HC-HD	Ecuador	HO-HP	Panama	4U1VIC	VIC - Vienna
YS	El Salvador	ZP	Paraguay		

Notes:

Since 1970, there has been an informal agreement between the United Kingdom and the US, permitting Pitcairn and US amateurs to exchange messages concerning medical emergencies, urgent need for equipment or supplies, and private or personal matters of island residents.

Please note that Region 2 of the International Amateur Radio Union (IARU) has recommended that international traffic on the 20 and 15 meter bands be conducted on 14.100 – 14.150, 14.250 – 14.350, 21.150 – 21.200 and 21.300 – 21.450 MHz. The IARU is the alliance of Amateur Radio societies from around the world; Region 2 comprises member-societies in North, South and Central America and the Caribbean.

At the end of an exchange of third-party traffic with a station located in a foreign country, an FCC-licensed amateur must transmit the call sign of the foreign station as well as his own call sign.

Current as of January 2015; see **www.arrl.org/third-party-operating-agreements** for the latest information.

Another type of prohibited transmission is codes that are intended to obscure the meaning of the message. What about Q-signals and prosigns? Those are well-known abbreviations intended to make normal communications more efficient and not more obscure, so they're perfectly acceptable. [G1B07] Are encryption or "secret codes" ever allowed? Only when used to control a space station (not the ISS, but any station operating in space, such as an amateur satellite [§97.3(a)(40)]) or a radio-controlled model aircraft. In the first instance, codes are necessary to prevent unauthorized stations from transmitting commands to the space station. In the second, the FCC has ruled that the coded commands are not intended to obscure the message — they are the message! [G1B06]

Speaking of space stations, some satellites have uplinks or downlinks in the 10 meter amateur band. If the downlink is on 10 meters, is it okay for a Technician licensee to transmit on the VHF or UHF uplink and have the satellite retransmit their signals on the 10 meter band? The satellites are acting as repeater stations that simultaneously retransmit the signals of other stations on another frequency. The same question applies to terrestrial *cross-band repeaters* that receive signals on one frequency band and retransmit them on another frequency band. Such transmissions are permitted if the control operator of the repeater transmitter that operates on the HF band has a General class license or higher. [G1E02]

Much is made as well over the prohibition of business-related and pecuniary (monetary) interests in activity on the amateur bands. In your Technician studies, you learned about what is considered business and what is incidental personal interest in a communication. Among the most common such situations are the regular "swap nets" held in many areas for amateurs to trade or sell equipment related to Amateur Radio. This is perfectly legitimate as long as other amateurs are being notified of the sale of apparatus normally used in an amateur station and such activity is not done on a regular basis. That means household goods may not be sold and no selling radios every week at a profit either! [G1B09]

WRITTEN RECORDS

In Chapter 2, we discussed station records and why it is a good idea to keep a record or "log" of your HF contacts. A detailed log is an asset to any amateur station. Practically, the log can help with a reply if the FCC requests information on who was control operator of your station at a given date and time. Even so, there are only two types of written records that the FCC requires you to keep:

● The call signs of other amateurs operating your station.

● For 60 meter operation only, if you are using an antenna other than a dipole, record the antenna gain calculations or manufacturer's data for antennas used — this is to ensure that the 100 W ERP restriction is met. [G2D07]

Before you go on, study test questions G1A01 through G1A13, G1B02, G1B03, G1B05, G1B06, G1B07, G1B09, G1B10, G1E01, G1E02, G1E04 through G1E08, G2D05 and G2D07. Review this section if you have difficulty.

3.4 Technical Rules and Standards

Two sets of technical rules receive the most attention on the General class exam — those for transmitted power and for digital transmissions. These two areas represent the biggest changes for operators new to HF operating and practices.

GOOD AMATEUR PRACTICES

To be sure, there are many operating procedures and technical areas not covered by the exam or even by the FCC Part 97 rules. Setting exact rules for every type of operating would result in an impenetrable thicket of regulation and would work against one of the basic tenets of the Amateur Service — technical experimentation and innovation. What has worked well for amateurs is the general requirement by the FCC that in the absence of a specific rule, amateur stations should be operated in conformance with good engineering and good amateur practice. [G1B11] While the FCC reserves the right to rule on what is and isn't "good engineering and good amateur practice," amateurs themselves set the day-to-day operating standards. [G1B12]

How can you find out what those standards are? Amateurs are expected to educate themselves and assist others in doing so. To that end, the ARRL publishes a number of respected references, such as the *ARRL Handbook* and the *ARRL Antenna Book*. (The complete set of ARRL publications is available at **www.arrl.org/shop**.) Other publishers offer their own materials and there are ham websites for every technical topic you can think of. The *General Class License Manual* website (**www.arrl.org/general-class-license-manual**) lists several sources for technical reference information.

QRP or QRO?

Two Q-signals have been adopted to signify operation with high power (QRO — originally "increase power") or low power (QRP — originally "decrease power"). There is a thriving community of hams who prefer low power operation — the "QRPers." They achieve remarkable success with a minimum of transmitted power, usually less than 10 W and often 5 W. [G2D10] Nevertheless, other activities require higher power to be successful, such as wide area net control and traffic handling or contacting DX stations on difficult paths and bands. The power output from most amateur transceivers is about 100 W. If no amplifier is used, this level of operation is often referred to as "barefoot."

How do you decide what power level to use in order to make a contact or call CQ? The FCC rules are clear that the "minimum power necessary" should be used, but that doesn't mean to reduce your transmitter output until your signal is just barely audible. What that means is to use the minimum power necessary for the desired signal quality and coverage. This allows other amateurs that are out of range of your signal to share the frequency, reducing congestion. Experience will allow you to judge propagation and band conditions so as to make the appropriate choice — to use QRP or "go QRO."

TRANSMITTERS AND AMPLIFIER POWER

Because HF QSOs are almost always made directly from point to point without the assistance of repeaters, transmitter power becomes a more significant issue on the HF bands. Many HF operators use a *linear amplifier* to increase the transmitter output power and their signal's readability at the receiving end.

General, Advanced, and Amateur Extra licensees are limited to a maximum transmitter output power of 1500 W peak envelope power or PEP with two restrictions as noted below. [G1C02, G1C06] The legal limit of power is sometimes known as a "full gallon." Novice and Technician licensees operating on HF are limited to 200 W PEP output. (See Chapter 4 for the definition of PEP.) Of course, amateurs are always required to use the *minimum* power necessary to carry out the desired communication. [G1C04]

The power measurement must be made at the output of the transmitter or amplifier, whichever is the final piece of equipment that generates RF power before the connection to the antenna system. The antenna system includes feed lines and any impedance matching devices.

There are two restrictions that reduce maximum power for Generals and Extras:

● Amateurs are restricted to 200 W PEP on the 30 meter band (10 MHz) [G1C01]

Table 3.4
Maximum Symbol Rates and Bandwidth

Band	Symbol Rate (baud)	Bandwidth (kHz)
160 through 10 m	300	1
10 m	1200	1
6 m, 2 m	19.6k	20
1.25 m, 70 cm	56k	100
33 cm and above	no limit	no limit

Pending Changes in Digital Bandwidth Rules

As this book was being written in early 2015, the FCC was considering a revision of the HF digital signal rules to eliminate the restrictions on symbol rate in favor of specifying a maximum bandwidth for digital emissions (RM-11708). The final rulemaking decision may change the allowed symbol rates and bandwidth on amateur bands so watch the ARRL home page and other amateur publications for information on those changes.

• Amateurs are restricted to 100 W ERP on the 60 meter band (5 MHz) with a maximum signal bandwidth of 2.8 kHz. [G1C03]

To determine your ERP (effective radiated power), multiply your transmitter output power by the gain of your antenna. For example, assume your antenna has a gain of 3 dBd (dB of gain relative to a dipole). Your transmitter output power is 100 watts and 3 dB is a factor of 2, so your ERP is $100 \times 2 = 200$ watts. To use this antenna on the 60 meter band, your transmitter output power should be no more than 50 watts because $50 \times 2 = 100$ watts ERP. (For simplicity, this calculation did not include feed line loss.)

When Morse code testing was eliminated from amateur exams, Novice and Technician licensees were allowed the same 80, 40, and 15 meter CW frequency privileges as General class licensees. On 10 meters, Novices and Techs are allowed the same CW, RTTY and data privileges as other operators in the 28.0 to 28.3 MHz segment, plus SSB phone and CW operation from 28.3 to 28.5 MHz. Novice and Technician licensees operating on HF are limited to 200 W PEP output, but General, Advanced, and Extra licensees may use full 1500 W PEP output in the former Novice segments on 80, 40, and 15 meters. [G1C05]

DIGITAL TRANSMISSIONS

Technical standards for digital transmissions are primarily concerned with the bandwidth of the transmitted signal. (Chapter 6 covers digital signals in detail.) There are also requirements that the protocol used be publicly available so that any amateur can monitor it or use it to engage in communications. [§97.309(a)] The transmitted signal bandwidth is closely tied to its *symbol rate* which is a measure of how many individual signaling events take place every second (see the sidebar "Bits or Bauds" in Chapter 5). In general, the higher the symbol rate, the wider the bandwidth required to transmit the signal. Bandwidth has a very specific definition in FCC rule §97.3(a)(8) — the frequency range outside of which the signal components are at least 26 dB (400 times) below the average (mean) power of the signal inside that range.

FCC rules §97.305(c) and §97.307(f) restrict the symbol rate of transmitted signals to make sure that digital signals do not consume too much bandwidth at the expense of other modes. **Table 3.4** shows the limits by band. On the HF bands, symbol rate and bandwidth are restricted because those bands are relatively narrow and a wide bandwidth signal would cause a lot of interference. As the size of the amateur bands increases with frequency, faster (wider) signals are allowed. At 33 cm (902 MHz) and above, there is no limit except for the band edges themselves, creating the "autobahn" of amateur digital signaling. [G1C07 through G1C11]

Before you go on, study test questions G1B11, G1B12, G1C01 through G1C11, and G2D10. Review this section if you have difficulty.

Chapter 4

Components and Circuits

Get ready to "lift the hood" and learn more about electronics, the heart and soul of what makes a radio go! As a General, you'll understand the basic mechanics of how simple circuits work and how the components work together. That understanding enables to you to adjust your equipment and maintain your station knowledgeably. Even more importantly, you'll be able to respond effectively when things aren't working exactly right or when you need to operate under field or emergency conditions.

You've already learned the fundamentals of electricity and radio to pass the Technician exam and we'll dive one layer deeper for the General. Turn the ignition key and get warmed up with a short refresher of what you learned to pass the Technician exam.

4.1 Electrical Review

CURRENT, VOLTAGE AND POWER

Electronic current (represented by the letter I) is the flow of electrons, atomic particles with one unit of negative electric charge. Current is measured in *amperes* (A or amps) with an *ammeter*. *Voltage* (E) is the force that makes electrons move and is measured in *volts* (V) with a *voltmeter*. The *polarity* of a voltage refers to the direction from positive to negative. *Power* (P), measured in *watts* (W), is the product of voltage and current, $P = E \times I$.

Discussions of electronic circuits should be assumed to use *conventional current* in which positive charge flows in the direction of positive to negative voltage. This is the exact opposite of *electronic current* in which electrons move in the direction of negative to positive voltage. Although it results in confusion, this convention was assigned before the true nature of electricity was understood. Unless texts and references specifically refer to the flow of electrons, assume that conventional current is used.

RESISTANCE AND OHM'S LAW

The opposition of a material to current flow is called *resistance* (R) and is measured in *ohms* (Ω) with an *ohmmeter*. Georg Ohm discovered that voltage, current and resistance

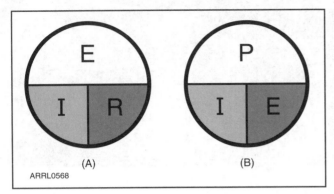

Figure 4.1 — These simple diagrams will help you re-member the Ohm's Law relationships and power equa-tions. If you know any two of the quantities, you can find the third by covering up the unknown quantity. The posi-tions of the remaining two symbols show if you have to multiply (side-by-side) or divide (one above the other).

are proportional. *Ohm's Law* states that $R = E \div I$. If you know any two of I, E or R, you can determine the missing quantity:

$$R = \frac{E}{I} \text{ and } I = \frac{E}{R} \text{ and } E = I \times R$$

The voltage caused by current flowing through a resistance ($E = I \times R$) is called a voltage drop.

Substituting the Ohm's Law equivalents for volt-age ($E = I \times R$) and current ($I = E \div R$) allows power to be calculated using resistance:

$$P = I^2 \times R \text{ and } P = \frac{E^2}{R}$$

The drawings in **Figure 4.1** are aids to remember-ing Ohm's Law and the power equations in any of their forms. Here are a few examples:

To find out how many watts of electrical power are used if 400 V dc is supplied to an 800-Ω resistor:

$$P = \frac{E^2}{R} = \frac{400 \times 400}{800} = \frac{160,000}{800} = 200 \text{ W} \quad [\text{G5B03}]$$

To find out how many watts of electrical power are used by a 12 V dc light bulb that draws 0.2 A:

$$P = E \times I = 12 \times 0.2 = 2.4 \text{ W} \quad [\text{G5B04}]$$

To find out how many watts are being dissipated when a current of 7.0 mA of current flows through a 1.25 kΩ resistor:

$$P = I^2 \times R = 0.007 \times 0.007 \times 1250 = 0.06125 \text{ W}$$
$$= 61.25 \text{ mW} \quad\quad\quad\quad\quad [\text{G5B05}]$$

Remember that 7 mA (milliamperes) is equal to 0.007 A, 1.25 kΩ (kilohms) is equal to 1250 Ω and 0.06125 W is equal to approximately 61 mW (mil-liwatts).

AC AND DC WAVEFORMS

Current that flows in one direction all the time is called *direct current*, abbreviated dc. Current that re-verses direction is called *alternating current*, abbre-viated ac. A voltage that has the same polarity all the time is a *dc voltage*. A voltage that reverses polarity is an *ac voltage*.

Frequency

A complete sequence of ac current flowing, stop-ping, reversing and stopping again is called a *cycle*. The number of cycles per second is the current's *frequency* (f) measured in *hertz* (Hz). A *harmonic* is a frequency at some integer multiple (2, 3, 4 and so on) of a lowest or *fundamental* frequency. The harmonic at twice the fundamental frequency is called the *second harmonic*, at three times the fundamental frequency the *third harmonic*, and so forth. There is no "first harmonic."

Wavelength

All radio waves travel at the *speed of light* (c) in whatever media they are traveling. The speed of light in space and air is 300 million (3×10^8) meters per second and somewhat slower in wires and cables. The *wavelength* (λ) of a radio wave is the distance it travels during one complete cycle.

$$\lambda = \frac{c}{f} \text{ and } f = \frac{c}{\lambda}$$

A radio wave can be referred to by wavelength or frequency because the speed of light is constant. As frequency increases wavelength decreases and vice-versa.

SERIES AND PARALLEL CIRCUITS

A *circuit* is any complete path through which current can flow. If two or more components are connected in a circuit so that the same current flows through all of the components, that is a *series circuit*. If two or more components are connected so that the same voltage is applied to all of the components, that is a *parallel circuit*.

DECIBELS

You were introduced to the decibel (dB) in your studies for the Technician class exam. As you become more and more experienced in ham radio, you'll notice the "deebee" everywhere — it's the standard way of referring to power or voltage ratios.

The formula for computing decibels is:

$$dB = 10 \log_{10} \text{ (power ratio)} = 20 \log_{10} \text{ (voltage ratio)}$$

If you are comparing a measured power or voltage (P_M or V_M) to some reference power (P_{REF} or V_{REF}) the formulas are:

$$dB = 10 \log_{10} \left(\frac{P_M}{P_{REF}} \right) = 20 \log_{10} \left(\frac{V_M}{V_{REF}} \right)$$

Positive values of dB mean the ratio is greater than 1 and negative values of dB indicate a ratio of less than 1. Ratios greater than 1 can be referred to as *gain*, while ratios less than 1 can be called a *loss* or *attenuation*. Note that loss and attenuation are often given as positive values of dB (for example, "a loss of 10 dB" or "a 6 dB attenuator") with the understanding that the ratio is less than one and the calculated value of change in dB will be negative.

For example, if an amplifier turns a 5-W signal into a 25-W signal, that's a gain of:

$$dB = 10 \log_{10} \left(\frac{25}{5} \right) = 10 \log_{10} (5) = 10 \times (0.7) = 7 \text{ dB}$$

On the other hand, if by adjusting a receiver's volume control the audio output signal voltage is reduced from 2 volts to 0.1 volt, that's a change of:

$$dB = 20 \log_{10} \left(\frac{0.1}{2} \right) = 20 \log_{10} (0.05) = 20 \times (-1.3) = -26 \text{ dB}$$

A very useful value to remember is that any time you double the power (or cut it in half), there is a 3 dB change. [G5B01] A two-times increase (or decrease) in power results in a gain (or loss) of:

$$dB = 10 \log_{10}\left(-\right) = 10 \log_{10}(2) = 10 \times (0.3) = 3 \text{ dB}$$

Calculating a Power or Voltage Ratio from dB

You already know how to turn power and voltage ratios into decibels. What if you are given a ratio in dB and asked to calculate the power or voltage ratio? Here are the formulas:

$$\text{power ratio} = \log^{-1}\left(\frac{dB}{10}\right) \text{ and}$$

$$\text{voltage ratio} = \log^{-1}\left(\frac{dB}{20}\right)$$

Note that the inverse log (written as $\log_{10}^{-1}$ or just $\log^{-1}$) is sometimes referred to as antilog. Most calculators use the inverse log notation. On scientific calculators the inverse log key may be labeled LOG^{-1}, ALOG, or 10^X, which means "raise 10 to the power of this value." Some calculators require a two-button sequence such as INV then LOG.

Example 1: A power ratio of 9 dB = $\log^{-1}(9/10) = \log(0.9) = 8$
Example 2: A voltage ratio of 32 dB = $\log^{-1}(32/20) = \log^{-1}(1.6) = 40$

Converting dB to Percentage and Vice Versa

$$dB = 10 \log\left(\frac{\text{Percentage Power}}{100\%}\right)$$

$$dB = 20 \log\left(\frac{\text{Percentage Voltage}}{100\%}\right)$$

$$\text{Percentage Power} = 100\% \times \log^{-1}\left(\frac{dB}{10}\right)$$

$$\text{Percentage Voltage} = 100\% \times \log^{-1}\left(\frac{dB}{20}\right)$$

Here's a practical application. Suppose you are using an antenna feed line that has a signal loss of 1 dB. You can calculate the amount of transmitter power that's actually reaching your antenna and how much is lost in the feed line.

$$\text{Percentage Power} = 100\% \times \log^{-1}\left(\frac{-1}{10}\right) = 100\% \times \log^{-1}(-0.1) = 79.4\% \text{ [G5B10]}$$

So 79.4% of your power is reaching the antenna and 20.6% is lost in the feed line.

Example 3: A power ratio of 20% = 10 log (20% / 100%) = 10 log (0.2) = −7 dB
Example 4: A voltage ratio of 150% = 20 log (150% / 100%) = 20 log (1.5) = 3.52 dB
Example 5: −3 dB represents a percentage power = $100\% \times \log^{-1}(-3/10) = 50\%$
Example 6: 4 dB represents a percentage voltage = $100\% \times \log^{-1}(4/20) = 158\%$

4.2 AC Power

RMS: DEFINITION AND MEASUREMENT

As ac electrical power became common, it was important to know how much ac voltage delivered the same average power in comparison to a dc voltage. The power equation is quite clear for dc: $P = E^2 / R$. But what value for E should be used for ac power? The peak voltage, an average…or what? The answer turns out to be the *root mean square (RMS)* voltage (often abbreviated V_{RMS}). If RMS voltage is used in the equations shown above for calculating power, the result for the ac signal is the same as for an unvarying dc voltage. [G5B07]

"Root mean square" refers to the method used to calculate the RMS voltage — it is the square root of the sum of the squares of the average (*mean*) values of the signal voltages that are present. If the voltages of more than one waveform are added together, first square the amplitude of each voltage ("square"), then sum them together and compute the average ("mean"), and take the square root of the mean ("root").

The RMS value of voltage can be calculated for any waveform, but for a sine wave, the most common ac waveform of all, the RMS value is simply 0.707 times the sine wave's peak voltage, V_{PK}, as shown in **Figure 4.2**.

For sine waves, use the following equations:

$$V_{RMS} = 0.707 \times V_{PK} = 0.707 \times \frac{V_{P-P}}{2}$$

$$V_{PK} = 1.414 \times V_{RMS}$$

$$V_{P-P} = 2 \times 1.414 \times V_{RMS} = 2.828 \times V_{RMS}$$

Do not use these formulas for waveforms that are not sine waves, such as speech, square waves or dc voltages combined with ac voltages!

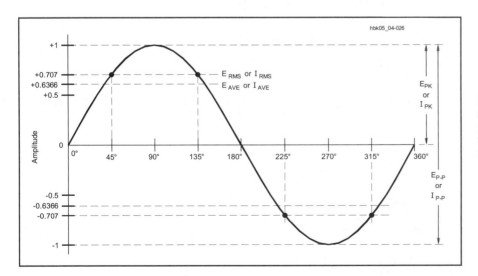

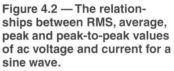

Figure 4.2 — The relationships between RMS, average, peak and peak-to-peak values of ac voltage and current for a sine wave.

Example 7: A sine wave with a peak voltage of 17 V has an RMS value of $V_{RMS} = 0.707 \times 17 = 12$ V [G5B09]

Example 8: A sine wave with a peak-to-peak voltage of 100 V has an RMS value of $V_{RMS} = 0.707 \times (100 / 2) = 35.4$ V

Example 9: A sine wave with an RMS voltage of 120 V has a peak-to-peak voltage of $V_{P-P} = 2 \times 1.414 \times 120 = 2.828 \times 120 = 339.4$ V

It is particularly important to know the relationship between RMS and peak voltages to choose components that have sufficient voltage ratings. Capacitors are often connected across ac power leads to perform RF filtering. The capacitor must be rated to withstand the ac peak voltage. For example, a capacitor placed across a 120 V ac power line will experience a peak voltage of $120 \times 1.414 = 169.7$ V. A capacitor with a 200 V rating or higher should be used.

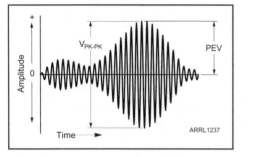

Figure 4.3 — The peak envelope voltage (PEV) for a composite waveform.

PEP: DEFINITION AND MEASUREMENT

You are sure to agree that the full amateur power limit of 1500 W certainly has a lot of "pep," but PEP (or *peak envelope power*) has a more formal definition. PEP is the average power of one complete RF cycle at the peak of the signal's envelope. (It is *not* the power at the peak of an RF cycle during a peak of the signal's envelope.) PEP is used because it is a convenient way to measure or specify the maximum power of amplitude-modulated signals.

To calculate average ac power, you need to know the load impedance and the RMS voltage. Measure the RF voltage at the very peak of the modulated signal's envelope — this is the *peak envelope voltage* (*PEV*) as shown in **Figure 4.3**. PEP is equal to one-half of the waveform's peak-to-peak voltage, V_{P-P}. PEP is then calculated as follows:

$$PEP = \frac{\left[\dfrac{0.707 \times V_{P-P}}{2}\right]^2}{R} = \frac{\left(PEV \times 0.707\right)^2}{R} = \frac{V_{RMS}^2}{R}$$

Example 10: If PEV is 50 V across a 50-Ω load, the PEP power is

$$PEP = \frac{\left(50 \times 0.707\right)^2}{50} = 25 \text{ W}$$

Example 11: If a 50-Ω load is dissipating 1200 W PEP, the RMS voltage is

$$V_{RMS} = \sqrt{PEP \times R} = \sqrt{1200 \times 50} = 245 \text{ V} \text{ [G5B12]}$$

Example 12: In Example 11, the peak voltage is

$$V_{PK} = 245 \text{ V} \times 1.414 = 346 \text{ V}$$

Example 13: If an oscilloscope measures 200 V_{P-P} across a 50-Ω load, the PEP power is

$$PEP = \frac{\left[\dfrac{0.707 \times 200}{2}\right]^2}{50} = \frac{4999}{50} = 100 \text{ W} \text{ [G5B06]}$$

For 500 VP-P, the PEP power is

$$PEP = \frac{\left[\dfrac{0.707 \times 500}{2}\right]^2}{50} = \frac{31241}{50} = 625 \text{ W} \text{ [G5B14]}$$

PEP is equal to the average power if an amplitude-modulated signal is not modulated. [G5B11] This is the case when modulation is removed from an AM signal (leaving only the steady carrier) or when a CW transmitter is keyed. Likewise, an FM signal is a constant-power signal, so PEP is always equal to average power for FM signals. If an average-reading wattmeter connected to your transmitter reads 1060 W when you close the key on CW, your PEP output is also 1060 W. [G5B13]

Before you go on, study test questions G5B06, G5B07, G5B09 and G5B11 to G5B14. Review this section if you have difficulty.

4.3 Basic Components

You were introduced to electronic components while studying for your Technician exam. In this section, you'll learn some basic characteristics of resistors, capacitors, inductors, and transformers. The symbols that represent each type of component on electronic schematics are presented in **Figure 4.4** for reference. Refer to this figure as you read this section. [G7A09 to G7A13]

The following terms apply to all components and may be important when selecting a component for a design or for repair.

- *Nominal value* — the quantity of a specific characteristic that the component is manufactured to exhibit, such as a 10-Ω resistor.
- *Tolerance* — the amount by which the actual value is allowed to vary from the nominal value, usually expressed in percent, such as a 5% tolerance resistor.
- *Temperature coefficient* — the variation of the component's actual value with temperature, such as 10 mΩ per degree Centigrade.
- *Power (or voltage or current) rating* — the rated ability of the component to withstand heat or dissipate power, such as a ¼ W resistor.

A more complete description of electronic components can be found in the *ARRL Handbook* and the website for this book contains links to more information.

RESISTORS AND RESISTANCE

A selection of resistors is shown in **Figure 4.5** ranging from subminiature *surface-mount technology* (*SMT*) packages to a *power resistor* that can dissipate several watts of power. Although all of the resistors could have the same nominal value, they obviously vary in other characteristics. There are several common types of resistors. **Table 4.1** illustrates how their characteristics differ and in what applications they are most commonly used.

Resistors of all types are available with nominal values from 1 Ω or less to more than 1 MΩ. The nominal value is printed directly on the body of the resistor as text or by using colored bands of paint. (This book's website, **www.arrl.org/general-class-license-manual**, has links to more information on component marking.) Several tolerances are available, from precision resistors with tolerances of 1% or less, to general-purpose resistors with tolerances of 5% or 10%.

Temperature coefficients (or "tempco") may be either positive or negative, depending on the material from which

Components

The three most basic types of electronic components are resistors, capacitors and inductors (coils). Resistors, designated with an R, have a resistance specified in ohms (Ω), kilohms (kΩ) or megohms (MΩ). Capacitors, designated with a C, store electric energy and have values measured in picofarads (pF), nanofarads (nF) and microfarads (μF). Inductors, designated L, store magnetic energy and have values measured in nanohenrys (nH), microhenrys (μH), millihenrys (mH) and henrys (H).

Use the following conversion factors to convert units with one metric prefix to another:

Divide by 1000 to convert: pico to nano, nano to micro, micro to milli, kilo to mega, and mega to giga.

Multiply by 1000 to convert: nano to pico, micro to nano, milli to micro, mega to kilo, and giga to mega. [G5C17,G5C18]

Common Schematic Symbols Used in Circuit Diagrams

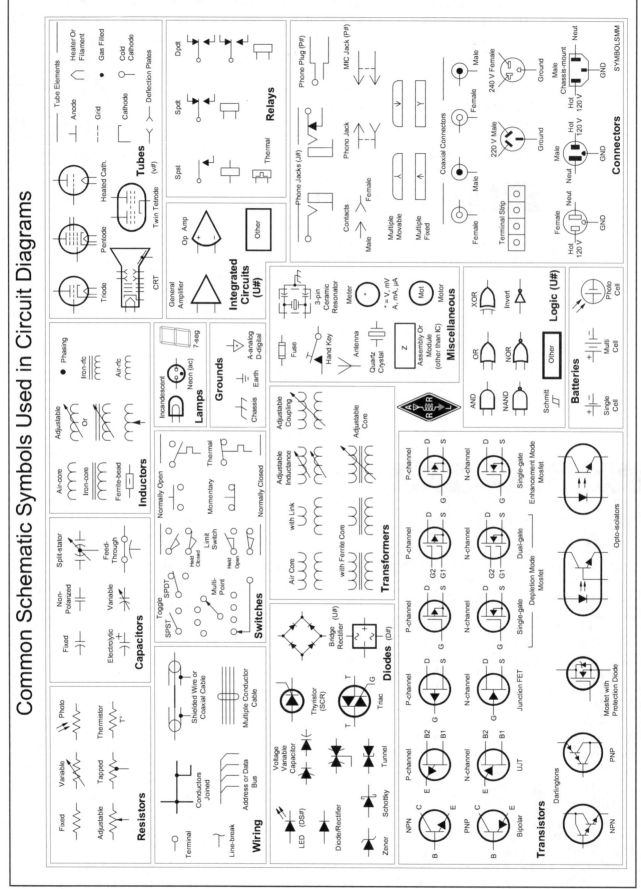

Figure 4.4 — These are the standard symbols used by the ARRL on schematic diagrams.

Table 4.1

Characteristics of Resistor Types

Resistor Type	Power Ratings	Applications
Carbon composition	⅛ – 2 W	General use, wire leads
Carbon film	¹⁄₁₀ – ½ W	General use, wire leads and SMT package
Metal film	¹⁄₁₀ – ½ W	Low-noise, wire leads and SMT package
Wirewound	1 W – 100 W or more	Power circuits
Metal oxide	½ – 10 W	Noninductive for RF applications

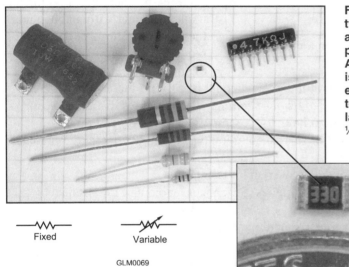

Fixed   Variable

GLM0069

Figure 4.5 — These examples of common resistor types include a 10-W power resistor at the upper left, a variable resistor at top center and a single in-line package (SIP) of several resistors at the upper right. A surface-mount technology (SMT) resistor package is barely visible next to the variable resistor but is enlarged in the inset photo. Several low-power resistors fill the bottom half of the photograph, from the large 1-W carbon composition resistor to the small ¼ W resistor at the bottom.

the resistor is made. [G6A16] For a positive temperature coefficient, as temperature increases so does resistance. Oppositely, resistors with a negative tempco will decrease in resistance as temperature increases. Most resistor types are available with several different values of tempco, specified in ohms per degree Centigrade (Ω/°C).

Parasitic Inductance

In radio electronics uses, the *parasitic inductance* of a resistor is important. (Parasitic means "an unwanted characteristic resulting from the component's physical construction.") Wire-wound power resistors are made by winding resistive wire on a ceramic form, making a small coil. This type of construction results in significant amounts of parasitic inductance that is generally unimportant at low frequencies or dc. If such a resistor is used in a radio frequency circuit, though, the inductance is often enough to disrupt the circuit's operation or affect the tuning. [G6A17] Be sure to use one of the non-inductive resistor types for circuits operating at radio frequencies: carbon composition, carbon film or metal oxide.

INDUCTORS AND INDUCTANCE

Figure 4.6 shows several common types of inductors and their corresponding schematic symbols. Double lines next to the inductor symbol indicate the presence of a magnetic core, as opposed to an air core. The variable inductor in the middle also has a magnetic core — showing the double lines in the variable inductor symbol is optional. Miniature

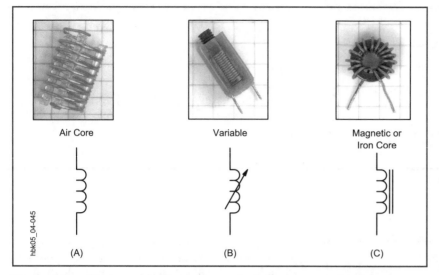

Air Core

Variable

Magnetic or Iron Core

(A)

(B)

(C)

hbk05_04-045

Figure 4.6 — Photos and schematic symbols for common inductors.

inductors (not shown in the figure) have the same style of package and are easily confused with resistors. (This book's website has links to more information on component marking and will take you to more information how these inductors are identified.)

The inductance of an inductor, the measure of its ability to store magnetic energy, is directly proportional to the square of the number of turns and the area enclosed by each turn. Making an inductor longer without changing the number of turns or diameter reduces inductance. The higher the inductance, the greater the amount of magnetic energy is stored for a given amount of current. Increasing the core's ability to store magnetic energy, called its *permeability*, also increases its inductance.

The type of core and winding of an inductor are important to the type of circuit in which it is to be used. Here is a list of several common types of inductors you'll encounter:

- *Laminated iron core* — dc and ac power and filtering
- *Powdered iron solenoid* — power supplies, RF chokes, audio and low-frequency radio circuits
- *Powdered iron* and *ferrite toroid*s — audio and radio circuits
- *Air core* — RF transmitting

Variable inductors are encountered in low-power receiving and transmitting applications. Low-power variable inductors are adjusted by moving a magnetic core in and out of the inductor. The core is threaded and moves when turned. In a transmitter or impedance matching circuit, high-power variable inductors are adjusted by moving a sliding contact along the inductor.

While resistors dissipate energy entirely within their bodies, the stored energy of an inductor is not quite so tame. As **Figure 4.7** shows, when two inductors are placed close together with their axes aligned, the magnetic field from one inductor can also pass through the second inductor, sharing some of its energy. This is called *coupling*. The ability of inductors to share or transfer magnetic energy is called *mutual inductance*.

Sharing of energy is useful in a transformer but may be undesired if it allows signals to transfer between circuits. Mutual inductance can be minimized in several ways. Small inductors can be shielded by wrapping them with a thin layer of magnetic material such as iron. If the coils are wound along a straight axis as shown in Figure 4.7 (called a *solenoidal winding*), the coils may be placed so that their axes are at right angles to each other. [G6A19]

Another way is to use a *toroidal winding* as shown at the right in Figure 4.6. The toroid core contains nearly all of the inductor's magnetic field. Since very little of the field extends outside of the core, toroidal inductors (or "toroids") can be placed next to each other in nearly any orientation with

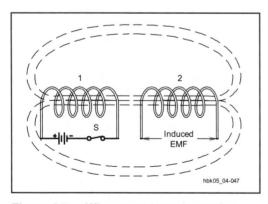

Figure 4.7 — When ac voltage is applied, current flows through coil number 1, setting up a shared magnetic field that causes a voltage to be induced in the turns of coil number 2.

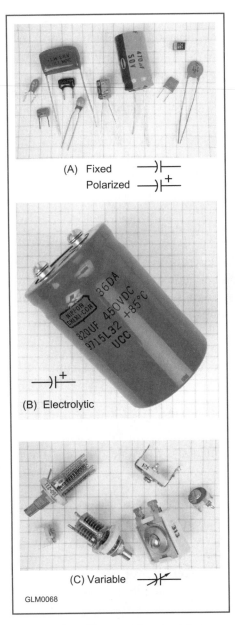

(A) Fixed

Polarized

(B) Electrolytic

(C) Variable

GLM0068

Figure 4.8 — Photo A shows fixed value capacitors, including aluminum electrolytic capacitors near the center. Film and mica capacitors are shown on the left and ceramic units on the right. Photo B shows a large "computer grade" electrolytic capacitor used in power supply filters. Photo C shows several small adjustable or "trimmer" capacitors.

minimal mutual inductance. This property makes them ideal for use in RF circuits, where you do not want interaction between nearby inductors.

Toroids may be wound on ferrite or powdered iron cores. (Ferrite is a ceramic containing iron compounds.) These core materials have high permeabilities, making it possible to obtain large values of inductance in a relatively small package (as compared to the number of turns that would be required with an air-core inductor). The material used to make the core is also optimized to work best over a specific range of frequencies. [G6A18]

CAPACITORS AND CAPACITANCE

Several types of capacitors or "caps" used in radio electronics are shown in **Figure 4.8** and additional symbols for capacitors in Figure 4.4. All capacitors have the same basic structure — two conducting surfaces separated by a *dielectric* that stores electrical energy while preventing dc current flow between the surfaces. The larger the surfaces, the closer the separation, and the more electrical energy the dielectric can store, the larger the resulting capacitance.

The simplest capacitor is a pair of metal plates separated by air. You can see examples of this type of capacitor in Figure 4.8C. These variable capacitors have two sets of plates, one fixed and the other moveable, so that as the moveable plates are rotated between the fixed plates, the changing area of overlap varies the capacitance as well.

Other types of capacitors use thin foils as the conducting surfaces. The foils are separated by a plastic film and rolled up. These are the film capacitors and as you might guess from the "rolled up" aspect of their construction, they have a significant amount of parasitic inductance. The ceramic capacitor is made from thin plates of ceramic with one side plated by a metal film and many such layers stacked together. As a result of this construction, ceramic capacitors have relatively little parasitic inductance. Ceramic and film capacitors are used in both audio and radio circuits with ceramics more common at high frequencies. Ceramic capacitors are also popular because of their low cost. [G6A14]

Two other popular styles of capacitors are designed to optimize their energy storage capabilities: aluminum and tantalum electrolytic capacitors. Aluminum electrolytic capacitors use metal foil for the conducting surfaces and the dielectric is an insulating layer on the foil created by a wet paste or gel of chemicals (the electrolyte). Tantalum capacitors are similar in that a porous mass of tantalum is immersed in an electrolyte. The electrolyte and the large surface area of these capacitors create large capacitances in comparatively small volumes. [G6A15] Electrolytic capacitors can be seen near the center of Figure 4.8A and in Figure 4.8B. The small "gumdrop" shaped capacitor toward the lower left of Figure 4.8A is a tantalum capacitor. Tantalum and electrolytic capacitors are also *polarized*, meaning that a dc voltage may only be applied in one direction without damaging the electrolyte in the capacitor. Electrolytics use the "rolled up" method of construction and have a high parasitic inductance. Tantalum capacitors have relatively little parasitic inductance compared to electrolytics.

After their value of capacitance, the most important rating for capacitors is their voltage rating. Practical capacitors have a voltage limit above which the dielectric material's insulating ability breaks down and an arc occurs between the capacitors' conducting surfaces. Except for air-dielectric capacitors, arcing usually destroys the capacitor. Some types of capacitors such as electrolytics and tantalum are *polarized*, meaning that to operate properly, voltage must be applied to them with a specific polarity. If the applied voltage is reversed, the capacitor may be damaged or destroyed. Look for the polarity markings on the capacitor to install it correctly. [G6A13]

There are many uses of capacitors in radio circuits. Each requires different characteristics that are satisfied by the various styles of capacitor construction. Here are some examples of common capacitor types and their uses:

- *Ceramic* — RF filtering and bypassing at high frequencies, inexpensive
- *Plastic film* — circuits operating at audio and lower radio frequencies
- *Silvered-mica* — highly stable, low-loss, used in RF circuits
- *Electrolytic and tantalum* —power supply filter circuits
- *Air and vacuum dielectric* — transmitting and RF circuits

Capacitors have many uses, but several are common enough to have a special name. *Blocking* capacitors pass ac signals while blocking dc signals. *Bypass* capacitors provide a low impedance path for ac signals around a higher-impedance component or circuit. *Filter* capacitors smooth out the voltage pulses of rectified ac to an even dc voltage. *Suppressor* capacitors absorb the energy of voltage transients or "spikes." *Tuning* capacitors vary the frequency of resonant circuits or filters or adjust impedance matching circuits.

COMPONENTS IN SERIES AND PARALLEL CIRCUITS

Now that you know about the basic electronic components, the next step is to learn how to combine them! First, let's review the two fundamental circuit rules illustrated in **Figure 4.9**:

- Voltages add in a series circuit, and
- Currents add in a parallel circuit.

Using an analogy between electricity and water pressure and flow, if a pump supplies pressure to a closed water system, the pressure drops around the system must add up to equal the pressure supplied by the pump. There can be no "spare" or "leftover" pressure. Whether voltage is applied by a battery, power supply or ac outlet, around a series circuit the voltages across the various components must add up to be equal to the voltage applied to the circuit. This is *Kirchoff's Voltage Law (KVL)*.

Parallel circuits also have a water analogy. Where several pipes come together, the sum of water flows entering the junction must be equal to the sum of water flows leaving the junction. Stated in a different way, the sum of water flows entering and leaving the junction must equal zero. Water in must equal water out. Electrical current works in just the same way: The total current entering a circuit junction must equal the sum of currents leaving the junction. This is *Kirchoff's Current Law (KCL)*. [G5B02]

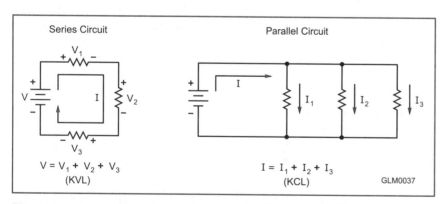
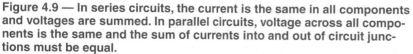

Figure 4.9 — In series circuits, the current is the same in all components and voltages are summed. In parallel circuits, voltage across all components is the same and the sum of currents into and out of circuit junctions must be equal.

Table 4.2
Calculating Series and Parallel Equivalent Values

Component	In Series
Resistor	Add values, R1 + R2 + R3 +...
Inductor	Add values, L1 + L2 + L3 +...
Capacitor	Reciprocal of reciprocals, 1/(1/C1 + 1/C2 + 1/C3 +...)

Component	In Parallel
Resistor	Reciprocal of reciprocals, 1/(1/R1 + 1/R2 + 1/R3 +...)
Inductor	Reciprocal of reciprocals, 1/(1/L1 + 1/L2 + 1/L3 +...)
Capacitor	Add values, C1+C2+C3+...

Table 4.3
Effect on Total Value of Adding Components in Series and Parallel

Component	Adding In Series	Adding In Parallel
Resistor	Increase	Decrease
Inductor	Increase	Decrease
Capacitor	Decrease	Increase

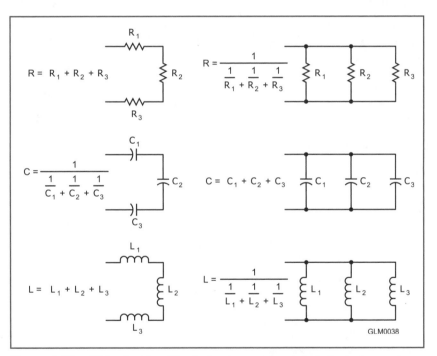

Figure 4.10 — This drawing illustrates how components in series and parallel can be combined into a single equivalent component value.

Components connected in series or parallel can be replaced with a single *equivalent* component. The rules for determining the equivalent component's value are summarized in **Table 4.2** and **Table 4.3**, and shown graphically in **Figure 4.10**. [G5C03, G5C13, G5C14] There are really only two formulas to remember — a simple sum (add the values) and the "reciprocal of reciprocals" as shown in Table 4.2.

When there are only two components, the reciprocal of reciprocals equation simplifies quite a bit, shown here for resistors:

$$R_{EQU} = \frac{R1 \times R2}{R1 + R2}$$

Example 14: What is the total resistance of three 100-Ω resistors in series?

$$R_{EQU} = 100 + 100 + 100 = 300 \ \Omega$$

In parallel?

$$R_{EQU} = \frac{1}{\dfrac{1}{100} + \dfrac{1}{100} + \dfrac{1}{100}} = \frac{1}{\dfrac{3}{100}} = \frac{100}{3} = 33.3 \ \Omega \ \text{[G5C04]}$$

Example 15: What is the total capacitance of three 100-μF capacitors in series?

$$C_{EQU} = \frac{1}{\dfrac{1}{100} + \dfrac{1}{100} + \dfrac{1}{100}} = \frac{1}{\dfrac{3}{100}} = \frac{100}{3} = 33.3 \ \mu F \ \text{[G5C09]}$$

In parallel?

$$C_{EQU} = 100 + 100 + 100 = 300 \ \mu F$$

Example 16: What is the total inductance of three 10-mH inductors in parallel?

$$L_{EQU} = \frac{1}{\dfrac{1}{10} + \dfrac{1}{10} + \dfrac{1}{10}} = \frac{10}{3} = 3.3 \ \text{mH} \ \text{[G5C10]}$$

In series?

$$L_{EQU} = 10 + 10 + 10 = 30 \ \text{mH}$$

Example 17: What is the total inductance of a 20-mH and 50-mH inductor in series?

$$L_{EQU} = 20 + 50 = 70 \ \text{mH} \ \text{[G5C11]}$$

In parallel?

$$L_{EQU} = \frac{L1 \times L2}{L1 + L2} = \frac{20 \times 50}{20 + 50} = 14.29 \ \text{mH}$$

Example 18: What is the total capacitance of a 20-μF and 50-μF capacitor in parallel?

$$C_{EQU} = 20 + 50 = 70 \ \mu F$$

In series?

$$C_{EQU} = \frac{C1 \times C2}{C1 + C2} = \frac{20 \times 50}{20 + 50} = 14.29 \ \mu F \ \text{[G5C12]}$$

Example 19: What is the total resistance of a 10-Ω, a 20-Ω and a 50-Ω resistor in series?

$$R_{EQU} = 10 + 20 + 50 = 80 \ \Omega$$

In parallel?

$$R_{EQU} = 10 + 20 + 50 = 80 \ \Omega \ \text{[G5C15]}$$

Example 20: What is the total capacitance of two 5 nF and one 750-pF capacitors in series? First, convert 5 nF to pF: 5 nF × 1000 = 5000 pF.

$$C_{EQU} = \cfrac{1}{\cfrac{1}{5000} + \cfrac{1}{5000} + \cfrac{1}{750}} = 577 \text{ pF}$$

In parallel?

$$C_{EQU} = 5000 + 5000 + 750 = 10750 \text{ pF} = 10.75 \text{ nF [G5C08]}$$

Knowing these equations for combinations of components can be used to create a specific equivalent value.

Example 21: What three equal-value resistors can be combined in series to create an equivalent value of 450 Ω? If R is the unknown value:

$$R_{EQU} = R + R + R = 3R = 450 \ \Omega \ \text{[G5C05]}$$

so

$$R = \frac{450}{3} = 150 \ \Omega$$

TRANSFORMERS

In the previous discussion on inductors, mutual inductance was introduced along with various methods of avoiding it. Mutual inductance is put to good use in the *transformer*. Transformers transfer ac power between two or more inductors sharing a common core (see Figure 4.4 for schematic symbols). The inductors are called *windings*. The winding to which power is applied is called the *primary winding* and the winding from which power is extracted is called the *secondary winding*. When voltage is applied to the primary winding, mutual inductance causes voltage to appear across the secondary winding. [G5C01] Transformers work equally well "in both directions," so the primary and secondary winding assignments are made based on construction and safety considerations.

Transformers can change power from one combination of ac voltage and current to another by using windings with different numbers of turns. This transformation occurs because all windings share the same magnetic field by virtue of being wound on the same core. If the energy in all windings is the same but the windings have different numbers of turns, then the current in each winding must change so that the total power into and out of the transformer are equal, regardless of what load is attached to the secondary windings. A significant change between primary and secondary voltage usually requires a change in the size of wire between windings. For example, in a step-up transformer, the primary winding carries higher current and is wound with larger-diameter wire than the secondary. [G5C16]

The ratio of the number of turns in the primary winding, N_P, to the number of turns in the secondary winding, N_S, determines how current and voltage are changed by the transformer. Most electronic circuits are primarily concerned with voltage, so the most common transformer equations are those that relate transformer input (or primary) voltage, E_P, to output (or secondary) voltage, E_S:

$$\frac{E_S}{E_P} = \frac{N_S}{N_P}$$

or

$$E_S = E_P \times \frac{N_S}{N_P}$$

Example 22: What is the voltage across a 500-turn secondary winding if 120 V ac is applied across the 2250-turn primary winding?

$$E_S = 120 \times \frac{500}{2250} = 26.7 \text{ V ac } \text{ [G5C06]}$$

Example 23: What would be the secondary-to-primary turns ratio to change 115 V ac to 500 V ac?

$$\frac{N_S}{N_P} = \frac{E_S}{E_P} = \frac{500}{115} = 4.35$$

Example 24: If the primary and secondary windings of a 4:1 step-down transformer are reversed, what happens to the secondary voltage? In the equation above for primary and secondary voltages, reverse E_P and E_S. Thus, the output voltage of the transformer would become 4 times the input voltage. [G5C02]

Before you go on, study test questions G5B02, G5C01 to G5C06, G5C08 to G5C18, G6A13 to G6A19 and G7A09 to G7A13. Review this section if you have difficulty.

4.4 Reactance and Impedance

REACTANCE

Capacitors and inductors resist the flow of ac differently than they do dc. The resistance to ac current flow caused by capacitance or inductance is called *reactance* (symbolized by *X*) and is measured in ohms, like resistance. [G5A02, G5A03, G5A04, G5A09] Reactance occurs because capacitors and inductors store energy. Let's find out how by starting with the capacitor.

Capacitive Reactance

If a dc voltage is applied to a capacitor that is fully discharged (that is, there is no stored energy and the voltage across the capacitor is zero), at first the current rushes in and the capacitor begins to store energy in its internal electric field. This causes the voltage across the capacitor to rise, opposing the voltage causing current to flow into the capacitor. This reduces the amount of current flowing into the capacitor. As shown in **Figure 4.11**, the more energy is stored and the higher the voltage across the capacitor, the smaller the current that flows. Eventually the capacitor charges to the same voltage as the source of the current and current flow stops. When voltage is initially applied, the capacitor looks like a short circuit to dc signals. After the capacitor is charged, it looks like an open circuit to dc signals and that is how a ca-

---

Omega — Angular Frequency

In engineering textbooks and other electronic references, you will see the equation for reactance written as:

$$X_C = \frac{1}{j\omega C} \text{ or } X_L = j\omega L$$

where $\omega = 2\pi f$ and is named *angular frequency*. Reactance and impedance are treated as complex numbers in which *j* represents the imaginary number square root of −1. You'll learn more about the use of angular frequency and complex numbers with reactance and impedance in your Extra class studies or you can study the references in the supplemental information online at **www.arrl.org/general-class-license-manual**.

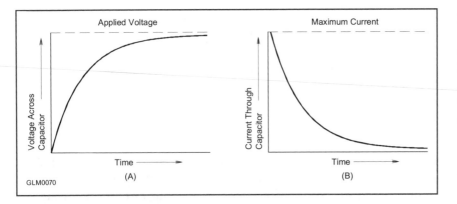

Figure 4.11 — When a circuit containing a capacitor is first energized, the voltage across the capacitor is zero and the current is very large. As time passes, the voltage across the capacitor increases, as shown at A, and the current drops toward zero, as shown at B.

pacitor blocks dc current.

For ac current, the situation is different. If the ac voltage is at a low enough frequency, it acts like a slowly varying dc voltage and the capacitor can stayed charged enough to reduce current to a small value. If the ac voltage is at a higher frequency, however, the capacitor never gets sufficiently charged to reduce current very much. So a capacitor blocks dc current, resists low-frequency ac current and passes high-frequency ac current.

The opposition to ac current flow from the stored energy in a capacitor is called *capacitive reactance* and is denoted with a subscript, X_C. Its behavior with frequency is described by the following equation:

$$X_C = \left(\frac{1}{2 \pi f C} \right)$$

where f is the frequency in Hz and C is the capacitance in farads. As the frequency of the applied signal increases, capacitive reactance decreases and vice-versa. [G5A06] Be sure to account for the units of frequency (such as kHz and MHz) and capacitance (such as pF, nF and µF).

Example 25: What is the reactance of a 1 nF capacitor at 2 MHz?

$$X_C = \left(\frac{1}{2 \times 3.14 \times (2 \times 10^6) \times (1 \times 10^{-9})} \right) = 79 \ \Omega$$

Inductive Reactance

Inductors also resist ac current but in a complementary way. If a dc voltage is applied to an inductor with no stored energy, the resulting current creates a changing magnetic field that opposes the incoming current. Initially, the current flow in the inductor is very small, but gradually builds up, storing more and more energy until opposition to the current disappears and the inductor is "fully charged" with magnetic energy. This is illustrated in **Figure 4.12**. When voltage is originally applied, the inductor looks like an open circuit to dc voltage. After the magnetic field is at full strength, the inductor looks like a short circuit to dc voltage.

This behavior is the opposite of a capacitor that blocks dc currents. If an ac voltage with a high frequency is applied to an inductor, the resulting magnetic field is always changing and so the current is always opposed. If the frequency of the ac voltage is low, the inductor's magnetic

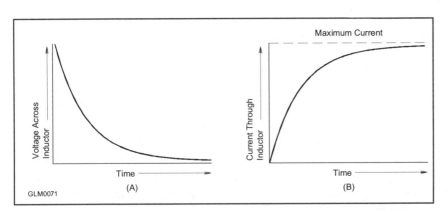

Figure 4.12 — When a circuit containing an inductor is first energized the initial current is zero and the full applied voltage appears across the inductor. As time passes, the voltage drops toward zero as shown at A, and the current increases, as shown at B.

field can be established and the opposition to current is low. So an inductor blocks high-frequency and passes low-frequency ac currents while acting like a short circuit to dc currents.

The opposition to ac current flow from the stored energy in a inductor is called *inductive reactance* and is denoted with a subscript, X_L. Its behavior with frequency is described by the following equation:

$$X_L = 2 \pi f L$$

where f is the frequency in Hz and L is the inductance in henrys. As the frequency of the applied signal increases, inductive reactance increases and vice-versa. [G5A05] As with the formula for capacitive reactance, be sure to account for the units of frequency and inductance.

Example 26: What is the reactance of a 10 µH inductor at 5 MHz?

$$X_L = 2 \times 3.14 \times (5 \times 10^6) \times (1 \times 10^{-6}) = 314 \ \Omega$$

Here's another way to look at the effect of the stored energy in capacitors and inductors: Capacitors oppose changes in voltage, while inductors oppose changes in current. Both oppose the flow of ac current, but in complementary ways.

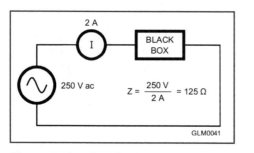

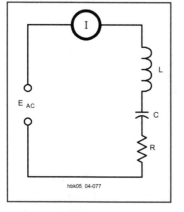

Figure 4.13 — In this circuit we know that the box presents 125 Ω of impedance (opposition to ac current), but we don't know what's in the box.

Figure 4.14 — This series circuit is resonant when the capacitive reactance of C equals the inductive reactance of L. At resonance the reactances cancel, leaving R as the only impedance in the circuit.

IMPEDANCE

Impedance is a general term for the opposition to current flow in an ac circuit caused by resistance, reactance or any combination of the two. [G5A01] Impedance is symbolized by the letter Z and it is also measured in ohms, just like resistance and reactance. [G5A10] Like resistance, impedance is the ratio of voltage to current. For example, in **Figure 4.13**, the impedance of whatever is in the "black box" is computed as the applied voltage of 250 V ac divided by the measured current of 2 A. The result is 125 Ω, regardless of whether the impedance is the result of a 125-Ω resistor or an inductor or a capacitor with a reactance of 125 Ω at the frequency of the ac voltage or even a combination of resistance and reactance that limited current to 2 A. How could you tell what was inside the box? Changing frequency and re-measuring current would be useful, since resistance does not change with frequency, while reactances do!

RESONANCE

In its broadest definition, *resonance* is the condition in which there is a match between the frequency at which a circuit or antenna naturally responds and the frequency of an applied signal. Resonance in a circuit or antenna occurs when the capacitive and inductive reactances present are equal. When a circuit's capacitive and inductive reactances are equal, their effects on ac current cancel out. In a resonant series circuit, such as shown in **Figure 4.14**, the reactances of L and C cancel, forming a short circuit, leaving only the resistance, R, as the circuit's impedance. In a resonant parallel circuit of L, C and R the reactances cancel, but this time L and C form an open circuit and again only R is left as the circuit impedance. Resonance is put to good use in filters and tuning circuits to select or reject specific frequencies at which resonance occurs..

IMPEDANCE TRANSFORMATION

A transformer can change the combination of voltage and current while transferring energy. The ratio of voltage to current in an ac circuit is impedance, so the transformer also changes or transforms impedance between the primary and secondary circuits. In this way, the transformer acts similarly to an automobile's transmission, transferring mechanical power while changing one combination of torque and rotating speed at the engine's drive shaft to a different combination at the wheels.

Electrically, the transformer changes the impedance connected to the secondary winding, Z_S, to a different impedance when measured through the primary winding, Z_P. The turns ratio controls the transformation in the same way as the ratio of gear teeth in a mechanical transmission.

$$Z_P = Z_S \left[\frac{N_P}{N_S} \right]^2 \text{ or } \sqrt{\frac{Z_P}{Z_S}} = \frac{N_P}{N_S}$$

Example 27: What is the primary impedance if a 200-Ω load is connected to the secondary of a transformer with a 5:1 secondary-to-primary turns ratio?

$$Z_P = 200 \left[\frac{1}{5} \right]^2 = 8 \, \Omega$$

Example 28: What turns ratio is required to change a 600-Ω impedance to a 4 Ω impedance? In this case, take the square root of the impedance ratio:

$$\text{Turns ratio} = \frac{N_P}{N_S} = \sqrt{\frac{Z_P}{Z_S}} = \sqrt{\frac{600}{4}} = \sqrt{150} = 12.25 \text{ [G5C07]}$$

Note that the impedance to be changed (in this case 600 Ω) can be connected to the primary or secondary but turns ratios are always stated with the larger number first. In this example, it is stated as 12.25:1, not 1:12.25.

IMPEDANCE MATCHING

The internal impedance of a source limits its ability to deliver power. For example, a hearing aid battery and a D-cell may both supply 1.5 V, but the internal impedance of the hearing aid battery is much higher, limiting it to supplying small currents. The D-cell's lower internal impedance enables it to supply high currents.

Knowing the impedance of a circuit is particularly important when the goal is to deliver the maximum power from a power source (such as a transmitter) to a load (such as an antenna). According to the *Maximum Power Transfer Theorem*, maximum power transfer occurs when the source's and load's output impedances are equal and purely resistive (meaning no reactance). [G5A07, G5A08]

Amateur transmitting equipment is designed so that the source impedance at the output (or output impedance) is 50 Ω. Most coaxial cables have a 50-Ω characteristic impedance. Most antennas are designed to have a feed point impedance of 50 Ω, but they rarely present that impedance over an entire amateur band. If the difference between the load impedance and the transmitter output impedance is great enough, the transmitter may reduce its output power to avoid damage. The solution is an *impedance-matching circuit* that transforms the undesired impedance to the desired value.

Most impedance-matching circuits are *LC circuits* made of inductors and capacitors. [G5A11] **Figure 4.15** shows two popular LC circuits used for impedance matching: the pi network (a *network* is a formal name for circuit) and the T network. The names are derived from the letters π and T, which the circuit schematics resemble. These can be made entirely of fixed-value components for loads such as a single-band antenna. Adjustable components

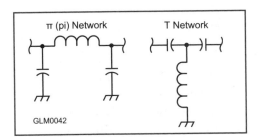

Figure 4.15 — The pi (π) and T networks are named for the letters that they resemble. The pi network is often used to transform the impedances between transistors or tubes in amplifiers and feed lines. The T network is common in stand-alone "antenna tuners" or "transmatches."

can also be used, allowing the circuit to be used at different frequencies or loads.

Another popular method of performing impedance matching was introduced in the section on transformers. Special RF *impedance transformers* are often employed in this role, equalizing impedances of source and load to maximize the transfer of power. [G5A12] Impedance-matching can also be performed by special lengths and connections of transmission line. [G5A13]

Regardless of what method is employed, it is important that the ratings of the components, transformer cores or transmission lines not be exceeded. Large transformation ratios (typically of 10:1 or more) or high power can put a lot of stress on the components used in the circuit. For example, using an impedance transformer at high power can result in core saturation, creating harmonics and causing signal distortion. Stay within the limit of the manufacturer's specification.

> *Before you go on, study test questions G5A01 to G5A13, and G5C07. Review this section if you have difficulty.*

4.5 Active Components

In order to amplify, switch, shape, or otherwise process a signal, it is necessary to use *active* components. These usually require a source of power and may include passive components, such as resistors or capacitors, as elements of a more complex device.

SEMICONDUCTOR COMPONENTS

The most common active components are made of semiconductors. Semiconductors are materials that conduct electricity better than an insulator but not as well as a metal. Silicon (chemical symbol Si) and germanium (Ge) are examples of semiconductors used in radio electronics. The electrical properties of semiconductors can be controlled by the addition of small amounts of other materials such as indium (In) or phosphorus (P). These impurities are called *dopants* and adding them to the base material is called *doping*. If the impurity's presence creates more electrons to conduct electricity, the result is N-type material. Otherwise, the impurity creates P-type material. All semiconductors are created from combinations of N-type and P-type material. Where the two types of material are in contact is a *PN junction*.

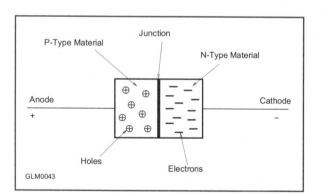

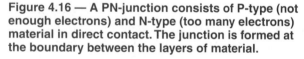

Figure 4.16 — A PN-junction consists of P-type (not enough electrons) and N-type (too many electrons) material in direct contact. The junction is formed at the boundary between the layers of material.

Diodes and Rectifiers

A semiconductor *junction diode* uses a PN junction to block current flow in one direction as shown in **Figure 4.16**. Wire leads are attached to each layer. Current flows when positive voltage is applied from the P-type to the N-type material, called *forward bias*, forcing electrons across the junction. Voltage applied in the reverse direction from N-type to P-type, called *reverse bias*, pulls electrons away from the junction so that no current flows. The voltage required to force electrons across the junction is the diode's *forward voltage* or *junction threshold voltage* and is abbreviated V_F. For silicon diodes, V_F is approximately 0.7 V and for germanium 0.3 V. [G6A03, G6A05] Typical diode packages are shown in **Figure 4.17**. (For more information about semiconductors, follow the links on the *General Class License Manual's* website.)

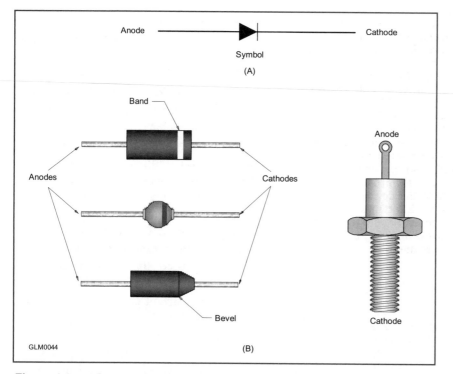

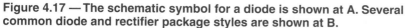

Figure 4.17 — The schematic symbol for a diode is shown at A. Several common diode and rectifier package styles are shown at B.

A semiconductor diode has several ratings that place limits on how it may be used. These are the two most important ratings:

- *Peak inverse (or reverse) voltage (PIV)* — the maximum reverse voltage (voltage in the non-conducting direction) that may be applied before *reverse breakdown* occurs, allowing current to flow in the reverse direction

- *Average forward current (I_F)* — because of the forward voltage, current through the diode dissipates a power of $I_F \times V_F$ in the form of heat. Exceeding this rating will destroy the diode's internal structure.

Another parameter that affects how a diode works at high frequencies is its *junction capacitance (C_J)*. When reverse-biased, the layers of P- and N-type material act like the plates of a small capacitor. The larger C_J becomes, the longer it takes the diode to switch from being reverse-biased to conducting forward current.

Different methods of construction create diodes with a different set of characteristics useful for certain types of circuits.

- *PIN diode* — conducts ac signals with low forward voltage drop, used for RF switching and control

- *Schottky diode* — low junction capacitance allows operation at high frequencies [G6A06]

- *Varactor* — the reverse-biased junction acts like a capacitor and can be used as a small variable capacitor

- *Zener diode* — extra levels of doping allow Zener diodes to be used as voltage regulators while in reverse breakdown

Diodes that are designed for circuits with low-power signals are called *signal* or *switching diodes*. Heavy-duty diodes for use in high-power circuits must carry high currents, withstand high voltages or dissipate a lot of power. These diodes are called *rectifiers* and may have PIV and I_F ratings as high as 1000 V or 100 A!

Bipolar and Field-Effect Transistors

The back-to-back layers of P- and N-type material cause the diode's unidirectional current flow. Adding another layer of semiconductor material, however, creates a device capable of amplifying a signal — the transistor. **Figure 4.18** illustrates the basic structure of a *bipolar junction transistor* or *BJT*. Bipolar transistors are made from P- and N-type material and use current to control their operation. Unlike the diode the transistor requires power to function.

Bipolar junction transistors have three electrodes — the *collector (C), emitter (E)* and *base (B)*. The collector and emitter leads carry the current controlled by the transistor. Transistor operation is controlled by current flowing between the base and emitter. The

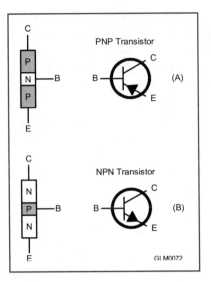

Figure 4.18 — Bipolar transistors are made from three layers of P- and N-type material. At A, a thin layer of N-type material is sandwiched between two layers of P-type material, forming a PNP transistor. The schematic symbol has three leads: collector (C), base (B) and emitter (E), with the arrow pointing in toward the base. At B, the opposite construction creates an NPN transistor, with the emitter arrow pointing out away from the base.

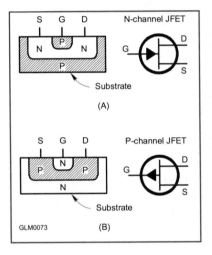

Figure 4.19 — JFET devices are made from P- and N-type material like bipolar transistors, but use a gate embedded in a channel to control electron flow. An N-channel JFET is shown at A and a P-channel JFET at B.

thin base layer of material creates a pair of back-to-back PN junctions that would seem to prevent current flow through the transistor no matter which way voltage is applied because one junction is always reverse-biased. When current flows between the base and emitter, however, the base is so thin that the current causes both junctions to break down, allowing current flow between collector and emitter.

The amount of base-emitter current required for collector-emitter current to flow is quite small. The control of a large current by a smaller current is *amplification* and the ratio of the collector-emitter current to base-emitter current is called *current gain*. Current gain for dc signals is represented by the symbol β (*beta*). Current gain for ac signals is represented by the symbol h_{fe}.

Another type of transistor, shown in **Figure 4.19** is the *field effect transistor* (FET). The FET has three electrodes like the bipolar transistor — the *drain (D)*, *source (S)* and *gate (G)*. Instead of controlling drain-source current with gate-source current, the voltage between the gate and source is used. Instead of current gain, the FET has *transconductance* (g_m) — the ratio of source-drain current to gate-source voltage. A *junction FET* or *JFET* is constructed with the gate material in direct contact with the material that connects the source and drain electrodes. The *metal-oxide-semiconductor FET* or *MOSFET* and a related device, the *insulated-gate FET* or *IGFET*, have an insulating layer of oxide between the gate and the rest of the transistor. [G6A09] Both JFETs and MOSFETs are very sensitive, with small amounts of voltage able to control the source-drain current.

The high amplification of transistors also makes them ideal for use as switches for both voltage and current. By applying enough base-emitter current or gate-source voltage, the transistor can be driven into *saturation* where further increases in input result in no output change. Similarly, the input signal can reduce output current to zero — the

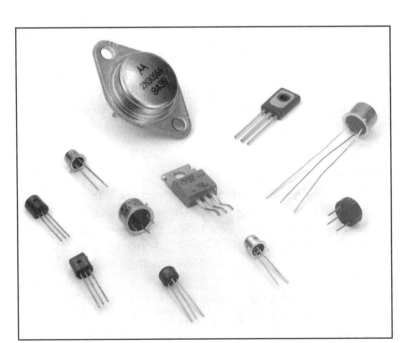

Figure 4.20 — Transistors come in a variety of package styles. The smaller packages are used in low-power circuits for small signals. The larger packages are used in power-control and transmitter circuits.

condition of *cutoff*. These two states make an excellent representation of digital ON/OFF signals in logic circuits. [G6A07]

Transistors come in many types of packages. The different styles are often identified with package numbers beginning with "TO" (for Transistor Outline), such as the TO-3, TO-92 and TO-220 packages shown in **Figure 4.20**. Low-power transistors usually have insulated, plastic packages. Plastic packaging is unsuitable for transistors that must dissipate larger amounts of power. Their packages have metal surfaces through which excess heat can be easily removed. The metal surface is often connected internally to the collector or source of the transistor so a direct connection to a metal heat sink or equipment chassis would short that electrode to ground. Some sort of insulation is often required between the case and heat sink. Be cautious when installing or replacing high-power transistors to avoid short circuits. [G6A08]

VACUUM TUBES

The vacuum tube, the oldest device capable of amplification, still makes a valuable contribution in high-power amplifiers. In addition to amplifiers, many amateurs enjoy using antique "tube gear," just as audiophiles do. As a General class licensee, you're likely to encounter vacuum tubes, so you'll need to know how they operate.

A vacuum tube has three basic parts: a source of electrons, an electrode to collect the electrons, and intervening electrodes that control the electrons traveling from source to collector. Each electrode of the tube is called an *element*. **Figure 4.21** shows the schematic symbol for a tube and the tube's elements. A tube with two elements is a *diode*, three elements a *triode*, four elements a *tetrode* and so forth. The most common tubes in amateur service today are triodes and tetrodes. Some tube terminology:

- *Filament or heater* — heats the cathode, causing it to emit electrons
- *Cathode* — the source of electrons
- *Control grid* — the grid closest to the cathode, used to regulate electron travel between the cathode and plate [G6A10]
- *Screen grid* — an electrode that reduces grid-to-plate capacitance that diminishes the tube's ability to amplify at high frequencies [G6A12]
- *Suppressor grid* — an electrode that prevents electrons from traveling from the plate to the control or screen grid
- *Plate* — the electrode that collects electrons, called *plate current*

All amplifying tubes have at least three electrodes — a cathode (and a filament to heat it), a grid and a plate. Heated to a high temperature by a heater or filament, the cathode emits electrons into the vacuum of the tube. The plate is placed at a positive voltage with respect to the cathode (plate-to-cathode voltage) to attract the electrons. The electrons travel toward the plate through holes in the control grid. If the control grid is at a negative voltage with respect to the cathode (grid-to-cathode voltage), the electrons are repelled and are either slowed down, decreasing plate current, or stopped altogether, called *cutoff*. Conversely, a positive grid-to-cathode voltage accelerates the electrons toward the plate, increasing plate current. Varying the control grid's voltage therefore varies plate current, amplifying the input signal.

Because the control grid is a fine mesh of wires with lots of empty space, relatively few electrons are collected by the grid, even when the grid-to-cathode voltage is positive. This means that grid current is low even for swings of tens of volts. Since impedance is the ratio of voltage to current that means the grid impedance is quite high — from several hundred ohms in large power tubes to more than a megohm in sensitive amplifiers. Compared to different types of semiconductors, the tube is most like the field-effect transistor (FET). [G6A11]

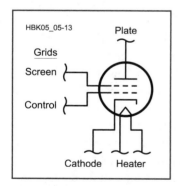

Figure 4.21 — The schematic symbol of a vacuum tube tetrode includes a heater, cathode, the control and screen grids and the anode or plate. The heavy circle represents the tube's enclosing envelope.

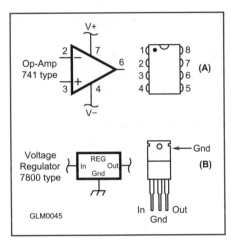

Figure 4.22 — The popular 741 op-amp symbol and dual in-line package (DIP) connections are shown at A. A common three-terminal voltage regulator, the 7800-series, is shown in the TO-220 package at B.

Vacuum tubes typically operate at hazardous voltages — as high as two or three thousand volts in power amplifiers. Equipment that uses high-voltage has numerous safety features to prevent electrical shock. Lower-voltage tube equipment relies on the operator or technician to exercise the proper procedures. Take extra safety precautions when servicing or maintaining tube equipment.

ANALOG AND DIGITAL INTEGRATED CIRCUITS

If one transistor is good, more must be better! The processes that make transistors on thin wafers of silicon can just as easily create many diodes, transistors, resistors, capacitors and even tiny spiral inductors and connect them with wires made of thin plated-on metal. The result is an *integrated circuit* (IC) also known as a "chip." The two most common types of integrated circuits are *analog* (or *linear*) and *digital* (or *logic*).

Analog ICs are used for applications such as signal amplification, filtering, measurement and power control. They operate over a continuous range of voltages and currents. **Figure 4.22** shows the schematic symbol and connection diagrams for two of the most common analog ICs, the operational amplifier and the linear voltage regulator. [G6B01, G6B06] The operational amplifier or "op amp" is widely used for dc and audio circuits as an inexpensive source of gain. Linear voltage regulators are used to maintain a power supply output at a constant voltage over a wide range of currents.

Digital ICs operate with discrete values of voltage and current representing the *binary number system* values 0 and 1. Digital electronic circuits operate with only two stable states of operation, ON and OFF, representing binary values. [G7B02] By combining digital circuits, those values can be used to perform computations or control functions.

There are several different types of digital circuits called *logic families* that use a specific style of circuit design that is used to create all of the different logic functions. Different families may use different power supply voltages or use different voltage and current levels to represent digital values. Complex digital circuits can be constructed by using ICs from the same family of circuits so that voltage and current levels are compatible for all of the individual circuits.

It is important to note that there is no hard and fast correspondence between TRUE and FALSE, 0 and 1, ON and OFF, or high and low voltage levels. The convention varies between logic families and even specific ICs may use voltage and current levels in different ways. The data sheets for each specific device describe the exact functions.

Characteristics of some common logic families are shown in **Table 4.4**. The oldest logic family is resistor-transistor logic (RTL) and is no longer in use. The transistor-transistor logic (TTL) logic family replaced RTL. The most popular logic family in use today is the *complementary metal-oxide semiconductor* (*CMOS*) logic family because of its high speed and low power consumption. [G6B03] CMOS devices are used in personal computers and in microprocessor-controlled equipment, such as most current amateur transceivers. There is also an older CMOS logic family represented by ICs with CD4000 part numbers that are designed for use in very low power circuits. Each logic family has a variety of subfamilies optimized for a particular use. One example is LSTTL, a low-power version of TTL. Information about

Table 4.4
Logic Family Characteristics

Family Name	Maximum Frequency of Operation	Power Consumption	Power Supply
TTL	100 MHz	High	5 V
CMOS	1 GHz	Low	3 – 5 V
CMOS (CD4000)	1 MHz	Very Low	3 – 15 V

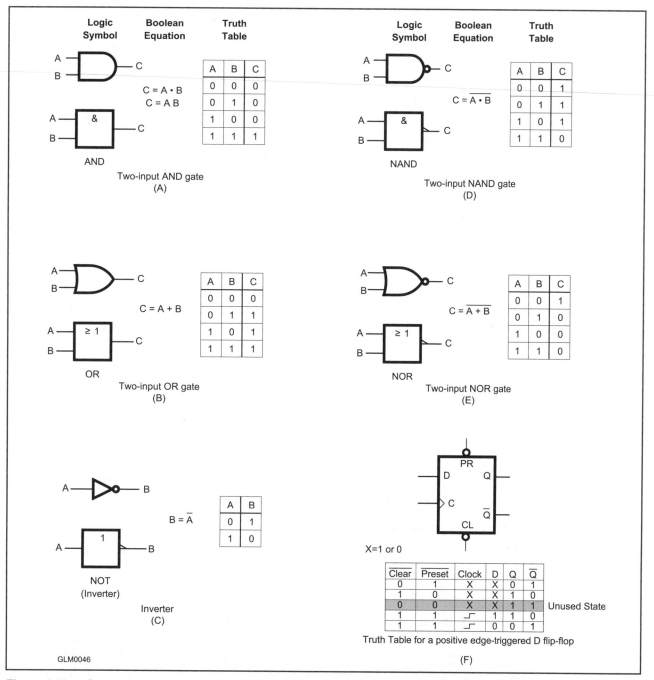

Figure 4.23 — Schematic symbols for the basic digital logic functions with the logic equations and truth tables that describe their operation. The two-input AND gate is shown at A, a two-input OR gate at B, an inverter at C, a two-input NAND gate at D and a two-input NOR gate at E. A D-type flip-flop is shown at F.

each logic family can be found on IC manufacturers' websites and in the *ARRL Handbook*.

Digital Logic Basics

The basic building block of digital circuits are circuits called *gates* that perform *inversion* (changing a 1 to a 0 and vice versa) and the OR and AND functions. Because of the way digital circuits are designed, the most common gates in actual use are the inverter, NAND and NOR. All three of these functions and their schematic symbols are shown in **Figure 4.23**. [G7B03, G7B04] More complex functions — all the way up to microprocessors and digital signal processors — are constructed from combinations of these three functions. Digital circuits that use gates to combine binary inputs to generate a binary output or combination of binary outputs are called *combinational logic*.

Another class of digital circuits combines binary signals in a way that depends on time and on the sequence of inputs to the circuits. These circuits are called *sequential logic*. The basic building block of sequential logic is the *flip-flop*, which has two stable states. The flip-flop responds to a *clock* signal that causes its outputs to change based on the input signals. The two outputs, Q and $\overline{Q}$ (the overbar indicates that the signal is inverted), are always in opposite states. There are several kinds of flip-flops and the most common, the D-type, is shown in Figure 4.23. When a digital signal, such as a pulse or square wave, is applied to the clock input, the rising edge (the edge that goes from low to high or from 0 to 1) causes the Q output to be 1 if the D input is 1 and vice versa. The Q and $\overline{Q}$ outputs stay in that state until the next rising edge is applied to the clock input.

By connecting flip-flops together so that one flip-flop's outputs feed the next flip-flop's input, two important types of circuits are created: *counters* and *shift registers*. In a counter, the outputs of the chain of flip-flops make up a binary number or state representing the number of clock signals that have occurred. Each flip-flop stores one bit of the total count. The highest number that a counter can represent is 2^N, where N is the number of flip-flops that make up the counter. For example, a 3-bit counter (one with three flip-flops) can count $2^3 = 8$ different states, a 4-bit counter can count 16 states, and so on. [G7B05]

Connecting the array of flip-flops slightly differently results in a shift register. The shift register stores a sequence of 1s and 0s from its input as the flip-flop outputs. Each clock signal causes the value at the shift register's input to pass or shift to the next flip-flop in the string. [G7B06] Some shift-register circuits can be configured to shift up or down (forward or backward) along the array. Shift registers are a simple form of digital memory. (For more information on flip-flops and digital circuits in general, see the website for this book, **www.arrl.org/general-class-license-manual**.)

RF INTEGRATED CIRCUITS

RF ICs are specially designed for functions commonly required at radio frequencies, such as low-level high-gain amplifiers, mixers, modulators and demodulators, and even filters. RF ICs greatly reduce the number of discrete devices required to build radio circuits.

An MMIC (monolithic microwave integrated circuit) is a special type of RF IC that works through microwave frequencies. [G6B02] Taking advantage of integration to combine many RF devices into a single package, some MMICs perform several functions. One example is an MMIC that acts as an entire receiver front end. The MMIC is what enables communications engineers to construct low-cost cell phones, GPS receivers and other sophisticated examples of wireless technology.

MICROPROCESSORS AND RELATED COMPONENTS

Where digital control and computing functions were once performed by complex circuits of many discrete ICs, today these functions are performed by the miniature computers called *microprocessors* that contain thousands of gates in a single IC (often called a "chip"). Microcontrollers are a special type of microprocessor with extra interfaces to external signal and control circuits. [G6B11, G7B01] Modern microprocessors are capable of performing millions of computing instructions per second and often include functions such as parallel and serial input-output ports, counters and timers right on the chip. Nearly all microprocessors are built from CMOS logic.

Table 4.5

Memory Types

Memory	Volatile/Nonvolatile
Static RAM (SRAM)	Volatile
Dynamic DRAM (DRAM)	Volatile, data must be continually refreshed
Programmable ROM (PROM)	Nonvolatile
EPROM (Erasable PROM)	Nonvolatile, can be erased by exposure to UV
EEPROM (Electrically-erasable PROM)	Nonvolatile, can be electrically erased, Flash EEPROM erased in sections
Mass storage	Nonvolatile, data stored on hard drive, CD-ROM or tape

Table 4.6

Common Computer Serial Interfaces

Interface	Typical Speed
RS-232	115 Kbits/sec
USB 1.1	1.5 Mbits/sec
USB 2.0	480 Mbits/sec
USB 3.0	5 Gbits/sec
Firewire	800 Mbits/sec

Memory

The machine language program must be stored in some kind of memory devices so that a microprocessor can read the instructions. There are several kinds of memory. *Volatile* memory loses the data it stores when power is removed. *Nonvolatile* memory stores data permanently, even if the power is removed. [G6B05] *Random-access memory* (RAM) can be read from or written to in any order. *Read-only memory* (ROM) stores data permanently and cannot be changed. [G6B04] There are several common types of each as shown in **Table 4.5**. Memory devices or systems are connected to the microprocessor by a high-speed interface called a *memory bus* that can transfer data at high rates.

Interfaces

Microprocessors and computers interact with the outside world through interfaces — special circuits, methods and connectors for data exchange. There are two types of interface, *serial* and *parallel*. Serial interfaces transfer one bit of data in each transfer operation. Some common computer serial interfaces are listed in **Table 4.6**. Parallel interfaces transfer multiple bits of data in each operation.

Serial interfaces are used as an inexpensive way of connecting two pieces of equipment to share digital data. The standard interface in amateur equipment has been the RS-232 interface (also known as a COM port). (RS-232 refers to the industry standard that describes the interface's electrical characteristics.) Computers sold today use the USB (Universal Serial Bus) interface although older models still provide RS-232 connections. RS-232 and USB serial interfaces in the ham shack are used to connect computers to transceivers, TNCs and multimode communications processors, as well as to accessories such as antenna switches and rotators. [G6B10] Converters are available for converting between USB and RS-232 interfaces.

Network connections are also serial interfaces. The most common physical network interface is Ethernet. For wireless connections, many computers use the popular WiFi interface, described by the IEEE 802.11 set of standards. Bluetooth and Zigbee wireless interfaces are used for short range "cable-replacement."

Parallel interfaces are used primarily to connect a computer's microprocessor to internal hard drives and memory devices but are being replaced with high-speed serial interfaces.

VISUAL INTERFACES

Amateur equipment uses two types of devices to present information visually, the *indicator* and the *display*. An indicator is a device that presents on/off information visually by the presence, absence or color of light. Common indicators are the incandescent light bulb and the light-emitting diode (*LED*). A display is a device that is capable of presenting text or graphics information in visual form. One example is the display showing frequency and operating information on the front panel of most transceivers.

Incandescent light bulbs have been largely replaced by LEDs in most amateur equipment. LEDs last longer, can be turned on and off far quicker, use less power and generate less heat than light bulbs. Some indicators include LEDs of different colors, creating more than one color or even white light. An LED is a diode made from special types of semiconductor material that emit light when the PN junction is forward biased. [G6B07, G6B08]

The most common type of display is the *LCD* (liquid crystal display) created by sandwiching liquid crystal material between transparent glass panels. A pattern of electrodes is printed in a thin, transparent film on the front glass panel with a single electrode covering the rear panel. As voltage is applied to the electrodes on the front panel, the liquid crystals twist into a configuration that blocks light. LCDs require ambient or *back lighting* (a light source behind the liquid crystal layer) since the liquid crystal layer does not generate light on its own. [G6B09]

> **Before you go on, study test questions G6A03, G6A05 to G6A12, G6B01 to G6B11, G7B01 to G7B06. Review this section if you have difficulty.**

4.6 Practical Circuits

RECTIFIERS AND POWER SUPPLIES

Almost every piece of amateur equipment requires power. Electronic equipment requires dc to operate, so a *power supply* (either built-in or external) is required to run equipment from household ac power. Most amateur equipment uses dc power at +13.8 V, a voltage chosen to be compatible with vehicle power systems for mobile operation.

A power supply has three basic parts — an input transformer, a rectifier and a filter-regulator output circuit. The input transformer converts the 120 V ac household power to a voltage closer to the desired 13.8 V. It also serves to isolate the power supply output from the ac power line. This is an important safety feature because the power supply's negative output is usually connected to the station's ground and metal equipment enclosures that are frequently in direct contact with the operator.

Rectifier Circuits

After the ac voltage has been reduced to a lower value by the input transformer, a rectifier circuit converts the bipolar ac waveform into dc pulses as shown in **Figure 4.24**. Don't confuse a single diode rectifier with the rectifier circuit — they both have the same name but one is a component and the other a circuit. There are two basic types of rectifier circuits — the *half-wave* and the *full-wave*.

A half-wave rectifier shown in Figure 4.24A permits current flow during one-half of the input ac waveform (180°) from the transformer. [G7A05] That creates a series of pulses of current in the load at the same frequency as the input voltage. There is an equal duration between pulses when no current flows. The rectifier output waveform's average voltage is 0.45 times the transformer winding's output voltage, or 0.45 E_{RMS}. There is also one diode forward voltage drop in series with the load current that reduces the peak output voltage by 0.6 V for regular silicon diodes.

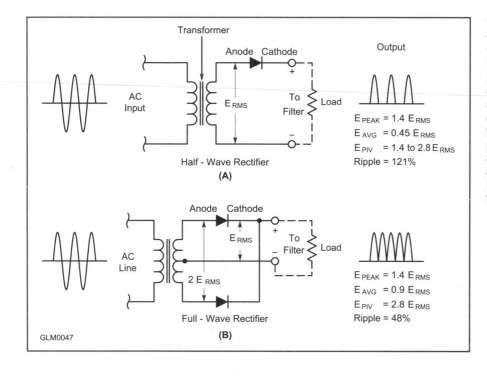

Figure 4.24 — Two basic rectifier circuits and their output waveforms. (A) Half-wave. (B) Full-wave center-tapped. The half-wave circuit converts only one-half of the input waveform (180°) while the full-wave circuit converts the entire input waveform (360°). In most power supplies, a capacitor is connected across the output of the rectifier and will charge to a voltage of E_{PEAK}, the normal peak output of the supply.

The full-wave rectifier shown in Figure 4.24B is really two half-wave rectifiers operating on alternate half-cycles. The advantage of the full-wave rectifier is that output is produced during the entire 360° of the ac cycle. [G7A06] The output voltage from this rectifier circuit is 0.9 E_{RMS} (minus one diode forward voltage drop). The output from full-wave rectifiers is a series of pulses at twice the frequency of the input voltage. [G7A07]

This *full-wave center-tapped* rectifier requires that the transformer output winding be center-tapped to provide a return path for current that flows in the load. Since the output winding is center-tapped, each half of the winding must be capable of generating the full output voltage, E_{RMS}, so the total winding must put out twice the full output voltage, 2 E_{RMS}.

A second type of full-wave

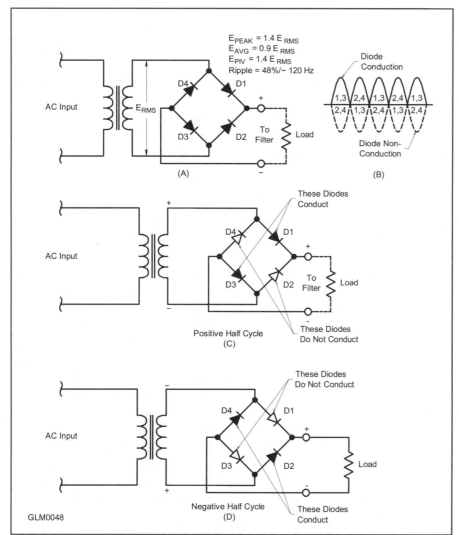

Figure 4.25 — The full-wave bridge rectifier has an equivalent output to the full-wave center-tapped rectifier without a center-tapped transformer winding, but requires twice as many rectifier diodes.

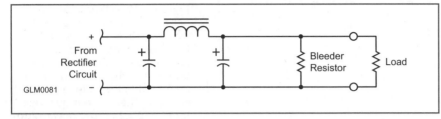
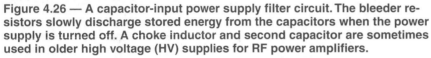

Figure 4.26 — A capacitor-input power supply filter circuit. The bleeder resistors slowly discharge stored energy from the capacitors when the power supply is turned off. A choke inductor and second capacitor are sometimes used in older high voltage (HV) supplies for RF power amplifiers.

rectifier called a *full-wave bridge* is shown in **Figure 4.25**. This circuit adds two diodes (a total of four), but eliminates the need for a center-tapped, double-voltage winding. The figure shows how it works, with a pair of diodes conducting on alternate half-cycles. The pairs of diodes work like a double-pole, double-throw switch synchronized to the ac waveform, connecting the winding to the load first with one polarity, then the other. Output voltage is again 0.9 E_{RMS}, but less two forward voltage drops because there are two diodes in series with the current at all times.

If the usual capacitor-input filter (see **Figure 4.26**) is used to construct a power supply, there are key differences in the peak inverse voltage and forward currents experienced by the diodes in these three circuits:

- In the full-wave center-tapped rectifier circuit, when a rectifier diode is not conducting it must withstand not only the negative peak voltage from its own half of the winding but also the positive voltage from the other winding. Thus the peak inverse voltage applied to the diodes is twice the normal peak output voltage of the supply.

- The peak inverse voltage applied to the diode in a half-wave rectifier circuit is twice the supply's peak output voltage. [G7A04]

- In a full-wave bridge rectifier circuit each rectifier diode only has to withstand the supply's peak output voltage. [G7A03]

- In the half-wave rectifier circuit the entire load current goes through one diode and so it must be rated to carry the average load current.

- In both full-wave rectifiers the diodes each supply only one-half of the load current, halving their current rating requirement. **Table 4.7** summarizes the maximum reverse voltage and average forward current for the diodes in all three rectifier circuits.

Filter Circuits

A rectifier's output pulses of dc current are unsuitable for direct use by electronic circuits. The pulses must be smoothed out so that the output is a relatively steady voltage. This smoothing is performed by a *filter network* consisting of capacitors or capacitors and inductors. [G7A02]

The variation in output voltage caused by the current pulses is called *ripple,* and it is measured as the percentage of the peak-to-peak variation compared to average output voltage. The most common way of reducing ripple is to use a large *filter capacitor* at the output of the rectifier. Shown in Figure 4.26, this is called a *capacitor-input filter.* You may encounter older high voltage (HV) supplies for RF power amplifiers which include a *choke* inductor with a second filter capacitor. Simple supplies rarely include an inductor since the capacitor alone provides sufficient filtering in most cases.

A sufficiently large capacitor maintains the power supply output voltage close to the average value of the rectifier output even for heavy load currents. (In

Table 4.7
Rectifier Diode Voltage and Current

Rectifier Type	Number of Diodes	PIV	Avg Forward Current
Half-wave	1	1.4 to 2.8 E_{RMS} (2 E_{PK})	I_{LOAD}
Full-wave	2	2.8 E_{RMS} (2 E_{PK})	0.5 I_{LOAD}
Full-wave bridge	4	1.4 E_{RMS} (E_{PK})	0.5 I_{LOAD}

practice, several capacitors in parallel may be used to increase the value of capacitance to the desired level.) The rectifier supplies current to the capacitor, charging it and raising its voltage whenever the rectifier output voltage is greater than the capacitor voltage. The capacitor then discharges the stored energy as current through the load until the rectifier can charge it up again. The percentage of variation in output voltage between no load and full load is called the supply's *regulation*. For a properly sized filter capacitor, the rectifier charges the capacitor in short pulses of high current while the load draws current from the capacitor more slowly.

The capacitor in a power supply output filter is continuously charging and discharging, with current flowing in and out of the capacitor. These currents can be quite high, so it is important to avoid losses caused by losses in the capacitor. There are several sources of capacitor losses such as the resistance of conducting surfaces and of the internal electrolyte paste. All of the losses are lumped together in a single parasitic resistance called the *equivalent series resistance* (ESR).

Power Supply Safety

Safety is important in power supply design because of the connection to the ac line power and because a lot of energy is supplied by and stored in the supply. Fuses in the primary are used to protect against the hazard of excessive current loads or short circuits, and all power supplies should have an on/off switch to remove ac power when not in use.

Another hazard encountered in power supplies is the stored energy in filter capacitors. If the supply is simply turned off with no load connected, the energy stored in the capacitor has nowhere to go and a significant voltage will be present at the capacitor terminals. *Bleeder resistors* are used to discharge the stored energy when power is removed. Connected across the filter capacitors as shown in Figure 4.26, these resistors have a high enough value that they do not affect normal operation. When power is turned off, if there is no load, the resistors slowly dissipate the stored energy as heat, reducing the capacitor voltage to a safe value within a few seconds. If you are working on a power supply, be sure to wait long enough for the bleeder resistors to do their work after turning power off. [G7A01]

Switchmode or Switching Supplies

Power supplies that use capacitor- or inductor-input filters and linear voltage regulators to provide filtering and regulation are called *linear supplies*. Another type of power supply filter and regulation circuit uses high-frequency pulses of current to control the output voltage. This is called a *switch-mode supply* or *switching supply*.

In the block diagram of a switching supply in **Figure 4.27**, the ac input is first rectified and filtered. A transistor switch then supplies current pulses to a small inductor or transformer at a very high frequency — 20 kHz or more compared to 60 Hz for a linear supply — which transfers the energy into another filter capacitor

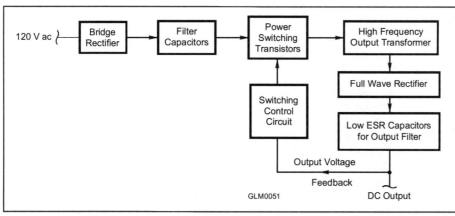

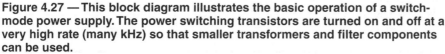

Figure 4.27 — This block diagram illustrates the basic operation of a switch-mode power supply. The power switching transistors are turned on and off at a very high rate (many kHz) so that smaller transformers and filter components can be used.

that smoothes the pulses for a steady output voltage. The high frequency of the pulses means that the supply can react quickly to changing current demands. The high frequency also means that small, lightweight inductors and capacitors can be used to smooth the pulses and filter the output. [G7A08]

BATTERIES AND CHARGERS

Battery power operation is important to amateurs. Everyday use of handheld and portable radios requires dependable, high-capacity batteries that can be easily recharged. Public service and portable operation depends on battery power. Because of these important roles for batteries, the General class exam focuses on the different types of batteries and how to recharge them.

There are two basic types of batteries: *primary* and *secondary*. A primary, or disposable, battery is discarded after it is discharged. Examples of primary batteries include carbon-zinc, alkaline and silver-nickel. Each of these types describes the chemicals that store energy in the battery, called the *battery chemistry*. For emergency operation, disposable batteries are preferred because battery chargers may not function if ac power is unavailable.

A secondary, or rechargeable, battery can be recharged and reused many times. Examples of secondary batteries include nickel-cadmium (NiCd), nickel-metal hydride (NiMH), lithium-ion (Li-ion) and lead-acid. **Table 4.8** lists several common types of batteries and their important characteristics. There is one schematic symbol for batteries with a single cell, and another for those with multiple cells. Note that these symbols are the same for all battery types (NiCd, NiMH, lead acid, and so on).

Larger secondary batteries are also known as *storage batteries*. Storage batteries, such as deep-cycle lead-acid marine or RV storage batteries are often used as a portable or emergency power source to replace a power supply operating from ac power. These batteries are available with liquid electrolyte for vehicle use or with the electrolyte in gel form ("gel-cells"). These batteries are rated as "12 V" batteries, but should actually be maintained at a voltage of 13.8 V. Lead-acid storage batteries can produce useful power until their output voltage drops to approximately 10.5 V, after which the voltage will fall quickly and the battery should be recharged. Discharging these batteries past their minimum voltage will reduce the life of the battery. [G6A01]

To get the most energy from a battery, limit the amount of current drawn. A low dis-

Table 4-8
Battery Types and Characteristics

Battery Style	Chemistry	Type	Full-Charge Voltage (V)	Energy Rating (average, mAh)
AAA	Alkaline	Disposable	1.5	1100
AA	Alkaline	Disposable	1.5	2600 – 3200
AA	Carbon-Zinc	Disposable	1.5	600
AA	Nickel-Cadmium (NiCd)	Rechargeable	1.2	700
AA	Nickel-Metal Hydride (NiMH)	Rechargeable	1.2	1500 – 2200
AA	Lithium	Disposable	1.7	2100 – 2400
C	Alkaline	Disposable	1.5	7500
D	Alkaline	Disposable	1.5	14,000
9 V	Alkaline	Disposable	9	580
9 V	Nickel-Cadmium (NiCd)	Rechargeable	9	110
9 V	Nickel-Metal Hydride (NiMH)	Rechargeable	9	150
Coin Cells	Lithium	Disposable	3 – 3.3	25 – 1000

Battery Schematic Symbols

+ − Single Cell   + − Multi Cell

charge rate keeps the battery cool inside and minimizes losses from the battery's natural internal resistance. Some types of batteries, such as NiCds or "Nicads," are specially designed to have low internal resistance to supply high discharge currents. [G6A02] A battery will also slowly lose its charge when not in use, called *self-discharge*. The rate of self-discharge varies with battery type. In general, self-discharge can be minimized by keeping the battery cool and dry. Do not freeze batteries because expanding water inside might crack the case or damage the electrodes. If a battery is damp, the moisture on the outside of the battery will supply a path for leakage current to flow directly between the battery terminals, discharging it.

Charging Batteries

Recharging batteries must be done properly to ensure that the battery is returned to its maximum level of charge without damage. First, never attempt to recharge a primary battery such as carbon-zinc or silver-nickel. [G6A04] The chemical reaction that produces energy is not intended to be reversed and often produces gasses and corrosive chemicals that can damage the charging equipment.

There are battery chargers designed specifically for each type of rechargeable battery. Using the correct charger maximizes the life and usefulness of the battery. Heed any manufacturer's warnings about heating or venting of gasses during recharging which should always be performed in a well-ventilated area.

ALTERNATIVE POWER

Sometimes batteries just aren't sufficient to get the job done and a longer-term source of power is required. Generators are widely used, but if you are really "off the grid" and don't have your own personal nuclear power plant, then solar and wind power can be put to work.

What is most often meant by "solar power" is really *photovoltaic conversion* of sunlight directly to electricity. [G4E08] Solar panels and solar cells are made of silicon PN-junctions that are exposed to sunlight. As opposed to transistors and diodes that are quite small, solar cells can be inches across with the PN-junction sandwiched between layers of P- and N-type material. The photons of sunlight are absorbed by electrons that then have enough energy to travel across the PN-junction and create dc current flow. The forward voltage created as the electron crosses the junction is approximately 0.5 V and can be measured as the *open-circuit voltage* of the solar cell. [G4E09]

Strings of 24 cells can be connected together to create a 12 V solar panel. Multiple strings are then connected in parallel to create a panel that can supply the desired amount of current. Solar arrays connect several panels together, further increasing available power.

Wind generators use a dc generator connected to a propeller though a gearbox that keeps the generator spinning at a fast rate even in low wind speeds. Larger wind generators use an electronic controller to regulate the generator output electrically or by controlling propeller blade pitch.

Energy Storage

Systems that create energy from wind and solar power require one more component that adds to the cost of using them — a substantial energy storage system. [G4E11] When the sun is down or the wind doesn't blow, no power is available. If excess energy has been stored during periods of peak generation, there can be enough power to supply the operating needs until the winds pick up or the sun rises again.

Storage batteries are the usual means of energy storage and most alternative energy systems are designed with battery backup capabilities. In solar power systems, the battery connection is made through a series-connected diode to prevent the battery from discharging back through the panel or panels during periods of low illumination when the voltage from the solar cells is reduced. [G4E10]

CONNECTORS

Connectors are a convenient way to make an electrical connection by using mating electrical contacts. There are quite a few connector styles, but common terms apply to all of them. Pins are contacts that extend out of the connector body, and connectors in which pins make the electrical contact are called "male" connectors. Sockets are hollow, recessed contacts, and connectors with sockets are called "female." Connectors designed to attach to each other are called "mating connectors." Connectors with specially shaped bodies or inserts that require a complementary shape on a mating connector are called *keyed connectors*. Keyed connectors ensure that the connectors can only go together one way, reducing the possibility of damage from incorrect mating. [G6B15]

Plugs are connectors installed on the end of cables and *jacks* are installed on equipment. *Adapters* make connections between two different styles of connector, such as between two different families of RF connectors. Other adapters join connectors of the same family, such as double-male, double-female and gender changers. *Splitters* divide a signal between two connectors.

Power Connectors

Amateur Radio equipment uses a variety of power connectors. Some examples are shown in **Figure 4.28**. Most low power amateur equipment uses coaxial power connectors. These are the same type found on consumer electronic equipment that is supplied by a wall transformer or "wall wart" style of power supply. Transceivers and other equipment that requires high current in excess of a few amperes often use Molex connectors (**www.molex.com** — enter "MLX" in the search window) with a white, nylon body housing pins and sockets crimped onto the end of wires.

Another standard, particularly popular among ARES and other emergency communications groups, is the use of Anderson Powerpole connectors (**www.andersonpower.com** — click "Product Brands"). These connectors are "sexless" meaning that any two connectors of the same series can be mated — there are no male or female connectors. By standardizing on a single connector style, equipment can be shared and replaced easily in the field.

Molex and Powerpole connectors use crimp terminals (both male and female) installed on the end of wires. A special crimping tool is used to attach the wire to the terminal and the terminal is then inserted into the body of the connector. Making a solid connection requires the use of an appropriate tool — do not use pliers or some other tool

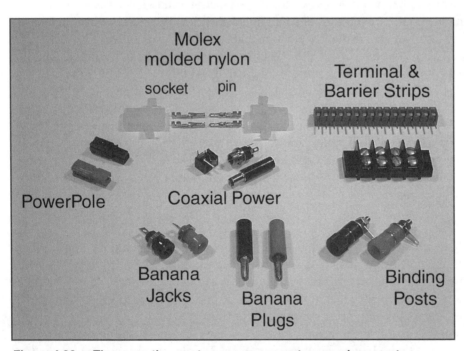

Figure 4.28 — These are the most common connectors used on amateur equipment to make power connections. (Courtesy of Wiley Publishing, *Ham Radio for Dummies*, or *Two-Way Radios & Scanners for Dummies*)

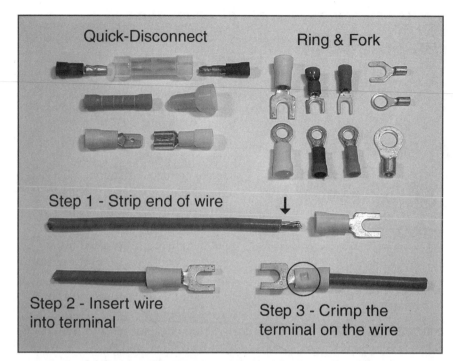

Figure 4.29 — Power connectors often use terminals that are crimped onto the end of wires with special crimping tools. (Courtesy of Wiley Publishing, *Ham Radio for Dummies*, or *Two-Way Radios & Scanners for Dummies*)

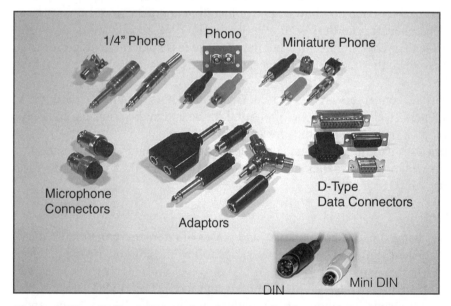

Figure 4.30 — Audio and data signals are carried by a variety of different connectors. Individual cable conductors are either crimped or soldered to the connector contacts. The popular DIN and Mini-DIN style of connectors are shown at the lower right.

to make a crimp connection.

Some equipment uses terminal strips for direct connection to wires or crimp terminals, often with screws. Other equipment uses spring-loaded terminals or binding posts to connect to bare wire ends. **Figure 4.29** shows some common crimp terminals that are installed on the ends of wires using special tools.

Audio and Control Connectors

Consumer audio equipment and Amateur Radio equipment share many of the same connectors for the same uses. *Phone* plugs and jacks are used for mono and stereo audio circuits. These connectors, shown in **Figure 4.30** come in ¼-inch, ⅛-inch (miniature) and subminiature varieties. The contact at the end of the plug is called the *tip* and the connector at the base of the plug is the *sleeve*. If there is a third contact between the tip and sleeve, such as for a stereo audio plug, it is the *ring*.

Phono plugs and jacks (sometimes called "RCA connectors" since they were first used on RCA brand equipment) are used for audio, video and other low-level RF signals. They are also widely used for control signals. [G6B14]

Multiple-pin DIN and Mini-DIN connectors seen in Figure 4.30 are the standard for accessory connectors on amateur equipment. DIN stands for the Deutsches Institut für Normung, the German standards organization. DIN and Mini-DIN connectors are keyed and have up to eight pins. [G6B17]

The most common microphone connector on mobile and base station equipment is an 8-pin round connector. On older transceivers you may see 4-pin round connectors used for microphones. Eight-pin RJ-45 modular connectors are often used in mobile and smaller radios.

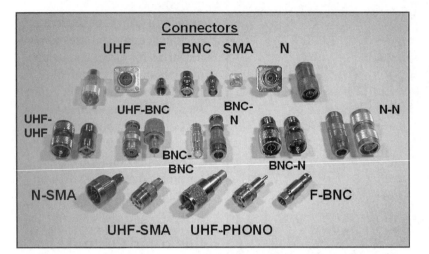

Figure 4.31 — Each type of RF connector is specially made to carry RF signals and preserve the shielding of coaxial cable. Adapters are available to connect one style of connector to another.

RF Connectors

Feed lines used for radio signals require special connectors for use at RF frequencies. The connectors must have approximately the same characteristic impedance as the feed line they are attached to or some of the RF signal will be reflected by the connector. Inexpensive audio and control connectors cannot meet that requirement, nor can they handle the high power levels often encountered in RF equipment. Occasionally, phono connectors are used for HF receiving and low-power transmitting equipment.

By far, the most common connector for RF in amateur equipment is the UHF family shown in **Figure 4.31**. (The UHF designation does not refer to frequency in this case.) A PL-259 is the plug that goes on the end of feed lines, and the SO-239 is the jack mounted on equipment. A "barrel" (PL-258) is a double-female adapter that allows two feed lines to be connected together. UHF connectors are typically used up to 150 MHz and can handle legal-limit transmitter power at HF. [G6B13]

UHF connectors have several drawbacks including lack of weatherproofing, poor performance above the 2 meter band and limited power handling at higher frequencies. The Type N series of RF connectors addresses all of those needs. Type N connectors are somewhat more expensive than UHF connectors, but they require less soldering and perform better in outdoor use since they are moisture resistant. Type N connectors can be used to 10 GHz. [G6B16]

For low power, BNC connectors are often used. BNC connectors are the standard for laboratory equipment, as well, and they are often used for dc and audio connections. BNC connectors are common on handheld radios for antenna connections.

SMA connectors are small threaded connectors designed for miniature coaxial cable and are rated for use up to 18 GHz. Handheld transceivers often use SMA connectors for attaching antennas. [G6B18]

Data Connectors

Digital data is exchanged between computers and pieces of radio equipment more than ever before in the amateur station. The connector styles follow those found on computer equipment.

D-type connectors are used for RS-232 (COM port) interfaces. The model number of a typical D-type connector specifies number of individual circuits and a "P" or "S" depending on whether the connector uses pins or sockets. For example, D-type 9-pin connectors often referred to as "DB-9" or "DE-9" are used for COM ports on PCs. [G6B12]

USB connectors are becoming more popular in amateur equipment as the computer industry moves to eliminate the bulkier and slower RS-232 interface. A number of manufacturers make devices for converting USB ports to RS-232 interfaces.

Before you go on, study test questions G4E08, G4E09 to G4E11, G6A01, G6A02, G6A04, G6B12 to G6B18, G7A01 to G7A08. Review this section if you have difficulty.

4.7 Basic Test Equipment

There's more to a radio than just operating it! As you gain experience with radios and accessories, you'll find yourself needing to make some simple checks and tests. You might try your hand at building some equipment and even repairing an ailing radio. To do so, you'll need some basic test equipment, and this section introduces you to some of the common items found on the radio workbench

ANALOG AND DIGITAL METERS

The *volt-ohm-meter* (VOM, also referred to as a voltmeter, volt-ohm-milliammeter, and multimeter) is the simplest piece of test equipment and amazingly versatile. A garden-variety meter that can be purchased new for $20 or less can measure voltage, current and resistance, act as a continuity checker, and even test diodes and transistors! For a few more dollars, you can add frequency counting, component value (capacitance, inductance) measurement, and a data interface to your PC to record readings.

There are two types of VOMs: analog and digital, as shown in **Figure 4.32**. The analog meter has a moving needle with calibrated scales on the meter face. While this type of meter can't perform more advanced functions, it is perfectly okay for basic go/no-go testing, tuning and troubleshooting. In fact, experienced hams prefer analog meters for finding a peak or minimum reading, such as when adjusting a tuned circuit, since it's easier to just watch the meter needle move than a numeric display. [G4B14]

The digital meter or DMM (for digital multimeter) has a microprocessor inside that takes care of all the basic functions and adds the ability to count and perform calculations. The digital meter also offers significantly greater precision (ability to resolve small changes) than an analog meter. [G4B06] Many hams have both a digital and an analog meter to use as the situation demands.

For both meter types, the instrument should affect the circuit being measured to the smallest degree possible. When measuring voltage, the meter should have a high input impedance so that it places the minimum load on the circuit being measured. [G4B05] In a sensitive circuit, the small current required by a voltmeter can affect the circuit's operation. Other useful features include fused current inputs to prevent damage from a temporary overload, peak hold to capture a maximum value, and autoranging to automatically select the proper display range.

Figure 4.32 — A digital voltmeter (DVM) shown at the left provides precise measurements of voltage, current and resistance. Many models can also act as a frequency counter or component tester. Analog meters (right) are often preferable for tuning and adjustments since the needle's movement makes adjusting for a maximum or minimum quite easy.

OSCILLOSCOPE

For working with fast-changing audio, data and RF signals, no instrument is more versatile or useful than the *oscilloscope*, often called a "scope." The oscilloscope provides a visual display of voltage against time as shown in **Figure 4.33**. The display can be updated thousands or even millions of times per second, giving the operator a real-time view of a signal's characteristics. This enables the technician to observe complex, fast-changing waveforms that are beyond the abilities of meters to measure. [G4B02] (For an on-line tutorial about oscilloscopes, see the ARRL's Technical Information Service web page **www.arrl.org/servicing-equipment**.)

An analog oscilloscope contains a *cathode-ray tube* (CRT) with a flat front surface. A beam of electrons is directed to the flat front surface, which is coated with a phosphor material that glows when struck by the electron beam. The electron beam is swept across the tube's surface by voltages applied to two sets of *deflection plates*. One set moves the beam horizontally and the other vertically.

External signals from the circuits under test are connected to the scope through horizontal and vertical *channel amplifiers*. The gain of the amplifiers is variable to adjust the sensitivity of the oscilloscope's display. [G4B01] An internal *time base* usually sweeps the electron beam along the horizontal axis at a highly stable, calibrated rate so that the scope can make accurate measurements of time and frequency. The track of the electron beam across the surface of the tube is called a *trace*.

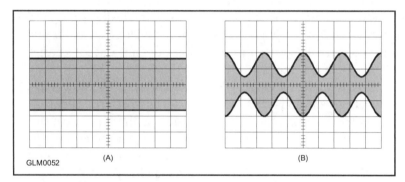

Figure 4.33 — Oscilloscope displays of RF signals. At A is an unmodulated carrier. The signal at B is from a full-carrier AM transmitter modulated with a single-frequency sine wave.

In the amateur station, a *monitoring oscilloscope* is very useful in monitoring transmitted signals by connecting the attenuated RF output of the transmitter to the vertical channel of the oscilloscope. [G4B04] Being able to monitor the transmitter output waveform in real time is of great assistance in adjusting keying waveforms, microphone gain and speech processing. Figure 4.33 shows an unmodulated carrier and an AM carrier modulated by a sine wave. **Figure 4.34** shows a typical keying waveform synchronized to the key closures that turn the transmitter on and off. The operator can clearly see the effects of any adjustments or conditions that might cause distortion or key clicks on the transmitted signal. [G4B03]

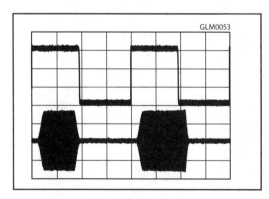

Figure 4.34 — It is easy to see the relationship between the key closure (top trace) and the transmitter output. If the transmitter turns on and off too abruptly or erratically, key clicks can result.

In recent years, oscilloscope manufacturers have begun replacing the bulky CRT with lightweight computer-type screens on digital oscilloscopes that simulate the CRT display. The input signals are converted to digital data and manipulated by a microprocessor to control how the signals are displayed. These digital scopes are becoming affordable for amateurs, both as new and used equipment. Some digital scopes do away with the separate display altogether and use a USB connection to display the signals on a computer.

IMPEDANCE AND RESONANCE MEASUREMENTS

It is often necessary to measure impedance when building or testing a new antenna or when performing maintenance on an existing antenna. An incredibly useful instrument that has made antenna testing much easier is the *antenna*

Figure 4.35 — An antenna analyzer, such as the MFJ-269 shown here, is handy for testing transmission lines and antennas. It displays SWR and impedance at frequencies of 1.5 to 170 MHz and across the 70 cm band.

Figure 4.36 — A field strength meter is used to check relative performance of an antenna by measuring the electric field intensity.

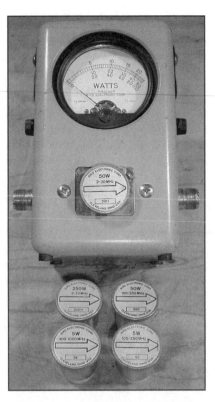

Figure 4.37 — The Bird Model 43 directional wattmeter uses sensing elements designed for a specific frequency range and power level. Forward and reflected power are read by rotating the sensing element. (One sensing element is plugged into the meter, and four other elements for different power levels and frequency ranges are shown below the meter.)

analyzer shown in **Figure 4.35**. The analyzer contains a CW signal generator, a frequency counter, an SWR bridge and an impedance meter. Different models of analyzers can display both resistive and reactance values of antenna impedance as well as the precise frequency at which the measurement is being made. By connecting the analyzer directly to the antenna feed line, SWR can be checked without having to transmit a signal at high power. [G4B11] The analyzers are also capable of measuring feed line velocity factor, electrical length, characteristic impedance and other parameters. [G4B13] The exact procedures for all measurements are explained in the analyzer user's manual.

The battery-powered analyzers are also small enough to be part of a tool kit so that antennas can be tested at the point of adjustment without having to go back into the shack to make measurements. A point of caution, however: Because the analyzer uses small signals to make measurements, its accuracy can be affected by strong signals from nearby transmitters. [G4B12]

FIELD STRENGTH AND RF POWER METERS

Another useful set of antenna tests and diagnostics concern the radiation efficiency and pattern of the antenna. A receiver can make these measurements, but it is often inconvenient to take a receiver into the field. A *field strength meter* is the better choice for that job, making calibrated readings of electric field strength. **Figure 4.36** shows a typical unit. While signal strength levels can be inferred from measurements of power and SWR, a field strength meter actually measures the transmitted signal level. It is often used to compare relative levels of RF output during antenna and transmitter adjustments. [G4B08]

By placing the field strength meter in one location and rotating the antenna, the radiation pattern of the antenna can be measured. Conversely, the meter can be carried to different locations to determine the radiation pattern of a fixed antenna, such as a wire beam or array. [G4B09]

Another power measurement tool is the *directional wattmeter* shown in **Figure 4.37**. Placed in a transmission line, usually at the transmitter output, the directional wattmeter can measure both forward (P_F) and reflected power (P_R) in the line. Some meters can measure both simultaneously with independent meters or by turning a switch or power sensing element. Power meters are used to adjust transmitter and amplifier output circuits and drive levels.

Standing wave ratio (SWR) can be calculated from forward and reflected power measurements made using a directional wattmeter. [G4B10] SWR is then calculated using the following formula:

$$SWR = \frac{1 + \sqrt{P_R / P_F}}{1 - \sqrt{P_R / P_F}}$$

Before you go on, study test questions G4B01 to G4B06, and G4B08 to G4B14. Review this section if you have difficulty.

Chapter 5

Radio Signals and Equipment

In this chapter, you'll learn about:
- **Basic signal concepts — a review**
- **Oscillators**
- **Mixers, multipliers and modulators**
- **Transmitter and amplifier fundamentals**
- **Receiver fundamentals**
- **Installing an HF station**

After learning about the fundamentals of electronics and components, you're ready to "build" on that knowledge. In this section, we study real radios and investigate what's going on as adjustments are made. We'll start with the building blocks and then put them together into complete packages — transmitters, receivers, and amplifiers. You'll be getting deeper into circuits and the structure of radio equipment, so you may need to brush up on your understanding of schematics and block diagrams. A helpful tutorial is available on the *General Class License Manual* website, **www.arrl.org/general-class-license-manual**. This chapter leads to the things you'll need to know about putting a station together and managing it. Set the power switch to ON and let's get busy!

5.1 Signal Review

Even though you studied the following terms and concepts for your Technician license, it helps to start by reviewing the basics of radio signals. A radio signal at one frequency whose strength never changes is called a *continuous wave*, abbreviated CW. Adding information to a signal by modifying it in some way, such as changing its frequency, phase angle, or amplitude, is called *modulation*. The method of modulation that carries the information is the signal's *mode*. The simplest mode is a continuous wave turned on and off in a coded pattern, such as Morse code.

Recovering the information from a modulated signal is called *demodulation*. A signal that doesn't carry any information is *unmodulated*. If speech is the information used to modulate a signal, the result is a *voice mode* or *phone* (short for *radiotelephone*) signal. If data is the information used to modulate a signal, the result is a *data mode* or *digital mode* signal. *Analog* modes carry information such as speech that can be understood directly by a human. Digital or data modes carry information as data characters between two computers.

Any characteristic of a signal can be varied to carry information if the variations are observable at the receiving end to recover the information. Three characteristics that can be modulated are the signal's amplitude or strength, its frequency, and its phase. The term *instantaneous* when applied to amplitude, frequency, or phase refers to the value of those characteristics at a specific instant in time.

AMPLITUDE MODULATED MODES

Varying the power or amplitude of a signal to add speech or data information is called *amplitude modulation* or AM. The information is contained in the signal's *envelope* —

the maximum values of the instantaneous power for each cycle. [G8A05] The process of recovering speech or music by following the envelope of an AM signal is called *detection*. An AM signal is composed of a *carrier* and two *sidebands*. The total power of an AM signal is divided between the carrier and sidebands. The AM signal's carrier is a continuous wave with an amplitude that does not change and contains no information.

An AM signal modulated by a tone has two sidebands that are present as steady, unchanging signals as long as the tone is transmitted. The *upper sideband* (USB) is higher in frequency than the carrier by the frequency of the tone. The *lower sideband* (LSB) is lower in frequency than the carrier. The information to recover the tone is contained in the amplitude of the sidebands and their differences in frequency from that of the carrier. Each sideband contains an exact copy of the modulating signal.

An AM signal with the carrier and one sideband removed is called a *single sideband* signal (SSB). SSB transmissions have more range compared to AM because all of an SSB signal's power is contained in the remaining sideband. SSB's smaller bandwidth also makes it possible to fit more signals in a fixed range of frequencies. The wider AM signals tend to have a fuller frequency response that sounds "warmer" on the air.

ANGLE MODULATED MODES

Modes that vary the frequency of a signal to add speech or data information are called *frequency modulation* or FM. The frequency is varied in proportion to the instantaneous amplitude of the modulating signal. The amount that an FM signal's frequency varies when modulated is called *deviation*. *Phase modulation* (PM) is created by varying a signal's *phase angle*. Receivers can demodulate FM and PM with the same demodulator circuits. [G8A02, G8A03]

FM and PM are called *angle modulation* because both techniques modulate the signal by varying the signal's *phase angle*. FM changes the amount of time it takes for the signal to make a 360° cycle. PM varies the relative phase difference between the signal and some reference phase. FM and PM signals have one carrier and many sidebands. These signals have a *constant power*, whether modulated or not.

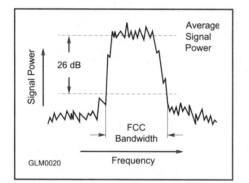

Figure 5.1 — The FCC defines bandwidth as "the width of a frequency band outside of which the mean [average] power of the transmitted signal is attenuated at least 26 dB below the mean power."

BANDWIDTH DEFINITION

Composite signals are groups of individual signals that combine to create a complex signal. Composite signals have *components* that may cover a range of frequencies. The difference in frequency between the lowest and highest component of a composite signal is the signal's *bandwidth*.

The FCC has a more specific definition of bandwidth in section §97.3(a)(8): "*Bandwidth*. The width of a frequency band outside of which the mean [average] power of the transmitted signal is attenuated at least 26 dB below the mean power within the band." **Figure 5.1** illustrates how this measurement is made.

The FCC limits signal bandwidth so that many stations and types of signals can share the limited amount of spectrum space. **Table 5.1** lists the bandwidth of the most common amateur signals. [G8A07]

Table 5.1
Amateur Signal Bandwidths

Type of Signal	Typical Bandwidth
AM voice	6 kHz
Amateur television	6 MHz
SSB voice	2 to 3 kHz
Digital using SSB	50 to 3000 Hz (0.05 to 3 kHz)
CW	100 to 300 Hz (0.1 to 0.3 kHz)
FM voice	5 to 16 kHz

5.2 Radio's Building Blocks

Nearly all radios are made up of a few fundamental types of circuits. The way in which the circuit designers choose to build those circuits varies quite a bit, but the basic functions of the circuit are the same. In this section we cover four of those circuits: *oscillators, mixers, multipliers* and *modulators*. You'll learn the functions and important characteristics of each.

OSCILLATORS

The function of most oscillators used in radio is to produce a pure sine wave with no noise or distortion — as close to a single-frequency signal as possible. The block diagram symbol for an oscillator (a circle with a sine wave inside) is shown in **Figure 5.2** along with the fundamental circuit that makes an oscillator work.

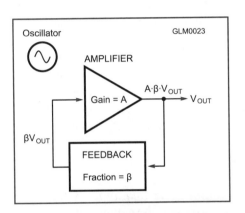

Figure 5.2 — An oscillator consists of an amplifier with feedback from the output to input. The product of gain and feedback ratio must be greater than 1 at the frequency of oscillation.

An oscillator consists of an amplifier (the triangle is the amplifier's block diagram symbol) that increases signal amplitude (*gain*) and a *feedback* circuit to route some of the amplifier's output signal back to its input. If at any frequency the product of the amplifier's gain and the amount of feedback is greater than unity, the circuit's output will be self-sustaining, called *oscillation*. To make an oscillator produce a single-frequency output, the feedback circuit must include a filter so that feedback is present at only the intended frequency. [G7B07]

An oscillator's output frequency can be fixed or variable. There are three basic types of fixed-frequency oscillators: RC, LC and crystal.

An RC oscillator's feedback circuit is made up of resistors (R) and capacitors (C). Because of the combination of reactance and resistance, the RC circuit shifts the phase of the feedback circuit so that the resulting signal, when applied to the amplifier's input, reinforces the output signal, building up a steady output signal.

The LC oscillator's feedback circuit consists of an inductor (L) and capacitor (C) connected in parallel or series to form a resonant circuit, often called a *tank circuit* because it stores electrical energy like a flywheel stores mechanical energy. The resonant frequency of the LC circuit, determined by the values of L and C, is the frequency of the oscillator. LC oscillators are more stable than RC oscillators and can be used throughout the radio frequency spectrum. [G7B09]

A quartz crystal is often substituted for the LC tank circuit, creating a *crystal oscillator*. The quartz crystal acts like a resonant LC circuit and is orders of magnitude more precise than an LC circuit. Crystal oscillators are used whenever an accurate, stable signal source is required.

A *variable-frequency oscillator* (VFO) whose output frequency can be adjusted is used to tune a radio to different frequencies. The frequency of the oscillator is adjusted by varying the value of one or more components in the feedback circuit. In radio circuits, VFOs are usually created by varying the capacitance of the LC feedback circuit, although some designs vary the inductance. Two other widely used VFO circuits are the *phase-locked loop* (PLL) and *direct digital synthesizer* (DDS). The DDS has the advantage of being controllable by software and having stability comparable to a crystal oscillator. [G7C05]

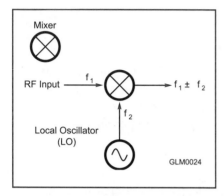

Figure 5.3 — The mixer combines signals of different frequencies, producing signals at the sum and difference frequency. Mixers are used to change or shift the frequency of signals.

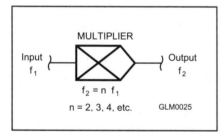

Figure 5.4 — A multiplier is a special type of tuned amplifier that creates harmonics of an input signal and then selects the desired harmonic at its output. The output of low frequency oscillators or modulators can be multiplied to frequencies at which it is difficult to build and modulate oscillators.

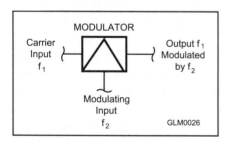

Figure 5.5 — The general symbol can be used for a modulator of any type — AM, FM or SSB.

MIXERS

A key function in both receivers and transmitters is to be able to change the frequency of a signal as you will see in the following sections. The circuit that performs this job is called a *mixer*. The block diagram symbol for a mixer is shown in **Figure 5.3**. The most common application of a mixer is also shown in the figure.

A mixer circuit combines two input frequencies, f_1 and f_2, and produces their sum and difference at its output. This process is called *heterodyning*. [G8B03] For example, if $f_1 = 14.050$ MHz and $f_2 = 3.35$ MHz, the output of the mixer will contain signals at both 10.7 MHz ($f_1 - f_2$) and at 17.4 MHz ($f_1 + f_2$). It is up to the following circuits to select the desired signal from the pair and make use of it. [G8B01] A mixer can change a signal to any other frequency — the input and output frequencies do not have to be related in any way.

In radio circuits, the input f_1 to the mixer is usually referred to as the RF input because that signal is usually associated with a received or transmitted signal. Input f_2 is usually labeled the *local oscillator* (LO) because it represents a reference signal produced locally by an oscillator within the equipment. All of the mixer outputs are called *mixing products*.

MULTIPLIERS

A circuit that acts similarly to a mixer is the *multiplier*. Instead of creating the sum and difference of two input frequencies, a multiplier creates a harmonic of an input frequency. [G8B04] The block diagram symbol for a multiplier circuit is shown in **Figure 5.4**. Multipliers are often used when a stable VHF or UHF signal is required, but constructing an oscillator at that frequency would be difficult. A low-frequency oscillator supplies the multiplier input and the output is tuned to the desired harmonic of the input signal. Multipliers are also used in FM transmitters as you will see in a following section.

MODULATORS

Modulators are the circuits which perform the neat trick of adding information to a carrier signal, either as amplitude, frequency, or phase variations. The block diagram symbol for a modulator is shown in **Figure 5.5**. The input signal on the left-hand side is usually the unmodulated input. The input from below is the signal containing information that is to be added to the unmodulated input, and the output is on the right. (You may have noticed that all four of the block diagram symbols support the left-to-right signal flow that is recommended for schematics and block diagrams.) The same symbol is used to represent demodulator circuits, as well.

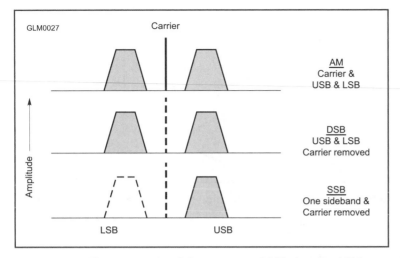

Figure 5.6 — The spectrum of three types of AM signals. AM has both sidebands and the carrier. DSB removes the carrier, but has the same bandwidth as AM. SSB removes one sideband and has the lowest bandwidth of the three.

Amplitude Modulators

AM was first generated by varying the power supply voltage to the output circuit of a CW transmitter. You can easily imagine this process: As the voltage is varied, the amplitude of the output signal's envelope follows along. This is called *plate* or *collector (or drain) modulation* because the voltage that is varied is connected to a vacuum tube plate or a transistor's collector or drain. A modulation transformer was used to add and subtract an amplified version of the operator's voice to the power supply voltage, creating the modulation.

After SSB became popular, transmitters were required to generate both SSB and AM signals. SSB cannot be generated by amplitude modulating an output circuit — different techniques must be used at lower signal levels. However, AM and double-sideband (DSB) can be generated by a *balanced modulator*. DSB is the same as AM with the carrier removed, leaving the upper and lower sidebands as shown in **Figure 5.6**.

A balanced modulator is a special type of mixer where f_1 is the carrier signal and f_2 is the modulating signal. Take another look at Figure 5.3. The output signal, shown as $f_1 \pm f_2$, is exactly a DSB signal — a pair of sidebands above and below the carrier frequencies without a carrier signal. The balanced modulator circuit produces DSB because it

How Close Is Too Close?

When you operate phone using SSB, it's important to know where your actual signals appear on the band. Nearly all radios display the carrier frequency of a SSB transmission. That means your actual signal lies entirely above (USB) or below (LSB) the displayed frequency. If the sidebands occupy 3 kHz of spectrum, you'll need to stay far enough from the edge of your frequency privileges to avoid transmitting a signal outside them. For example, Generals are permitted to use up to 14.350 MHz, so the displayed carrier frequency of a USB signal should be at least 3 kHz below the band edge — 14.347 MHz — so that the signal occupies 14.347 to 14.350 MHz. If your carrier frequency is higher than that, the sidebands begin to extend into the non-amateur frequencies above 14.350 MHz! Similarly, using LSB on 40 meters, Generals should operate with the carrier frequency at least 3 kHz above the edge of their band segment — 7.178 MHz — thus occupying the range of 7.175 to 7.178 MHz. See **Figure 5.7**. [G4D08 to G4D11]

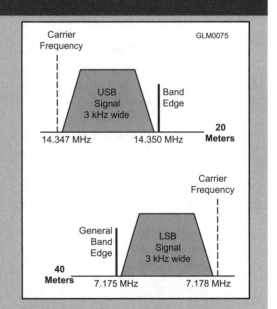

Figure 5.7 — When sidebands extend from the carrier toward a band edge or a band segment edge, operate with a displayed carrier frequency no closer than 3 kHz to the edge frequency and be sure your signal is "clean."

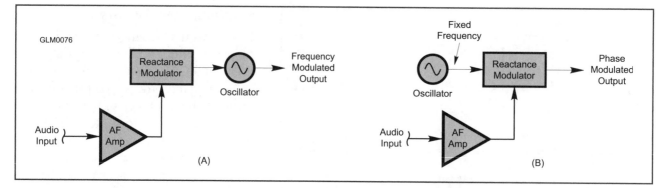

Figure 5.8 — Reactance modulators can be used to create frequency modulation (A) or phase modulation (B).

cancels the carrier signal internally. AM can be generated by a balanced modulator if the circuit is intentionally unbalanced, allowing the carrier to reappear in the output signal.

Starting with a DSB signal, SSB can be generated by filtering out the unwanted sideband. This is the filter method of generating SSB. The phasing method of generating SSB signals without filters uses a pair of balanced modulators fed by carrier and modulating signals that are 90° out of phase. The resulting DSB signals are then added together, with the result being an SSB signal. By only using one sideband, the transmitter's available output power can be used more effectively compared to full AM. [G8A06]

Frequency and Phase Modulators

Frequency modulation (*FM*) is the result when the frequency of the modulated signal deviates only in proportion to the modulating signal's amplitude. *Phase modulation* (*PM*) occurs if the deviation is proportional to both the modulating signal's amplitude and frequency. The design of the modulator circuit determines whether the output signal is FM or PM. It is important to note that except for very specific circumstances, FM and PM sound identical on the air and can both be demodulated by the same circuits.

The most common method of performing angle modulation is a reactance modulator, shown in **Figure 5.8**. If the modulator is connected to the tuned circuit that controls the oscillator's frequency then the frequency will change when modulation is applied, creating frequency modulation. To create phase modulation, the reactance modulator is connected to a tuned RF amplifier following the oscillator. When modulation is applied, the phase of the carrier will be changed but the average frequency will not be changed. [G8A04]

> *Before you go on, study test questions G4D08 to G4D11, G7B07, G7B09, G7C05, G8A04, G8A06, G8B01, G8B03, and G8B04. Review the section if you have difficulty.*

5.3 Transmitter Structure

From the building blocks are assembled the equipment of radio — transmitters and receivers. In this section, you'll learn how the components produce the many signals you hear on the air — CW, SSB and FM. Armed with that understanding, you'll understand the effects of transmitter controls and how to keep your signal "clean." We'll take a close look at amplifiers — the business end of a transmitter — and how to use them properly. The goal is for you to transmit a signal you can be proud of every time.

AM MODES

As you learned in previous sections, CW, AM and SSB are all types of amplitude modulation. They can all be generated by the same basic transmitter structure. Transmitters described in this section are all "analog," meaning they generate and modify signals with discrete electronic circuits. Transmitters using DSP and SDR (software defined radio) techniques perform the same functions as mathematical operations in a microprocessor.

CW TRANSMITTERS

The simplest transmitter is a two-stage CW rig, shown in **Figure 5.9**. It consists only of an oscillator and an amplifier, with the amplifier turned on and off by a key or keyer. Many amateurs began their on-the-air operating careers with a simple transmitter just like this — one tube or transistor for a crystal-controlled oscillator and a larger tube or transistor for the amplifier! Using a crystal restricts the transmitter to one frequency per crystal, but the output frequency is quite stable. If the crystal oscillator is replaced with a variable-frequency oscillator, it becomes a VFO-controlled transmitter.

The oscillator frequently includes a buffer amplifier that isolates the oscillator from the output amplifier. This makes the signal cleaner and less prone to chirp — a rapid change in frequency during key-down periods caused by power supply or load changes. The output amplifier often includes two amplifiers, as well: a driver stage and a power amplifier (PA) stage. The driver amplifier brings the low-power oscillator output signal to a sufficient strength to drive the PA to full power.

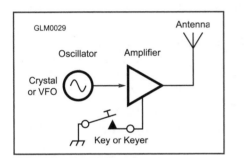

Figure 5.9 — The simplest transmitter consists of the oscillator and amplifier and a means of turning the output signal on and off — the key.

In a VFO-controlled transmitter that operates on more than one band, mixers are used to change the transmitter output frequency band without changing the VFO frequency range. This keeps the VFO design simple and stable for good signal quality. **Figure 5.10** shows a simple scheme for a three-band, VFO-controlled transmitter. The mixer input from the VFO always covers the same frequency range. The local oscillator (LO) outputs a signal on one of three frequencies determined by which crystal is switched in. A filter tuned to one of the three bands follows the mixer to eliminate the undesired sum or difference frequency.

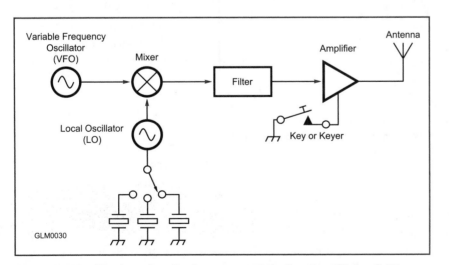

Figure 5.10 — By changing the frequency of the local oscillator (LO), the VFO's output can be shifted from band to band, creating a multi-band transmitter.

The use of microprocessor-controlled dual VFOs in modern transceivers makes it easy to use the time-honored technique of operating "split" — that is, listening on one frequency and transmitting on another. This is often encountered when a rare DX station is on the air with many callers. Operating simplex — transmitting and receiving on the same frequency — can result in a lot of confusion with stations trying to hear the DX station while others transmit on the same frequency. By transmitting on one frequency and having callers transmit on adjacent frequencies, everyone can hear the DX station and keep "in sync" for more orderly, effective operating. By swapping the VFOs, you can also listen to your transmit frequency to avoid interfering with other contacts or find out precisely where the DX station is listening! [G4A03, G4A12]

Many transceivers also feature the ability to listen to a second frequency, independently of the main receive frequency. This is accomplished by switching a single receiver very rapidly between two frequencies or with a second, independent receiver. This allows you to listen to both the DX station and the pileup at the same time, a very valuable capability allowing you to quickly find the right transmit frequency.

SSB PHONE TRANSMITTERS

Figure 5.11 shows how to change the CW transmitter to SSB phone. Starting with the three-band CW transmitter in Figure 5.10, a balanced modulator stage is added between the oscillator and mixer. Voice signals from a microphone (mic) are processed by a speech amplifier and input to the balanced modulator. The variable-frequency carrier oscillator is the other input to the balanced modulator. [G7C02] The output is a DSB signal, so a filter is required to remove the undesired sideband. (USB signals are the standard on 20 meters and LSB on 80 and 40 meters.) [G7C01] A mixer then converts the signal to the correct frequency as before. This SSB transmitter can also produce AM signals by unbalancing the modulator so that the AM carrier is present in the modulator output. For SSB signals, the FCC requires that the carrier must be reduced or suppressed to at least 40 dB below the signal's peak power output on the air to prevent unnecessary interference.

Note that the output amplifier is now labeled a "Linear Amplifier." That change is necessary because the transmitter must accurately reproduce the rapidly changing speech waveform. In a CW transmitter, it is only necessary to turn a sine wave on and off. In an AM or SSB transmitter, however, all of the stages must be designed to accurately reproduce the input signal, whether they amplify, mix, or filter it. Distortion anywhere in the "transmit chain" (meaning the sequence of circuits that produce the transmitted signal) will generate unwanted spurious signals such as harmonics, mixing products, or splatter.

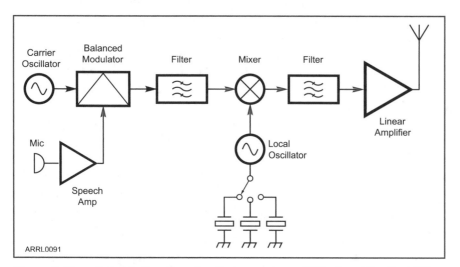

Figure 5.11 — Substituting the circuits to create an SSB signal for the VFO creates a multiband SSB transmitter.

The FCC does not specify bandwidth limits on any phone signal except to say that signals should not occupy more bandwidth than is dictated by "good amateur practice" [§97.307(a)]. Generally speaking, that means an SSB signal should have a bandwidth of no more than 3 kHz and an AM signal about 6 kHz. There is one exception. On 60 meters, the FCC specifies in §97.303(s) that the USB signals should occupy no more than 2.8 kHz of bandwidth as defined in §97.3(a)(8).

FM TRANSMITTERS

Modulation and frequency changing are performed differently in FM transmitters. While it is possible to generate an FM signal and then use mixers, it is much less expensive and more practical to generate the FM signal at a low frequency and multiply it to reach the desired band. This technique is illustrated in **Figure 5.12**. In a 2 meter band FM transmitter, the modulated oscillator frequency is approximately 12 MHz and the multiplier selects the 12th harmonic for transmission. For example, for an output on 146.52 MHz, the oscillator must produce a $146.52 \div 12 = 12.21$ MHz signal.

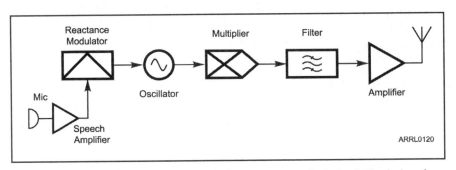

Figure 5.12 — The carrier and modulation are generated at relatively low frequencies in an FM transmitter. The modulated signal is then multiplied to the desired output frequency. The amount of signal deviation is also multiplied.

It's important to realize that the deviation of the modulated oscillator output is also multiplied, increasing with each harmonic. The radio designer must compensate for that factor when designing the modulator circuit. For example, if that same 146.52 MHz signal is to have no more than the standard deviation of 5 kHz, the maximum deviation of the oscillator can only be $5 \div 12 = 416.7$ Hz. [G8B07]

Just as for AM signals, the FCC requires amateurs to limit the bandwidth (BW) of FM signals to that which represents good amateur practice. Any angle modulated signal has a theoretically infinite number of sidebands, so what is the bandwidth of an FM signal? While there may be a lot of sidebands, except for those close to the carrier they have negligible power. *Carson's Rule* is a formula that gives a good approximation of an FM signal's bandwidth: BW = 2 × (peak deviation + highest modulating frequency).

As an example, if an FM phone signal's peak deviation is limited to 5 kHz and the highest modulating frequency is 3 kHz, then BW = 2 × (5 + 3) = 16 kHz. [G8B06] This signal will stay safely within the 20 kHz channels used by repeater coordinators. Thus, it is important to control both deviation (the swings in frequency from the amplitude of the modulating signal) and the frequency content of the modulating signal.

Another thing you might have noticed about Figure 5.12 is that the output amplifier is no longer required to be a linear amplifier. FM and PM signals have a constant power level, so it doesn't matter whether an amplifier can faithfully reproduce the input waveform or not. The only important characteristic of the FM signal is its frequency. Amplifiers in an FM transmitter can be highly nonlinear as long as harmonics are removed from the transmitted signal!

SIGNAL QUALITY

Operating a transmitter so that the on-the-air signal is intelligible and does not have excessive bandwidth is an important part of operating. This section discusses the causes of poor signal quality and what the operator should do about them.

Harmonics and Spurs

Harmonics and parasitics are examples of *spurious emissions*. Harmonics are generated by nearly all circuits because of minor nonlinearities in their operation. Transmitters use filters to remove harmonics from their output signals. Nevertheless, you should be aware that a misadjusted or overdriven transmitter or defective equipment external to the transmitter can produce harmonics.

Parasitics (sometimes called *spurs*) are unwanted outputs that are not harmonically related to the desired output. They may even be low-level replicas of the desired output signal! They are usually caused by excessive drive levels or mistuning of the output stage of a transmitter or amplifier.

The solution to reducing or eliminating harmonics and parasitics is often to simply reduce the overall power level of the transmitted signal and check to be sure the power stages are tuned properly.

Overmodulation — AM Modes

If the amplitude of an AM or SSB signal is varied excessively in response to the modulating signal, this is called *overmodulation*. Overmodulation is caused by speaking too loudly or by setting the microphone or audio gain too high. Examples of properly modulated and overmodulated signals are shown in **Figure 5.13**. The figure shows the *modulation envelope* of an AM signal, the waveform created by connecting the peaks of the modulated signal. (The modulation envelope of an SSB signal is similar.) [G8A11]

Figure 5.13B shows an example of *cutoff* in which the transmitter output is turned off instead of following the modulating signal. *Flattopping* occurs when the transmitter output reaches a maximum limit and cannot increase further even though the modulating signal is still increasing. Overmodulation distorts the transmitted audio and increases the signal's bandwidth by creating unwanted spurious signals that are transmitted on nearby frequencies and interfering with other communications. These spurious signals are *distortion products*, commonly referred to as *splatter* or *buckshot*.

Microphone (or mic) gain is the control used to adjust the amount by which speech modulates the transmitter output signal. To prevent overmodulation, reduce microphone gain or speak more quietly. If you have a monitoring oscilloscope in your shack, you can watch the transmitter output on voice peaks to see if your signal appears "clean." It also helps to have a friend check your signal on the air to make sure you are not causing interference to other operators. Once your transmitter is operating properly, take note of the transmitter settings, meter behavior and oscilloscope images so that you can keep your signal properly adjusted in the future.

If the drive level to transmitter output stages or external amplifiers is increased beyond the point of maximum output power level, the result is *flat-topping* or *clip-*

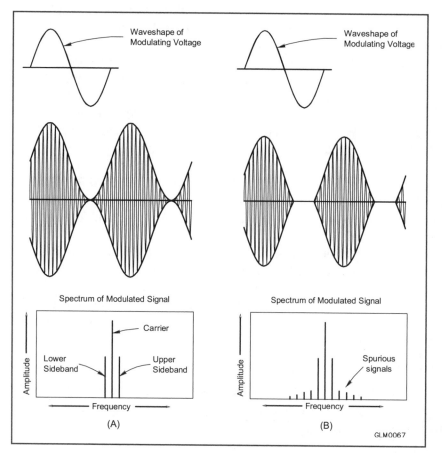

Figure 5.13 — A properly modulated signal at A. The results of overmodulation are visible at B. This distorted signal causes interference on nearby frequencies.

ping. [G8A10] The peaks of such a transmitted signal appear "flattened" on a monitoring oscilloscope. If the output signal is completely cut off between peaks, the result is *carrier cutoff*. Both cause interference to nearby channels by generating spurious signals beyond the normal signal bandwidth.

Audio level adjustment is somewhat different for each radio and style of signal monitoring equipment. The basics are similar, however. First, use normal speech or audio levels during both testing and on the air contacts. It's natural under difficult conditions to raise your voice but that usually only reduces intelligibility. Next, make use of the monitor function to listen to your own signal while you transmit. This is not an exact copy of your output signal, but is helpful in controlling your own speech volume and in catching any distortion in the audio circuits of the transmitter.

The automatic level control (ALC) circuits of your transmitter also help prevent overmodulation. ALC reduces output power during voice peaks. Your radio's manual will have some instructions on how to use ALC to properly set your transmit audio levels. In general, the microphone gain should be adjusted to cause the ALC to activate only on voice peaks. [G8A09]

Finally, the *two-tone test* for transmitter linearity is very helpful in keeping your signal clean. This test consists of modulating your transmitter with a pair of audio tones that are not harmonically related (700 and 1900 Hz are typical frequencies) while watching the transmitted signal on a monitoring oscilloscope. The transmitter and any external amplifier are then adjusted for an output free of distortion. This test needs only to be performed occasionally to note the appropriate settings of gain and level adjustments. [G4B07, G4B15]

Watch the Noise!

A common downfall of speech processing is background noise, such as fans, wind or other conversations. Noise entering a microphone is indistinguishable from soft speech and can mask speech components, with the expected loss in signal quality. When using a processor, be sure to reduce room noise as much as possible.

Speech Processing

Compared to modes such as CW, the average power of an AM or SSB signal is quite low. Human speech spreads its energy out over a wide frequency range with only short periods of high sound levels. When transmitted over HF as an amplitude-modulated signal in the presence of noise, interference or fading, the received signal can be difficult to understand. *Speech processing* addresses this problem by increasing the average power of the speech signal without excessively distorting the signal. The result is improved intelligibility of the received signal in poor conditions. [G4D01, G4D02] Speech processors are available that work on the audio input to the transmitter and on the low-level RF signal before amplification.

A common technique for speech processing is *compression*, which increases gain at low input levels while holding gain constant for louder speech components. The amount of compression is measured in dB as the difference in gain for different levels of input. For example, if low-level input signals are amplified with 10 dB more gain than for high-level signals, it is referred to as "10 dB of compression." Modest amounts of compression make a voice "sound louder" because the low-level speech components are easier to hear in the received signal.

Any kind of speech processing is, by definition, distortion. Too much processing (called *overprocessing*) results in a signal with plenty of power, but is more distorted and harder to understand than the unprocessed signal! A processed signal also requires careful adjustment of transmitter modulation to avoid causing splatter on adjacent channels. Speech processors can also amplify low-level background noise, further reducing intelligibility. The proper use of speech processing balances the increase in average power against any reduction in intelligibility. [G4D03]

Overdeviation — FM and PM

FM signals can be overmodulated as well, but instead of distorting the signal envelope, the result is excessive deviation. This increases the strength of the extra FM signal sidebands that are usually too small to cause interference. The result of overdeviation is distortion of the received signal and interference to adjacent channels, just as it is for overmodulation of AM signals. [G8A08]

Most FM rigs have limiting circuits that prevent overdeviation caused by speaking too loudly. Your voice may be distorted, but it won't cause interference. Multimode rigs with adjustable microphone gain may allow overmodulation, however. Read your owner's manual to learn the proper operating procedure for your radio.

Key Clicks

Key clicks are sharp transient clicking sounds heard on adjacent frequencies as a transmitter turns on and off too rapidly during CW transmissions. Clicks can also be generated if the transmitter turns on and off erratically. These can be quite disruptive to nearby contacts. Key clicks can often be reduced by adjusting a transmitter configuration setting or by modifying the transmitter's keying control circuits. An oscilloscope can be used to monitor the CW waveform as shown in **Figure 5.14**. If the leading and trailing edges of the CW output are 4 to 8 ms long, clicks are not generated. Be sure to look closely at the keying waveform for transients or sharp steps.

AMPLIFIERS

Many HF operators use an amplifier (sometimes called a *linear*) so that they can make contacts when conditions are poor, over difficult propagation paths, or in situations such as running a net for which a strong signal is necessary. VHF and UHF amplifiers are most commonly available as solid-state "bricks" that require no tuning or adjustment — turn them on, hook up the rig and the antenna and go. On HF, high-power amplifiers often use vacuum tube circuits that require operator adjustment, although high power "no tune" solid-state amplifiers are gaining popularity. Modes such as SSB require linear amplifiers that accurately reproduce the input signal waveform. [G7B14]

An amplifier circuit or *stage* is designed to operate in one of several different *classes*. Each different class is best suited for different radio uses. Hams use four common amplifier classes:

• *Class A* — The most linear (lowest signal distortion) of all classes and also the least efficient. The amplifying device in a Class A amplifier is on all the time. Gain is limited. [G7B10]

• *Class B* — Also known as *push-pull* with a pair of amplifying devices each active during complementary halves of the signal's cycle. Efficiency is good and linearity can be good with careful design and adjustment.

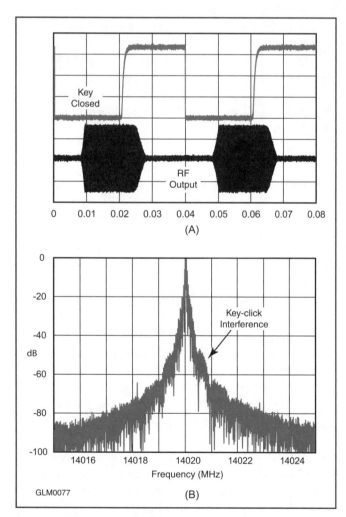

Figure 5.14 — CW waveforms can be inspected by using a monitoring oscilloscope. Key clicks that result from rising and falling edges that are too abrupt or not smooth cause interference on nearby frequencies.

- *Class AB* — Midway between Classes A and B, the amplifying device is active for more than one-half but less than an entire signal cycle. Linearity is not as good as Class A, but efficiency is improved.
- *Class C* — Amplifying devices are active for less than one-half of the signal's cycle. This class of amplifier has the highest efficiency, but Class C amplifiers are only suitable for CW and FM because they have very poor linearity. [G7B11, G7B12]

Some linear amplifiers can be operated in either Class AB for SSB operation or in Class C for CW. The efficiency of an amplifier is defined as the RF output power divided by the dc input power. [G7B08]

Along with the RF input from the transceiver, the transceiver should provide a *keying circuit* that tells the amplifier when to activate. When the keying circuit is inactive, signals from the antenna are bypassed around the amplifier circuit by a transmit-receive *changeover relay* (TR relay) so they can be received. Transceivers often include a delay in the keying circuit timing so that the changeover relay is completely switched before the transceiver is allowed to supply any RF output. This prevents *hot-switching* in which the amplifier is already supplying RF at the time the changeover relay is switching. This can destroy the relay or other external devices. [G4A09]

Tuning and Driving a Linear Amplifier

Amplifiers have three primary operator adjustments: BAND, TUNE and LOAD (or COUPLING). No-tune or auto-tune amplifiers do not require these operator adjustments because of their circuit design or because a microprocessor makes the adjustments automatically. The BAND switch configures the input and output impedance matching or filter circuits for the band on which signals will be applied to amplifier. TUNE and LOAD controls adjust components in the output matching circuit, often a pi-network that was introduced in Chapter 4.

With the band switch set properly, a small amount of drive power is applied to the amplifier while watching the amplifier's plate current meter and adjusting the TUNE control for a minimum setting (or "dip"). This means the output matching circuit is resonant at the operating frequency. The LOAD control is adjusted to maximize (or "peak") output power and TUNE readjusted for the dip in plate current so that maximum output power is obtained without exceeding maximum plate current. Input power to the amplifier may also be adjusted during that process. [G4A04, G4A08]

Drive power is important, particularly for *grid-driven* amplifier circuits in which the input power is applied to the tube's control grid. It is easy to destroy an expensive tube by applying too much drive, observed as excessive grid current on the amplifier's metering circuits. Most modern amplifiers have protective circuits to prevent excessive grid drive. Excessive drive power or mistuning can also result in excessive plate current. This overheats the tube and can cause it to fail. Operate the amplifier according to the manufacturer's specifications and procedures to obtain the longest life from transmitting tubes. Similar cautions apply to solid-state amplifiers with power transistors that can be damaged or destroyed by excessive drive power. [G4A07]

Many amplifiers also generate an ALC signal that can be connected to your transmitter in order to limit excess drive that causes distorted output signals and splatter. You should read both the amplifier and transceiver manuals to be sure the signals are compatible and that you know how to use the ALC meter readings on your transceiver. [G4A05]

Neutralization

In the section on oscillators, you learned that to make an amplifier oscillate, positive feedback must reinforce the input signal at some frequency for which the amplifier has gain greater than 1. HF amplifiers using triode tubes such as the popular 3-500Z are often capable of becoming an oscillator (called *self-oscillation*) at VHF frequencies because the physical construction of the tube and the circuit creates positive feedback. The main path for positive feedback in a grid-driven circuit is though *inter-electrode capacitance* between the plate and control grid.

Self-oscillation creates spurious output signals and can even damage the tube or amplifier components. The technique of preventing self-oscillation is called *neutralization*. Neutralization is performed by creating negative feedback at VHF. Negative feedback consists of connecting some of the output signal back to the input, but out-of-phase with the input signal to cancel the unwanted positive feedback. For an HF amplifier, this is done by connecting a small variable capacitor between the amplifier's output and input circuits. The amplifier's operating manual will show the appropriate procedure for making the adjustments. Once an amplifier is neutralized, no further adjustment is needed unless the amplifier tubes are replaced or some other circuit changes are made. [G7B13]

> *Before you go on, study test questions G4A03 to G4A05, G4A07 to G4A09, G4A12, G4B07, G4B15, G4D01 to G4D03, G7B08, G7B10 to G7B14, G7C01, G7C02, G8A08 to G8A11, G8B06, and G8B07. Review the section if you have difficulty.*

5.4 Receiver Structure

As the wise old radio saying goes, "You can't work 'em if you can't hear 'em!" That makes the receiver just about the most important part of the ham shack. HF receivers also have more adjustments than HF transmitters by far — why? This section explains how receivers are constructed — clean out your ears and tune in!

As with transmitters, DSP and SDR techniques are rapidly replacing analog receiver electronic circuits with digital calculations in a microprocessor. While this section focuses on analog receivers, many of the very same functions are performed as mathematical operations in a modern digital receiver.

BASIC SUPERHETERODYNE RECEIVERS

Most analog receivers in use by amateurs today are some type of *superheterodyne*, a design invented in the 1920s by Edwin Armstrong. As you learned earlier, the mixing together of signals to obtain sum and difference frequencies is called heterodyning. The "superhet" is built around that process.

Received signals are incredibly weak — on the order of nano or picowatts. Thus, a receiver must be quite sensitive to make it possible for an operator to hear such a signal. Simultaneously, a single signal must be picked out of a crowded spectrum where nearby signals might be billions of times stronger. So the receiver must be very selective, as well. Both of these requirements are satisfied by the basic superheterodyne receiver structure shown in **Figure 5.15**. Let's trace the signal through the receiver from antenna to speaker.

Received signals are first strengthened by the RF amplifier, and then applied to the RF input of a mixer. [G7C03] The local oscillator (LO) is adjusted so that the desired signal creates a mixing product at the *intermediate frequency* (IF). An IF filter removes signals outside the receiver's passband and whatever signals remain are amplified by the IF amplifier. A detector or demodulator stage follows the IF to recover the modulating information. The simplest possible superhet consists of a mixer connected to the antenna, an HF oscillator to act as an LO, and a detector that operates directly on the resulting IF signal. [G7C07]

An IF stage is used because it is much easier to create high quality filters and high gain amplifiers at a single frequency that does not need to be tuned to a signal's frequency.

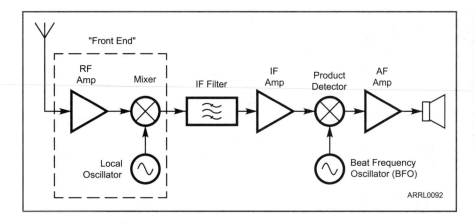

Figure 5.15 — A superhetero-dyne receiver converts signals to audio in two steps. The front end converts the frequency of a signal to the intermediate frequency (IF) where most of the gain of the receiver is provided. A second mixer — the product detector — converts the signal to audio frequencies.

Only the LO needs to be tuned in a superhet receiver. For example, to convert an RF signal on 14.250 MHz to an IF of 455 kHz, the LO must be tuned to either 14.250 – 455 kHz = 13.795 MHz or to 14.250 + 455 kHz = 14.705 MHz.

To cover the entire 20 meter band and assuming the difference mixing product is used, the LO would be tuned from 14.000 – 0.455 MHz = 13.545 MHz to 14.350 – 0.455 MHz = 13.895 MHz.

Once amplified to a more usable level, SSB and CW signals are demodulated by a *product detector*, a special type of mixer. [G7C04] If an AM signal is being received, either a product detector or an *envelope detector* is used to recover the modulating signal. The output of the product or envelope detector is an audio signal that is amplified by an audio frequency (AF) amplifier and applied to a speaker or headphones or sound card.

The RF amplifier and mixer comprise the receiver's "front end." This section of the receiver processes weak signals at their original frequencies, so it must work over a wide frequency range and for both strong and weak signals. A tunable filter or *preselector* is sometimes used between the antenna and RF amplifier to reject strong *out-of-band* signals, such as those from broadcasters or commercial stations. These out-of-band signals are not in the desired frequency band, but they could overload the circuitry. If additional sensitivity is needed, an additional stage of RF amplification called a *preamplifier* (or *preamp*) is used.

FM receivers are very similar to an AM/SSB/CW superhet, but they have key differences as shown in **Figure 5.16**. The only information that matters in an FM signal is the frequency, so a special, non-linear IF amplifier called a *limiter* replaces the linear IF amplifier in an AM receiver. A limiter amplifies the received signal until all of the amplitude modulated information, such as noise, is removed and only a square wave of varying frequency remains. The audio information is recovered by a *discriminator* or a *quadrature detector* that replaces the product detector. [G7C08] The audio is then amplified as before.

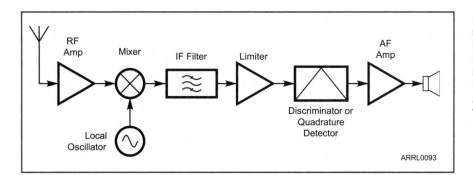

Figure 5.16 — Once the FM signal is converted to the IF, high-gain amplifiers called limiters change the signal to a square wave that only varies in frequency (not amplitude). A discriminator converts the frequency variations to audio.

Removing Received Interference

Every analog receiver uses IF filters to narrow the receiver's passband and remove unwanted signals. (A digital receiver implements filters in software.) An assortment of filters is available to suit the common operating modes and styles. Once an interfering signal is in the receiver's passband, however, removing it can be difficult. You can apply several techniques to get rid of these signals.

✔ *Notch filters* remove signals in a very narrow band of frequencies, such as a single tone from an interfering carrier. [G4A01]

✔ *Passband or IF shift* adjusts the receiver's passband above or below the displayed carrier frequency to avoid interfering signals. This results in a shift in tone of the received signal, but often improves intelligibility. [G4A11]

✔ *Reverse sideband* controls allow the operator to switch between receiving CW signals above the displayed carrier frequency (USB) and below it (LSB). This can help avoid nearby signals causing interference by placing them on the "other side" of the carrier frequency where filtering rejects them. [G4A02]

Like every design, the superheterodyne has some weaknesses. Because the mixers produce both sum and difference frequency signals (and to some degree, other combinations), undesired signals can also create their own mixing products at the IF. For example, if the IF is 455 kHz and the LO frequency is 13.800 MHz, signals at both 14.255 and 13.345 MHz will create a mixing product at 455 kHz. The first is 14.255 – 13.800 MHz = 455 kHz and the second is 13.800 – 13.345 MHz = 455 kHz. Assuming the receiver is supposed to receive the 14.255 MHz signal, the undesired signal at 13.345 MHz is called an *image*. [G8B02] Filters in the receiver front end are required to remove signals that might produce images.

Another flaw is caused by the LO and other oscillator circuits inside the receiver. Leakage of these signals into the signal path can cause steady signals to appear. These signals are called *birdies*. Even if no signals are present at the receiver input, birdies will still be audible because they are caused by signals inside the receiver.

The receiver shown in Figures 5.15 and 5.16 is a *single-conversion* receiver, with only one mixer converting the signal from RF to IF. The IF stages provide most of the receiver's gain and almost all of its selectivity (the ability to reject unwanted signals). Depending on how many different frequency bands the receiver must cover and the demands for selectivity, superhet receivers may have one, two, or three IF stages, resulting in a single, double or triple-conversion receiver. Filtering is applied at each IF, allowing the receiver use to match the received bandwidth to that of the desired signal. This gives the best received signal quality with the lowest unwanted noise and interference, maximizing the *signal-to-noise ratio* or (*SNR*). [G8B09]

DIGITAL SIGNAL PROCESSING (DSP)

While the superheterodyne receiver design continues to be the most common type of amateur receiver, DSP technology replaces analog circuits with software. The general term for converting signals from analog to digital form, operating on them with a microprocessor, and converting them back to analog is digital signal processing (DSP). **Figure 5.17** shows the basic structure of a digital signal processor in a communications receiver.

DSP technology requires an analog receiver front end to tune in a signal, convert it to the IF frequency and amplify it to suitable levels. Once prepared by the front end, the signal is converted to digital form by an *analog-to-digital converter* (ADC). In digital form, a specialized microprocessor called a *digital signal processor* performs filtering and other functions mathematically. The data is then converted back to analog form for the human operator by a *digital-to-analog converter* (DAC). If the receiver is intended to be used for digital modes, the data may be converted directly to characters instead of to analog form. [G7C09, G7C10]

DSP technology has two major advantages over analog circuitry — performance and flexibility. Current DSP components can achieve performance as good as or better than

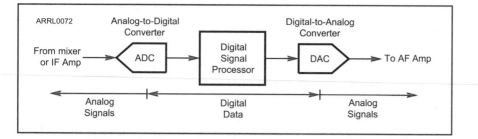

Figure 5.17 — DSP systems use an analog-to-digital converter (ADC) to change the signal to digital data. A special type of microprocessor then performs the mathematical operations on the data to accomplish filtering, noise reduction, or other functions. A digital-to-analog converter (DAC) changes the processed data back to analog form for output as audio.

the best analog filters. Functions that would be prohibitively expensive in analog circuitry can be implemented in DSP as a program without any additional hardware cost. DSP is also much more flexible than analog circuitry, limited only by processor speed and available memory as to how many options, functions and adjustments can be implemented. DSP functions can even react automatically to the received signals and adjust the function's characteristics.

The most common DSP functions are:

• *Signal filtering* — Radios with DSP offer selectable preprogrammed filters and allow the operator to adjust the filter bandwidth and shape and even to define new filters. [G4C12]

• *Noise reduction* — It is possible for DSP to distinguish noise and remove a great deal of it, leaving only the desired speech or CW for the operator to copy. [G4C11]

• *Notch filtering* — Interfering signals in the receiver's passband, particularly carriers from broadcast stations, can be sensed and removed by DSP. An *automatic notch filter* can track them as they change frequency and even eliminate more than one at a time! [G4C13]

• *Audio frequency equalization* — The operator can adjust receive or transmit audio frequency response to suit his or her preferences, compensating for hearing loss or optimizing microphone audio.

As digital processing performs more and more functions at higher and higher frequencies, a new type of radio has emerged — the *software defined radio* or *SDR*. In an SDR, all major signal processing functions are performed by software. [G7C11] The only analog circuits that handle signals are the RF input and output to the radio and the audio for and from the operator or whatever system is connected to the radio. If a different type of radio function is desired, new software can be developed and installed in the transceiver without having to redesign or change any hardware elements. There are several manufacturers of SDRs for Amateur Radio with very active groups of users developing and experimenting with this technology. SDR is rapidly becoming the dominant technology used to construct high-performance transceivers.

MANAGING RECEIVER GAIN

Receivers need to have a lot of gain to bring those weak signals up to a level where their information can be recovered by ear or by computer. Just as too little gain can cause weak signals to be missed, too much gain can cause its own set of problems. There are several controls and displays that the operator can use to get the gain setting "just right."

RF Gain and Automatic Gain Control

The amount of receiver gain is set by the RF gain control. If you are tuning your receiver and looking for weak signals, you will likely set the RF gain to maximum so that receiver sensitivity is highest. Once you've tuned in a signal, unless it's very weak, maximum gain isn't required and so RF gain can be adjusted for the most comfortable listening. Lower values of RF gain also reduce the volume of the background noise heard in the output audio.

The automatic gain control (AGC) circuits vary the gain of the RF and IF amplifiers so that the output volume of a signal stays relatively constant for both weak and strong signals. The AGC control of the receiver can be set so that the circuit responds quickly or slowly (or not at all) to volume changes, depending on the operator's preference. Fast AGC response is usually used for CW and data signals, while slow response works best for phone.

The AGC circuit adjusts receiver gain by changing a voltage that controls the IF amplifier gain. This voltage is also read by the *S meter* of the receiver, which is used to measure received signal strength. ("S" stands for "signal.") [G4D04, G4D06] The more the AGC circuit has to reduce gain to keep volume constant, the higher the reading on the S meter, since stronger signals require less gain to produce the same output volume. You'll notice that turning down the RF gain also increases the S meter reading because the RF gain control uses the same control voltage as the AGC circuit.

S meters are calibrated in *S units*, with a change of one S unit usually equal to a 6 dB (fourfold) change in signal strength, although this may vary with manufacturer. [G4D07] An AGC circuit may also respond differently at different signal strengths. Nevertheless, the S meter is a useful indicator of signal strength, with a signal strength of S-9 being a strong signal. You'll notice that S-9 is at the midpoint of the S meter display. To the right are additional markings of "20", "40" and "60." These correspond to "dB above S-9," so a reading of "S-9 + 20 dB" corresponds to a signal 20 dB (100 times) stronger than an S-9 signal. [G4D05]

Receiver Linearity

It is important that a receiver respond linearly to received signals, just as it is important for a transmitter to amplify linearly. If the received signal is distorted, spurious signals will appear just as if the transmitting station were emitting them!

Before you go on, study test questions G4A01, G4A02, G4A11, G4A13, G4C11 to G4C13, G4D04 to G4D07, G7C03, G4C04, G7C07 to G7C11, G8B02 and G8B09. Review the section if you have difficulty.

The most common form of receiver nonlinearity is *overload* or *gain compression*. (Overload is also called *front-end overload*.) This occurs when an input signal is simply too strong for the circuitry to handle and distortion results. The usual symptom is strong distortion of all signals when the overloading signal is present. The solution to overload is to either filter out the offending signal or reduce receiver gain using the *attenuator* circuit to reduce signal levels overall. Proper use of the attenuator and RF gain controls can dramatically reduce received noise and distortion caused by strong signals. [G4A13]

Accessory circuits in the receiver can also affect its linearity. Using a preamplifier makes it easier for strong signals to overload a receiver. Noise blankers that work by shutting off the receiver when a strong noise pulse is detected can confuse strong signals with the pulses, creating severe distortion as a result. Use these circuits only when necessary and to the minimum amount needed.

5.5 HF Station Installation

Along with understanding the structure of the equipment itself, assembling it into a working station at home or in a vehicle creates another set of concerns. HF operating, with longer wavelengths and typically higher field strengths, makes grounding and interference control much more important. The General class exam focuses on three related areas: mobile installations, RF grounding and RF interference.

MOBILE INSTALLATIONS

Once quite popular, mobile HF operation took a back seat, so to speak, during the 1980s and early 1990s as hams turned to VHF and UHF on the road and HF at home. Over the past decade however, the introduction of compact all-band, all-mode radios and a new generation of mobile antennas have accelerated HF mobile operation growth. Not only is it an enjoyable change of pace from the home shack, but in this era of antenna restrictions it offers an HF operating opportunity to many hams who might otherwise be unable to use those bands. There are no restrictions on which bands may be used while mobile, so give operating-in-motion a try!

To help you get rolling, review some of the mobile operating references on the *General Class License Manual* website (**www.arrl.org/general-class-license-manual**) before installing your mobile system. Don't hesitate to ask other mobile operators for advice — they're often glad to relate their own experiences and act as an Elmer.

Power Connections

Unlike low power radios, a mobile rig capable of putting out 100 W requires a solid power connection capable of supplying 20 A or more with a minimum amount of voltage drop. Solid-state radios perform unpredictably when input voltage drops below a specified minimum.

Smaller gauge wire should never be used to extend or replace the power cable provided by the manufacturer. The best power connection is direct to the battery using heavy gauge wire with a fuse in both the positive and negative leads. Do not use the cigarette lighter socket, as that circuit is usually rated at only a few amperes which is insufficient to supply a 100-W HF radio. [G4E03, G4E04]

Do not assume that the vehicle's metal chassis is a suitable dc ground connection. Many vehicle bodies are constructed from independent sections, which leads to erratic ground connections over time. Some pieces may be made from plastic or other nonmetallic materials. Connect the radio power ground either directly to the battery or to the battery ground strap where it attaches to the engine block or vehicle chassis.

Antenna Connections

The most significant limitation of mobile operating is that the antenna system must be smaller in terms of a wavelength than at a home station. This is particularly true on the lower frequencies, such as 75 meters, a popular mobile band. [G4E05] When mobiling, the entire vehicle becomes part of the antenna system and attention to every detail can pay big benefits in signal strength. For example:
- Use the most efficient antenna you can.
- Make sure RF ground connections to the vehicle are solid.
- Mount the antenna where it is as clear as possible of metal surfaces.

Mobile Interference

When operating HF mobile, there are interference concerns quite different from those in the home station. Ignition noise caused by the spark plugs firing can be quite strong,

Tame That High-Pitched Whine

A good power connection also helps cut down on electrical noise from the vehicle's power system. Alternator whine, a high-pitched tone that changes with engine speed, is caused by current pulses from the alternator as it charges the battery. Connecting the rig's power cable directly to the battery uses the battery as a filter, greatly reducing alternator whine and all other electrical noise conducted to the radio through the power leads.

although the noise blanker of modern radios can be quite effective at this reducing this type of noise. (Vehicles with diesel engines don't have this problem!) Another common problem is interfering signals generated by the vehicle's accessories and other systems. (See the sidebar, "Tame That High-Pitched Whine.") Common sources of interfering signals include the vehicle's onboard control computers, electric motor-driven devices such as fuel pumps and windows, and battery charging systems. [G4E07] Online mobile resources and manufacturer service bulletins can help you deal with mobile interference and noise problems.

RF GROUNDING AND GROUND LOOPS

Although a good station ground is important to prevent electrical shock, at HF and higher frequencies, ac safety ground wiring usually acts more like an antenna than a ground! In amateur stations, it's necessary to manage RF separately from the ac safety ground by bonding equipment enclosures together as shown in **Figure 5.18**. The goal of RF bonding is to keep all equipment at as close to the same RF voltage as possible. This and reduces RF current flowing between pieces of equipment which can cause audio distortion or improper operation of station equipment. [G4C07]

Keeping all of your equipment at the same RF voltage minimizes "hot spots" where high RF voltage is present that can cause an "RF burn." It also reduces RF current flowing between pieces of equipment on power and signal cabling. For example, during digital operation, unwanted RF currents can cause audio distortion or erratic operation of computer interfaces, activate the transmitter improperly (such as when using VOX), and garble digital protocols which causes data or connections to be lost. [G4A15]

The basics for RF bonding in your shack are:

• Connect all metal equipment enclosures directly together or to a common RF bonding bus.

• Keep all connections, straps and wires short.

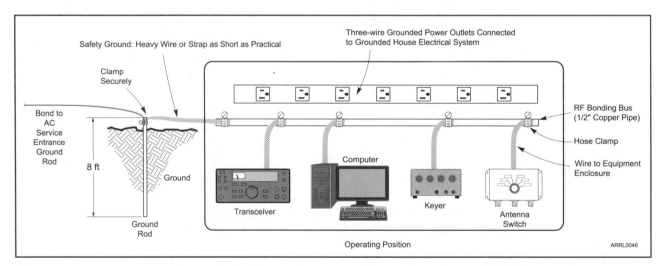

Figure 5.18 — This example of a typical RF bonding bus at the operating position helps keep all of the equipment at the same RF voltage. The connection between the bus and the external ground rod for lightning protection should be as short as possible. The ground rod must also be bonded to the ac service entry ground with a heavy wire.

- Use short, wide conductors such as heavy wire (#12 or #14 AWG) or strap.
- In difficult situations, a piece of wide flashing or screen can be placed under the equipment and connected to the RF bonding bus.

If your station includes an external ground rod for lightning protection, make the connection as short as possible. If the ground connection approaches resonance at an odd number of ¼-wavelengths at any frequency, it will present a high impedance, enabling RF voltages to exist on your equipment enclosures and connecting cables. [G4C05, G4C06] Avoiding a high impedance on the ground connection may be difficult, particularly for upper-floor or apartment stations! In such cases, keeping the equipment at the same RF voltage is the most effective strategy.

Ground loops are created when a continuous current path (the loop) exists around a series of equipment enclosures. This loop acts as a single-turn inductor that picks up voltages from magnetic fields generated by power transformers, ac wiring, and other low-frequency currents. The result is a "hum" or "buzz" in audio signals or an ac signal that interferes with control or data signals. [G4C10] Ground loops can be avoided by using a RF bonding bus to which all pieces of equipment are connected. [G4C09]

The ARRL Technical Information Service's Safety web page (**www.arrl.org/safety**) provides an entire page of resources about grounding and RF management in your station with several *QST* magazine articles and web references. Each station is a little different and you may have to experiment to get the results you expect.

RF INTERFERENCE

Radiating a good signal means that you'll probably discover some unintentional listeners in nearby receivers and consumer electronics. A license study manual cannot provide a thorough discussion of the causes and effects of RF interference (RFI), but the ARRL's Technical Information Service offers a lot of information. You can also learn more from the *ARRL RFI Book* and *The ARRL Handbook*.

Here are some common causes and solutions of RF interference to consumer electronics and broadcast receivers:
- *Fundamental overload* — usually exhibited by radio or TV receivers unable to reject a strong signal that causes the internal circuits to act improperly, distorting or wiping out the intended signal. Prevent the offending signal from entering the equipment by using filters in the path of the signal.
- *Common-mode and direct pickup* — any type of electronic equipment with internal electronics, including telephones, computers, music players and so on, can be affected by strong local signals. The signal is picked up as common-mode current on the outside of cable shields or on all conductors of an unshielded connection. This can occur for power connections, speaker leads, telephone cable — any external wiring. The unwanted signal is then conducted into the equipment where it can cause erratic operation or audio noise. The solution is to prevent RF signals from entering the equipment by using RFI filters, RF suppression chokes, or bypass capacitors on the cables or connections picking up the RF current. Direct pickup occurs when the signal is received directly by the internal wiring of a device and can be very hard to eliminate without adding shielding to the device.
- *Harmonics* — spurious emissions from an amateur station may be received by radio or TV equipment. The solution is to use a low-pass filter to remove the spurious emissions at the amateur station. Remember to match the low-pass filter's impedance with the characteristic impedance of the feed line into which it is inserted. [G7C06]
- *Rectification* — Poor contacts between conductors picking up RF signals can create a mixer and mixing products from the signals. If the mixing products are on the frequency that the receivers are tuned to, they will cause interference to the desired signal. The solution is to find and repair the poor contact.

• *Arcing* — Any spark or sustained arc creates radio noise over a wide range of frequencies and will interfere with both amateur and consumer reception. [G4C02] When created by the ac power lines, the result will be a crackling buzz. If the arc is from a motor or welding equipment, the buzz will come and go when the equipment is energized. In general, poor contact between any current-carrying conductors will cause interference. The solution for power line noise is to isolate it to a single installation and then request that the power company make the necessary repairs. Noise from specific equipment may require filtering of that equipment.

RF INTERFERENCE SUPPRESSION

The best solution to many types of interference caused by proximity to an amateur station is to keep the RF signals from entering the equipment in the first place. If filters can be used, they are generally the most effective and least troublesome to install. The next approach is to prevent RF current flow by placing inductance or resistance in its path. This is done by forming the conductor carrying the RF current into an RF choke by winding it around or through a ferrite core.

Ferrite beads and cores can also be placed on cables to prevent RF common-mode current from flowing on the outside of cable braids or shields ("common mode" interference). [G4C08] The same beads and cores can be used to prevent signals from computers and computer accessories from causing interference to amateur communications. Interference to audio equipment and appliance switch and sensor connections can sometimes be eliminated by placing a small (100 pF to 1 nF) bypass capacitor across balanced connections or from each connection to chassis ground. [G4C01]

Before you go on, study test questions G4A15, G4C01 to G4C10, G4E03 to G4E05, G4E07 and G7C06. Review the section if you have difficulty.

Chapter 6

Digital Modes

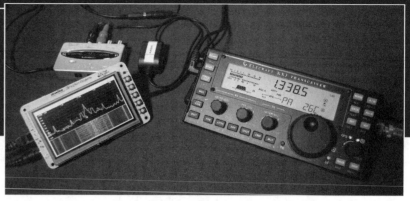

In this chapter, you'll learn about:
- **Digital data definitions**
- **Digital codes and protocols**
- **Rules for digital modes**
- **Digital operating procedures**
- **Receiving and transmitting digital signals**

Digital communications systems exchange digital data over the air between two computing systems. This includes email, digital files, keyboard-to-keyboard typing, and control data, just to name a few examples. Amateur Radio experimenters are developing new digital protocols and modes while more hams are using digital modes such as radioteletype, PSK31, PACTOR, MFSK, and others every day. As a General class licensee you'll have access to all of Amateur Radio's digital technology, so it's important to learn about it as part of studying for your licensing exam.

6.1 Introduction to Digital Modes

Communications are considered to be digital modes if information is exchanged as individual characters encoded as digital bits. For example, the character "A" can be sent as "didah" in Morse code or the bit pattern 01000001 in the ASCII code. There are many digital modes used in Amateur Radio. Some are quite old, such as radioteletype which was invented in the 1930s. Others are adaptations of modes used commercially and some, such as PSK31, are purely amateur creations. New digital modes are being added regularly — an area in which amateur inventiveness shines brightly.

WHERE TO FIND DIGITAL ACTIVITY

Digital mode signals are restricted to the CW/data segments of each HF band. Most digital mode operation is found close to the top of the CW segment. Calling frequencies for the popular digital modes are incorporated into band plans and are usually the lowest frequency of operation with operators moving up in frequency as activity increases. For example, on 20 meters most PSK31 signals are found near 14.070 MHz. RTTY and other digital mode signals are found above that. [G2E04, G2E08] Segments of the HF bands where you'll find signals of the popular digital modes are listed in **Table 6.1**. [G2E07]

The automatically-controlled connection and message transfer ability of modes such as PACTOR and WINMOR have made them popular choices for transferring email and digital files. Stations making up the message transfer systems are found in the band segments allowed for automatically-controlled data transmission.

Digital voice modes are regulated as voice emissions by the FCC. This includes modes such as Icom's D-STAR, Yaesu's SystemFusion, AOR's digital voice, WinDRM, and the public domain FreeDV. Slow-scan TV is also converting from the analog system to digital file transfer systems which are regulated as image modes. These modes are reviewed in

Table 6.1

Digital Signal Band Plan

Where to Find Digital Signals on the HF Bands

Band (Meters)	Frequency Range (MHz)	Notes/
160	1.800 – 1.810	
80	3.570 – 3.600	
60	5332, 5348, 5358.5, 5373 and 5405 kHz	Channel center frequencies.*
40	7.070 – 7.125	RTTY DX calling frequency 7.040 MHz
30	10.130 – 10.150	
20	14.070 – 14.0995 and 14.1005 – 14.112	PSK31 calling frequency 14.070 MHz
17	18.100 – 18.110	
15	21.070 – 21.110	
12	24.920 – 24.930	
10	28.070 – 28.189	

*On 60 meters, the FCC continues to require that all digital transmissions be centered on the channel-center frequencies, which the Report and Order defines as being 1.5 kHz above the suppressed carrier frequency of a transceiver operated in the Upper Sideband (USB) mode. This is typically the frequency shown on the frequency display. Automatic operation is not permitted.

The Winlink System

With the steady improvement of amateur digital modes on the HF bands, transferring email messages and digital files has become a very common method of communication. Along with these improvements, the Winlink system (**www.winlink.org**) has grown from a few stations to a robust, worldwide system. Winlink uses the Internet to connect its system of email servers with gateway and mailbox stations around the world on HF, VHF, and UHF frequencies. [G2E13]

Winklink stations do not connect an amateur directly with the Internet but provide an effective means of email access for stations out of local Internet connection range and for when the Internet is not available due to disasters or local outages. Even without Internet connectivity, Winlink's RMS (Radio Messaging System) stations can act as standalone mailboxes or communicate directly with each other to provide messaging capabilities. A list of stations providing access to the Winlink system is published on the system's home page.

Many amateurs upgrade to General class to take advantage of these and other messaging capabilities. If that sounds like something you'd like to try, remember that it is necessary to share the amateur bands with other users of the spectrum operating on different modes. All of us need to be good neighbors by following the time-honored practices of listening first, keeping our signals clean, and recognizing that no individual or system has exclusive rights to any frequency.

the *ARRL Handbook* and are not covered on the General Class exam.

DIGITAL MODE OVERVIEW

The following paragraphs present a short summary of some popular digital modes on HF. More detailed definitions are provided later in this chapter. Maximum data rates and signal bandwidths are specified by the FCC rules in §97.307 to limit signal bandwidth on congested bands. FCC rules identify several types of digital codes (the method of encoding the characters for transmission) [§97.309]. If you intend to use a digital code other than those specified, you must first make sure that the protocol rules are public (amateurs are not allowed to use secret or private codes) and you must comply with bandwidth and symbol rate limitations. (As this edition was being completed in early 2015, the FCC is considered changing how it regulates amateur digital mode transmissions to be based on bandwidth. News of any changes will be made available on the ARRL home page (**www.arrl.org**) and by other amateur publications.)

The following do not by any means include all of the different digital modes used in Amateur Radio. More digital modes are being invented by hams all the time! If you'd like to know more about digital communications in Amateur Radio, check out some of the references at **www.arrl.org/general-class-license-manual**.

Radioteletype (RTTY)

RTTY (pronounced "ritty") is a mode that was originally designed to be copied and printed off the air by a mechanical teleprinter. Today, amateurs use a computer instead. RTTY operation is popular on all of the HF amateur bands. Most stations operate toward the bottom of the ranges given in Table 6.1.

PSK31

PSK31 has several attractive features. It requires a very narrow bandwidth (<100 Hz) and performs very well even as a weak signal on HF. PSK31 can be generated and decoded with an inexpensive PC sound card. No special equipment is required; you need only an audio interface to connect the radio and sound card. You'll find PSK31 signals near the PSK calling frequencies published in various band plans. Other similar modes, such as PSK63, are also becoming more widely used.

PACTOR and WINMOR

PACTOR stands for *PACket Teletype Over Radio* and WINMOR stands for *Windows Messaging Over Radio*. These modes improve on RTTY with the ability to detect and correct errors. Both use advanced modulation techniques and transmit the data as packets to make the transmitted information easier to recover from the noisy and fade-prone HF channel. PACTOR has four different levels (PACTOR-I through PACTOR-4) and is a proprietary mode developed by SCS.

Packet Radio

You may already be familiar with packet radio which is common on the VHF and UHF bands. Packet radio is not commonly used on HF because transmission errors from noise and fading and the much lower transmission speeds permitted on the HF bands greatly reduce the effectiveness of this mode compared to VHF and UHF.

Miscellaneous Digital Modes

There are numerous other digital modes on the HF bands. Here are some of the better known modes:

● G-TOR: forerunner of PACTOR that sends data as FSK tones in short bursts at a net data rate of 100 to 300 baud that varies depending on conditions.

● MFSK16: On the air, the 16 tones of an MFSK16 signal sounds like a set of whistles being played in a narrow bandwidth.

● JT65 and JT9, recent variations of protocols in the WSJT family, are very effective at communicating in the presence of noise and ionospheric distortion at extremely low signal levels. [G8C01]

● CLOVER: A family of MFSK modes developed by HAL Communications to provide high bit rates on HF by structuring the data in blocks and paying careful attention to the transmitted waveform.

● ALE (Automatic Link Establishment) searches through a set of frequencies automatically to find where the best contact with the desired station can be established before transferring data.

- WSPR (Whisper) is designed to experiment with propagation paths at very low signal-to-noise ratios. It is similar to JT65.

To help you tell what mode you are hearing, a set of digital recordings of many modes are available for you to listen to at **www.kb9ukd.com/digital**.

Before you go on, study test questions G2E04, G2E07, G2E08, G2E13, and G8C01. Review this section if you have difficulty.

6.2 Digital Basics

DEFINITIONS

Before diving into the details of the many amateur digital modes, it's helpful to define some useful terms.

- *Air link* — the part of the communication system that involves radio transmission and reception of signals.
- *Bit* — the fundamental unit of data; a 0 or 1 representing all or part of a binary number.
- *Bit rate* — the number of digital bits per second sent from one computing system to the other.
- *Baud or bauds* — the number of symbols per second that are sent from one computing system to the other, also known as *symbol rate*.
- *Duty cycle* — the ratio of time that the transmitter is on to the total of on time plus off time.
- *Protocol* — the rules that control the method used to exchange data between two systems.
- *Mode* — the combination of a protocol with a modulation method.

In some modes, such as RTTY or PSK31, bits are transmitted one at a time as audio tones over an air link. A *modem* (short for modulator-demodulator) translates the bits into tones (and back again). Typically, additional bits are added at lower levels of the system to help control the flow of data.

There is a lot of confusion about bit rate and baud. Is it 1200 bits per second or 1200 baud? Bit rate refers to the number of bits per second (bps) carried by the transmission. Baud (just "baud" or "bauds," not "baud rate") refers to the number of digital *symbols* sent each second. A symbol is defined as whatever combination of signal characteristics make up each distinct state of the transmitted signal. For example, a CW symbol is the ON or OFF state of the transmitted signal and in RTTY the symbols are represented by tones.

In simple coding methods such as Baudot or ASCII, each symbol sent by the transmitter represents one bit. More sophisticated codes use complex audio signals to carry the data and encode more than one bit in every symbol. That is how modems exchange data at such high rates over a narrow voice channel — each symbol sent by the transmitter at 9600 baud represents 2 bits (19.2 kbps), 4 bits (38.4 kbps) or 6 bits (56.6 kbps) of data. If one bit is sent in each symbol, then bit rate and baud are the same. As more and more bits are encoded in each symbol, the bit rate will be higher than the symbol rate.

A digital mode combines a protocol and a method of modulation. A protocol is the set of rules that control the encoding, packaging, exchanging and decoding of digital data. For example, packet radio uses the AX.25 protocol. The rules for that protocol specify how each packet is constructed, how packets are exchanged, what characters are allowed, and so forth. The protocol rules don't say what kind of transmitter to use or what the signal will sound like on the air. The method of modulation, such as SSB or FM, is determined by conventional operating practices.

Modulation used for digital modes can be simple *On-Off Keying* (*OOK*) such as for CW or pulse-coded modulations. For the modes most of us think of as true digital modes, the data is transmitted as tones or as combinations of tones. The data may be represented by the tone frequency (*frequency shift keying* or *FSK*) or as phase differences (*phase shift keying* or *PSK*). Another popular method is to transmit two carriers with a 90° phase difference and vary their amplitude and/or phase relationship independently. This is called *I/Q modulation*. Each distinct combination of tones or amplitudes or phase shifts constitutes one symbol

FREQUENCY SHIFT KEYING (FSK)

Frequency shift keying is a method of digital communications in which the individual bits of data are encoded as tones. As the stream of bits is transmitted, different tone frequencies are used. If you listen to a slower modem or RTTY signal, you can hear the bits being exchanged as a rapidly changing pattern of two different tones shifting from one frequency to another. The frequencies in a two-tone FSK signal are called *mark* and *space*. [G8C11] Space represents 0 and mark represents 1.

In true or "direct" FSK, the frequency of the transmitter's VFO is controlled directly by a digital data signal from the computer representing the 1s and 0s of the code. [G8A01] *Audio frequency shift keying* (*AFSK*) is also used in which the audio tones modulate an SSB or FM transmitter through the microphone input. AFSK is a convenient method, but the operator must be careful to manage the audio level to avoid noise and distortion that could adversely affect signal quality or cause interference to nearby stations.

Whether FSK or AFSK is used, the rate at which symbols are sent affects the amount of frequency shift required. The faster the symbol rate (or keying rate), the greater the frequency shift required. This is because the closer the tones are in frequency, the longer it takes the receiving system to discriminate between them. Tones must be spaced far enough apart in frequency for the receiver to be able to determine which tone is being sent during the time interval in which the tone is present.

PHASE SHIFT KEYING (PSK)

If you listen to a modern dialup modem making a call, initially you'll hear the warbling whistle of frequency shift keying at the beginning of the "conversation," followed by what sounds like buzzing noise. You are listening to the modems changing from simple FSK to include PSK in which the data is encoded as the phase relationship between tones.

The most common type of phase shift is to simply invert one of the tone waveforms, shifting its phase by 180°. The difference in phase can be measured with respect to the phase of the same signal at an earlier time or with respect to some other tone. The rapid changes in phase are heard by the human ear as a raspy noise or buzz — the signature of PSK signals on the air received by a CW or SSB receiver.

Before you go on, study test questions G8A01 and G8C11. Review this section if you have difficulty.

6.3 Character-Based Modes

The simplest use of digital communications is a mode in which individual characters are entered by an operator, then transmitted to another station where they are read by another operator. CW is an example of this type of communication. The speed of these modes is low but they are convenient to use and require little additional equipment beyond a sound card or a modem. This is often referred to as *keyboard-to-keyboard* operation. Because these modes simply transmit their characters without any additional data, they are often referred to as *unstructured* modes.

RADIOTELETYPE (RTTY)

RTTY is the oldest (and still very popular) form of ham radio digital communication. Originally, bulky military and commercial surplus teleprinters and terminal units (modems) were used by hams to communicate using RTTY. Today a sound card and modem software does the conversion between audio tones and characters simply and at low cost. RTTY is identified in the FCC rules as "narrowband, direct-printing telegraphy."

RTTY uses the Baudot code which represents (encodes) each text character as a sequence of 5 bits as shown in **Figure 6.1**. Baudot is the origin of the term baud. An initial bit (the *start bit*) and an inter-character pause (the *stop bit*) are used to synchronize the transmitting and receiving stations. [G8C04] With only 5 bits for encoding data, there can be only 32 different characters, not enough for the entire English alphabet, numerals, and punctuation. Thus, two special codes, LTRS and FIGS, are used to switch between two sets of characters, increasing the number of available characters to 62 (not including the LTRS and FIGS codes).

The standard audio mark and space frequencies for encoding a RTTY signal are 2125 Hz (the mark tone) and 2295 Hz (the space tone). The difference between them is called the signal's *shift*. The rate of shifting between mark and space tones determines the character speed. On HF, the most common speeds are 60, 75 and 100 WPM (corresponding to 45, 56 and 75 baud). You should always answer a RTTY station at the same speed it is using. Most RTTY conversations on HF are conducted at 45 baud and the most common shift between the mark and space frequencies is 170 Hz. [G2E06] Other tone pairs and shifts are used, but are not common.

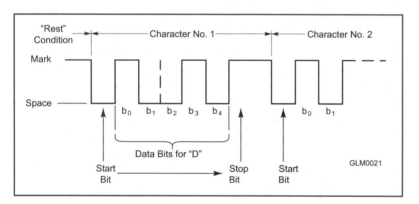

Figure 6.1 — The Baudot timing sequence for the bit pattern that encodes the letter "D." The start bit is sent first. Start and stop bits are required to allow the receiving and transmitting systems to synchronize. Mark and space are represented as audio tones in the transmitted signal.

MULTIPLE FREQUENCY SHIFT KEYING (MFSK)

Multiple-frequency shift keying or *MFSK* uses more than two tones to encode the data. There are a number of MFSK modes that have been developed by amateurs and this is an active area of experimentation. Some examples of MFSK modes are described below.

MFSK16 uses 16 separate tones, all 15.625 Hz apart, so that the entire set can be received through one HF CW 500 Hz filter. By carefully shaping the signal and controlling how the tones are turned on and off, MFSK16 modulation withstands the fading and distortion associated with sky-wave signals better than two-tone FSK signals.

DominoEX is an improvement on basic MFSK that encodes data as the difference between successive tones. This makes it less sensitive to tuning errors and drift. Data rates range from slightly less than 4 baud to 21.5 baud in bandwidths up to 524 Hz.

OLIVIA is a wider-bandwidth MSFK mode that occupies from 125 to 1000 Hz depending on the number of tones in use. It can be used at very low signal levels and includes forward error correction.

In MT63, "MT" stands for "multi-tone." The data signal is composed of 64 tones and uses advanced DSP techniques which enable it to perform well under the noisy and fading conditions typical of amateur HF communications.

PSK31

The most popular PSK mode is PSK31. The "31" stands for the symbol rate of the protocol, actually 31.25 baud. [G8C09] That may sound slow, but it is just right for keyboard-to-keyboard communication and is sufficient to keep up with most typists. PSK31 can support typing rates of up to 50 WPM under good conditions. Instead of a fixed-length character code of 5, 7 or 8 bits, PSK uses a variable length code called *Varicode* that assigns shorter codes to common characters, just like Morse code does. [G8C02] PSK63 at 63.5 baud is also becoming popular and there are higher-speed variations as well. PSK31 signals are generally found on or near the calling frequency because the mode has such a narrow bandwidth.

PSK31 sends a single tone, encoding each symbol as reversals of the tone's phase at regular intervals. Symbols are sent continually, with a reversal of phase from one interval to the next representing a "0" and no reversal a "1." (Two intervals of transmission are required to send one symbol.) If you listen to a PSK31 signal on the air, you'll hear a steady buzz with short variations as characters are transmitted. Zeroes are sent continuously when no other data is present so that the transmitter and receiver stay synchronized — you can hear the pauses as periods of consistent, unvarying buzz.

Saving Time with Varicode

An important innovation of PSK31 is its use of Varicode. [G8C12] (**en.wikipedia.org/wiki/Varicode**) Instead of using a fixed number of bits to represent each character, Varicode uses short codes for common characters (such as "e") and longer codes for others. Just as for Morse code, this saves a great deal of time. Note that most capital letters and punctuation characters take more bits than lower case. Thus, it will take longer to send "MY NAME IS HIRAM" than "My name is Hiram." If you are used to RTTY operation which has no lower-case characters, you should be sure you have turned off your CAPS LOCK key! [G8C08]

Before you go on, study test questions G2E06, G8C02, G8C04, G8C08, G8C09, G8C12. Review this section if you have difficulty.

6.4 Packet-Based Modes

Packet-based or *structured* modes are derived from early teletype-over-radio modes (TOR) and computer-to-computer network protocols. The networked protocols, developed in the early days of computing, are the basis of the modern protocols used for the Internet and digital mobile telephones today. Hams adapted those protocols to be used over radio links, creating packet radio, PACTOR, WINMOR and other communications systems.

PACKET BASICS

Packet refers to the transmission of data in structured groups as shown in **Figure 6.2**. While there are many different packet protocols, all of them use the same basic structure.

● *Header* — contains bit patterns that allow the receiver to synchronize with the packet's structure, control and routing information, and for some protocols, error detection and correction information. [G8C03]

● *Data* — the data to be exchanged between computing systems, usually as ASCII characters. Data in packets is often compressed for efficiency.

● *Trailer* — additional control or status information and data used for error detection.

The process of packaging data within a packet structure is called *encapsulation*. Packets from one protocol can be treated as data by another protocol, so that entire protocols can be encapsulated. In fact, that is the basis for the popular TCP/IP protocol pair used on the Internet. The Internet Protocol (IP) encapsulates packets from the Transport Control Protocol (TCP) and carries them to the destination.

By using error detection, it is possible for a protocol to provide *reliable transport* in which corrupted data is never accepted. The most common error detection mechanism is a *cyclic redundancy check* or *CRC*. A CRC is calculated from the contents of the packet and transmitted with the data. (A *checksum* is a weaker version of error detection than the CRC.) The receiving system performs the same calculation and if the results match, accepts the data as transmitted without error and responds with an ACK (acknowledged) message.

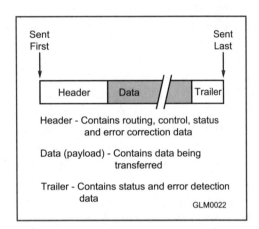

Figure 6.2 — Packet communication systems package data with control and routing information and add error detection information. Different packet protocols use different sets of information and methods of packaging.

Forward error correction (FEC) goes beyond simply detecting errors. By including additional redundant encoded information with the data being transmitted, it is possible for the receiver to correct certain types of data errors. [G8C10]

If a mismatch is detected, the receiving system responds with a NAK (not acknowledged) message and the protocol requests that the packet be retransmitted. The transmitting system will continue to send a packet until it is received without errors or the limit for retransmission is exceeded. This type of protocol or mode is called *ARQ* for *Automatic Repeat reQuest*. [G8C05, G8C07]

Because they were originally developed for connections over wired networks and not radio, ARQ protocols, such as PACTOR, are designed to transfer data between two stations: the transmitter and a single receiver. An ACK or NAK transmission can only be received from one receiving station during the connection. This means you can't "break in" to an ongoing contact between two stations using an ARQ mode. [G2E09]

So that a station can advertise its presence, ARQ protocols provide a "broadcast" mode to transmit without another station having established a connection. In addition, a monitoring or "MON" mode is provided so that other stations can listen to the conversation and even receive the data but without error correction. Using a monitoring mode allows you to determine if a frequency is occupied by two stations having an ARQ mode contact. [G2E02]

PACKET RADIO

Packet radio, used almost exclusively on VHF and UHF bands, is based on the computer network protocol X.25. Amateurs adapted it to radio transmission instead of transmission over wired networks and renamed the protocol AX.25. Packets are exchanged using VHF FM voice transceivers at 1200 or 9600 baud. Packet does not work well on HF because the data is easily disrupted by noise and fading, even at the slow maximum signaling rates of 300 baud permitted on HF.

PACTOR AND WINMOR

The RTTY protocol is not designed to manage transmission errors. As a result, text is frequently garbled, particularly over noisy, fading HF signal paths. To improve communications reliability, *Teletype Over Radio* (*TOR*) systems were developed, such as AMTOR, G-TOR and others. These systems send short bursts of characters with error detection and correction data. TOR modes are definitely more reliable, but the original versions were quite slow, particularly in the presence of interference or noise. PACTOR (Packet-based TOR) and WINMOR (Windows TOR) were developed to apply microprocessor technology to extend the capability of TOR modes.

PACTOR-I uses FSK modulation while PACTOR-II, PACTOR-III, and PACTOR-4 use more advanced PSK modulation. (PACTOR-4 is not legal for US amateurs to transmit but that may change if the FCC modifies the bandwidth and symbol rate rules.) WINMOR can use either FSK or PSK. Both employ error detection methods and an ARQ protocol to insure the reliability of the transferred data. These modes are the most popular on HF radio today for exchanging large amounts of information. PACTOR modes and WINMOR are the preferred method of HF data transmission for the popular Winlink Amateur Radio e-mail system (**www.winlink.org**).

> *Before you go on, study test questions G2E02, G2E09, G8C03, G8C05, G8C07, and G8C10. Review this section if you have difficulty.*

6.5 Receiving and Transmitting Digital Modes

Most digital modes on HF are transmitted as LSB signals except for JT65 and JT9 which use USB. [G2E01, G2E05] Modern radios may be set up to select the conventional sideband automatically when using a data mode.

Just as when trying to receive a USB voice signal on an LSB receiver, it is not possible to receive a digital signal on the wrong sideband because the relationship between the tones and the digital data will be inverted. Similarly, you'll need to have your receiving modem or software configured to the correct baud rate and the correct tone frequencies. Mistakes in any of these important settings will make it impossible to receive the data even if the signal seems tuned in correctly. [G2E14]

BANDWIDTH OF DIGITAL MODES

The FCC rules define the bandwidth of a digital mode signal in the same way as any other signal. [97.3(a)(8)] However, the bandwidth of a signal changes with the symbol rate. As the symbol rate increases, so does the bandwidth needed for the signal needed to transmit them. [G8B10] Many common protocols offer several different data rate settings and can even adjust the data rate during a contact as conditions change.

Table 6.2 shows the approximate bandwidths for several popular digital modes used on HF. [G8B05] The most common method of generating and transmitting these modes is to

Table 6.2

Bandwidth Comparison of Digital Modes

Mode	Bandwidth (Hz)
PSK31	50
RTTY	200
MFSK16	300
JT65	350
DominoEX	524
Olivia	1000
WINMOR	1600
MT63	2000
PACTOR-III	2300
PACTOR-4	2300

Bandwidths are approximate for the highest commonly used symbol rate and are not specifications

connect the audio output from a computer sound card to the microphone input of an SSB transceiver. The standard is thus for all of the modes to be capable of being transmitted within a standard SSB voice channel bandwidth.

A reminder — the FCC is considering changes to the rules regulating signal symbol rate and bandwidth on HF. The decision may affect the bandwidth and symbol rate questions on this exam. The NCVEC will announce any changes to the exam following the release of any FCC rule change.

Staying in the Band

Be careful when you are operating near the edge of a data signal band segment! When using LSB for an FSK mode, the sidebands will be *below* the displayed carrier frequency on your radio. For example, if the carrier frequency displayed is 18103 kHz, when transmitting a RTTY signal's 2295 Hz tone, the RF signal's frequency will be $18103 - 2295 = 18100.705$ kHz. Similar calculations must be applied when using a digital mode on USB.

TRANSMITTER DUTY CYCLE

It is also important to know the typical duty cycle for a digital mode because most amateur transmitters are not designed to operate at full power output for an extended time. When you are operating CW, for example, the transmitter is turned on and off to form the characters so that the transmitter is only operating at full power about 40 to 50% of the time. During the off times, the amplifier stage cools sufficiently to allow full power operation. When you are using SSB, the transmitter is producing full power only when your voice reaches maximum amplitude. For a typical SSB conversation, the transmitter is operating at full power only about 20 to 25% of the time.

When you are operating some data modes, however, your transmitter may be operating at full power the entire time you are transmitting. For Baudot radioteletype the transmitter is continually switching between the mark and space tones of the code, so the duty cycle is 100%. For PSK31 and similar modes, the transmitter is producing full power for virtually the entire transmit time, so the duty cycle is nearly 100%. ARQ modes have slightly reduced duty cycles because the transmitter sends some data and then waits to receive an acknowledgement. If you are operating a high-duty-cycle mode you should reduce your transmit power to prevent overheating the amplifier. Reduce your transmitter power to about 50% of maximum output power for most digital modes. [G8B08]

DIGITAL MODE SIGNAL QUALITY

Digital mode operation involves the same concerns about signal quality as phone and CW. Digital signals are just as capable of generating interference to nearby channels, plus the audio signals between the computer and radio can also be a source of problems.

For digital modes that use an SSB transmitter to transmit AFSK, the most common problem is supplying too much or too little audio from the computer to the radio's microphone input. A microphone input is easy to overdrive, resulting in splatter and spurious outputs. Some radios have direct digital inputs that can connect directly to a computer data interface. This eliminates the audio interface and level setting problems entirely.

If you are using a waterfall display (discussed later in this chapter), it will be quite obvious if a signal is distorted because there will be additional lines to each side of the main signal which may itself look broader than the usual signal. Each of those vertical lines represents a spurious emission, usually caused by overmodulation of the transmitter from the audio level at the microphone input being too high. [G2E11] If you listen carefully by ear, you'll be able to hear those "extra" tones. A distorted waveform is more difficult to decode and the spurious emissions occupy bandwidth that could be used by other stations. After adjusting transmit audio level yourself, have a friend check your signal to confirm that your audio level is set properly.

ALC AND DIGITAL MODES

Automatic Level Control (*ALC*) is used to prevent excessive drive to amplifier inputs. Inside a transceiver, ALC prevents overdrive of the output amplifier stage. The ALC signal from an external amplifier prevents a transceiver from putting out too much power for the amplifier's input. This sounds like a good thing but ALC and digital signals do not work well together.

ALC circuits reduce gain when power levels get too high so that higher amplitude input signals are amplified less than low ones. In effect, this compresses the signal similarly to how a speech processor works. For a voice signal, the resulting distortion is an acceptable trade for the higher average power because your ears can make up the difference. But for a digital signal, the distortion caused by ALC makes the signal harder to decode and creates interference just like overmodulation does. [G4A14]

When using a digital mode, your ALC system should be either disabled or the microphone input level and gain turned down to the point where the ALC system does not activate. You can usually monitor ALC action on the same transceiver meter that monitors power output and SWR. Resist the temptation to turn up the gain because you will only be making your signal harder to understand and creating interference for others.

> *Before you go on, study test questions G2E01, G2E05, G2E11, G2E14, G4A14, G8B05, G8B08, and G8B10. Review this section if you have difficulty.*

6.6 Digital Operating Procedures

LISTENING FIRST

Just as with voice and CW contacts, you must listen to the channel first to be sure it's not occupied with an ongoing contact — digital or not. It's important that you, the control operator, use your ears to listen to the received audio or your eyes to watch a waterfall-style display. It's not enough to just check a BUSY light on a modem or in a software window because those may only indicate the presence of signals that can be decoded. If a contact using another mode is in progress and your software doesn't understand that mode, you could start transmitting right on top of the stations and never know unless you listen first. Follow good amateur practice and listen, listen, listen!

INITIATING AND TERMINATING DIGITAL CONTACTS

Digital QSOs usually follow the general structure established by the long tradition of RTTY operating. A CQ on a digital mode looks similar to the other modes:

CQ CQ CQ DE W1AW W1AW W1AW
CQ CQ CQ DE W1AW W1AW W1AW K

The usual method of responding looks like this:

W1AW W1AW W1AW DE WB8IMY WB8IMY K

As on CW, if signals are loud and clear, you may reduce the number of times you send the call signs.

Terminating an RTTY or PSK31 keyboard-to-keyboard connection is very much like ending a CW contact. Digital operators often use the same prosigns and abbreviations as for CW operation. For example, K is used at the end of a transmission to indicate the other station is to transmit as shown above. SK is used to indicate "signing off" or "end of contact."

If you are using a mode such as PACTOR or WINMOR, your software or modem will have a specific "disconnect" message or command such as BYE or D which initiates the contact termination sequence. If band conditions change and one station fades out, for example, after a preset number of unacknowledged message transmissions, the transmitting station will *timeout* and return to the disconnected state.

Gateway and Mailbox Stations

Unmanned *gateway* and *mailbox* stations monitor a fixed frequency until another station attempts to connect to them. Because they respond without requiring a human control operator, the FCC classifies them as automatically-controlled digital stations. [G1E11] As such, they are restricted to certain segments of the amateur bands. Automatically-controlled stations are only permitted to use RTTY and data modes below 220 MHz (1.25 meters) in the band segments listed in **Table 6.3**. [G1E13]

You may hear stations operating under automatic control outside the US amateur allocations. Stations in areas outside FCC administration may operate under automatic control on other amateur frequencies. A station operating under FCC rules must be operating under local or remote control (that is, with a control operator in charge of all transmissions) to contact these stations legally. [G1E03]

The exact method of establishing a connection will vary with the equipment and mode being used but beginning the contact starts with sending a CONNECT message to the station with which you want to connect. [G2E10] If your signal is received without errors, a *training sequence* of packets may be exchanged to determine the type and version of protocol to use. If your signal is weak or experiencing interference, the connection may not be made or the available data rate may be too low for efficient use. Once the connection is established, a message can then be transferred.

Table 6.3

Automatic Control Band Segments for RTTY and Data

Band (Meters)	Frequency Range (MHz)
80	3.585 – 3.600
60	Not permitted
40	7.100 – 7.105
30	10.140 – 10.150
20	14.095 – 14.0995 and 14.1005 – 14.112
17	18.105 – 18.110
15	21.090 – 21.100
12	24.925 – 24.930
10	28.120 – 28.189
6	50.1 – 50.4
2	144.1 – 148

DURING THE CONTACT

Operating Displays

A waterfall display as seen in **Figure 6.3A** displays the presence of signals as a series of lines each representing a scan across the frequency range. The strength of the signals or noise present is represented as the brightness, intensity, or color of the line at each frequency. As new lines are captured and displayed, the older lines are moved down or to one side, giving the impression of a "waterfall" as the information slows "flows" across the screen. [G2E12] Waterfall displays show the presence of any type of signal and a skilled operator can often tell what type of mode is in use from its appearance.

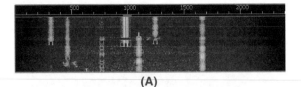

(A)

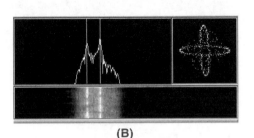

(B)

Figure 6.3 — At A, the waterfall display shows seven different digital signals being received in an audio frequency range of 0 to 2400 Hz. B shows an RTTY tuning display with a filter output window and a crossed-ellipse display for fine tuning.

Figure 6.3B shows two common tuning aids for RTTY signals. On the left is a window showing the spectrum of the filtered received audio. Two vertical lines at the mark and space frequencies help tune in a signal so that the peaks are on the lines, indicating the right tone frequencies. At right is a crossed-ellipse display used for fine tuning. When the ellipses have approximately the same size and are at right angles, the signal is precisely tuned.

Third-Party Traffic

Digital contacts are no different than voice or CW in the rules governing message content. All of the FCC rules about third-party messages apply to digital transmissions. [G1E12] This includes all information included in email, digital images, or web pages transmitted via Amateur Radio. This is why Internet access through gateways and other services must be very limited. Commercial messages such as advertisements may not be transmitted via Amateur Radio and neither may information pertaining to your business or finances.

Interfering Signals

There are certain symptoms of interference you can recognize while using a digital mode. One of the most common is the "hidden transmitter" problem that occurs with all modes, not just digital. If you are located in a skip zone for one of the stations involved in an ongoing contact or that is trying to connect to the same digital station, you will not hear the hidden transmitter's signals but the receiving station might hear both of you. The resulting interference is completely unintentional but generally prevents both you and the hidden transmitter from completing a contact with the desired station.

Keyboard-to-keyboard modes, such as RTTY or PSK31, tolerate interference fairly well but it's your job to interpret any garbled information that appears in the decoded output. Packet modes, such as PACTOR or WINMOR, do their best to automatically recover from reception difficulties but you should be aware of how they respond in the presence of interference. The result is generally one of these problems [G2E03, G8C06]:

● Failure to connect — the receiver won't be able to decode your connect request and your connect attempt will fail.

● Frequent retries or transmission delays — because of the interference, your transmissions will be received with errors and the data will be garbled so your station must retransmit the data multiple times, causing the data transfer progress to be slow or erratic.

● Timeouts or dropped connections — in cases of strong or persistent interference, the number of requested retransmissions may exceed a preset limit which causes the other station to drop the connection or disconnect from your station, ending the contact.

Those symptoms are a clue for you to listen to the channel or watch your operating displays to see if another signal is present. Remember, the interference may be accidental or the other station may not hear your signal at all! Use a different frequency or aim directional antennas in another direction.

Before you go on, study test questions G1E03, G1E11, G1E12, G1E13, G2E03, G2E10, G2E12, and G8C06. Review this section if you have difficulty.

Chapter 7

Antennas

In this chapter, you'll learn about:
- Antenna basics
- Dipoles and ground-planes
- Effects of antenna height and polarization
- How Yagis work
- Loop antennas
- Antennas with special characteristics
- Feed line basics
- SWR and impedance matching

Any conductor can act as an antenna for radio waves but selecting an efficient and useful antenna takes a little bit of know-how. It's not necessary for General class licensees to be antenna designers but you should understand the basic principles of antennas. You're going to learn more detail about how simple antennas and feed lines work, then extend your understanding of common directional antennas. Building on what you already know from your Technician studies, the things you learn for your General exam will help you make better choices about what sort of antenna to use and what sort of performance to expect.

7.1 Antenna Basics

Making a quick review of your existing knowledge of antennas and feed lines is a good way to be ready to learn. We'll start this section by brushing up on definitions:

Elements are the conducting portions of an antenna that radiate or receive a signal. *Polarization* refers to the orientation of the electric field radiated by the antenna and is determined by the physical orientation of the elements with respect to the Earth's surface. If an element is horizontal, then the signal it radiates is horizontally polarized.

Feed point impedance is the ratio of RF voltage to current at an antenna's feed point. An antenna is *resonant* when its feed point impedance is completely resistive with no reactance.

An antenna's *radiation pattern* is a graph of signal strength in every direction or at every vertical angle. An *azimuthal* pattern shows signal strength in horizontal directions. An *elevation* pattern shows signal strength in vertical directions. An antenna transmits and receives with the same pattern. *Lobes* are regions in the radiation pattern where the antenna is radiating a signal. *Nulls* are the points at which radiation is at a minimum between lobes.

An *isotropic* antenna radiates equally in every possible direction, horizontal and vertical. Isotropic antennas do not exist in practice and are only used only as a reference. An *omnidirectional* antenna radiates a signal of equal strength in every horizontal direction. A *directional* antenna radiates preferentially in one or more directions.

Concentrating transmitted or received signals in a specific direction is called *gain*. Signal strength is increased in that direction for both receiving and transmitting. Antenna gain is specified in decibels (dB) with respect to an identified reference antenna. Gain with respect to an isotropic antenna is called dBi. Gain with respect to a dipole antenna's maximum radiation is called dBd. You can convert dBd to dBi by adding 2.15 dB and from dBi to dBd by subtracting 2.15 dB. [G9C19, G9C20]

The ratio of gain in the preferred or forward direction to the opposite direction is called *front-to-back ratio* (F/B). The ratio of gain in the preferred or forward direction to directions at right angles called the *front-to-side ratio* (F/S). All such ratios are measured in dB.

7.2 Dipoles, Ground-planes and Random Wires

Simple antennas are by far the most popular antennas used by hams. They are inexpensive, easy to install and give good performance. The design of more sophisticated antennas is often based on these simple "skyhooks."

DIPOLES

The most fundamental antenna is a *dipole* (from "two electrical polarities") — a straight conductor that is ½ wavelength (λ/2) long with its feed point in the middle. (*Doublet* is another name for a dipole but that term is generally applied to similar center-fed wire antennas that are not resonant.) A dipole radiates strongest broadside to its axis and weakest off the ends as shown in **Figure 7.1**. This "figure-eight" is the shape of the azimuth pattern for a dipole in free space. [G9B04] When installed over actual ground, the resulting reflections will change both the azimuth and elevation radiation patterns as described later in this section.

Current in a half-wave dipole is highest in the middle and zero at the ends. Voltage along the dipole is highest at the ends and lowest in the middle. (See **Figure 7.2**.) The feed point impedance (the ratio of RF voltage to current) of a center-fed dipole in free-space is approximately 72 Ω but it varies widely depending on its height above ground as we discuss later in this section. Impedance increases as the feed point is moved away from the center and is several thousand ohms at the ends. [G9B08]

In free space, ½ wavelength in feet equals 492 divided by frequency in MHz. If you cut a piece of wire that length, however, you'll generally find it somewhat too long to

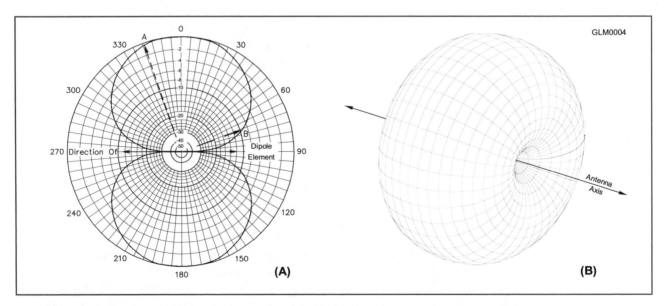

Figure 7.1 — Part A shows the radiation pattern in the plane of a dipole located in free space. The dipole element is located on the line from 270 to 90 degrees in this figure. Part B shows the three-dimensional radiation pattern in all directions around the dipole.

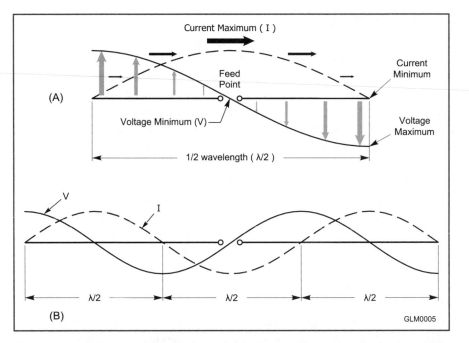

Figure 7.2 — The half-wave dipole at A has its maximum current in the middle and maximum voltage at each end. Feed point impedance is lowest in the middle. At odd harmonics of the fundamental frequency, the dipole's feed point impedance is low at the midpoint once again as shown at B.

resonate at that frequency. At resonance, a ½-wave dipole made of ordinary wire will be shorter than the free-space ½ wavelength for several reasons. First, the physical thickness of the wire makes it look a bit longer electrically than it is physically. The lower the *length-to-diameter (l/d) ratio* of the wire, the shorter it will be when it is resonant. Second, the dipole's height above ground also affects its resonant frequency. In addition, nearby conductors, insulation on the wire, the means by which the wire is secured to the insulators and to the feed line also affect the resonant length. For these reasons, a single universal formula for dipole length, such as the common 468/f, is not very useful. You should be start with a length near the free-space length and be prepared to trim the dipole to resonance using an SWR meter or antenna analyzer.

The exam only requires that you identify an approximate resonant length for a dipole. Use the free-space length, calculated as 492 / f (in MHz), and select the closest choice.

Example 1: What is the approximate length in feet of a ½-wave dipole resonant at 3.550 MHz? [G9B11]

$$\text{free-space length} = \frac{492}{3.55} = 139 \text{ ft}$$

The choices are 42, 84, 131, and 263 feet. The closest length and correct answer is 131 feet.

Example 2: What is the approximate length in feet of a ½-wave dipole for 14.250 MHz? [G9B10]

$$\text{free-space length} = \frac{492}{14.250} = 34.5 \text{ ft}$$

The choices are 8, 16, 24, and 32 feet. The closest length and correct answer is 32 feet.

Center-fed dipoles are easiest to use on the band for which they are resonant. The feed point impedance of such an antenna is a good match for the 50 or 75-Ω coaxial cable used by most hams. The feed point impedance of a half-wave dipole is also a good match for coax on odd multiples of the fundamental frequency. For example, a dipole for the 40 meter band (7 MHz) can also be used on 15 meters (21 MHz). On its third harmonic, the dipole "looks like" the three half-wave dipoles in Figure 7.2 connected end to end. On even-numbered harmonics and non-resonant bands, the feed point impedance of the dipole can be high, just as it is near the antenna's end.

GROUND-PLANES (VERTICALS)

The ground-plane antenna is one-half of a dipole with the missing portion made up by an electrical mirror, called the *ground plane*. The ground plane can be made from sheet metal or a screen of *radial* wires. The basic ground-plane antenna is ¼-wavelength (λ/4) long with the feed point at the junction of the antenna and the ground plane. Currents in the ground plane create the effect of an electrical image of the physical portion of the antenna as shown in **Figure 7.3**. For HF ground-plane antennas mounted at ground level, the radial wires are laid on the surface of the ground or buried within a few inches of the surface. [G9B06]

Ground-planes are often called simply "verticals" because that is the usual way of constructing and installing them. Like a dipole, the ground-plane radiates best broadside to its axis. If installed vertically, this means the ground-plane antenna is omnidirectional. This is a very useful characteristic for VHF and UHF communications while mobile or portable and for an HF antenna where signals may come from all directions.

The feed point impedance at the base of the ideal ground-plane is 35 Ω, half of a complete dipole's impedance, because only half of the antenna is physically there and able to radiate energy. Sloping the radials of an elevated ground-plane antenna downward raises the feed point impedance. A droop angle between 30 and 45 degrees as shown in **Figure 7.4** results in the feed point impedance increasing to approximately 50 Ω which matches coaxial cable. [G9B02, G9B03]

If the droop angle continues to increase, the antenna functions more and more like a physical dipole and the feed point impedance eventually reaches the 72 Ω of the dipole. Also as with the dipole, moving the feed point away from the base — the midpoint of the combined physical antenna and its image — raises the impedance.

As with the dipole antenna, it is not useful to provide a one-size-fits-all formula for length of a ground-plane antenna. Since the ground-plane is one-half the size of a dipole, start with one-half the free-space length (246 / f in MHz) and be prepared to trim the antenna's length.

Example 3: What is the approximate length in feet of a ¼-wave ground-plane antenna resonant at 28.5 MHz? [G9B12]

$$\text{free-space length} = \frac{246}{28.5} = 8.6 \text{ ft}$$

The choices on the exam question are 8, 11, 16 and 21 feet. The closest length and correct answer is 8 feet.

Mobile HF Antennas

Mobile HF antennas are often some form of ground-plane antenna. The most popular mobile antenna by far is the vertically-oriented *whip* — a thin steel rod mounted over the conducting surface of the vehicle, giving omnidirectional coverage. Whips are common on the VHF and UHF bands. A full-sized λ/4 mobile whip is not feasible on the HF bands below 10 meters, so *loading* techniques are used to increase

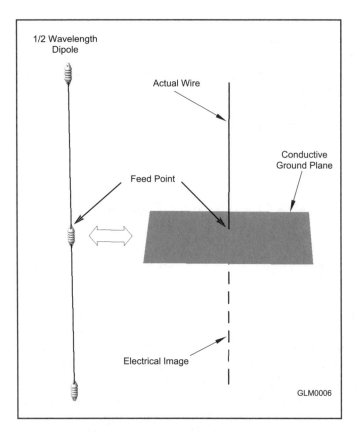

Figure 7.3 — The ground plane, whether made of solid metal or radial wires, creates an electrical mirror image of the ¼-wavelength antenna. This creates the electrical equivalent of a dipole antenna.

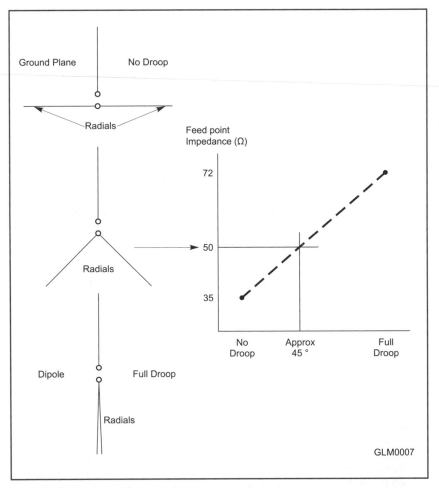

Figure 7.4 — The feed point impedance of a ground-plane antenna with radials perpendicular to the antenna is approximately 35 Ω, resulting in a 1.4:1 SWR with 50-Ω coaxial cable. Drooping or sloping the radials gradually raises the feed point impedance until, with the radials drooped so far as to become the other half of a dipole, feed point impedance becomes 72 Ω. A 50-Ω feed point is reached with radials drooping approximately 45 degrees.

Loading Techniques for Mobile Antennas

As a practical matter, mobile HF antennas must be small to be safe and manageable on a vehicle. Some common loading techniques are used to electrically lengthen the physically-short antennas:

✔ *Loading coils* — a coil is added at the base or somewhere along the length of the antenna.

✔ *Capacitance hats* — spokes or a wheel-shaped structure is added near the top of the antenna. [G4E01]

✔ *Linear loading* — part of the antenna is folded back on itself.

Another common feature on mobile whips is the *corona ball* at the tip of the antenna. While this does add a small amount of loading capacitance, its primary function is to eliminate any high-voltage discharges from the sharp tip of the antenna while transmitting. [G4E02]

a physically small antenna's electrical size. (See the sidebar, "Loading Techniques for Mobile Antennas.")

While loading can cause an antenna to present reasonable feed point impedances, a loaded antenna is not as efficient as a full-sized straight whip and will have a small operating bandwidth without retuning. [G4E06] The "screwdriver" antenna design — a whip with an adjustable loading coil at the base — has gained popularity for HF mobile operation as a good compromise between performance and convenience.

RANDOM WIRES

It is not always practical to have a ½ or ¼-wavelength long resonant antenna. For portable operation and in other special circumstances, a *random wire* antenna can be used. The antenna is just what the name suggests, a random length of wire deployed however possible. The feed point impedance and radiation pattern of a random wire are unpredictable. The antenna's radiation pattern may have several lobes at different vertical and horizontal angles.

A true random wire is connected directly to the output of the transmitter (more commonly to the output of an antenna tuner) without a feed line. The station equipment and its ground connection are thus part of the antenna system as well. Using this type of an antenna may result in significant RF currents and voltages on the station equipment that could cause RF burns. [G9B01] Nevertheless, this simple antenna can give excellent results on any band for which the transmitter or tuner can accept the feed point impedance.

EFFECTS OF HEIGHT ABOVE GROUND

An antenna's feed point impedance and radiation pattern are both affected by the antenna's physical height above ground. The effects are caused by the presence of the electrical image of the antenna created in the electrically conducting ground below the antenna. The ground may not be a very good conductor, but the image is still present and affects antenna performance.

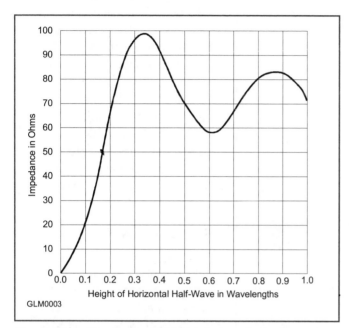

GLM0003

Figure 7.5 — The feed point impedance of a horizontal dipole over perfect ground varies dramatically with height. At ground level, the antenna is effectively "shorted out" by its electrical image. As the antenna is raised, the impedance gradually approaches the 72-Ω feed point impedance of a dipole in free space.

Feed point impedance is affected because the electrical image, like all mirror images, is electrically reversed from the actual antenna. As the image and antenna get closer together, the actual antenna begins to be "shorted out" by the image. Below ½ wavelength in height, the antenna's feed point impedance steadily decreases until it is close to zero at ground level. [G9B07] Above ½ wavelength, the impedance varies as suggested by **Figure 7.5**, eventually reaching a stable value at a height of several wavelengths.

Height above ground also affects radiation patterns because of reflection of the antenna's radiated energy by the ground. The actual radiation pattern is composed of energy received directly from the antenna and energy that has been reflected by the ground. The direct and reflected signals take different amounts of time to travel to the receiving antenna so they can add together, cancel each other, or any combination in between. This creates a new pattern of lobes and nulls not present for an antenna in free space.

Figure 7.6 shows what happens when a dipole is raised in steps from a very low height to more than one wavelength above ground. At heights below ½ wavelength, the dipole's pattern is almost omnidirectional and is maximum straight up. [G9B05] As a height of ½ wavelength is reached, the reflected and direct energy cancel in the vertical direction and add together at intermediate angles, creating a pattern of peaks and nulls in the radiation pattern for the antenna. Selecting the proper antenna height is important to achieving the desired goals for the antenna!

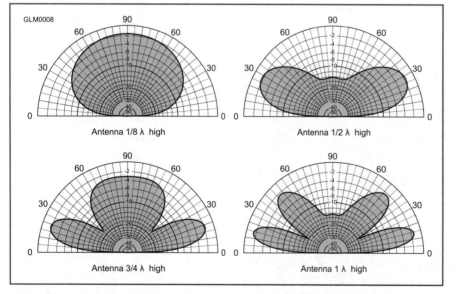

Figure 7.6 — As a low dipole starting at ⅛ wavelength above ground is raised, the effects of its electrical ground image cause the elevation pattern to flatten out. At multiples of ½ wavelength in height, the pattern has a null in the vertical direction.

EFFECTS OF POLARIZATION

Polarization also affects the amount of signal that is lost from the resistance of the ground. Radio waves reflecting from the ground have lower losses when the polarization of the wave is parallel to the ground. That is, when the waves are horizontally polarized. Because the antenna's radiation pattern is made up of the reflected waves combining with the direct waves that are not reflected, lower reflection loss results in stronger maximum signal strength. [G9B09]

Ground-mounted vertical antennas, however, are able to generate stronger signals at low angles of radiation than horizontally polarized antennas at low heights. This means they are often preferred for DX contacts on the lower HF bands where it is impractical to raise horizontally polarized antennas to the height necessary for strong low-angle signals.

> *Before you go on, study test questions G4E01, G4E02, G4E06 and G9B01 to G9B12, G9C19, and G9C20. Review the section if you have difficulty.*

7.3 Yagi Antennas

For the combination of economy, performance and simplicity it's hard to beat the Yagi antenna. More accurately called the Yagi-Uda antenna, the design was first described in 1927. With the end of World War II, coaxial cable, inexpensive aluminum tubing, and steel towers placed the rotatable antenna within reach of amateurs.

Aiming Antennas

There are two reasons you want to be able to aim an antenna: 1) to be heard better by a desired station, and 2) to hear a desired station better. The radiation pattern of a unidirectional antenna like a Yagi usually has one main lobe and at least three nulls — two side nulls and one rear null. If you know where each of those nulls is pointing, it's a simple matter to use the pattern to accomplish your goals.

The device that does the actual mechanical moving is called a *rotator* (not a "rotor"). The rotator's control box in your shack has a meter or digital readout that you can calibrate to provide the compass heading of where the main lobe of the antenna is pointing — usually along the boom of the antenna. From that heading, you know that the side nulls will be at 90 degrees to either side where the ends of the elements face the signal. The rear null is usually aligned directly opposite to the direction of the main lobe. (The direction of the rear null may shift slightly from asymmetries in the antenna's installation or for signals arriving from different vertical angles.) To minimize noise or interference, try pointing one of these nulls at the source of the interference.

Being heard better by the station you're contacting means that you need to point the main lobe at the station. To aim the antenna accurately if that station is beyond your line of sight, you'll need a special kind of map called an *azimuthal projection* map. This map shows the world squashed into a circle centered on a particular location (such as your station) so that the paths to all other locations are shown as *great circle* paths, giving the true bearing and distance to any other point. By aiming your antenna in the direction shown on the azimuthal projection map, you will be beaming your signal directly at the other station. [G2D04]

Once you have the antenna pointed in what you think is the right direction, don't hesitate to search or hunt for a slightly better signal somewhat off the direct path. It is not uncommon, particularly on HF, for the ionosphere to skew the signal path by up to 15 degrees. To minimize noise or interference, you rarely know the exact location, so you'll have to find the best direction for a null by using your ears and your radio's S meter.

HOW YAGIS WORK

Directional antennas are used widely because they create gain as well as reject interference and noise from other than the desired direction. The venerable Yagi remains the most popular of all directional antennas because of its simple construction and good performance. Even a simple Yagi can reduce interfering signals and noise from unwanted directions to the rear and sides of the antenna— an important feature on a crowded band such as 20 meters. [G2D11]

While the dipole, ground-plane, and random wire use a single radiating element, the Yagi uses more than one. It is an example of an *array* antenna, in which two or more elements are used to create maximum field strength in a specific direction, called the *main*

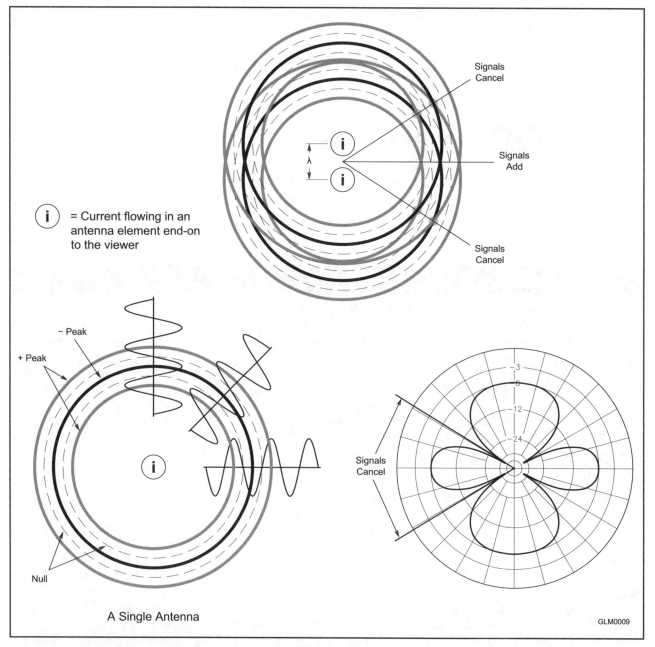

Figure 7.7 — For two antennas 1 wavelength apart (seen on-end) and fed identical, in-phase signals, the radiated signals add and cancel at different angles around the antennas. This creates the lobes and nulls of the radiation pattern seen at right.

lobe or *major lobe* of the radiation pattern. [G9C08] There are two types of arrays: *driven* and *parasitic*. In a driven array, all of the antenna elements are connected to the transmitter and are called *driven elements*. In a parasitic array, one or more of the elements are not connected to the feed line but influence the antenna's pattern by interacting with the radiated energy from the driven element(s).

Whether an array is a driven or parasitic array, its radiation pattern is determined by *constructive* and *destructive interference*. When two waves interfere with each other, they can reinforce each other if they are in phase and cancel if they are out of phase. Partial cancellation occurs otherwise.

If two antenna elements are separated by more than a small fraction of a wavelength, the differences in travel time to a distant antenna from each are enough to result in cancellation that varies with the position of the distant antenna. **Figure 7.7** shows an example of cancellation for a pair of dipole antennas. The radiated fields from each antenna add and subtract at different angles around the antennas so that lobes and nulls are formed.

In a driven array, power is applied to all of the elements, such as in Figure 7.7. In a parasitic array, the antenna elements are so close together that energy from the driven element induces a current to flow in the parasitic element. That current radiates a field — called *re-radiation* — just as if it had been supplied by a feed line! By careful placement and tuning of the parasitic and driven elements, a directional antenna pattern can be created.

YAGI STRUCTURE AND FUNCTION

The Yagi is a parasitic array with a single driven element and at least one parasitic element as shown in **Figure 7.8**. The elements are physically arranged to create gain in a single *major* or *main lobe* and cancel signals in the opposite direction. The parasitic elements placed in the direction of maximum gain are called *directors* and are slightly shorter than the driven element. [G9C03] Parasitic elements in the direction of minimum gain are called *reflectors* and are slightly longer than the driven element. [G9C04] For a Yagi antenna, the front-to-back ratio is the ratio of signal strength at the peak of the radiation pattern's major lobe to that in exactly the opposite direction. [G9C07]

The following description of how a Yagi works is somewhat oversimplified but illustrates the general principles. The simplest two-element Yagi consists of a driven element and a reflector. The driven element (DE) is a resonant dipole, approximately ½ wavelength long. [G9C02] The reflector is slightly longer than the DE by about 5% and placed about 0.15 to 0.2 wavelength behind the DE, opposite the direction of maximum signal.

The original signal from the DE travels to the reflector where it causes current to flow, re-radiating a signal. Re-radiated signals are 180 degrees out of phase with the original signal, so the re-radiated and DE signals cancel in the direction of the reflector (to the back of the antenna). To the front of the antenna, the extra travel time for the re-radiated signal from the reflector causes it to reinforce the DE signal.

So why is the reflector slightly longer than the DE? The physical separation and the 180 degrees of re-radiation phase shift don't quite add up to complete cancellation and reinforcement. Additional phase shift is needed and that

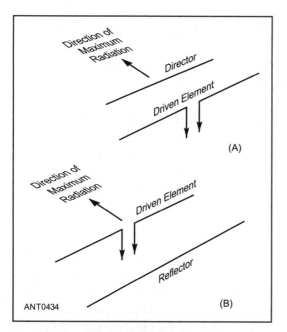

Figure 7.8 — Two-element Yagi antennas using a single parasitic element. At A the parasitic element acts as a director, and at B as a reflector. The arrows show the direction of maximum radiation.

comes from the reflector being slightly longer than ½ wavelength so that its impedance is inductive. The additional phase shift to the current in the reflector from the inductive reactance is just enough to cause the original and re-radiated signals to add and cancel in the desired directions.

A director element, placed in front of the DE by the same amount, increases forward gain. It works similarly but is somewhat shorter than the DE by about 5%. The resulting capacitive reactance subtracts a small amount of phase shift so that the DE and director signals add to the front of the antenna in the direction of the director.

Neglecting the effects of height above ground, a two-element Yagi with a driven element and a reflector has a gain of approximately 7 dBi (over an isotropic antenna) and about 5 dBd (over a dipole). The front-to-back ratio is 10 to 15 dB. By adding a single director, a three-element Yagi's forward gain improves to a theoretical maximum of 9.7 dBi and the front-to-back ratio to 30 to 35 dB. This is a very useful antenna!

Additional reflectors make little difference in either gain or front-to-back ratio. Therefore, most Yagi antennas have a single reflector. Adding more directors does not have a big effect on front-to-back ratio but does increase antenna gain, so it is not uncommon at HF to see Yagis with two to four directors. At VHF and UHF, there may be as many as a dozen or more directors, although each only adds a fraction of a dB in gain.

· DESIGN TRADEOFFS

Once the basic design principles are established, there are many ways to optimize the design of an actual antenna to fit a specific need. Is it more important to have the maximum gain or the best front-to-back ratio? How much variation of SWR is allowed across the entire band? Making a "one size fits all" antenna is quite difficult!

The primary variables for Yagi antennas are the length and diameter of each element and their placement along the *boom* of the antenna (the central support). These affect gain, SWR, and front-to-back ratio in different ways:

- More directors increase gain.
- A longer boom with a fixed number of directors increases gain up to a maximum length beyond which gain is reduced. [G9C05]
- Larger diameter elements reduce SWR variation with frequency (increases SWR bandwidth). [G9C01]
- Placement and tuning of elements affects gain and feed point impedance (and SWR).

To be sure, there are other general rules of cause-and-effect, but these are typical of the decisions that antenna designers (and purchasers) should consider. [G9C10]

The process of modifying a design for a certain level of performance is called *optimizing*. Some antenna modeling programs can start with a basic design and then modify it so as to obtain the best gain, front-to-back ratio, feed point impedance and so on. For example, if you purchase a garden-variety commercial antenna, you could experiment with it to get more gain or better front-to-back ratio. Antenna design and modification is a very popular activity for hams.

IMPEDANCE MATCHING

Most Yagi designs that have desirable radiation patterns also have a feed point impedance somewhat below the 50 Ω of regular coaxial cable; typically the feed point impedance is 20 to 25 Ω. This results in an undesirable SWR of greater than 2:1. To change the feed point impedance back to 50 Ω, various impedance matching techniques are used.

The most common technique is the *gamma match* shown in **Figure 7.9**. The gamma match is actually a short section of parallel-conductor transmission line that uses the driven element as one of its conductors. The transmission line transforms the low impedance of the feed point to a higher value. [G9C11] An adjustable capacitor — either an actual

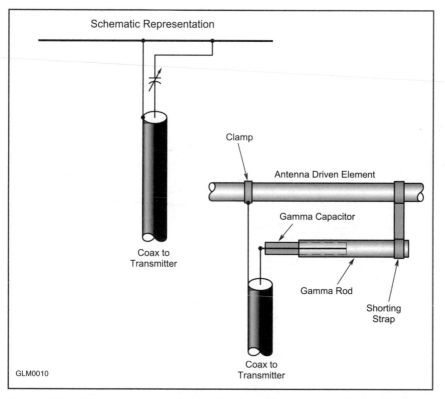

Figure 7.9 — The gamma match is a short section of transmission line that transforms a low impedance at the center of the driven element to a higher impedance closer to that of coaxial cable. The gamma match is tuned with the gamma capacitor and by moving the shorting strap.

variable capacitor or a short piece of insulated wire inside a hollow gamma rod — is used to adjust the gamma match for an SWR of 1:1. A mechanical advantage of the gamma match over other techniques is that the driven element need not be insulated from the boom, simplifying construction. [G9C12]

There are other techniques of impedance matching Yagi antennas, such as the beta match (or "hairpin"), the omega match, impedance transformers and transmission line stubs. These are described in references such as *The ARRL Antenna Book*. At VHF and UHF, it is also possible to use relatively large-diameter elements so that the feed point impedance is close to 50 Ω without any external matching devices.

Before you go on, study test questions G2D04, G2D11, G9C01 to G9C05, G9C07, G9C08, G9C10, G9C11, and G9C12. Review the section if you have difficulty.

7.4 Loop Antennas

Loop antennas completely enclose an area, usually one wavelength or more in circumference. Loop antennas can be oriented vertically or horizontally. On the HF bands, loops are made of wire because of their large size. At VHF and UHF, loops may be made of tubing or metal strap. The loop is cut to attach the feed line.

Loops can be circular, square, triangular or any simple open shape that is not too narrow. A square loop with each leg λ/4 long is called a *quad loop*. Triangular or *delta loops* are usually symmetrical, with each leg λ/3 long. Some delta loops shorten one leg and lengthen the other two equally. The radiation pattern of the loop in **Figure 7.10** shows that the direction of maximum signal is broadside to the plane of the loop, whether round, quad or delta. If the loop is oriented horizontally most of its signal will go straight up, making it a good antenna for local and regional contacts. Orienting the loop vertically aims the maximum signal toward the horizon, where it would be better for making DX contacts.

A one-wavelength loop acts electrically like two dipoles connected end-to-end with the open ends brought together. The location at which a loop's feed line is attached becomes

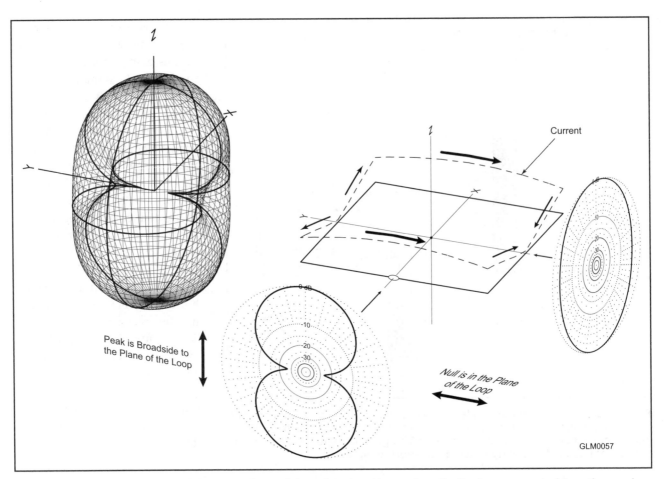

Figure 7.10 — The 1-wavelength loop can be envisioned as two ½-wavelength dipoles connected together and stretched into a square, circle, or triangle. Radiation is highest perpendicular to the plane of the loop.

a high current point, just like at the middle of a dipole. No matter where the feed point is attached, a mirror image of the high current point then appears ½ wavelength from the feed point across the loop as shown in Figure 7.10. Shorter and longer loops (not integer multiples of 1 λ) can't form the same pattern of current and have a higher feed point impedance.

Loops can be used in arrays, just as dipoles can. In fact, a popular variation of the Yagi beam uses quad loops for elements. Not surprisingly, this beam antenna is called a *quad*. The quad has two or more full-sized loops mounted on a boom just like a Yagi's elements: reflector, driven element and director(s). The quad or delta loop beam driven elements are approximately 1 λ in circumference and operate on the same principles of re-radiation and phase shift as does the Yagi. The driven element of a quad is about ¼ wavelength per side and of a symmetrical delta loop about ⅓ wavelength per side. [G9C13, G9C17] Quad and delta loop reflectors are about 5% longer in circumference than the driven element and the directors about 5% shorter. [G9C06, G9C15] A two-element quad or delta loop with a driven element and a reflector has approximately the same forward gain as a three-element Yagi. Front-to-back ratio is generally better for the Yagi. [G9C14, G9C16]

The quad is mechanically more complex than the Yagi, requiring cross-arms to hold the loop. A quad has more surface area and wind loading than a Yagi with the same number of elements, which can be a drawback in environments with severe weather. Quad and delta loop beams with the same number of elements have about the same gain.

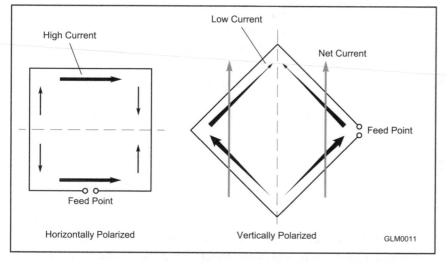

Figure 7.11 — The polarization of a vertical loop depends on the location of the feed point. Feeding the loop in the middle of a horizontal section forces maximum current to flow horizontally and the fields from vertical currents to cancel for a net horizontal polarization. Rotating the antenna 90 degrees also rotates the resulting polarization.

The polarization of a loop oriented horizontally is always horizontal, no matter where the feed point is located. The polarization of a vertical loop antenna depends on where the feed point is attached as shown in **Figure 7.11**. Taking the quad loop as an example, attaching the feed point at the midpoint of the bottom or top side of the loop results in horizontal polarization. Moving the feed point of the loop to one of the vertical sides results in vertical polarization. It doesn't matter whether the loop is constructed with the top and bottom legs parallel to or at 45 degrees to the ground. [G9C18]

Before you go on, study test questions G9C06 and G9C13 to G9C18. Review the section if you have difficulty.

7.5 Specialized Antennas

This section covers several interesting topics associated with specific types of antennas or special ways of using them. There are literally hundreds of different types of specialty antennas, but the following examples are common on the HF bands. You will also find that an ordinary antenna can be made to give unexpected results if constructed and installed in the just the right way!

NVIS

NVIS stands for *near-vertical incidence sky-wave*, a fancy way of saying, "Signals that go straight up!" [G9D01] When most hams think of an optimum antenna, they imagine one that sends a signal out at a low vertical angle so that it will be heard at the maximum distance for those great DX contacts. But it is not always desirable to work someone far away. Sometimes it's more important to make local and regional contacts, such as for emergency communications or nets.

If you've ever seen a searchlight sweeping across the clouds at night, you've observed something similar to NVIS. The beam of light is reflected down and visible over a much wider range than if the beam had been pointed toward the horizon. Radio NVIS works the same way. An antenna that sends most of its signal at a high angle or straight up is used and the ionosphere reflects the signal back to Earth over a wide area as "short skip." On 75 meters, NVIS can cover an area several hundred kilometers across. Therefore it is recommended for emergency communications. This works even during the day when low-angle signals would likely be absorbed by the ionosphere. [G9D02]

What kind of an antenna is used for NVIS signals? You may be surprised to find out that a simple dipole mounted a dozen or so feet above the ground is all that's required! You'll recall from earlier in this section that a dipole antenna mounted at a height lower than $\lambda/4$ has a more-or-less omnidirectional pattern with the peak signal at 90 degrees — straight up. The best antenna heights for NVIS communications are between $\lambda/10$ and $\lambda/4$. [G9D03] Below that the feed point impedance becomes too low to provide a good match to coaxial cable. Higher than that and the main lobe starts to send more signal at lower angles.

STACKED ANTENNAS

You may have seen an installation with a pair (or more!) of identical parallel Yagi antennas mounted one above the other or side-by-side. *Stacking* antennas in the manner of **Figure 7.12** results in more gain.

There is an additional benefit to stacking antennas. If you study the azimuthal radiation patterns of Yagis, you notice that as more and more directors are added, the *beamwidth* of the main lobe (the angle between the points on the main lobe at which gain is 3 dB less than maximum) narrows. If you look at the elevation pattern however, adding more directors doesn't have as great an effect. Vertically stacking antennas increases gain and narrows the elevation beamwidth. [G9D05]

Most *vertical stacks*, with the antennas directly above each other, space the antennas about $\lambda/2$ apart although spacings of up to more than 1 λ are sometimes used. Spaced $\lambda/2$ apart, the additional gain for a vertical stack of two horizontally-polarized beams is about 3 dB. [G9C09] Sometimes the antennas are aligned such that the elements are parallel but end-on to each other, in a *horizontal stack*. In this arrangement, the spacing is larger to keep the antennas from interacting too strongly.

LOG PERIODICS

If you don't look too closely at a TV antenna, you might think it is just another Yagi. Take a closer look and you'll be surprised — that's a *log periodic* antenna! Usually referred to as "logs," the log periodic antenna in **Figure 7.13** is designed to have a consistent radiation pattern and low SWR over a wide frequency bandwidth — as much as 10:1 — meaning the log periodic can be used over several bands. A log periodic will not have as much gain or front-to-back ratio as a Yagi antenna, however. [G9D06]

The "log" in log periodic refers to "logarithmic," and "periodic" means the spacing of the elements along the boom. The length and the spacing of the elements increases logarithmically from one end to the other. [G9D07] The result is that the part of the antenna doing the radiating and receiving shifts with frequency — the short elements are active at the high frequencies and the long elements at low frequencies. The elements are approximately the length of $\lambda/2$ dipoles at the frequency on which they are active. A log

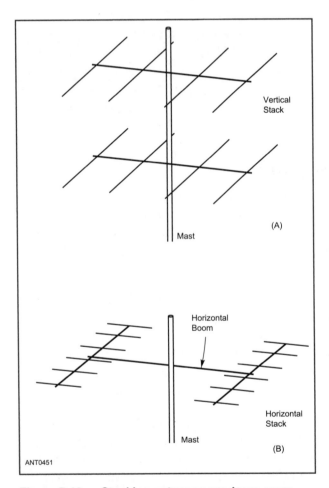

Figure 7.12 — Stacking antennas produces more gain in a main lobe that is carefully controlled. At A, two Yagis are stacked vertically on the same mast. At B, two Yagis are stacked horizontally side-by-side.

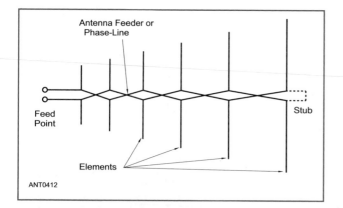

Figure 7.13 — The log periodic dipole array (LPDA) consists of dipoles fed by a common feed line that alternates polarity between elements. TV antennas sweep the elements slightly forward — there are many variations on the basic design.

periodic antenna can be a good choice if only one rotatable antenna can be installed for several bands.

The log periodic is one member of an entire family of *frequency independent* antennas whose characteristics are consistent over wide frequency ranges. There are spirals and conicals and discones and many other interesting designs. They are designed so that the shape of the antenna is consistent from very small to very large scales. In that way, the radio waves will always find some area of the antenna to their liking!

BEVERAGE ANTENNAS

Invented in 1922 by Harold Beverage, this antenna was designed not to have terrific gain (it's actually quite inefficient) but to reject noise. At the low frequencies used in the early days of radio, atmospheric noise was intense. Rejecting it meant big improvements in receiving range, so Beverage designed a simple antenna that would reject noise and interfering signals in all but the desired direction. It consists of a long, low wire (usually less than 20 feet high) aligned with the preferred signal direction. [G9D10] If one end is terminated in a resistor the antenna receives best toward the termination.

The Beverage of **Figure 7.14** is a *traveling wave antenna*. As the incoming wave moves along the antenna wire it builds up a voltage wave just as wind blowing across

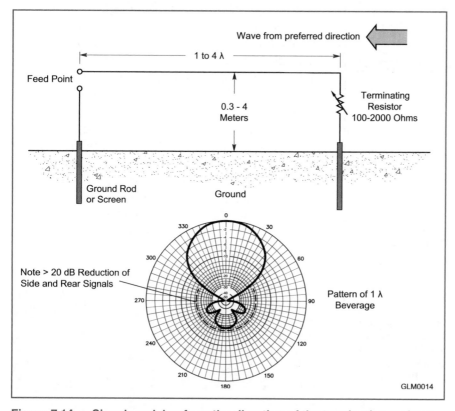

water builds up a water wave. When the wave reaches the end of the antenna, the energy is transferred to the feed line. Voltage waves from signals arriving from the opposite end of the antenna are absorbed by the terminating resistor. Signals arriving from the side cannot create voltage waves, so the Beverage favors signals only in the desired direction, dramatically improving the ratio of received signal to noise.

Used exclusively for directional receiving on the lower HF bands (40 meters and longer wavelengths), the Beverage has high ground losses and is too inefficient for use as a transmitting antenna. The Beverage works by throwing away more noise than it does signal, not by acquiring more signal. [G9D08, G9D09]

Figure 7.14 — Signals arriving from the direction of the terminating resistor induce a traveling voltage wave along the wire transferred to the feed line at the feed point. Signals arriving from other directions are either absorbed by the terminating resistor or do not induce voltage waves in the antenna.

MULTIBAND ANTENNAS

So far, the discussion has been mainly about antennas that are designed for a single band. It is terrific to be able to put up a separate antenna for each band, but that's rarely practical. The solution is *multiband* antennas with good performance on more than one band, often several.

As discussed before, a half-wave dipole can be used on its odd harmonics without a tuner and gives good performance. A random wire or nonresonant antenna can also be used on multiple bands with a tuner. What hams generally mean by multiband antenna, however, is a design that reconfigures itself electrically for each band of operation.

The most basic multiband antenna, the *trap dipole*, is shown in **Figure 7.15**. Each trap is a parallel LC circuit. At resonance it acts like an open circuit, below resonance like an inductor, and above resonance like a capacitor. At their resonant frequencies, traps act like open electrical switches, effectively cutting off the rest of the antenna beyond their location. At lower frequencies, the traps add inductance to the antenna, making the antenna look electrically longer. At higher frequencies, the capacitance electrically shortens the antenna. [G9D04]

For the trap dipole in Figure 7.15, at the lowest frequency of operation the antenna acts like a regular dipole, shortened by the inductance of the trap. On the band where the trap is resonant, the outer segments of the antenna are electrically disconnected and only the inner segment is active. Some trap antenna designs are useful on higher frequencies as well. Yagis can also use traps to work on several bands. The three-element *tribander* Yagi with traps in the elements is a time-proven performer on 20, 15, and 10 meters.

There are a few drawbacks of using techniques such as traps to make antennas work on multiple bands. First, because the antenna does work on multiple bands, it will happily radiate harmonics and spurious signals just as if they were intentional. It is up to the transmitter operator to be sure those signals are not generated. [G9D11] Second, the traps have losses and do reduce the efficiency of the antenna to some degree. Third, because the antenna is shortened on the lowest or lower frequencies of operation, it will not radiate quite as well as a full-sized antenna. Nevertheless, using trap antennas is often an excellent compromise between performance and available space and budget for antennas.

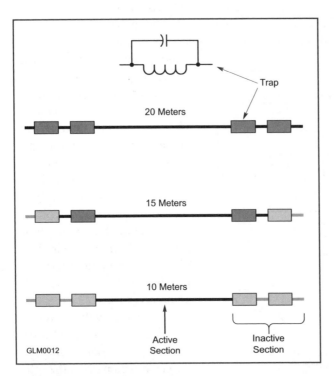

Figure 7.15 — Traps are parallel LC circuits. They may be made from discrete inductors and capacitors or may use coaxial cable or metal sleeves. The traps act like open circuits at their resonant frequency, causing different sections of the antenna to be active on different bands.

Before you go on, study test questions G9C09 and G9D01 to G9D11. Review the section if you have difficulty.

7.6 Feed Lines

As a General class licensee, you'll be assembling more sophisticated collections of equipment, trying bigger and better antennas and using more and more feed lines — more accurately, transmission lines — to connect everything together. Getting the best performance out of your equipment requires a basic understanding of how feed lines work, the goal of this section. Let's start by reviewing what you learned for the Technician class exam.

CHARACTERISTIC IMPEDANCE

All feed lines have two conductors. Coaxial cable has an inner or center conductor and an outer shield or braid. The inner conductor is insulated from the outer conductor by air or by foamed or solid plastic. *Balanced* feed lines consist of two parallel conductors separated by insulating material in the form of strips or spacers. **Figure 7.16** shows some examples of common feed lines used by hams.

Just as pipes and tubes have different "acoustic impedances" to the flow of sound or air through them, feed lines have different *characteristic impedances* (Z_0) that characterize how electromagnetic energy is carried by the feed line. This is not the same as the resistance of the feed line's conductors.

The geometry of the feed line conductors determines the characteristic impedance. For parallel feed lines, the radius of the conductors and the distance between them determine Z_0. [G9A01] Flat ribbon TV-type *twin lead* has a characteristic impedance of 300 Ω. [G9A03]

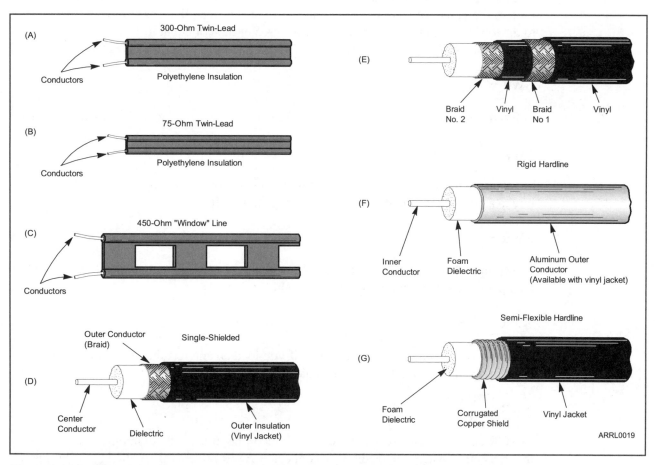

Figure 7.16 — Some common types of parallel conductor and coaxial cables used by amateurs. Parallel conductor line (A, B, C) has two parallel conductors separated by insulation (dielectric). Coaxial cable (D, E, F, G) or "coax" has a center conductor surrounded by insulation. The second conductor, called the shield, covers the insulation and is in turn covered by the plastic outer jacket.

Amateurs also use parallel-conductor feed lines (also called *open-wire* and *ladder* or *window line*) that have impedances of 300 to 600 Ω.

In a coaxial feed line, Z_0 is determined by the diameters of the inner and outer conductors and the spacing between them. The characteristics of the insulating material has some effect on characteristic impedance, but has a larger effect on *feed line loss* and the *velocity of propagation*. The most common characteristic impedances for coaxial feed lines used by amateurs are 50 Ω and 75 Ω. [G9A02]

FORWARD AND REFLECTED POWER AND SWR

A feed line transfers all of its power to an antenna when the antenna and feed line impedances are *matched*. If the feed line and antenna impedances do not match, some of the power is *reflected* by the antenna. Power traveling toward the antenna is called *forward power*. Power reflected by the antenna is called *reflected power*. Power in a feed line is reflected at any point at which the impedance of the feed line changes. This can be at an antenna, at a connector, or from a different type of feed line. [G9A04]

The waves carrying forward power and reflected power form stationary interference patterns inside the feed line. These are *standing waves*. The ratio of the peak voltage in the standing wave to the minimum voltage is called the *standing wave ratio* (SWR) and is used to measure how well the antenna and feed line impedances are matched. SWR of 1:1, a "perfect match," indicates that none of the power is reflected, all of it transferred to the antenna. An SWR of infinity indicates that all of the power was reflected.

SWR is always greater than 1:1 (for example, 3:1 and not 1:3). SWR is equal to the ratio of the higher of antenna feed point impedance or feed line characteristic impedance to the lower. That means the ratio is always greater than or equal to 1:1.

Example 4: What is the SWR in a 50-Ω feed line connected to a 200-Ω load? [G9A09]

$$SWR = \frac{50}{25} = 2:1$$

Example 5: What is the SWR in a 50-Ω feed line connected to a 10-Ω load? [G9A10]

$$SWR = \frac{50}{10} = 5:1$$

Example 6: What standing wave ratio will result from the connection of a 50-Ω feed line to a non-reactive load having a 50-Ω impedance? [G9A11]

$$SWR = \frac{50}{50} = 1:1$$

Example 7: What would be the SWR if you feed a vertical antenna that has a 25-Ω feed point impedance with 50-Ω coaxial cable? [G9A12]

$$SWR = \frac{50}{25} = 2:1$$

Example 8: What would be the SWR if you feed an antenna that has a 300-Ω feed point impedance with 50-Ω coaxial cable? [G9A13]

$$SWR = \frac{300}{50} = 6:1$$

SWR can be measured anywhere along a feed line. It is most commonly measured at the transmitter where the feed line is connected. SWR meters (also called SWR bridges) are used to measure the SWR present in the feed line between the transmitter and the antenna.

Most amateur transmitting equipment is designed to work at full power with an SWR at the input to the feed line of 2:1 or lower. SWR greater than 2:1 may cause the transmitter to reduce power. The higher the SWR, the harder it is for a transmitter to transfer power to a feed line. High SWR may damage a transmitter. Antennas that are much too short or too long will not work well and will have extreme feed point impedances, causing high SWR. High SWR can be caused by a mismatch of the feed line and transmitter impedances, a mismatch of the antenna and feed line impedances, or by a faulty feed line.

IMPEDANCE MATCHING

Matching feed line and load (antenna) impedances eliminates standing waves from reflected power and maximizes power delivered to the load. [G9A07] This is not always practical however, so the impedance matching is more often done at the transmitter end of the feed line as shown in **Figure 7.17**.

The device used to reduce SWR at the transmitter connection to the feed line has many names: *impedance matcher, transmatch, antenna coupler* and *antenna tuner*. [G4A06]

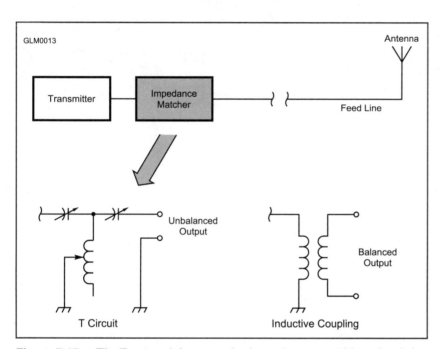

Figure 7.17 — The T network is a popular impedance matching circuit for HF antennas. Installed at the transmitter end of the feed line, a T network is designed to be used with unbalanced, coaxial feed lines. To use balanced feed lines, such as open-wire lines, the output of a T network can be inductively coupled to the output so that neither of the feed line conductors is connected to ground.

Remember that an "antenna tuner" does not tune the antenna at all — it only changes the impedance of your antenna system at the end of the feed line to match that of your transmitter.

Impedance matching devices are constructed from inductors and capacitors that are adjustable by the operator. The most common circuit configuration is the T network shown in Figure 7.17. This circuit can match a wide range of impedances at the feed line connection to 50 Ω that matches transmitter output impedance.

Regardless of what technique is used to transform impedances, it is important to remember that the SWR in the feed line between the impedance matching device and the antenna does not change! If the SWR in the feed line is 5:1 and an impedance matching device causes a 50-Ω load to be presented to the transmitter, the SWR is still 5:1 in the feed line. [G9A08]

Feed Line Loss

All feed lines dissipate a little of the energy they carry as heat — this is *attenuation* or *loss*. Loss occurs because of the resistance of the conductors and because the insulating material between the conductors absorbs

Table 7.1
Feed Line Characteristics

Type	Impedance (Ω)	Loss per 100 ft (dB) at 28.4 MHz	Loss per 100 feet (dB) at 144 MHz
RG-174	50	4.4	10.2
RG-58	50	2.4	5.6
RG-8X	50	1.9	4.5
RG-213	50	1.2	2.8
9913	50	0.64	1.6
LMR-400	50	0.65	1.50
LMR-600	50	0.41	0.94
¾ inch CATV hardline	75	0.26	0.62

some of the energy. Air-insulated cables such as parallel conductor feed lines and certain types of hardline have the lowest loss. Teflon insulation also has extremely low loss. Polyethylene, both solid and foamed, is used in most cables and has the highest loss, although it is still a very good insulating material.

Loss is measured in dB per unit of length, usually dB/100 feet of cable. [G9A06] Typical values for loss of different types of cable are given in **Table 7.1**. Loss increases with frequency for all types of feed lines. [G9A05] Small coaxial cables generally have higher loss at a given frequency than larger diameter cables.

As SWR increases, more power is reflected by the load. That reflected power must travel through the line and on each round trip, some of it is dissipated as heat due to feed line loss. Thus, increasing SWR in a feed line also increases the total loss in the line. [G9A14] Higher feed line loss also affects SWR measurement at the input to the line. The increased loss in the feed line means that less of reflected power returns to the input where it can be measured. This makes SWR look artificially low. The higher the feed line loss, the lower the measured SWR will be at the input to the line. [G9A15] In fact, a long length of lossy feed line can be used as a good dummy load!

Before you go on, study test questions G4A06 and G9A01 to G9A15. Review the section if you have difficulty.

Chapter 8

Propagation

In this chapter, you'll learn about:
- **The structure of the ionosphere**
- **Reflection and absorption**
- **Sky-wave and ground-wave signals**
- **Sunspots and sunspot cycles**
- **How to assess propagation**
- **Solar phenomena**
- **Scatter propagation**

You've now studied electronics, signals, transmitters, receivers and antennas. Only one thing is missing — how the waves get from point A to point B! That's propagation and it's the subject of this section. On the HF bands, propagation is strongly affected by what's happening on the Sun so you'll need to learn a few things about solar phenomena. The effects of those events on the ionosphere are also important to HF operators. By learning some basic terms and relationships, HF propagation will be much easier to understand and use.

8.1 The Ionosphere

The upper reaches of the Earth's atmosphere get thinner and thinner with distance above the Earth. Beginning at about 30 miles in height, the remaining gas is thin enough that solar ultraviolet (UV) radiation can break the molecules of gas into individual atoms and then knock electrons away from them. The gas is *ionized* by the loss of an electron, causing the atom to become a positively charged *ion* and the electron a *free electron*. These ions and the electrons can respond to voltages just as electrons do in a conductor and so this region of the atmosphere becomes a very weak conductor called the *ionosphere*.

REGIONS

The ionosphere extends to 300 miles above the Earth where the gas molecules, atoms, ions and electrons are so far apart that it is essentially the vacuum of space. Orbiting at 200 miles above the Earth, the International Space Station is actually inside the ionosphere! Because of various physical processes, the ionosphere organizes itself naturally into several regions in which the density of the free electrons is higher than at adjacent altitudes. The main regions of the ionosphere are the D, E and F layers as shown in **Figure 8.1**. (The words region and layer mean the same thing.)

- The *D layer* (30 to 60 miles in altitude) is only present when illuminated by the Sun. It disappears at night because the ions and free electrons are close enough together to recombine quickly when no UV is present, returning to a neutral condition. [G3C01]
- The *E layer* (60 to 70 miles in altitude) acts similarly to the D region. Because it is

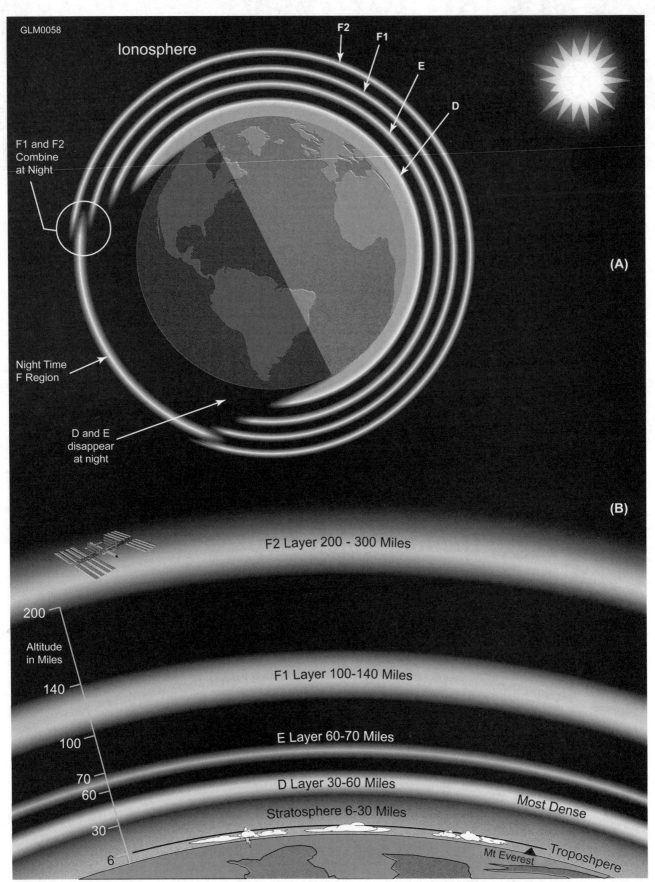

GLM0058

Ionosphere

F2

F1

E

D

(A)

F1 and F2
Combine
at Night

Night Time
F Region

D and E
disappear
at night

(B)

F2 Layer 200 - 300 Miles

200

Altitude
in Miles

F1 Layer 100-140 Miles

140

E Layer 60-70 Miles

100

70
60

D Layer 30-60 Miles

Most Dense

30

Stratosphere 6-30 Miles

Troposhpere

6

Mt Everest

**Figure 8.1 — The ionosphere consists of several regions of ionized particles at different heights above the Earth.
At night, the D and E regions disappear and the F1 and F2 regions combine to form a single F region.**

higher and less dense than the D region, it lasts longer after sunset but still disappears at night, returning to its neutral state.

- The *F layer* (100 to 300 miles in altitude) is the least dense of the three and can remain partially ionized at night. During the day, the F region splits into the F1 and F2 layers, which combine back into the single F layer at night. The height of the F region and the F1 and F2 layers varies quite a bit with local time, season, latitude and solar activity. At any particular location, the stronger the illumination from the Sun, the higher the F2 layer will be, so the maximum height is reached at noon in the summer when the Sun is overhead. [G3C02]

REFLECTION AND ABSORPTION

That the ionosphere is a weak conductor enables it to affect radio waves passing through it by gradually bending or *refracting* them as shown in **Figure 8.2**. The ability of the ionosphere to bend radio waves depends on how strongly the region's gases are ionized and the frequency of the wave. The higher the region's ionization, the more the wave will be bent. The higher the frequency of the wave, the less it is bent. In fact, at VHF and UHF, the waves are hardly bent at all and are usually lost to space. (Scatter propagation, discussed later, is an exception.) The continually shifting combination of ionization and frequency makes ionospheric propagation an exciting phenomenon! [G3B05]

At HF, the waves can often be bent enough to return to Earth as if they were reflected from a mirror high in the ionosphere. Figure 8.2 illustrates how the height of this "mirror" is determined, called the region's *virtual height*. Remember that radio waves are actually refracted by the ionosphere, however.

Some combinations of frequency and ionization level result in weak bending. In these cases, the wave must leave the Earth's surface at a low enough angle for the bending of the wave to send it back. The highest takeoff angle at which a wave can be returned to Earth is the critical angle. If the wave enters the ionosphere at a steeper angle, it might be diffracted, but not enough and it is lost to space, as shown in **Figure 8.3**. The critical angle depends on ionospheric conditions and frequency. [G3C04]

The companion to critical angle is *critical frequency*, the highest frequency on which a wave transmitted straight up will be returned to Earth. Measuring the critical frequency with ionosonde equipment gives the height of all the ionosphere's regions and helps provide a day-to-day picture of the ionosphere's status and activity. (An ionosonde is a special type of radar instrument for measuring ionospheric parameters.)

The enemy of propagation is *absorption*. In the D and E regions, waves passing through the denser gas are partially absorbed, even as they are refracted. In fact, the D region is not very good at refraction. In the HF bands below 10 MHz, the AM broadcast bands, and at lower frequencies, the D region completely absorbs radio

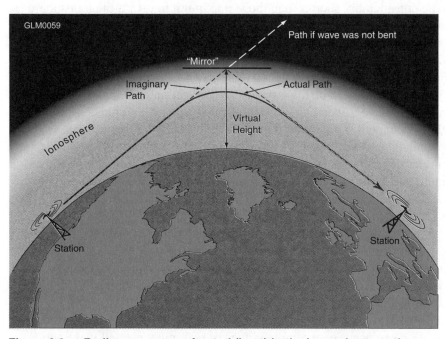

Figure 8.2 — Radio waves are refracted (bent) in the ionosphere, so they return to Earth far from the transmitting station. Without refraction in the ionosphere, radio waves would pass into space. (Not to scale)

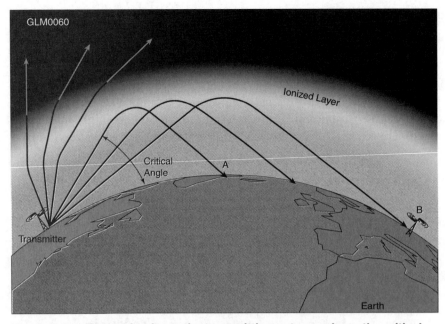

GLM0060

Ionized Layer

Critical
Angle

A

B

Transmitter

Earth

Figure 8.3 — Waves that leave the transmitting antenna above the critical angle are refracted in the ionosphere, but not enough to return to Earth. Waves at and below the critical angle will return to Earth. The lowest angle waves return to Earth at the greatest distance, which is why low angles of radiation are often best for contacting DX stations. (Not to scale)

waves during the day, preventing those waves from returning to Earth until after dark. [G3C05, G3C12] In general, absorption increases in the daytime and when solar UV is more intense. Lower frequency waves are most susceptible to ionospheric absorption.

SKY-WAVE AND GROUND-WAVE PROPAGATION

Each reflection from the ionosphere is called a *hop* and allows radio waves to be received hundreds or thousands of miles away. Signals received in this way are called sky-wave and propagation via the ionosphere is called *skip*.

The higher the region from which the reflection takes place, the longer the hop. Waves reflected from the uppermost F2 layer can travel up to 2500 miles before returning to the ground! Hops that use the E layer are shorter, up to 1200 miles, because of the lower reflecting height. [G3B09, G3B10, G3C03]
• Sky-wave propagation can consist of multiple hops because the Earth's surface also reflects radio waves. The ocean's highly conductive saltwater is a particularly good reflector of radio waves. Propagation between Europe and the United States, for example, requires up to seven hops depending on location and time of day!

Hops can also be considerably shorter than those maximum figures if the ionosphere is sufficiently ionized so that the critical angle is high. Signals received via sky-wave at much shorter than maximum hop distances are called *short skip*. Short skip is also a good indicator that there is sufficient ionization to support longer skip distances on higher frequency bands. For example, short skip on the 10 meter band is a good indication that sky-wave propagation may be available on the 6 meter band at low takeoff angles. [G3B02]

Sky-wave signals also have a characteristic sound caused by the variations in density and height they encounter in the ionosphere. The ionosphere is not a smooth, stable medium through which the waves travel. The ionosphere is in motion itself and there are large variations in density and ionization at different heights and locations. This allows a sky-wave signal to take multiple paths before returning to Earth. Receiving several of these *multipath* signals at once gives the signal a characteristic echo or flutter as the quality of reflection changes or as signals combine from different paths.

Ground-wave signals travel along the surface of the Earth between stations. Rock and soil and concrete are not very good conductors and so a ground-wave signal loses strength much more rapidly than if it were traveling through air. The higher the frequency of the wave, the greater the loss as it travels. Ground-wave propagation on 40 meters, for example, may be up to 100 miles, but on 10 meters, only a few miles at best.

Depending on the critical angle for a particular frequency, a ring-shaped region around the transmitting station can occur between the ranges of maximum ground-wave and minimum sky-wave. This region is called the *skip zone* and stations located in the skip zone of a particular station can't be contacted on that particular frequency.

LONG PATH AND SHORT PATH

As you become more skilled in observing and understanding propagation, you'll begin to take advantage of unusual and short-term propagation effects. One of the most exciting is *long path* in which stations are contacted over a path that takes "the long way 'round." Most contacts are made via the *short path*, which is the shorter of the two great circle paths between stations. When the ionosphere along the short path does not support propagation, sometimes the long path will. The bearing of the long path is 180 degrees away from the short path bearing as illustrated by **Figure 8.4**. [G2D06]

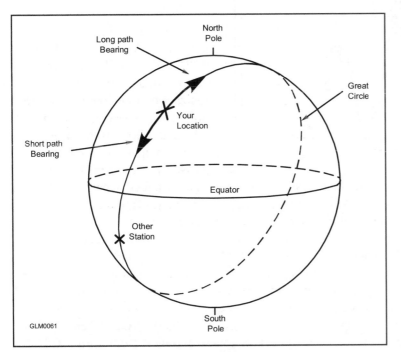

Figure 8.4 — This sketch of the Earth shows both great circle paths drawn between two stations. The bearings for the short path and the long path are shown from the Northern Hemisphere station.

Occasionally, propagation over both the long and short paths will be supported. Unless the long and short paths are almost equal (such as between stations located at each other's *antipode*) there will be an echo as the more delayed signal arrives a fraction of a second later. [G3B01] Occasionally, *round-the-world* propagation is supported and you can hear your own signal coming all the way around to your location about 1/7 of a second later!

Before you go on, study test questions G2D06, G3B01, G3B02, G3B05, G3B09, G3B10, G3C01 to G3C05, and G3C12. Review the section if you have difficulty.

 The Sun

SUNSPOTS AND CYCLES

In the previous discussion, you learned that the ionosphere is dependent on solar UV to separate the electrons from their host atoms. The Sun is always generating UV radiation (even at night!) but there is a considerable amount of variation over time. A lot of this variation has been shown to be caused by sunspots, the slightly cooler (and comparatively darker) regions of the Sun's surface.

Sunspots vary in number over an approximately 11-year period known as the sunspot cycle. [G3A11] The number of sunspots and sunspot groups present on the solar disk at a particular time is the sunspot number. [G3A01] Sunspot number is used as an important parameter in assessing overall solar activity which rises and falls along with the presence of sunspots. As this book is written in early 2015, the sunspot cycle has gone through a second maximum (some cycles have two peaks) and is expected to soon start declining to a minimum. The chart in **Figure 8.5** shows how the sunspot number has varied during the past several cycles.

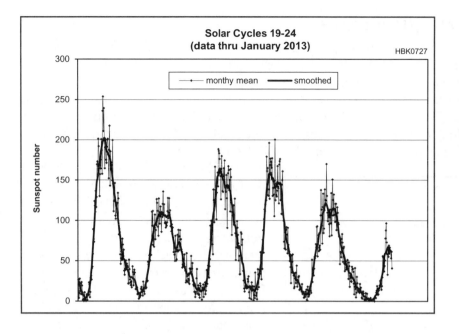

Solar Cycles 19-24
(data thru January 2013)

HBK0727

Figure 8.5 — One complete sunspot cycle lasts about 11 years, ramping up and down gradually. This graph shows the monthly mean sunspot numbers for several past cycles through February 2013. The NASA Solar Physics web page maintains complete data on the sunspot cycle (see solarscience.msfc.nasa.gov/SunspotCycle.shtml).

At the same time more sunspots are observed on the face of the Sun, more UV is being generated, creating more intense ionization in the ionosphere and improving propagation on the HF bands above 10 MHz and even into the lower VHF range. [G3A09] At the peak of the sunspot cycle, there may be sufficient solar UV to cause higher frequency bands such as 10 meters to stay open for long-distance contacts at night. The high ionization takes a toll on the low frequency bands such as 80 and 160 meters as it increases absorption. Conversely, at the bottom of the sunspot cycle when solar activity is low, the lower HF bands have good propagation and the higher HF bands above 20 MHz (15 meters and up) are often closed. [G3A04] One band that seems to do well at all times in the sunspot cycle is 20 meters (14 MHz), supporting daytime communications worldwide nearly every day! [G3A07]

Sunspots also seem to move across the Sun's surface because the Sun rotates once every 28 days. That is why propagation conditions (good and bad) on the HF bands often repeat themselves in 28-day cycles as sunspots rotate back into view from Earth. [G3A10]

There are strong daily and seasonal variations in HF propagation at any point in the sunspot cycle. **Table 8.1** shows the typical variations in propagation on a daily basis across the HF bands for average solar activity. The seasons also affect propagation as the hemispheres receive more or less solar illumination. In summer, the higher illumination and absorption make daytime HF propagation more difficult, shifting activity toward the evenings. The opposite happens in the winter. Propagation around the equinoxes in March and September can be very interesting at any time of the sunspot cycle.

Table 7.1
Daytime/Nighttime HF Propagation

HF Band (meters)	Daytime	Nighttime
160, 80, 60	Local and regional to 100 – 200 miles	Local to long distance with DX best near sunset or sunrise at one or both ends of the contact
40, 30	Local and regional to 300 – 400 miles	Short-range (20 or 30 miles) and medium distances (150 miles) to worldwide
20, 17	Regional to long distance, opening at or near sunrise and closing at night	20 meters is often open to the west at night and may be open 24 hours a day
15, 12, 10	Primarily long distance (1000 miles and more), opening to the east after sunrise and to the west in the afternoon	10 meters is often used for local communications 24 hours a day

MEASURING SOLAR ACTIVITY

Solar activity is so important to propagation and communications that it is monitored around the clock by solar observatories all over the world. The results are available from websites, email distribution and radio broadcast announcements. By using this information, along with their experience and software tools to predict propagation, amateurs can confidently plan their on-the-air activity and be alerted of sudden changes in conditions.

Along with the sunspot number, there are three primary indices that are used to measure solar activity:

• *Solar-Flux Index (SFI)* — describes the amount of 2800 MHz (10.7 cm wavelength) radio energy coming from the Sun. This index corresponds well to the amount of solar UV that is hard to measure at ground level. SFI starts at a minimum of 65 and has no maximum value. Higher levels indicate higher solar activity and generally better HF propagation above 10 MHz. **Figure 8.6** shows the correlation between SFI and sunspot number. [G3A05]

• *K index* — K values from 0 to 9 represent the short-term stability of the Earth's *magnetic* or *geomagnetic field*, updated every three hours at the National Institute of Science and Technology (NIST) in Boulder, Colorado. Steady values indicate a stable geomagnetic field. Higher values indicate that the geomagnetic field is disturbed, which disrupts HF communications. [G3A12]

• *A index* — based on the previous eight K index values from around the world, the A index gives a good picture of long-term geomagnetic field stability. A index values range from 0 (stable) to 400 (greatly disturbed). [G3A13]

All three indices and other solar data is available from the NASA Spaceweather website. (**spaceweather.com**) An announcement of the values of SFI, K, and A indices can be heard on the air by tuning in WWV or WWVH (**www. nist.gov/pml/div688**) at 18 or 45 minutes past the hour, respectively.

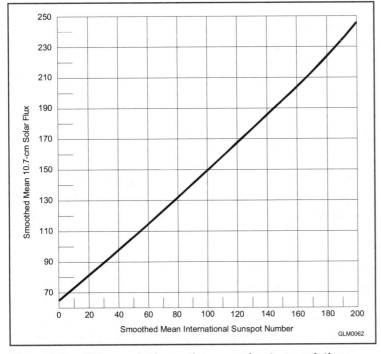

Figure 8.6 — This graph shows the approximate correlation between solar flux and sunspot number. Note that the minimum solar flux is 65, corresponding to a sunspot number of 0.

ASSESSING PROPAGATION

Given the solar activity indices and a reasonably good model of the Earth's geomagnetic field, scientists and communications engineers have developed fairly effective software tools for predicting propagation. Amateurs make extensive use of these programs and as a General class ham operating on HF, you'll want to give them a try.

Two key terms used by prediction programs are of particular importance to hams: *MUF* — *maximum usable frequency* and *LUF* — *lowest usable frequency*. [G3B07, G3B08] Both the MUF and LUF depend on the specific path between two points — their location and distance apart. MUF and LUF also vary with time of day, season, the amount of solar radiation and ionospheric stability. [G3B12]

The MUF represents the highest frequency at which propagation exists between two points. Waves at or below the MUF will be refracted back toward the Earth. Note that

MUF accounts for propagation at all points along the path between the two stations. The MUF will be different on every path between your station and any other station. It must account for variations in the ionosphere at every likely reflection as the wave hops its way from place to place. Waves above the MUF will at some point in the journey penetrate the ionosphere and be lost to space. MUF must also take into account the likely takeoff angles from your antenna system, since this affects the ability of the ionosphere to reflect your signal.

The LUF specifies the lowest frequency for which propagation exists between two points. Waves below the LUF will be completely absorbed by the ionosphere. [G3B06] To make contact with a distant station, you will have to use a frequency between the LUF and the MUF. If the MUF drops below the LUF, then no propagation exists between those two points via ordinary skywave. [G3B11]

Short-term variations in solar activity or the geomagnetic field can make predictions useless. There is no substitute for turning on the radio and listening with your own ears! Predictions do not take into account unusual propagation modes or paths, so you might be surprised.

One way to check the actual band conditions between two points is to listen for propagation beacons. There is an international network of beacon stations maintained by the Northern California DX Foundation (**www.ncdxf.org**) that transmit continuously. In addition, there are many beacon stations between 28.190 and 28.225 MHz that are excellent sources of information about 10 meter propagation. [G3B04] A recent amateur innovation, the Reverse Beacon Network (RBN — **www.reversebeacon.net**) coordinates a system of automated receivers that report call sign and strength of signals on the HF bands.

SOLAR DISTURBANCES

It would be wonderful if the Sun just beamed steadily, pumping up the ionosphere and never causing any trouble up there. That's not the case, unfortunately. The Sun is very dynamic, particularly during the years of peak activity during the sunspot cycle. There are several common events on the Sun that affect HF propagation. Their characteristics are measured by solar observatories and included in regular bulletins and broadcasts to alert users of the HF spectrum.

● *Solar flare* — a large eruption of energy and solar material when magnetic field disruptions occur on the surface of the Sun.

● *Coronal hole* — a weak area in the Sun's corona (the outer layer) through which plasma (ionized gas and charged particles) escapes the Sun's magnetic field and streams away into space at high velocities.

● *Coronal mass ejection (CME)* — an ejection of large amounts of material from the corona. A CME may direct the material in a relatively narrow stream or in a wide spray.

Sudden Ionospheric Disturbances

UV and X-ray radiation from a solar flare travels at the speed of light to impact the ionosphere about 8 minutes later. [G3A03] When the radiation hits the ionosphere, the level of ionization increases rapidly, particularly in the D region (see **Figure 8.7**). This increases absorption dramatically, causing a *sudden ionospheric disturbance* (SID) also known as a *radio blackout*. After a large flare, the HF bands can be completely devoid of sky-wave signals for a period of many seconds to hours, returning gradually to normal. The lower bands are more strongly affected so communication may still be possible on

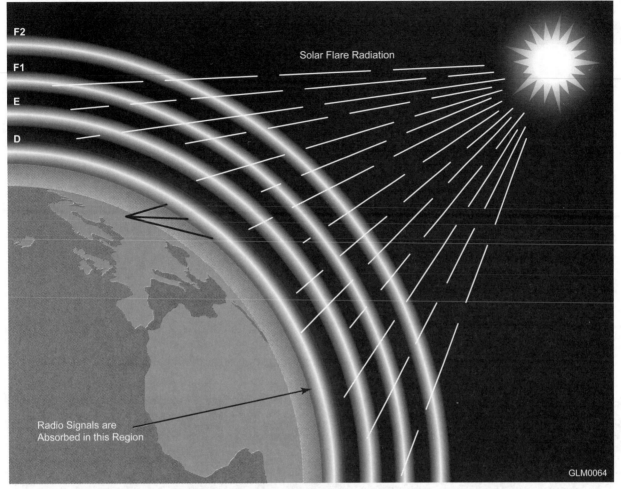

Figure 8.7 — Approximately eight minutes after a solar flare occurs on the Sun, the ultraviolet and X-ray radiation released by the flare reaches the Earth. This radiation causes increased ionization and radio wave absorption in the D region.

a higher band. SIDs affect only the sunlit side of the Earth so dark-side communications may be relatively unaffected. [G3A02]

Geomagnetic Disturbances

The Sun continually gives off a stream of charged particles called the *solar wind*. The interaction between the solar wind and the Earth's geomagnetic field creates a region of space called the *magnetosphere*. Charged particles and other material from coronal holes and coronal mass ejections travel considerably slower and take longer to reach Earth, up to 20 to 40 hours. [G3A15] When the charged particles arrive they can be trapped in and disturb the Earth's magnetosphere near the north and south magnetic poles. By depositing their energy into the Earth's geomagnetic field they increase ionization in the E region of the ionosphere, causing auroral displays and creating a *geomagnetic storm*. [G3A06]

The sudden change in the geomagnetic field disrupts the upper layers of the ionosphere, causing propagation on the higher HF bands to be affected first. Long-distance paths that traverse high latitudes, particularly those that pass near the magnetic poles, may be completely wiped out for a period of hours to days. [G3A08, G3A14]

Auroras are actually the glow of gases ionized by the incoming charged particles as they flow vertically down into the atmosphere, guided by the magnetic field. The resulting

Before you go on, study test questions G3A01 to G3A16, G3B03, G3B04, G3B06 to G3B08, G3B11 and G3B12. Review the section if you have difficulty.

conductive sheets that light up the night sky also reflect radio waves above 20 MHz. In particular, auroral propagation is strongest on 6 and 2 meters, modulating the signals with a characteristic hiss or buzz. [G3A16]

8.3 Scatter Modes

As you may have experienced on VHF, radio waves often propagate by reflections from terrestrial objects and disturbances in the atmosphere. The same is true for HF radio waves on a larger scale. In particular, the ionosphere is not nearly so neatly organized into horizontal layers or regions as we imagine. There are regions that are tilted at significant angles and that reflect waves somewhat horizontally. Other regions may have significant variations in density that support localized reflections, such as the sporadic E propagation common on 6 meters. These are scatter modes of propagation and can be quite useful when regular sky-wave is unavailable.

SCATTER CHARACTERISTICS

Signals received via HF scatter are usually weaker than those received by normal sky-wave propagation because the reflection is not very efficient and tends to spread out

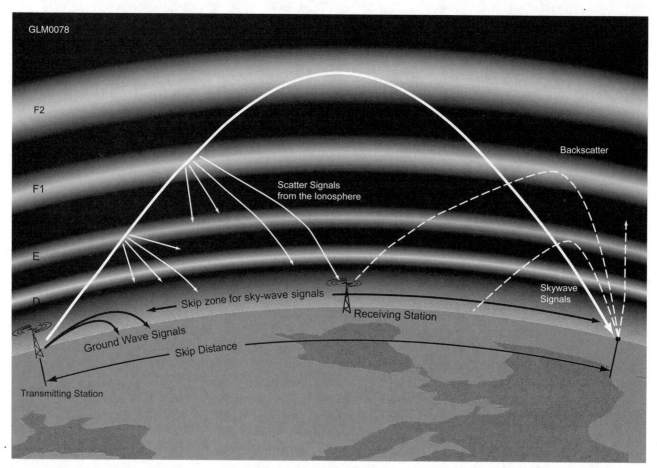

Figure 8.8 — On striking the ground after ionospheric reflection, radio waves may be reflected back toward the transmitting station. Backscatter consists of signals reflected by the ground back into the skip zone. Backscatter supports communication between stations that would otherwise be in each other's skip zone.

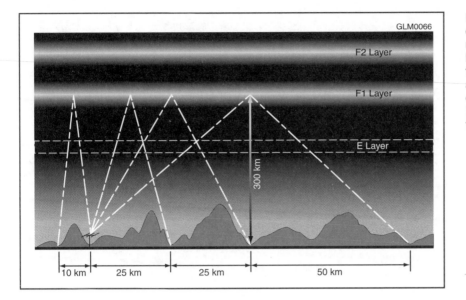

Figure 8.9 — Near vertical incidence sky-wave (NVIS) communications relies on signals below the critical frequency transmitted at high vertical angles. The signals are reflected by the ionosphere back to Earth in the region around the transmitter.

the signal, delivering only a small fraction of the signal to the receiving station. Scatter signals often sound distorted because the reflected waves may arrive at the receiver from many different directions, resulting in multipath interference, just as on VHF and UHF. The usual effect is a fluttering or wavering characteristic. [G3C06, G3C07, G3C08]

If the wave is very close to the MUF, reflections from features on the Earth's surface such as the ocean or a mountain range may return some of the wave back toward the transmitting station. This is called backscatter and is illustrated in **Figure 8.8**. Waves can also be scattered from within the ionosphere, allowing signals to be heard from stations too distant to be heard by ground wave and on frequencies too high for short hop sky-wave propagation. Scatter and backscatter help fill in the skip zone where signals would otherwise not be heard. [G3C09, G3C10]

NVIS

You will recall that for waves below the critical frequency, the ionosphere reflects waves arriving at any angle — even vertical. At most locations, the critical frequency is always above 5 MHz and frequently rises above the 40 meter band. For a signal below the critical frequency, when it is radiated vertically the reflection scatters the signal back to Earth over a wide area around the transmitter. Communication using this special scatter mode is called *near vertical incidence sky-wave* (*NVIS*). [G3C13]

To make use of NVIS as shown in **Figure 8.9**, horizontally polarized dipoles are placed low to the ground so that their radiation pattern is almost omnidirectional and concentrated at high elevation angles. Best results are obtained with the antenna ⅛ to ¼ wavelength high. [G3C11] The resulting skip will provide good signals throughout a region of up to 200 to 300 miles centered on the transmitter. Higher frequencies can be used during the day as the critical frequency rises due to solar illumination.

Before you go on, study test questions G3C06 to G3C11 and G3C13. Review the section if you have difficulty.

Chapter 9

Electrical and RF Safety

In this chapter, you'll learn about:
- **Basic electrical safety practices**
- **Electrical shock hazards**
- **Safety grounding and protective components**
- **RF exposure fundamentals**
- **Evaluating RF exposure**
- **Antenna installation practices**

Radio is basically quite safe but no activity is completely without risk. As a General class licensee, you'll be using more different types of equipment, larger antennas and towers, and more complex stations. With this broader set of privileges comes an increased responsibility to be aware of potential hazards. Doing so helps you to take the necessary steps to protect yourself and others.

9.1 Electrical Safety

With the exception of mobile and portable operating, radio equipment gets its power from the ac power grid. Since that ac line voltage from the wall doesn't care whether a powerful radio or a tiny indicator light is connected, the same safety practices apply for both low-power and high-power stations.

BASIC SAFETY

It's important to have a master OFF/ON switch for your station and workbench, just as in a shop full of power tools and machinery. If you are shocked, your rescuers should have been trained to remove power first so they are not also exposed to shock. The switch should be clearly labeled and somewhat away from the equipment. Don't place the OFF/ON switch in an obscure, hard-to-find or reach location. Show your family how to turn off power at the master switch and at your home's circuit-breaker box.

Don't put yourself in a position to be shocked or hard to rescue. Don't work on "live" equipment unless absolutely necessary. Avoid working alone on energized equipment. Never assume equipment is off or de-energized — check with a meter or tester first. If you are working on feed lines or antennas, be sure that a transmitter or amplifier can't be activated while you're working. Keep one hand in your pocket while probing or testing energized equipment, wear shoes with an insulated sole and remove unnecessary jewelry.

When working inside equipment, remove, insulate or otherwise secure loose wires and cables. Remember that the residual charge on a capacitor can present hazardous voltages for a long time and use bleeder resistors to drain it off. A grounding stick (shown in **Figure 9.1**) should be used to positively remove charge from capacitors and be sure that all exposed conductors are at ground potential.

Soldering and Lead

Soldering is part of the electronic experience and has been for more than 100 years. Solder is primarily lead-based, with tin added to lower the melting point. Lead is a known toxin and so it is prudent to avoid unnecessary exposure. Solder in a well-ventilated area to avoid breathing the small amounts of lead vapor that result from melting the solder. The rosin flux smoke is also likely not good for you in high doses. After you are finished soldering, wash your hands to remove any solder or flux residue. [G0B10]

In 2006, a new set of environmental regulations called "Reduction of Hazardous Substances" or RoHS went into effect. The goal of those regulations is to reduce the amount of toxic materials used in electronics manufacturing, reducing them when the equipment is discarded or recycled, as well. Part of the regulations require that solder become lead-free.

Most amateurs will never be exposed by soldering to enough lead to pose a health hazard, but as industry changes, so will amateur practices. Lead-based solder will continue to be available for some time, but newer equipment will likely contain the new solders. Consult the owner's manual or manufacturer of your equipment to find out what type of solder was used. Mixing types of solder may lead to unreliable solder joints and erratic operation.

ELECTRICAL SHOCK

Shocks result from current flow through the body, and shocks that result from ac current are the most dangerous. Remember that it is not voltage that causes the shock, but current flow. **Table 9.1** (from OSHA Publication 3075, "Controlling Electrical Hazards" — **www.osha.gov/Publications/3075.html**) shows that even shocks from small currents can be painful. Electrical current of more than a few milliamperes can cause involuntary muscle spasms that in turn cause falls and sudden large movements. Burns can be caused by large ac or dc currents through the body or along the skin. The largest current that has been shown to have no adverse effects is 50 µA.

The most dangerous currents are those that travel through the heart, such as arm-to-arm or arm-to-foot. The current flow disrupts the heart's normal beating rhythm. Low-frequency ac current, such as 50 or 60 Hz household power, is the most dangerous because it penetrates the body easily and is of a frequency that can disrupt the heart.

After a shock, the heart may resynchronize to its usual rhythm, enter an uncoordinated state called *fibrillation*, or stop beating altogether. Depending

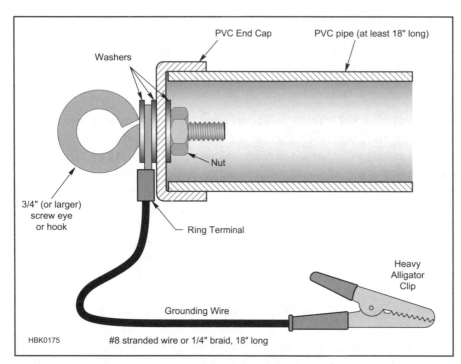

Washers

PVC End Cap

PVC pipe (at least 18" long)

3/4" (or larger) screw eye or hook

Nut

Ring Terminal

Heavy Alligator Clip

Grounding Wire

HBK0175

#8 stranded wire or 1/4" braid, 18" long

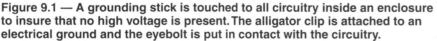

Figure 9.1 — A grounding stick is touched to all circuitry inside an enclosure to insure that no high voltage is present. The alligator clip is attached to an electrical ground and the eyebolt is put in contact with the circuitry.

Table 9.1

Effects of Electric Current Through the Body of an Average Person

Current	Effect (1 sec contact)
50 µA	Maximum harmless current.
1 mA	Faint tingle
5 mA	Slight shock felt; not painful but disturbing. Average individual can let go. Strong involuntary reactions can lead to other injuries.
6 – 25 milliamperes (women)	Painful shock, loss of muscular control*
9 – 30 milliamperes (men)	Painful shock, loss of muscular control*
50 – 150 milliamperes	Extreme pain, respiratory arrest, severe muscular contractions. Death is possible.
1,000 – 4,300 milliamperes	Rhythmic pumping action of the heart ceases. Muscular contraction and nerve damage occur; death likely.
10,000 milliamperes	Cardiac arrest, severe burns; death probable

*If the extensor muscles are excited by the shock, the person may be thrown away from the power source.

Source: W.B. Kouwenhoven, "Human Safety and Electric Shock," Electrical Safety Practices, Monograph, 112, Instrument Society of America, p. 93. November 1968.

on the body's resistance, voltages as low as 30 V can cause enough current flow to be dangerous.

Both fibrillation and lack of beating cause immediate unconsciousness from which you'll need assistance to recover. It is a good idea for you and every other adult to get CPR training from your local fire or police department or from the American Red Cross (**www.redcross.org**). It could come in handy not just for you, but as a lifesaver to anyone in need. A comprehensive discussion of electrical injury is available on the website **www.healthopedia.com/electrical-injury**.

WIRING AND SAFETY GROUNDING

When you are performing electrical maintenance in your home or in the shack, how can you tell what practices are safe? The National Electrical Code (NEC) contains detailed descriptions of how to handle ac wiring in your home and shack in a safe manner. [G0B14] (You can get a copy at many home improvement stores or at the library.) Local building codes should also be followed so that your home is properly wired to meet any special local conditions. This may be important for insurance purposes, as well. If you are in doubt about your ability to do the work properly, hire a licensed professional electrician!

When wiring or repairing an ac power cord plug, be sure to follow the standard wire color conventions as shown in **Figure 9.2** and **Figure 9.3**:

● Hot (the wire or wires carrying voltage) is black or red insulation, connect to the brass terminal or screw

● Neutral is white insulation, connect to the silver terminal or screw

● Ground is green insulation or bare wire, connect to the green or bare copper terminal or screw

Table 9.2

Current Carrying Capacity of Some Common Wire Sizes

Copper Wire Size (AWG)	Allowable Ampacity (A)	Max Fuse or Circuit Breaker (A)
6	55	50
8	40	40
10	30	30
12	25 (20)*	20
14	20 (15)*	15

*The National Electrical Code limits the fuse or circuit breaker size (and as such, the maximum allowable circuit load) to 15 A for AWG #14 copper wire and to 20 A for AWG #12 copper wire conductors.

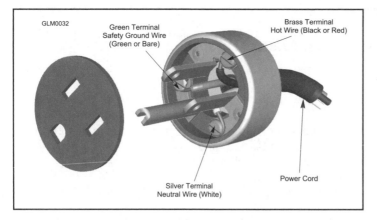

Figure 9.2 — The correct wiring of a 120-V ac line cord to a new plug: Connect the black or red wire (hot) to the brass terminal, the white wire (neutral) to the silver terminal, and the green or bare wire (ground) to the green terminal.

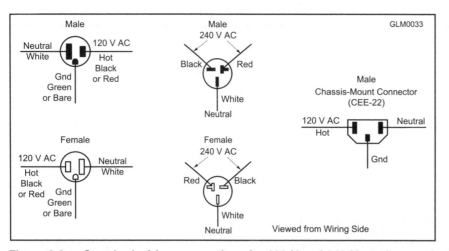

Figure 9.3 — Standard wiring conventions for 120-V and 240-V ac plugs and receptacles. It is critically important to follow the correct wiring techniques for ac power wiring. The white wire is neutral, the green wire is ground, and the black or red wire is the hot lead. Note that 240 V circuits have two hot wires and a neutral.

When connecting an ac power cord inside equipment, use the three-wire/three-prong cords. If the equipment has a metal chassis, always connect the ground wire or terminal to the chassis. This prevents hazardous voltages from appearing on the chassis. [G0B06] Do not use water or waste piping or structural metal as a safety ground unless you have verified that there is enough direct metal-to-ground contact to act as a ground rod. Many new homes and buildings use plastic piping in parts of the system.

Whether you are installing a new power circuit in your home or selecting a power cord, use cable and wire sufficiently rated for the expected current load as shown in **Table 9.2**. The rating of wire to carry current is called its *ampacity*. For house ac wiring, the two most common sizes are #12 AWG for 20-A circuits and #14 AWG for 15-A circuits. [G0B02, G0B03] When you are finished with the wiring job, verify that you have the connections correct by using an ac circuit tester.

PROTECTIVE COMPONENTS

Protective components are used to prevent equipment damage or safety hazards such as fire or electrical shock caused by equipment malfunction. Those that are aimed at preventing shock hazards act when they detect current or voltage where it shouldn't be or indications that current is going where it's not supposed to go. Power control devices such as fuses and circuit breakers prevent equipment damage and fire by interrupting potentially large currents and disconnecting substantial voltages.

Fuses and Circuit Breakers

Fuses interrupt excessive current flow by melting a short length of metal. When the metal melts or "blows," the current path is broken. The rating of a fuse is the maximum current it can carry without blowing. Fuses also have a voltage rating showing how much voltage they will withstand. Do not substitute a fuse rated at 12 V for one with a 120/240 V rating or the result may be that the fuse arcs over instead of removing voltage from the circuit. "Slow-blow" fuses can withstand temporary overloads, but will blow if the overload is sustained.

Circuit breakers act like fuses and "trip" when current overloads occur, opening the circuit and interrupting current flow. Unlike fuses, circuit breakers can be reset once the cur-

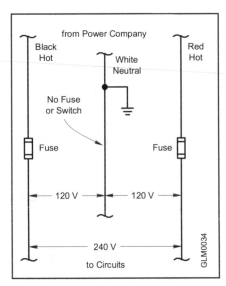

Figure 9.4 — Fuses and circuit breakers should be placed in the hot wire or wires of ac power wiring. Never install a fuse or circuit breaker in the neutral or ground wire of ac wiring. If a neutral or ground wire is disconnected, ac voltage is not removed from the equipment and may still present a shock or fire hazard.

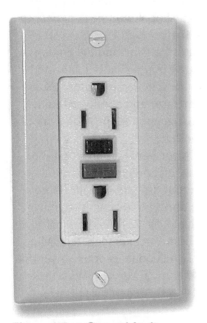

Figure 9.5 — Ground fault circuit interrupter (GFCI) circuit breakers are used in ac power circuits to prevent shock hazards. They are usually found in bathrooms, kitchens and other areas of the home with running water.

rent overload is removed. If a circuit breaker repeatedly trips, it is an indication that too much power is being drawn on that circuit. Either move some of the loads to a different circuit or increase the circuit's current capacity by increasing the wire size and circuit breaker rating.

Use properly sized fuses and circuit breakers. Equipment manufacturers will specify the required fuse rating. Along with minimum wire size, building codes specify the size of the circuit breakers required at the power distribution panel. Never replace a fuse or circuit breaker with one of a larger current rating — fix the problem!

When installing fuses or circuit breakers in an ac power wiring circuit, be sure to place them only in the correct lines. Power is generally delivered to your home as a two-wire, 240 V circuit as shown in **Figure 9.4**. There is 120 V between each of the hot wires and the neutral wire. Most of your household circuits are connected between one of the hot wires and the neutral wire. Large household appliances and amplifiers should be connected between the two hot wires supplying 240 V because running from the higher voltage reduces the required amount of current for the same power consumption. Modern 240-V household appliances use a separate ground wire in addition to the neutral wire and two hot wires (four conductors total). For both types of wiring, only place a fuse or circuit breaker in the hot wire, never in the neutral or ground wire. [G0B01] The reason is that opening the neutral does not remove voltage from the equipment and an electrical hazard may still be present.

Shock Prevention

A *safety interlock* is an example of a shock prevention device. Safety interlocks are switches that prevent dangerous voltages or intense RF from being present when a cabinet or enclosure is opened. [G0B12] One type of interlock physically disconnects high voltage (HV) or RF when activated. A second type shorts or grounds a HV circuit when activated, possibly blowing a circuit breaker or fuse in a power supply. Never bypass an interlock during testing unless specifically instructed to do so and then only in the way directed by the instructions. Be sure to enable the interlock before returning the equipment to service.

Ground fault circuit interrupter (GFCI) circuit breakers (**Figure 9.5**) are used in ac power circuits to prevent shock hazards. A GFCI circuit breaker will trip if an imbalance is sensed in the currents carried by the hot and neutral conductors. Current imbalances indicate the presence of an electrical shock hazard because the unbalanced current must be flowing through an unintended path, such as through a person from the hot wire to ground! GFCI breakers can be sensitive to just a few mA of imbalance between hot and neutral, well below the threshold for electrical injury. [G0B05]

GENERATOR SAFETY

Emergency and portable operation often makes use of an electrical generator driven by a gasoline, diesel or propane engine. With generators easier and more convenient to use than ever, it's easy to overlook basic safety procedures.

Fueling and ventilation problems cause more injuries associated

Figure 9.6 — Install your generator in a well ventilated area, away from living areas.

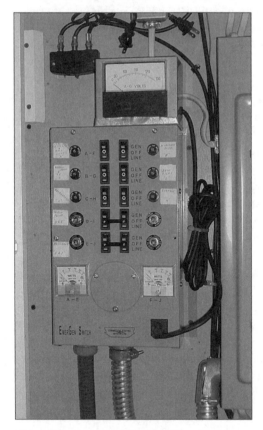

Figure 9.7 — A transfer switch connects your household circuits to the ac line or to a generator and isolates the generator from the line. This device eliminates the dangerous practice of "back-feeding" generator power into the ac line or the possibility of damaging the generator if ac power is restored.

with generators than from any other cause. A generator should never be operated in an enclosed space or basement, or even a garage, where people are present or nearby. Install it outdoors, away from living areas, as shown in **Figure 9.6**. Carbon monoxide (CO) in the exhaust can quickly build up to toxic levels. (For more information about CO safety, visit **www.epa. gov/iaq/pubs/coftsht.html.**) Even outside, exhaust fumes can be drawn into air intakes or windows or build up in poorly ventilated areas. If you plan on using a generator regularly, install CO detector alarms in living and working areas. [G0B04, G0B15]

Flammable liquid fuels pose their own hazards. Generators should always be shut off when refueling to avoid igniting fumes or splashed liquid from the spark plug. Even if the generator engine is shut off, the engine block or exhaust may remain hot enough to pose an ignition hazard. Refueling should be done by a team of two, with one person equipped with a fire extinguisher. Store fuel well away from the generator, particularly from its hot exhaust, in approved containers. A fire extinguisher should be kept near the generator and separated from the fuel.

The metal frames of the generator housing and the engine act as an electrical ground, but they are not physically connected to the Earth. The best way to provide a generator safety ground is to use a ground rod near the generator and connected to the frame with heavy gauge wire. Most generators provide a special ground terminal just for this purpose.

If the generator is to be used at your home, connecting it to your household circuits requires special precautions. If you intend to connect the generator output directly to your home's wiring system, you must have the ability to disconnect your power service from the utility lines. [G0B13] This is usually accomplished by a pair of large circuit breakers labeled "Main." Opening these breakers completely disconnects your power distribution panel from the external electrical service. With these breakers open, you can then safely use a generator to power your home.

By not opening the main breakers, power supplied to your home's system is also connected back to the utility grid. The power system transformer that normally supplies your home works just as well in reverse — the voltage from your generator will be stepped up to lethal levels and placed on the utility lines. Known as *back-feeding*, this poses a serious hazard to electrical workers working on the system and to neighbors whose homes are likely still connected to the power system. If your generator is connected and running when power is restored, the resulting conflict between the utility and generator power is likely to cause damage to your generator.

The best way to connect a generator to your home is by using a *transfer switch* that transfers the power source for your distribution panel from the utility lines to a special connector for your generator. Once the transfer switch is thrown, the power from your generator is connected only to your home's wiring and nothing else. The type of transfer switch in **Figure 9.7** switches selected household circuits between the ac line and the generator. A transfer switch should be installed by a licensed professional electrician.

LIGHTNING

The goal of lightning protection is to provide fire prevention for your home and to reduce or prevent electrical damage to your equipment. The best protection is to disconnect all cables outside the house and unplug equipment power cords inside the house *before* a storm. Don't forget that ac power lines, telephone and computer wiring can also conduct lightning.

When installing your station, a metal entry panel where signal and control cables enter the house is a good place to provide a lightning ground (see **Figure 9.8**). The panel should be grounded to a nearby ground rod with a heavy, short metal strap. Lightning arrestors should be installed at the entry panel. The ground rod must then be connected to the ac service entry ground rod with a heavy bonded conductor.

Grounding wires and straps should be as short and direct as possible. All towers, masts and antenna mounts should be grounded. Lightning grounds should be bonded to other safety grounds. [G0B11] Do not use solder to make the connections since solder joints would likely be destroyed if hit with a lightning-sized current pulse. Use mechanical clamps, brazing, or welding to be sure the ground connection is heavy enough. [G0B09]

Finally, you should also determine whether your renter's or homeowner's insurance covers lightning damage. Be sure to check for coverage of "external structures" and other types of property improvements that may be recognized by the insurance underwriters.

Figure 9.8 — A metal entrance panel serves as a common grounding point for all cables and feed lines entering your home. The ground rod to which the panel is attached must also be connected to the ac service entry ground rod with a heavy bonding wire. This helps to prevent damage from lightning.

> *Before you go on, study test questions G0B01 to G0B06 and G0B09 to G0B15. Review this section if you have difficulty.*

9.2 RF Exposure

Exposure to RF at low levels is not hazardous. At high power levels, for some frequencies, the amount of energy that the body absorbs can be a problem. There are a number of factors to consider: power level or density, frequency, average exposure time, and duty cycle of the transmission. [G0A02] The two primary factors that determine how much RF the body will absorb are power density and frequency. This section discusses how to take into account the various factors and arrive at a reasonable estimate of what RF exposure results from your transmissions and whether any safety precautions are required.

Radiation

If there is a word guaranteed to cause apprehension, it is "radiation." Amateur Radio uses the word in a much broader sense — radiation pattern, feed line radiation, antennas radiate — and that can be confusing to the layman. It is true that radio frequency energy is a form of radiation, but it is far different from the radiation used for cancer treatment or emitted by radioactive materials.

Radiation from antennas is not the same as ionizing radiation from radioactivity. Radio frequencies are not nearly high enough for a photon of radio energy to cause an electron to leave the atom (ionize) as was discussed in the earlier section on ionospheric propagation. That is the difference between *ionizing* and *non-ionizing radiation* of which radio waves are the latter type.

Before radio waves can be considered ionizing, their frequency would have to be increased far beyond microwaves, through visible light and on to the upper reaches of the ultraviolet and x-ray spectrum. The radiation from radioactivity is atomic particles such as the nucleus of a helium atom (alpha radiation), an electron (beta radiation), neutrons, or gamma-ray photons with frequencies even higher than X-rays. These are billions of times more energetic than the radio waves used by amateurs.

Biologic (athermal) effects such as genetic damage have never been observed at amateur frequencies and power levels. That requires the energy of ionizing radiation. The only demonstrated hazard from exposure to RF energy is heating (thermal effects) and that occurs only in very strong fields. RF "burns" are caused by touching conducting surfaces that have a high RF voltage present and are a very localized instance of heating that carries no more risk than thermal burns from hot objects.

POWER DENSITY

Heating from exposure to RF signals is caused by the body tissue absorbing RF energy. [G0A01] The intensity of the RF energy is called *power density* and it is measured in mW/cm^2 (milliwatts per square centimeter), which is power per unit of area. For example, if the power density in an RF field is 10 mW/cm^2 and your hand's surface area is 75 cm^2, then when exposed to that RF field, your hand is exposed to a total of 10 × 75 = 750 mW of RF power. RF field strengths can also be measured in V/m and A/m, but mW/cm^2 is the most useful for amateur requirements.

Power density is highest near antennas and in the directions in which antennas have the most gain. Increasing transmitter power increases power density around the antenna. Increasing distance from an antenna lowers power density.

ABSORPTION AND LIMITS

The rate at which energy is absorbed from the power to which the body is exposed is called the *specific absorption rate* (SAR). SAR is the best measure of RF exposure for amateur operators. The SAR varies with frequency, power density, average amount of exposure, and the duty cycle of transmission. Injury is only caused when the combination of frequency and power cause too much energy to be absorbed in too short a time.

SAR depends on the frequency and the size of the body or body part affected and is highest where the body and body parts are naturally resonant. The limbs (arms and legs) and torso experience the highest SAR for RF fields in the VHF spectrum from 30 to 300 MHz. The head is most sensitive at UHF frequencies from 300 MHz to 3 GHz and the eyes are most affected by microwave signals above 1 GHz. The frequencies with highest SAR are between 30 and 1500 MHz. At frequencies above and below the ranges of highest absorption, the body responds less

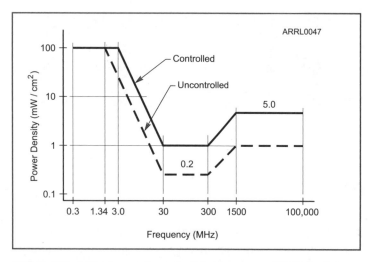

Figure 9.9 — Maximum Permissible Exposure (MPE) limits vary with frequency because the body responds differently to energy at different frequencies. The controlled and uncontrolled limits refer to the environment in which people are exposed to the RF energy.

Table 9.3
Maximum Permissible Exposure (MPE) Limits

Controlled Exposure (6-Minute Average)

Frequency Range (MHz)	Power Density (mW/cm²)
0.3-3.0	(100)*
3.0-30	(900/f²)*
30-300	1.0
300-1500	f/300
1500-100,000	5

Uncontrolled Exposure (30-Minute Average)

Frequency Range (MHz)	Magnetic Field Power Density (mW/cm²)
0.3-1.34	(100)*
1.34-30	(180/f²)*
30-300	0.2
300-1500	f/1500
1500-100,000	1.0

* = Plane-wave equivalent power density.
f = frequency in MHz

and less to the RF energy, just like an antenna responds poorly to signals away from its natural resonant frequency.

Safe levels of SAR based on demonstrated hazards have been established for amateurs by the FCC in the form of *Maximum Permissible Exposure* (MPE) limits that vary with frequency as shown in **Figure 9.9** and **Table 9.3**. These take into account the variations in the body's sensitivity to RF energy at different frequencies.

AVERAGING AND DUTY CYCLE

Exposure to RF energy is averaged over fixed time intervals because the body responds differently to heating for short duration and long duration exposures. Time-averaging evaluates the total RF exposure over a fixed time interval. [G0A04]

Controlled and Uncontrolled Environments

Because of variations in the time a person might be exposed to RF, there are two types of averaging periods: one for *controlled* and another for *uncontrolled environments*. People in controlled environments are considered to be aware of their exposure and are expected to take reasonable steps to minimize exposure. Examples of controlled environments are transmitting facilities (including Amateur Radio stations) and near antennas. In a controlled environment, access is restricted to authorized and informed individuals. The people expected to be in controlled environments would be station employees, licensed amateurs, and the families of licensed amateurs.

Uncontrolled environments are areas in which the general public has access, such as public roads and walkways, homes and schools, and even unfenced personal property. People in uncontrolled environments are not aware of their exposure, but are much less likely to receive continuous exposure. As a result, RF power density limits are higher for controlled environments and the averaging period is longer for uncontrolled environments. The averaging period is 6 minutes for controlled environments and 30 minutes for uncontrolled environments.

Duty Cycle

Duty cycle is the ratio of the time the transmitter is on to the total time during the exposure. Duty cycle has a maximum of 100%. (*Duty factor* is the same as duty cycle expressed as a fraction, instead of percent, such as 0.25 instead of 25%.) The lower the transmission duty cycle (the less time the transmitter is on), the lower the average exposure. A lower transmission duty cycle permits greater short-term exposure levels for a given average exposure. [G0A07] This is the *operating duty cycle*. For most amateur operating, listening and transmitting time are about the same, so operating duty cycle is rarely higher than 50%.

Along with operational duty cycle, the different modes themselves have different *emission duty cycles* as shown in **Table 9.4**. For example, a normal SSB signal without speech processing to raise average power is considered to have an emission duty cycle of 20%. In contrast, FM is a constant-power mode so its emission duty cycle is 100%. Transmitter

Table 9.4
Operating Duty Factor of Modes Commonly Used by Amateurs

Mode	Duty Cycle	Notes
Conversational SSB	20%	1
Conversational SSB	40%	2
SSB AFSK data	100%	
SSB SSTV	100%	
Voice AM, 50% modulation	50%	3
Voice AM, 100% modulation	25%	
Voice AM, no modulation	100%	
Voice FM	100%	
Digital FM	100%	
ATV, video portion, image	60%	
ATV, video portion, black screen	80%	
Conversational CW	40%	
Carrier	100%	4

Notes
1) Includes voice characteristics and syllabic duty factor. No speech processing.
2) Includes voice characteristics and syllabic duty factor. Heavy speech processing.
3) Full-carrier, double-sideband modulation, referenced to PEP. Typical for voice speech. Can range from 25% to 100% depending on modulation.
4) A full carrier is commonly used for tune-up purposes.

PEP multiplied by the emission duty cycle multiplied by the operating duty cycle gives the average power output.

Example 1: A station is using SSB without speech processing, transmitting and listening for equal amounts of time and with a PEP of 150 W. The average power output = 150 × 20% × 50% = 15 W.

Example 2: A station is sending a series of messages using SSB AFSK to transmit a digital signal at 100 W PEP, listening only ¼ of the time. The average power output = 100 × 75% × 100% = 75 W.

Antenna System

You must also take into account the amount of gain provided by your antenna and any significant losses from the feed line. High gain antennas increase a signal's average power considerably. For example, let's modify the two examples above by using an antenna with 6 dB of gain. In Example 1, the transmitter PEP is increased to 600 W by the antenna, increasing average power to 60 W. In Example 2, the same antenna would increase the average power to 300 W, larger than the transmitter PEP output.

Table 9.5
Power Thresholds for RF Exposure Evaluation

Band	Power (W)
160 meters	500
80	500
60	500
40	500
30	425
20	225
17	125
15	100
12	75
10	50
6	50
2	50
1.25	50
70 cm	70
33	150
23	200
13	250
SHF (all bands)	250
EHF (all bands)	250

• ESTIMATING EXPOSURE AND STATION EVALUATION

All fixed amateur stations must evaluate their capability to cause RF exposure, no matter whether they use high or low power. [G0A08] (Mobile and handheld transceivers are exempt from having to calculate exposure because they do not stay in one location.) A routine evaluation must then be performed if the transmitter PEP and frequency are within the FCC rule limits. The limits vary with frequency and PEP as shown in **Table 9.5**. You are required to perform the RF exposure evaluation only if your transmitter output power exceeds the levels shown for any band. For example, if your HF transmitter cannot output more than 25 W, you are exempt from having to evaluate exposure caused by it.

You can perform the evaluation by actually measuring the RF field strength with calibrated field strength meters and calibrated antennas. [G0A09] You can also use computer modeling to determine the exposure levels. However, it's easiest for most hams to use the tables provided by the ARRL (**www.arrl.org/rf-exposure**) or an online calculator, such the one listed on the ARRL website. [G0A03]

If you choose to use the ARRL tables or calculators, you will need to know:

• Power at the antenna, including adjustments for duty cycle and feed line loss

Multitransmitter Environments

In a multitransmitter environment, such as at a commercial repeater site, each transmitter operator may be jointly responsible (with all other site operators) for ensuring that the total RF exposure from the site does not exceed the MPE limits. Any transmitter (including the antenna) that produces more than 5% of the total permissible exposure limit for transmissions at that frequency must be included in the site evaluation. (This is 5% of the permitted power density or 5% of the square of the E or H-field MPE limit. It is *not* 5% of the total exposure, which sometimes can be unknown.) The situation described by this question is common for amateur repeater installations, which often share a transmitting site.

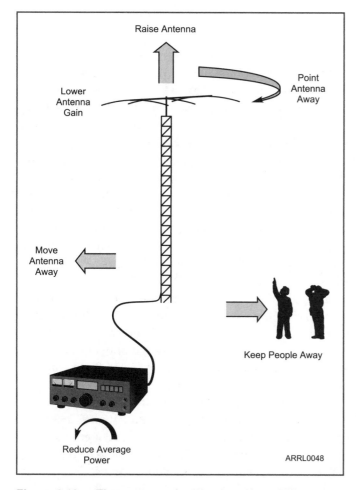

Figure 9.10 — There are many ways to reduce RF exposure to nearby people. Whatever lowers the power density in areas where people are present will work. Raising the antenna will even benefit your signal strength to other stations as it lowers power density on the ground!

- Antenna type (or gain) and height above ground
- Operating frequency

The ARRL tables are organized by frequency, antenna type and antenna height, and they show the distance required from the antenna to comply with MPE limits for certain levels of transmitter output power.

Exposure can be evaluated in one of two ways. The first way is to determine the power density at a known distance to see if exposure at that distance meets the MPE limit. The second way is to determine the minimum distance from your antenna at which the MPE limit is satisfied. Either way, the goal is to determine if your station meets MPE limits for all controlled and uncontrolled environments present at your station.

If you make changes to your station, such as changing to a higher power transmitter, increasing antenna gain or changing antenna height, you must re-evaluate the RF exposure from your station. If you reduce output power without making any other changes to a station already in compliance, you need not re-evaluate RF exposure.

EXPOSURE SAFETY MEASURES

The measures you can take if your evaluation results exceed MPE limits are summarized in **Figure 9.10**. These are all "good practice" suggestions and can save time and expense if they are followed before doing your evaluation. All of them satisfy the basic requirement to prevent human exposure to the excessive RF fields. [G0A05]

- Locate or move antennas away from where people can be exposed to excessive RF fields. Raise the antenna or place it away from where people will be. Keep the ends (high voltage) and center (high current) of antennas away from where people could come in contact with them. Locate the antenna away from property lines and place a fence around the base of ground-mounted antennas. [G0A06]

- Don't point gain antennas where people are likely to be. Use beam antennas to direct the RF energy away from people. [G0A10] Remember that high-gain antennas have a narrower beam, but exposure in the beam will be more intense. Take special care with high-gain VHF/UHF/ microwave antennas (such as long Yagis and dish antennas) and transmitters — don't transmit when you or other people are close to the antenna or when the antenna is pointed close to the horizon.

• If you have to use stealth or attic or other indoor antennas, make sure MPE limits are not exceeded in your home's living quarters. [G0A11]

• On VHF and UHF, place mobile antennas on the roof or trunk of the car to maximize shielding of the passengers. Use a remote microphone to hold a handheld transceiver away from your head while transmitting.

• From the transmitter's perspective, use a dummy load or dummy antenna when testing a transmitter. You can also reduce the power and duty cycle of your transmissions. This is often quite effective and has a minimal effect on your signal.

Before you go on, study test questions G0A01 to G0A11. Review this section if you have difficulty.

9.3 Outdoor Safety

Focusing on electrical safety associated with wiring and equipment is certainly justified, but there are many components of an Amateur Radio station outside the shack, as well. Outdoor safety involves mostly mechanical concerns that can be just as important as electrical safety indoors. A complete treatment of antenna and antenna support safety is available in the *ARRL Antenna Book*.

INSTALLING ANTENNAS

The most important rule for installing antennas is violated every year, usually with tragic results: *Place all antennas and feed lines well clear of power lines!* Poles and transmission lines like those in **Figure 9.11** are a common sight and must be given wide clearance. Safety rules dictate that no part of your antenna system should be closer than 10 feet from power lines and a good rule of thumb is to separate all parts of the antenna and support from the power lines by at least 150% of total height of tower or mast plus antenna. For example, if the combination of antenna and support mast is 40 feet tall, they should be 60 feet from the power lines. This effectively prevents an antenna from toppling over or blowing into power lines. Similarly, should a power line come down, it will have plenty of clearance from your antenna.

Speaking of power lines, don't run feed lines over power lines or service drops from a transformer to the house. Even though they are "just" 240 V ac lines, they pack plenty of punch! If you are shooting lines through or over trees to support a wire antenna, be sure the projected flight path is completely safe and clear of people and power lines. Power lines can be hidden in or just beyond trees!

Once the antenna is up, people should not be able to come in contact with it. Place a fence around a ground-mounted antenna if there is a chance that people could come in contact with the antenna while you are transmitting. This also helps reduce RF exposure and reduces the chance of your antenna being knocked over.

Perhaps the most ignored safety advice is to follow the manufacturer's directions! Read the directions thoroughly

Figure 9.11 — Utility poles and power lines must be given wide clearance from your antenna system.

before starting the job. The manufacturer wants you to have good results from their product and for you to be able to install it safely. Make sure you understand every step and that every part is on hand. When the mast is halfway up or the antenna is pulled up to the top of the tower is no time to discover that you didn't really understand the instructions or that a crucial part is missing!

TOWERS, MASTS AND HARDWARE

To increase range and reduce interference, a tower or mast is used to raise antennas above buildings and other obstructions. A fixed-length pipe mast of up to 20 feet is the simplest method of raising small antennas, such as ground planes or small directional antennas. Telescoping push-up masts for TV antennas can hold small amateur antennas. They are available up to 40 feet in height and require guy lines.

If the mast or tower requires guying, keep all lines and guys above head height wherever possible. If the guy anchor is low to the ground, flag or fence guy lines where they are lower than head height.

Building permits are generally required for lattice, crank-up and tilt-over towers. When erecting a tower near an airport, be sure to comply with FCC and FAA rules about maximum structure height near an airport. Make sure you follow grounding rules for external metal structures. Check with your local building codes. Towers should be grounded with separate 8-foot ground rods for each tower leg, with the ground rods bonded to the tower and each other.

PERFORMING ANTENNA AND TOWER MAINTENANCE

Once you have the antenna and mast or tower up, regular maintenance is not something to scrimp on. You'll probably be experimenting with new antennas, as well. Whether you're climbing a tree, your roof or a tower, following basic safety rules will get the job done properly and without risking life and limb. Ignore that little voice saying, "Oh, I can just run up there in five minutes and do the job — why go to all the bother?"

First, both the climbers and ground crew should wear appropriate protective gear at all times. The climber must have a proper safety belt, or better yet a harness such as the one shown in **Figure 9.12**. Other needed gear includes a hard hat, gloves, sun block and even goggles. Wear boots or work shoes to protect your feet and prevent sore arches from standing on tower rungs for extended periods. Plan for extra time on the job to handle the unexpected chores.

The ground crew is an important part of the team. Round up enough crew to do the job safely. If you don't have enough people, postpone the work. With everybody present and paying attention, review the job in detail and agree on who gives instructions. Make sure you can communicate clearly. Handheld unlicensed FRS radios or ham radios are a lot easier to use than yelling and pointing. If you're going to use hand signals, make sure everybody understands them and uses the same ones!

Before climbing or starting work, run through a safety checklist every time:
- Inspect all tower guying and support hardware.
- Crank-up towers must be fully nested and blocked.
- Double-check all belts and lanyards.
- Inspect all ropes and load-bearing hardware such as pulleys.
- Secure all electrical and RF equipment. Transmitters should be off and disconnected from the feed line to avoid shock or excessive RF exposure. Turn off and unplug all ac equipment, locking the circuits out and tagging them if possible (**Figure 9.13**). [G0A12, G0B08]
- Check the weather report and don't be caught on the tower in a storm!

Figure 9.12 — A harness specifically designed for tower climbing makes working on the tower more comfortable as well as providing essential safety features.

Figure 9.13 — Before working on a tower or antenna, disconnect and if possible lock out the ac power circuits for your radio equipment.

As you are climbing up or down, remember to take your time — it's not a race! Be sure your climbing gear is fully secure:

● Belts and harnesses must be within their service life and adequately rated for weight [G0B07]

● Carabiners should be completely closed

● Always use a safety lanyard or redundant lanyards

And remember that often forgotten rule to follow the manufacturer's directions!

> *Before you go on, study test questions G0A12, G0B07 and G0B08. Review this section if you have difficulty.*

Chapter 9

Electrical and RF Safety

Absorption — The dissipation of the energy of a radio wave as it travels through a medium such as the ionosphere.

Accredited — Formally recognized and qualified by a **VEC**.

Active — A device that amplifies, switches or changes the characteristics of a signal and which usually requires a source of power to operate.

Adapters — Special connectors that convert one style of connector to another.

AFSK (see **FSK**)

Air core — An inductor without any magnetic material in its core.

Air link — That part of a digital communications system implemented using radio transmission and reception.

Allocation — The assignment of frequencies or other privileges to a particular service.

Alternating current (ac) — Electrical current that flows first in one direction and then in the other. The applied voltage is also changing polarity. This direction reversal continues at a rate that depends on the frequency of the ac.

Amateur Auxiliary — A formally-organized amateur group that supports the FCC with enforcement issues.

Amateur Radio Emergency Service (ARES) — Sponsored by the ARRL and provides emergency communications by working with groups such as the American Red Cross and local Emergency Operations Centers.

Amateur television (ATV) — A wideband TV system that uses commercial transmission standards. ATV is only permitted on the 70 cm band (420 to 450 MHz) and higher frequencies.

American Radio Relay League (ARRL) — The national association for Amateur Radio in the United States.

Ammeter — A test instrument that measures current.

Ampacity — A wire's current rating.

Ampere (A) — The basic unit of electrical current, also abbreviated **amp**. Current is a measure of the electron flow through a circuit. 1 ampere is the flow of 1 **coulomb** per second.

Amplifier — A device or piece of equipment used to increase the strength of a signal, called *amplification*.

Amplitude modulated (AM) phone — Radiotelephone (phone) transmission in which voice signals modulate the carrier. Most AM transmission is *double-sideband* (AM-DSB) in which the signal is composed of two sidebands and a carrier. Shortwave broadcast stations use this type of AM as do stations in the Standard Broadcast Band (535-1710 kHz). The most popular form of AM phone on the amateur bands is **single sideband (SSB)** although AM-DSB is used by amateurs who enjoy the mode's characteristics.

Amplitude modulation (AM) — The process of adding information to a signal or *carrier* by varying its amplitude characteristics.

Analog (linear) — Circuits or devices that operate over a continuous range of voltage and current.

Analog signals — A signal (usually electrical) that can have any amplitude (voltage or current) value and whose amplitude can vary smoothly over time. When referring to a communications **mode**, refers to **modulation** in which the modulating signal is an analog signal. Also see **digital signals** and **digital communications**.

Analog-to-digital converter (ADC) — A circuit that converts an analog signal to a digital value. (see also **Digital-to-analog converter**)

Angle modulation — Modulation by varying a signal's phase angle. (see also **Frequency modulation** and **Phase modulation**)

Anode — In semiconductor diodes and vacuum tubes (the **plate**) the electrode to which electrons flow during conduction.

Antenna — A device that radiates or receives radio frequency energy.

Antenna analyzer — Test equipment that contains a low-power **signal generator**, **frequency counter**, and impedance measuring circuit; used for measuring the impedance characteristics of antennas and transmission lines.

Antenna switch — A switch used to connect one transmitter, receiver or transceiver to several different antennas.

Antenna tuner — A device that matches the antenna system input impedance to the transmitter, receiver or transceiver output impedance. Also called an *antenna coupler*, *antenna-matching network* or *unit (ATU), impedance matcher* or *transmatch*.

Antipode — Location at the diametrically opposite point on the Earth's surface.

ARQ mode — Automatic Repeat reQuest; a digital mode that returns ACK (OK) or NAK (not OK) messages based on error checking so that corrupted data can be retransmitted.

Array — An antenna that uses more than one element to direct radiated energy in a specific direction. A *driven array* is one in which all elements receive power via a feed line from the transmitter. A *parasitic array* is one in which at least one element picks up and re-radiates power without a direct connection to the transmitter.

Attenuation — To reduce the strength of a signal.

Audio frequency shift keying (AFSK) — Frequency shift keying (FSK) performed by modulating the transmitter with audio tones.

Automatic gain control (AGC) — Receiver circuitry used to maintain a constant audio output level.

Automatic level control (ALC) — Transmitter circuitry that prevents excessive modulation of an AM or SSB signal.

Automatic operation — A station being operated under the control of a computer or other device, also known as **automatic control**.

Average forward current (I_F) — The maximum average current that a rectifier is rated to carry.

Back-feeding — Supplying electrical power to the utility grid through a home power distribution panel when using a generator.

Back light — Illuminating a display from behind.

Backscatter — (see **Scatter modes**)

Balun — Contraction of "balanced to unbalanced." A device to couple a balanced load to an unbalanced feed line or device, or vice versa.

Band plan — Voluntary organization of communications activity on a frequency band.

Bandwidth — (1) Bandwidth describes a range of frequencies occupied by a signal. (2) FCC Part 97 defines bandwidth for regulatory purposes as "The width of a frequency band outside of which the mean power is attenuated at least 26 dB below the mean power of the transmitted signal within the band." [§97.3 (8)]

Balanced (feed line) — See **parallel-conductor feed line**.

Battery — A device that converts chemical energy into electrical energy.

Battery chemistry — The type of chemicals used to store energy in a battery.

Battery pack — A package of several individual batteries connected together (usually in series to provide higher voltages) and treated as a single battery.

Baud (also **bauds**) — The rate at which individual data symbols are transmitted (see also **symbol rate**).

Beacon station — An amateur station transmitting communications for the purposes of observation of propagation and reception or other related experimental activities.

Beam antenna — A directional antenna. A beam antenna must be rotated to provide coverage in different directions.

Beamwidth — The angle between the points in the main lobe at which gain is 3 dB less than the maximum value.

Bias — An applied voltage to a circuit or component. *Forward bias* causes current to flow. *Reverse bias* prevents current from flowing.

Binary data (number) — Information represented by 1s and 0s. A binary number consists entirely of 1s and 0s representing powers of 2.

Bipolar transistor — (See **Transistor**).

Birdie — An unwanted receiver response to an internal signal.

Bit rate — The rate at which digital bits are carried by a transmitted signal.

Bleeder resistor — A high-value resistor that discharges a filter capacitor when power is removed.

BNC connector — A type of connector for RF signals.

Boom — The central support of an **array** antenna.

Break-in — Switching rapidly between transmit and receive so that signals can be heard between keying elements (*full break-in* or *QSK*) or words (*semi-break-in*).

Breaking in — Interrupting an ongoing contact to join the conversation or contribute to the discussion.

Bridge — A circuit with two parallel current paths and a path between the midpoints of the two paths. In a *bridge rectifier*, ac voltage is applied to rectifier diodes that make up the parallel current paths and dc voltage is obtained across the midpoints of the parallel paths.

Buffer — An amplifier intended to isolate a circuit from loads connected to its output.

Call district — The ten administrative areas established by the FCC.

Calling frequency — A frequency on which amateurs establish contact before moving to a different frequency. Usually used by hams with a common interest or activity.

Capacitance (C) — The ability of a **capacitor** to store energy in an **electric field**.

Capacitor — An electrical component usually formed by separating two conductive plates with an insulating material. A capacitor stores energy in an **electric field**.

Carrier — A steady, single-frequency signal that is modulated to add an information signal to be transmitted. For example, a voice signal added to a carrier produces a **phone emission** signal.

Cathode — In semiconductor diodes and vacuum tubes, the electrode from which electrons flow during conduction.

Cathode-ray tube (CRT) — A vacuum tube with a flat, phosphor coated face used for visual displays. *Deflection plates* in the tube use varying voltage created by *channel amplifiers* to steer an electron beam across the tube's face, creating a visible *trace*, while a *time base* controls the timing of the beam.

Center tapped — A transformer winding that is split into two equal halves with a connection (tap) at the center point.

Centi (or lower case **c**) — The metric prefix for 10^{-2}, or divide by 100.

Certificate of Successful Completion of Examination (CSCE) — A document that verifies that an individual has passed one or more exam elements. A CSCE is good for 365 days and may be used as evidence of having passed an element at any other amateur license exam session.

Changeover relay (see **Transmit-receive relay**)

Characteristic impedance — The ratio of RF voltage and current for power flowing in a feed line.

Chassis ground — The common connection for all parts of a circuit that connect to the metal enclosure of the circuit. Chassis ground is usually connected to the negative side of the power supply.

Checksum — A general term for an algorithm that allows the receiving system to detect errors in transmitted data. A *Cyclical Redundancy Check (CRC)* is a strong type of checksum.

Chip (see **Integrated circuit**)

Choke — An inductance used to resist or "choke off" ac current flow. An inductor used in a power supply to reduce **ripple** is called a *filter choke* and a power supply filter that uses inductors as the primary means of reducing **ripple** is a *choke filter.*

Circuit — Any path in which **current** can flow.

Class A — Amplifier operation in which the amplifying device is active during the entire cycle of the signal.

Class AB — Amplifier operation in which the amplifying device is active for between one-half of and the entire signal cycle.

Class B — Amplifier operation in which the amplifying device is active for one-half of the signal's cycle. Also known as *push-pull* if two amplifying devices operating in Class B are combined in a single circuit.

Class C — Amplifier operation in which the amplifying device is only active during a fraction of the cycle.

Clock — In a digital circuit, a signal that synchronizes circuit operation.

CMOS (complementary metal oxide semiconductor) — A popular type of low-power digital logic circuit.

Coaxial cable — Coax (pronounced kó-aks). A type of feed line with one conductor inside the other and both sharing a concentric central axis.

Combination logic — Digital circuits with an output determined solely by the current state of the input signals.

Common-mode — Currents that flow equally on all conductors of a multiconductor cable, such as speaker wires or telephone cables, or on the outside of shielded cables, such as coaxial or twisted-pair.

Composite signal — A signal composed of one or more *component* signals.

Conductor — A material whose electrons move freely in response to voltage, so an electrical current can pass through it.

Constant power — A signal whose power is constant, regardless of modulation, such as FM or PM.

Continuous wave (CW) — Radio communications transmitted by on/off keying of a continuous radio-frequency signal. Another name for international Morse code.

Controlled environment — Any area in which an RF signal may cause radiation exposure to people who are aware of the radiated electric and magnetic fields and who can exercise some control over their exposure to these fields. The FCC generally considers amateur operators and their families to be in a controlled RF exposure environment to determine the maximum permissible exposure levels.

Conventional current — Current in which the moving particles are assumed to be positively charged, the opposite of **electronic current**.

Conversion — The process of converting a signal from one frequency to another by a receiver. A *single-conversion* receiver has a single conversion step, a *double-conversion* two steps, and so forth.

Conversion efficiency — The percentage of solar energy that is converted to electricity by a solar cell.

Coordinated repeater — A repeater system whose input and output frequencies are approved by the regional frequency coordination organization.

Coordinator (see **Frequency coordinator**)

Corona ball — A round ball placed at the tip of **whip** antennas to prevent high-voltage discharge.

Coronal hole (mass ejection) — Small or large-scale ejections of plasma through the Sun's corona

Coulomb (C) — The basic unit of charge. 1 coulomb is the quantity of 6.25×10^{18} electrons. 1 ampere equals the flow of 1 coulomb of electrons per second.

Counter — A circuit that accumulates a total number of events or a device that displays the frequency of an input signal.

Coupling — The sharing or transfer of energy between two components or circuits.

CRC (see **Checksum**)

Clipping — Overmodulating an AM signal so that the envelope reaches the maximum or minimum value for an extended period. Also known as *flat-topping*.

Critical angle — The largest angle at which a radio wave of a specified frequency can be returned to a specific point on Earth by the ionosphere.

Critical frequency — The highest frequency for which a signal transmitted straight up is returned to Earth.

Cross-band — Able to receive and transmit on different amateur frequency bands. For example, a cross-band repeater might retransmit on 2 meters a signal received on 70 cm.

Current (I) — The flow of electrons in an electrical circuit.

Current gain (beta) — The control of a large collector-emitter current by a small base-emitter current, numerically equal to the ratio of collector-emitter current to base-emitter current. Beta (β) is the symbol for dc current gain. h_{fe} is the symbol for ac current gain.

Cutoff — The point at which current flow in a transistor or vacuum tube is reduced to zero.

CW (Morse code) — Radio communications transmitted by on/off keying of a continuous radio-frequency signal. Another name for international Morse code.

Cycle — One complete repetition of an **ac** waveform.

D region — The lowest region of the ionosphere. The D region (or layer) contributes very little to short-wave radio propagation. It acts mainly to absorb energy from radio waves as they pass through it.

Data modes — see **digital communications**

Decibel (dB) — In electronics decibels are used to express ratios of power, voltage, or current. One dB = 10 log (power ratio) or 20 log (voltage or current ratio). The smallest change in sound level that can be detected by the human ear is approximately 1 dB.

Deci (or lower case **d**) — The metric prefix for 10^{-1}, or divide by 10.

Delta loop antenna — A variation of the **quad antenna** with triangular elements.

Demodulate or **demodulation** — Recovering information from a **modulated** signal.

Detector — The stage in a receiver in which the modulation (voice or other information) is recovered from the RF signal without reversing the process of modulation (*detection*). An *envelope detector* recovers information from an AM signal's **envelope**.

Deviation — The change in frequency of an FM carrier due to a modulating signal.

Dielectric — The insulating material that separates the two conducting surfaces of a capacitor and in which electrical energy is stored.

Diffract — To alter the direction of a radio wave as it passes by the edges of obstructions such as buildings or hills.

Digital (logic) — Circuits or devices that operate with discrete values of voltage and current. A *digital logic family* is a group of digital circuits with a common set of characteristics.

Digital communication (digital mode) — Computer-to-computer communication, such as by **packet radio** or **radioteletype (RTTY)**, which transmit and receive digital information.

Digital signal — (1) A signal (usually electrical) that can only have certain specific amplitude values, or steps — usually two; 0 and 1 or ON and OFF. (2) On the air, a digital signal is the same as a **digital mode** or **digital communication**.

Digital-to-analog converter (DAC) — A circuit that converts a digital value to an analog signal. (see also **Analog-to-digital converter**)

Digital signal processing (DSP) — The process of converting an **analog signal** to **digital** form and using a microprocessor to process the signal in some way such as filtering or reducing noise.

Diode — An electronic component that allows electric current to flow in only one direction.

Dipole — From "two electric polarities", an antenna consisting of a straight conductor approximately ½ wavelength long and fed in the middle. An *off-center fed dipole* (OCF) has a feed point away from the center. (see also **Doublet**)

Direct current (dc) — Electrical current that flows in one direction only.

Direct digital synthesis (DDS) — The technique of creating a signal with a rapid sequence of digital signal values.

Direct pickup — A type of **RF interference** caused by a device's internal wiring receiving the interfering signal directly.

Directional antenna — An antenna with **gain** in one or more preferred directions.

Directional wattmeter — An RF power meter that can measure both forward and reflected power in a transmission line (also see **wattmeter**).

Director — A parasitic element in front of the driven element in a directional antennas.

Discriminator — A type of **detector** used in some FM receivers. Also known as a *frequency discriminator*.

Display (visual) — A device that is capable of presenting text or graphics information in visual form.

Doping — Adding impurities (*dopants*) to semiconductor material in order to control its electrical properties.

Doublet — A general term for a center-fed antenna similar to a dipole but which is generally non-resonant.

Driven array (see **Array**)

Driven element — The part of an antenna that connects directly to the feed line.

Driver — An amplifier that brings low-power signals to a level suitable to drive a power amplifier to full power output.

Dummy antenna or **dummy load** — A station accessory that allows you to test or adjust transmitting equipment without sending a signal out over the air.

Duty cycle — A measure of the amount of time a transmitter is operating at full output power during a single transmission. A lower duty cycle reduces **RF radiation** exposure for the same PEP output. *Duty factor* is the same as duty cycle expressed as a fraction instead of in percent. *Emission duty cycle* includes the transmission characteristics associated with a particular mode. *Operating duty cycle* includes the transmit/receive behavior associated with a particular and style of communication.

DX — Distance, distant stations, foreign countries.

E region — The second lowest ionospheric region, the E region (or layer) exists only during the day. Under certain conditions, it may refract radio waves enough to return them to Earth.

Earth ground — A circuit connection to a ground rod driven into the Earth or to a metallic cold-water pipe that goes into the ground.

Effective radiated power (ERP) — The power level that would be required to be applied to a dipole to achieve the same signal strength in the direction of maximum radiation.

Electric field — An electric field exists in a region of space if an electrically charged object placed in the region is subjected to an electrical force.

Electrical potential — The amount of energy that would be acquired or given up by charge moving between two points in space. (see also **electromotive force**)

Electromagnetic wave — A wave of energy composed of electric and magnetic fields.

Electromotive force (EMF) — The force that causes electrons to move, creating current through a circuit. The unit of EMF is the **volt**.

Electron — A tiny, negatively charged particle, normally found in the volume surrounding the nucleus of an atom.

Electronic current — The flow of electrons. (see also **Conventional current**)

Electronic keyer — A device that makes it easier to send well-timed Morse code. It sends a continuous string of either dots or dashes, depending on which lever of the *paddle* is pressed.

Element — (1) The conducting part or parts of an antenna designed to radiate or receive radio waves. (2) An electrode in a vacuum tube used to control the tube's operation.

Encapsulation — The process of packaging information from one protocol inside another.

Encoding — Changing the form of a signal into one suitable for storage or transmission. *Decoding* is the process of returning the signal to its original form.

Energy — The ability to do work; the ability to exert a force to move some object.

Envelope — The shape formed by the maximum values of the instantaneous amplitude of an **AM** signal.

Equalization (audio) — Adjusting the frequency response of a circuit or signal.

Equivalent — An electrically identical circuit or component.

Equivalent series resistance — A single **parasitic** resistance that accounts for all of a capacitor's losses.

Equivalent series inductance — A single **parasitic** inductance that accounts for all of the inductance exhibited by a capacitor.

Error correction (detection) — Techniques of detecting and correcting transmission errors in digital data.

F region — A combination of the two highest ionospheric regions (or layers), the F1 and F2 regions. The F region refracts radio waves and returns them to Earth. Its height varies greatly depending on the time of day, season of the year and amount of sunspot activity.

Farad (F) — The basic unit of capacitance.

FEC (Forward error correction) — A technique of sending redundant data so that common transmission errors can be corrected without retransmission.

Feedback — The technique of routing some fraction of an output signal back to the system's or circuit's input.

Feed line — The wires or cable used to connect a transmitter, receiver or transceiver to an antenna. The feed line connects to an antenna at its **feed point**. Also see **transmission line**.

Feed point — The point at which a feed line is electrically connected to an antenna.

Feed point impedance — The ratio of RF voltage to current at the feed point of an antenna.

FET (JFET) — See **Transistor**

Ferrite — A ceramic material that can store or dissipate magnetic energy. A ferrite core can be used to increase inductance and ferrite beads can be used to block RF current flow.

Field strength meter — A calibrated meter that measures the electric field strength of a transmitted signal.

Filter (network) — A circuit that will allow some signals to pass through it but will greatly reduce the strength of others.

Filter capacitor — A capacitor used to reduce **ripple** in a power supply.

Flat-topping (see **Clipping**)

Flip-flop — Digital circuit with two stable output states controlled by the sequence of input signals.

Form 605 — An FCC form that serves as the application for your Amateur Radio license, or for modifications to an existing license.

Forward power — The power traveling along a transmission line from the transmitter to the load or antenna.

Forward voltage — The voltage required to cause current to flow through a **PN junction**. The voltage at which current starts to flow is the *junction threshold*.

Frame — A single image in a video signal.

Free electron — An electron not bound to an atom.

Frequency — The number of complete cycles of an alternating current that occur per second.

Frequency band — A continuous range of frequencies. An **amateur band** is a frequency band in which amateur communications take place.

Frequency coordination — Allocating repeater input and output frequencies to minimize interference between repeaters and to other users of the band.

Frequency coordinator — An individual or group that recommends repeater frequencies to reduce or eliminate interference between repeaters operating on or near the same frequency in the same geographical area.

Frequency counter — Test equipment used to measure frequency. (see also **Counter**)

Frequency modulation (FM) — The process of adding information to an RF signal or *carrier* by varying its frequency.

Frequency shift keying (FSK) — Frequency shift keying in which different bit values are represented by different transmitted frequencies. *AFSK (audio FSK)* is created by inputting tones into the voice modulation circuitry of a voice-mode transmitter.

Front-to-back (front-to-side) ratio — The ratio in dB of an antenna's radiation in the main lobe to that in the directly opposite direction (at ±90° to the direction of maximum radiation).

Full-wave rectifier — A rectifier circuit that converts every half-cycle (360 degrees) of the input waveform to dc.

Fundamental (see **Harmonic**)

Fundamental overload — Overload of a receiver by the fundamental of a transmitted signal. (see also **Receiver overload**)

Gain — (1) Focusing of an antenna's radiated energy in one direction. Gain in one direction requires that gain in other directions is diminished. (2) The amount of amplification of a signal in a circuit. (3) A control that determines the amount of amplification by a piece of equipment, such as AF Gain (volume) or RF Gain (sensitivity).

Gain compression (blocking) — A reduction in gain due to the presence of strong signals.

Gamma match — A type of **impedance matching** structure used to transform the low impedance of an antenna's driven element to a higher value closer to that of standard feed lines.

Gate (logic) — A circuit that performs a specific logic function such as inversion, NOR, NAND, XOR, and so on.

Gateway — A station that transfers communications between Amateur Radio and commercial networks such as the Internet.

Geomagnetic field — The Earth's magnetic field. Disruption of the geomagnetic field can result in a *geomagnetic storm* that alters ionospheric propagation.

GFCI (or GFI) — Ground-fault interrupting circuit breaker that opens a circuit when an imbalance of current flow is detected between the hot and neutral wires of an ac power circuit.

Giga (or lower case **g**) — The metric prefix for 10^9, or multiply by 1,000,000,000.

Great circle — The direct path across the surface of the Earth between two points.

Grid-driven (cathode-driven) — Vacuum tube amplifier for which the input signal is applied to the control grid (cathode) of the amplifying tube.

Ground loop — A current path that connects two or more pieces of equipment in a loop in which voltage can be induced by RF or magnetic fields.

Ground rod — A copper or copper-clad steel rod that is driven into the earth. A heavy copper wire or strap connects all station equipment to the ground rod.

Ground plane — A conducting surface of continuous metal or discrete wires that acts to create an electrical image of an antenna. **Ground-plane antennas** require a ground-plane in order to operate properly.

Ground wave propagation — Propagation in which radio waves travel along the Earth's surface.

Half-wave rectifier — A rectifier circuit that converts every other half-cycle (180 degrees) of the input waveform to dc.

Harmful interference — Interference that seriously degrades, obstructs or repeatedly interrupts a radio communication service operating in accordance with the Radio Regulations. [§97.3 (a) (22)] (see also **malicious interference**)

Harmonic — Signals from a transmitter or oscillator occurring at integer multiples (2×, 3×, 4×, etc) of the original or **fundamental** frequency. Frequencies of signals at harmonics of a fundamental are *harmonically related*, such as 3.5, 7, 14, 21 and 28 MHz.

Header — The portion of a packet that contains information about the packet for routing or other control functions.

Henry (H) — The basic unit of inductance.

Hertz (Hz) — The basic unit of frequency. One hertz is the same as one cycle per second.

Heterodyne — Combining two signals in order to obtain signals at the sum and difference of the frequencies of the original signals.

Hop (see **Skip**)

Hot switching — Opening or closing relay or switch contacts while current is flowing through them, often a destructive practice.

Hum — Unwanted 60- or 120-Hz modulation of a RF signal due to inadequate filtering in a power supply. Also called *buzz*, particularly 120 Hz and higher frequency artifacts.

Image — An unwanted response by the receiver to signals that create **mixing products** at the same **IF** as desired signals.

Impedance (Z) — The opposition to electric current in a circuit. Impedance includes both reactance and resistance, and applies to both alternating and direct currents.

Impedance match — To adjust impedances to be equal or the case in which two impedances are equal. Usually refers to the point at which a feed line is connected to an antenna or to transmitting equipment. If the impedances are different, that is a *mismatch*.

Impedance matcher — (circuit) A circuit that transforms impedance from one value to another. Adjustable impedance matching circuits are used at the output of transmitters and amplifiers to allow maximum power output over a wide range of load impedances. (equipment) A device that matches one impedance level to another. For example, it may match the impedance of an antenna system to the impedance of a transmitter or receiver. (see also **Antenna tuner**)

Impedance transformer — A transformer designed specifically for transforming impedances in RF equipment.

Indicator — Characters added after a slash or other separating phrase at the end of a call sign to modify the license class or location implied by the call sign. For example, "portable AG" added after a call sign indicates that the operator has obtained General class privileges.

Indicator (visual) — A device that presents on/off information visually by the presence, absence, or color of light.

Inductance (L) — A measure of the ability of a coil to store energy in a *magnetic field*.

Inductor — An electrical component usually composed of a coil of wire wound on a central core. An inductor stores energy in a *magnetic field*.

Integrated circuit (IC) — Multiple semiconductor devices in a circuit created on a single substrate.

Inter-electrode capacitance — The capacitance between the elements of a vacuum tube.

Interference (constructive and destructive) — The reinforcement (constructive) or cancellation (destructive) of signals caused by their relative phase.

Intermediate frequency (IF) — The stages in a receiver that follow the input amplifier and mixer circuits. Most of the receiver's gain and selectivity are achieved at the IF stages.

Intermodulation — Two signals mixing together in a receiver circuit or non-linear contact in a strong RF field to produce mixing products that are received along with actual signals.

International Telecommunication Union (ITU) — The organization of the United Nations responsible for coordinating international telecommunications agreements.

Inversion — (digital) the function of changing 0 to 1 and vice-versa. An *inverter* is a circuit that performs inversion.

Ion (ionized) — An atom that is missing one or more electrons.

Ionizing radiation — Electromagnetic radiation that has sufficient energy to knock electrons free from their atoms, producing positive and negative ions. X-rays, gamma rays and ultraviolet radiation are examples of ionizing radiation. Radiation below this energy (such as RF waves) is called *non-ionizing radiation*.

Ionosphere — A region of electrically charged (ionized) gases high in the atmosphere. The ionosphere bends radio waves as they travel through it, returning them to Earth. Also see **sky-wave propagation**.

Isotropic antenna — An antenna that radiates and receives equally in all possible directions.

Jack — Connector intended to be mounted on equipment and into which a mating connector (the *plug* or *male*) is inserted. Also referred to as the *female* connector or a *receptacle*.

JFET — Junction FET (see **Transistor**)

Junction (see **PN junction**)

Junction capacitance (C_J) — The capacitance created by a PN junction.

Junction threshold (see **Forward voltage**)

Keyed connector — Connectors with a contact arrangement or body shape that only allows mating in one orientation.

Keyer or **electronic keyer** — A piece of equipment that generates Morse code automatically.

Kilo (or lower case **k**) — The metric prefix for 10^3, or multiply by 1000.

Kirchoff's Laws — Electrical laws that describe the distribution of voltage (Kirchoff's Voltage Law, KVL) and current (Kirchoff's Current Law, KCL) in electrical circuits.

Ladder line (feed line) — See **Parallel-conductor feed line**.

Lamination — Strips of metal in an inductor or transformer core.

LCD — Liquid crystal display.

LC circuit — A circuit made entirely from inductors (L) and capacitors (C).

LED — Light-emitting diode.

Limiter — A type of high-gain **IF amplifier** that strips all AM information from the signal, leaving only frequency variations.

Linear amplifier — Also known as a *linear*, a piece of equipment that amplifies the output of a transmitter, often to the full legal amateur power limit of 1500 W PEP.

Linear supply — A power supply that uses capacitor- or inductor-filter output circuits and a passive rectifier circuit.

Loading — The technique of increasing an antenna's electrical size by adding inductive (coils) or capacitive (capacity hats) reactance to the antenna. *Linear loading* folds the antenna back on itself to reduce physical size.

Local oscillator (LO) — An oscillator used to generate one of the input signals to a **mixer**.

Log — A record of a station's operation. In cases of interference-related problems, it can be used as supporting evidence and for troubleshooting.

Log periodic antenna — A frequency-independent antenna whose element dimensions and placement are arranged in a logarithmic pattern.

Logic (see **Digital**)

Long path — The longest of the two great circle paths between two stations.

Loop antenna — An antenna with element(s) constructed as continuous lengths of wire or tubing. A symmetrical square loop is called a *quad loop* and a symmetrical triangular loop is a *delta loop*.

Loss — A reduction in power, voltage, or current due to dissipation of energy. (see also **attenuation**).

Lower sideband (LSB) — (1) In an AM signal, the sideband located below the carrier frequency. (2) The common single-sideband operating mode on the 40, 80 and 160-meter amateur bands.

Magnetosphere — The interface between charged particles from the Sun (the *solar wind*) and the Earth's **geomagnetic field**.

Malicious (willful) interference — Intentional, deliberate obstruction of radio transmissions. (see also **Harmful interference**)

Match (impedance) — Equal impedance values

Maximum Power Transfer Theorem — The statement that the maximum energy can be transferred between a source and a load when the source and load impedances are equal.

Maximum useable frequency (MUF) — The highest-frequency radio signal that will reach a particular destination using **sky-wave propagation**, or *skip*. The MUF may vary for radio signals sent to different destinations.

Maximum permissible exposure (MPE) — The maximum intensity of RF radiation to which a human being may be exposed. FCC rules establish maximum permissible exposure values for humans to RF radiation. [§1.1310 and §97.13 (c)]

Mean — The average value.

Mega (or capital **M**) — The metric prefix for 10^6, or multiply by 1,000,000.

Memory bus — The interface between a microprocessor and memory devices that supports high-speed data transfer.

Micro (or **μ**) — The metric prefix for 10^{-6}, or divide by 1,000,000.

Microprocessor — An integrated circuit that contains all of the digital circuitry necessary to perform digital control and computing functions. A **microcontroller** is a microprocessor combined with circuitry designed to interface with external signal and control circuits.

Microwave — Radio waves or signals with frequencies greater than 1000 MHz (1 GHz). This is not a strict definition, just a conventional way of referring to those frequencies.

Milli (or lower case **m**) — The metric prefix for 10^{-3}, or divide by 1000.

Mismatch — A difference between the impedance of a load from the equipment or feed line to which it is connected.

Mixer — Circuitry that combines two signals and generates signals called *mixing products* at both their sum and difference frequencies.

Mode — The combination of a type of information and a method of transmission. For example, FM radiotelephony or *FM phone* consists of using FM modulation to carry voice information.

Modem — Short for *mo*dulator/*dem*odulator. A modem changes data into audio signals that can be transmitted by radio and demodulates a received signal to recover transmitted data.

Modulate or **modulation** — The process of adding information to an RF signal or *carrier* by varying its amplitude, frequency, or phase.

Modulation envelope — The waveform created by connecting the peak values of a modulated signal.

Monitor — Observe by listening or watching.

Morse code (see **CW**)

MOSFET — Metal-oxide semiconductor FET (see **Transistor**), also known as an insulated-gate FET (IGFET).

Multiband antenna — An antenna capable of operating on more than one amateur frequency band, usually using a single feed line.

Multihop propagation — Long-distance radio propagation using several skips or hops between the Earth and the ionosphere.

Multipath propagation — Propagation by multiple paths to a single receiver.

Multimeter — An electronic test instrument used to measure current, voltage and resistance in a circuit. Describes all meters capable of making these measurements, such as the *volt-ohm-milliammeter (VOM)* or *digital multimeter (DMM)*.

Multiplier — A circuit that creates a signal that is a **harmonic** of the input signal.

Mutual inductance — The ability of inductors to share or transfer energy through a common magnetic field

N or **Type N connector** — A type of RF connector.

National Electrical Code — A set of guidelines governing electrical safety, including antennas.

Near vertical incidence sky-wave (NVIS) — The use of high-angle radiation for local and regional communication.

Network — (1) A term used to describe several digital stations linked together to relay data over long distances. (2) A general term for any circuit or set of electrical connections.

Neutralization — The technique of preventing self-oscillation in an amplifier.

Noise reduction — Removing random noise from a receiver's audio output.

Nominal value — The rated amount of ohms, farads, henrys, or other electrical characteristics that a component is supposed to present to a circuit.

Nonionizing radiation — Electromagnetic radiation that does not have sufficient energy to knock electrons free from their atoms. Radio frequency (RF) radiation is nonionizing.

Notch filter — A filter that removes a very narrow range of frequencies, usually from a receiver's audio output to remove interfering tones. An *automatic notch filter (ANF)* can detect the presence of one or more such tones and adapt to remove them.

OCF Dipole (see **Dipole**) — Off-center fed dipole.

Ohm — The basic unit of electrical **resistance**.

Ohm's Law — A basic law of electronics. Ohm's Law states the relationship between voltage (E), current (I) and resistance (R). The voltage applied to a circuit is equal to the current through the circuit times the resistance of the circuit ($E = I \times R$).

Ohmmeter — A device used to measure resistance.

Omnidirectional — An antenna that radiates and receives equally in all horizontal directions.

Open circuit voltage — The voltage at the output of a circuit with no load connected.

Open-wire (feed line) — See **Parallel-conductor feed line**.

Optimization — Adjustment of design parameters for a circuit or antenna to improve performance.

Oscillate — To vibrate continuously at a single frequency. An **oscillator** is a device or circuit that generates a signal at a single frequency.

Oscillator — A circuit that produces a single frequency output signal. An *LC oscillator* uses inductors and capacitors to form a resonant circuit that determines the oscillator's frequency. A *crystal oscillator* replaces the LC circuit with a quartz crystal.

Oscilloscope — Test instrument that visually displays voltage versus time on a **cathode-ray tube**.

Overload (see **Receiver overload**)

Overdeviation (overmodulation) — Applying excessive modulation so that the recovered information is distorted or that distortion products create a modulated signal with an excessive bandwidth.

Paddle — Instrument with one or two lever-operated contacts for controlling an electronic **keyer** that generates Morse code automatically.

Parallel circuit — An electrical **circuit** in which the electrons may follow more than one path in traveling between the negative supply terminal and positive terminal.

Parallel-conductor line — A type of transmission line that uses two parallel wires spaced apart from each other by insulating material. Also known as *balanced, open-wire, ladder, or window line*.

Parallel interface — A data interface through which multiple bits of data are transferred at one time. A byte-wide interface transfers eight data bits in each operation.

Parasitic component — An unwanted characteristic of an electrical component whose effects are represented by a component of a different type, such as parasitic inductance of a resistor lead.

Parasitic element (see **Array**)

Parasitic (signal) — Unwanted signal generated by a circuit and not harmonically related to the circuit's input or output frequencies.

Parity bit — A bit that indicates whether there is an odd or even number of 1 bits in an encoded character.

Part 97 — The section of the FCC's rules that regulate Amateur Radio.

Passive — A device that functions without requiring a source of power.

Peak envelope power (PEP) — The average power of an RF signal during one complete cycle at the peak of a signal's modulation envelope.

Peak envelope voltage (PEV) — The voltage at the peak of a modulated signal's **envelope**.

Peak inverse (reverse) voltage (PIV) — The maximum reverse bias that a rectifier is rated to withstand.

Permeability — The ability of a material to contain magnetic energy.

Phase — A measure of position in time within a repeating waveform, such as a sine wave. Phase is measured in degrees or radians. There are 360 degrees or 2ϖ radians in one complete cycle.

Phase angle — The phase angle of a signal is a measure of the relative difference in phase between the signal and a reference signal or some point in time.

Phase-locked loop (PLL) — A circuit that adjusts the frequency of an oscillator to have the same phase as that of a reference circuit.

Phase modulation (PM) — The process of adding information to a signal by varying its **phase angle**.

Phone — Another name for voice communications. An abbreviation for *radiotelephone*.

Phone emission — The FCC name for voice or other sound transmissions.

Phone patch — Using radio to transmit and receive audio from the public telephone system.

Photovoltaic conversion — The direct conversion of sunlight to electricity.

Pi (π) — A mathematical constant approximately equal to 3.14159. The ratio of a circle's circumference to its diameter.

Pico (or lower case **p**) — The metric prefix for 10^{-12}, or divide by 1,000,000,000,000.

Plug (see **Jack**)

PN junction — The interface between two types of semiconductor material, forming a *junction diode*.

Polarity — The convention of assigning positive and negative directions or quantities. (see also **phase**)

Polarization — The orientation of the electrical-field of a radio wave with respect to the surface of the Earth. An antenna that is parallel to the surface of the Earth, such as a dipole, produces horizontally polarized waves. One that is perpendicular to the Earth's surface, such as a quarter-wave vertical, produces vertically polarized waves. An antenna that has both horizontal and vertical polarization is said to be *circularly polarized*.

Polarized capacitor — A capacitor to which dc voltage may only be applied with one polarity without damage (non-polarized capacitors are insensitive to the polarity of the applied voltage).

Powdered iron — Finely ground iron particles combined with an electrically inert material and used as a core for inductors at high frequencies.

Power — The rate of energy consumption or expenditure. Calculate power in an electrical circuit by multiplying the voltage applied to the circuit times the current through the circuit ($P = I \times E$).

Power amplifier (see **linear amplifier**)

Power (or **voltage** or **current**) **rating** — The rated ability of the component to withstand electrical stress.

Power density — The concentration of RF energy in a certain area.

Power resistor — A resistor designed to dissipate several watts of power or more.

Power supply — A circuit that provides a direct-current output at some desired voltage from an ac input voltage.

Preamplifier — An amplifier placed ahead of a receiver's input circuitry to increase the strength of a received signal.

Preselector — A filter at the input to a receiver to reject strong out-of-band signals.

Primary battery — A battery that can only be charged once and is discarded after it is discharged.

Primary service — When a frequency band is shared among two or more different radio services, the primary service is preferred. Stations in the **secondary service** must not cause harmful interference to, and must accept interference from stations in the primary service. [§97.303]

Product detector — A type of mixer circuit that allows a receiver to demodulate CW and SSB signals.

Propagation — The process through which radio waves travel.

Prosign — A Morse code character used to control contact flow or indicate status

Protocol — A method of encoding, packaging, exchanging, and decoding digital data.

Push to talk (PTT) — Turning a transmitter on and off manually with a switch, usually thumb- or foot-activated.

QRL — A Q-signal used to inquire if a channel is occupied or if an operator is busy.

QRM — Interference from other signals.

QRN — Interference from natural or man-made static or noise.

QRS — A Q-signal used to ask a station sending CW to send slower. **QRQ** means to speed up.

QSK — A Q-signal indicating a station can receive between individual dots and dashes, called "full break-in".

QSL (card) — QSL is a Q-signal meaning "received and understood." QSL cards or QSLs are postcards which serve as a confirmation of communication between two hams. The exchange of QSLs is *QSLing*.

Quad antenna — An antenna built with its elements in the shape of four-sided loops.

Quadrature detector (see **Discriminator**)

Radial — Wires connected to the feed point of a **ground-plane** antenna that act as an electrical mirror for the physical portion of the antenna.

Radiation pattern — A graph showing how an antenna radiates and receives in different directions. An *azimuthal pattern* shows radiation in horizontal directions. An *elevation pattern* shows how an antenna radiates and receives at different vertical angles. *Lobes* are regions in which the antenna radiates and receives and *nulls* are the minima between lobes. The strongest lobe is the *major lobe*.

Radio frequency (RF) exposure — FCC Rules establish maximum permissible exposure (MPE) values for humans to RF radiation. [§1.1310 and §97.13 (c)]

Radio-frequency interference (RFI) — Disturbance to electronic equipment caused by radio-frequency signals.

Radioteletype (RTTY) — Radio signals sent from one teleprinter machine to another machine using the *Baudot code* encoded as *mark* and *space* tones using. Also known as narrow-band direct-printing telegraphy.

Random access memory (RAM) — Computer memory whose locations can be read from or written to in any order.

Random wire (antenna) — An antenna of any length and generally connected directly to the transmitter or impedance matching device.

Range — The longest distance over which radio signals can be exchanged.

Rating — A maximum value of electrical stress to which a component can be subjected and still perform properly.

Reactance (X) — The opposition to ac current flow by a capacitor or inductor.

Read-only memory (ROM) — Stores data permanently and cannot be changed.

Receiver incremental tuning (RIT) — Adjustment of the receive frequency without changing the main tuning control.

Receiver overload — Interference to a receiver caused by a RF signal too strong for the receiver input circuits. A signal that overloads the receiver RF amplifier (front end) causes *front-end overload*. Receiver overload is sometimes called *RF overload*.

Rectification — The process of changing ac current into pulses of dc current.

Rectifier — (Circuit) A circuit that performs **rectification**. (Component) A diode intended for high current or voltage **rectification**. A *rectifier string* is several rectifiers connected in series to withstand reverse voltages higher than a single diode's **PIV** rating.

Reflected (reverse) power — The power flowing in a transmission from the antenna or load back towards the transmitter.

Reflector — A parasitic element behind the driven element in a directional antennas.

Refract — Bending of an electromagnetic wave as it travels through materials with different properties.

Region — One of the three administrative areas defined by the **ITU**; I — Europe and Africa, II — North and South America, and III — Asia and the Pacific.

Regulation — The ability to maintain a voltage or current at a specified level.

Reliable transport — A protocol capable of delivering only data in which no transmission errors have occurred within the limits of its error correction and detection mechanisms.

Re-radiation — Radiation from a parasitic antenna element resulting from energy received from a driven element.

Resistance (R) — Opposition to electric current in which some of the energy carried by the current is dissipated as heat.

Resistor — An electronic component specifically designed to oppose or control current through a circuit.

Resonance — (1) The frequency at which the maximum response of a circuit or antenna occurs. (2) The frequency at which a circuit's capacitive and inductive reactances are equal and cancel, leaving a purely resistive impedance.

Resonant frequency — The desired operating frequency of a tuned circuit. In an antenna, the resonant frequency is one at which the feed point impedance is composed only of resistance.

Reverse breakdown — Flow of current in the reverse direction across a **PN junction** due to excessive applied voltage.

RF burn — A burn produced by coming in contact with RF voltage.

RF feedback — Distortion caused by RF signals disturbing the function of an audio circuit.

RF safety — Preventing injury or illness to humans from the effects of radio-frequency energy.

Ring — The middle contact in a multiple-circuit phone-type connector between the *tip* contact at the end of the plug and the *sleeve* contact usually connected to circuit common or ground.

Ripple — Variations in power supply output voltage due to current pulses in a rectifier circuit.

Root mean square (RMS) — A measure of voltage of an ac signal that would deliver the same amount of power as a dc voltage of the same value. Root Mean Square refers to the method used to calculate the voltage.

Rotator — A device used to turn an antenna.

Rotor — A part of a device or motor that turns. (see **Rotator**)

S meter — A meter that provides an indication of the relative strength of received signals. The meter's calibration is in *S units* that are generally represent 5 to 6 dB changes in signal strength.

Safety interlock — A switch that automatically turns off power to a piece of equipment when the enclosure is opened.

Saturation — The point at which an increase in input signal results in no change in the output signal.

Scatter modes — HF propagation by means of multiple reflections in the layers of the atmosphere or from the ground (*backscatter*).

Secondary battery — A battery that can be recharged and reused (also known as a **storage battery**).

Secondary service or allocation — When a frequency band is shared among two or more different radio services, the **primary service** is preferred. Stations in the secondary service must not cause harmful interference to, and must accept interference from stations in the primary service. [§97.303]

Selectivity — The ability of a receiver to distinguish between signals. Selectivity is important when many signals are present and when it is desired to receive weak signals in the presence of strong signals.

Self policing — The practice of amateurs encouraging and assisting other amateurs to abide by FCC regulations.

Self-resonance — Resonance caused by the reactance from a component's parasitic reactance cancelling the component's intended reactance.

Self-discharge — The gradual loss of stored energy by a battery.

Sensitivity — The ability of a receiver to detect weak signals.

Sequential logic — Digital circuits with an output determined by the history of the input signal states.

Serial interface — A data interface through which data is transferred one bit at a time.

Series circuit — An electrical **circuit** in which all the electrons must flow through every part of the circuit because there is only one path for the electrons to follow.

Shack — Slang for a room or building containing an amateur's station.

Shielding — Surrounding an electronic circuit to block RF signals from being radiated or received.

Shift — In an AFSK or FSK signal, the difference between the tones that represent different bit values.

Shift register — Digital circuit that stores information as a sequence of internal states.

Short path — The shortest of the two great circle paths between two stations.

Sidebands — Signals adjacent to a **carrier** generated by the process of **modulation**.

Signal diode (switching diode) — A diode designed for use with low power signals that operate at high frequencies.

Signal generator — A device that produces low-level signals similar to those received over the air; used for testing receivers and other equipment.

Signal to noise ratio (SNR) — The ratio of a signal's amplitude to that of the noise in a specific bandwidth.

Single sideband (SSB) phone — SSB is a form of double-sideband **amplitude modulation** in which one sideband and the carrier are removed.

Skip — Propagation by means of ionospheric reflection. Traversing the distance to the ionosphere and back to the ground is called a *hop*. *Short skip* is propagation that covers distance much shorter than the maximum range for skip propagation.

Skip zone — A ring-shaped area of poor radio communication, too distant for ground waves and too close for sky waves.

Sky-wave propagation — The method by which radio waves travel through the ionosphere and back to Earth. Sometimes called *skip*, sky-wave propagation has a far greater range than **line-of-sight** and **ground-wave propagation**.

Sleeve (see **Ring**)

SMA connector — A type of RF connector.

Software-defined radio (SDR) — A transceiver in which all major signal processing functions are performed by software.

Solar cycle — The 10.7 year period of variation in solar activity.

Solar flare — A sudden eruption of energy and material from the surface of the Sun.

Solar indices — Measurements of solar activity. *Solar-flux index (SFI)* is a measure of solar activity at 10.7 cm. The *A* and *K indices* are measures of long-term and short-term geomagnetic field stability, respectively.

Solenoid (solenoidal winding) — An inductor wound around a cylindrical core.

Specific absorption rate (SAR) — A term that describes the rate at which RF energy is absorbed into the human body. Maximum permissible exposure (MPE) limits are based on whole-body SAR values.

Speech compression or **processing** — Increasing the average power and intelligibility of a voice signal by amplifying low-level components of the signal more than high-level components.

Splatter — A type of interference to stations on nearby frequencies. Splatter occurs when a transmitter is **overmodulated**.

Splitter — A circuit or connector that divides a signal between two or more circuits.

Sporadic E — A form of enhanced radio-wave propagation that occurs when radio signals are reflected from small, dense ionization patches in the E region of the ionosphere. Sporadic E is observed on the 15, 10, 6 and 2-meter bands, and occasionally on the 1.25-meter band.

Spurious emissions — Signals from a transmitter on frequencies other than the operating frequency.

Spurs (see **Parasitic**).

SSB (see **Amplitude modulation**)

Stacking — The process of increasing forward gain and controlling the vertical angle of radiation by adding antennas vertically or horizontally.

Stage — One of a sequence of circuits that process signals.

Standing-wave ratio (SWR) — Sometimes called *voltage standing-wave ratio* (VSWR), the ratio feed line's characteristic impedance and the load (usually an antenna). VSWR is the ratio of maximum voltage to minimum voltage along the feed line which is the same the ratio of antenna impedance to feed-line impedance. SWR is always stated so as to be greater than 1:1.

Start bit — A bit preceding the data bits in a character in order to synchronize the receiving system.

Step rate (size) — The smallest increment by which frequency changes as a **VFO** control is operated.

Stop bit — A bit following the data bits in a character in order to synchronize the receiving system.

Storage battery (see **secondary battery**)

Straight key — manual instrument for sending Morse code

Stub (transmission line) — A section of transmission line that is used to modify the impedance of an antenna system.

Sudden ionospheric disturbance (SID) — Short-term disruption of ionospheric propagation called a *radio blackout* as a result of a sudden increase in solar radiation.

Sunspot cycle — The number of **sunspots** increases and decreases in a predictable cycle that lasts about 11 years.

Sunspots — Dark spots on the surface of the Sun. When there are few sunspots, long-distance radio propagation is poor on the higher-frequency bands. When there are many sunspots, long-distance HF propagation improves.

Surface-mount technology (SMT) — Printed-circuit board components that solder directly to connection pads without mounting holes.

Switch-mode supply (switching supply) — A power supply that uses active devices to create high-frequency current pulses in an inductor to regulate output voltage.

SWR bridge (meter) — A measuring instrument that senses forward and reflected power to display SWR.

Symbol rate (signaling rate) — The rate at which individual data *symbols* are transmitted (see also **baud**).

Tank circuit — A resonant circuit that stabilizes the frequency of an oscillator or amplifier.

Temperature coefficient — The variation of a component's actual value with temperature.

Thermistor — A resistor manufactured with a precisely controlled **temperature coefficient** so as to be used as a temperature sensor.

Third-party — An unlicensed person on whose behalf communications is passed by Amateur Radio.

Third-party communications — Messages passed from one amateur to another on behalf of a third person.

Third-party communications agreement — An official understanding between the United States and another country that allows amateurs in both countries to participate in third-party communications.

Third-party participation — An unlicensed person participating in amateur communications. A control operator must ensure compliance with FCC rules.

Through-hole — Printed-circuit board components that have wire leads that are inserted into holes through connection pads and then soldered to the pads.

Timeout — In digital communications, for a station to terminate a contact because of excessive errors or delays.

Tip (see **Ring**)

Tolerance — The amount the actual value is allowed to vary from the nominal value, usually expressed in percent.

Toroidal winding — An inductor wound around a circular core with a central hole (a toroid).

Trailer — Control or error correction/detection information added after the data in a digital packet.

Transconductance (g_m) — The ratio of output current to input voltage.

Transfer switch — A switch that connects a home power distribution panel to either a generator or the utility lines.

Transform (impedance) — To alter the ratio of voltage and current (impedance) from an undesired value to a desired value.

Transceiver (XCVR) — A radio transmitter and receiver combined in one unit.

Transistor — A solid-state device made of semiconductor material and used as a switch or amplifier. A *bipolar junction transistor (BJT)* is made of three layers of doped material forming two **PN junctions** and is controlled by current. A *field-effect transistor (FET)* consists of a *channel* and a *gate* and is controlled by voltage.

Transformer — Two or more inductors wound on a common core for the purpose of transferring energy between them.

Transmission line — The wires or cable used to connect a transmitter or receiver to an antenna. Also called **feed line**.

Transmit-receive (TR) relay (switch) — A relay that switches an antenna or transceiver between transmit and receive functions. Also known as a *changeover relay*.

Transmitter (XMTR) — A device that produces radio-frequency signals.

Transmitter incremental tuning (XIT) — Adjustment of the transmit frequency without changing the main frequency control.

Trap — A tuned circuit that acts as an electrical switch in a multiband antenna, such as a *trapped dipole* or *trapped Yagi*.

Traveling-wave antenna — An antenna whose characteristics are determined by radio waves moving along or across it.

Triband Yagi (tribander) — A common design that operates on each of the three main HF bands, 20, 15, and 10 meters, through the use of **traps** or other features.

Turns ratio — The ratio of the number of turns in a transformer's primary winding to the number of turns in the secondary winding.

Twin-lead (feed line) — See **Parallel-conductor feed line**.

Two-tone testing — Using a pair of non-harmonically related tones to evaluate the linearity of an AM transmitter.

UHF connector — A type of RF connector.

Unbalanced feed line — Feed line with one conductor at ground potential, such as coaxial cable.

Uncontrolled environment — Any area in which an RF signal may cause radiation exposure to people who may not be aware of the radiated electric and magnetic fields. The FCC generally considers members of the general public and an amateur's neighbors to be in an uncontrolled **RF radiation** exposure environment to determine the maximum permissible exposure levels.

Upper sideband (USB) — (1) In an AM signal, the sideband located above the carrier frequency. (2) The common single-sideband operating mode on the 60, 20, 17, 15, 12 and 10-meter HF amateur bands, and all the VHF and UHF bands.

Variable-frequency oscillator (VFO) — An oscillator used in receivers and transmitters. The frequency is set by a tuned circuit using capacitors and inductors and can be changed by adjusting the components of the tuned circuit.

Varicode — A digital code in which the codes for each value have a different number of bits.

Velocity Factor (VF) — velocity of electromagnetic waves in a specific medium relative to free space and expressed as a percentage or a value between 0 and 1.

Velocity of propagation — The speed at which electromagnetic waves propagate through a media or a transmission line. The constant c is often used to represent the speed of light.

Vertical antenna — A common amateur antenna whose radiating element is vertical. There are usually four or more radial elements parallel to or on the ground.

Virtual height — The height at which a reflecting surface would have to be to create **sky-wave propagation** between two points.

Voice-operated transmit (VOX) — Activating the transmitter under the control of the operator's voice.

Volatile (memory) — Memory that loses its stored data when power is removed (**nonvolatile** memory retains the data when power is removed).

Volt (V) — The basic unit of electrical potential.

Voltage — Another term for electrical potential.

Voltage drop — The difference in voltage caused by current flow through an **impedance**.

Voltmeter — A test instrument used to measure **voltage**.

Volt-ohm-meter (VOM) — See **Multimeter**

Volunteer Examiner (VE) — A licensed amateur who is accredited by a Volunteer Examiner Coordinator (VEC) to administer amateur license examinations.

Volunteer Examiner Coordinator (VEC) — An organization that has entered into an agreement with the FCC to coordinate amateur license examinations.

Waterfall display — A method of displaying signal strength and frequency on a sequence of lines with newer lines appearing at the top or left of the display, giving the appearance of flow.

Watt (W) — The unit of power in the metric system. The watt describes the rate at which a circuit uses electrical energy.

Wattmeter — Also called a *power meter*, a test instrument used to measure the power output (in watts) of a transmitter in a feed line.

Wavelength (λ) –– The distance a radio wave travels in one RF cycle. The wavelength relates to frequency. Higher frequencies have shorter wavelengths.

Whip antenna — An antenna with an element made of a single, flexible rod or tube.

Willful interference (see **Malicious interference**)

Windings — The inductors that share a common core in a **transformer.** Energy is supplied via the *primary windings* and extracted via the *secondary windings.*

Winlink 2000 — A system of email transmission and distribution using Amateur Radio for the connection between individual amateurs and mailbox stations.

Window line (feed line) — See **Parallel-conductor feed line**.

XCVR — Transceiver.

XIT (see **Transmitter incremental tuning**)

XMTR — Transmitter.

Yagi antenna — The most popular type of directional (beam) antenna. It has one driven element and one or more additional parasitic elements.

Chapter 11

Question Pool

2011-2015 General Class (Element 3) Syllabus

SUBELEMENT G1 — COMMISSION'S RULES
[5 Exam Questions — 5 Groups]

G1A   General Class control operator frequency privileges; primary and secondary allocations

G1B   Antenna structure limitations; good engineering and good amateur practice; beacon operation; prohibited transmissions; retransmitting radio signals

G1C   Transmitter power regulations; data emission standards

G1D   Volunteer Examiners and Volunteer Examiner Coordinators; temporary identification

G1E   Control categories; repeater regulations; harmful interference; third party rules; ITU regions; automatically controlled digital station

SUBELEMENT G2 — OPERATING PROCEDURES
[5 Exam Questions — 5 Groups]

G2A   Phone operating procedures; USB/LSB conventions; procedural signals; breaking into a contact; VOX operation

G2B   Operating courtesy; band plans; emergencies, including drills and emergency communications

G2C   CW operating procedures and procedural signals; Q signals and common abbreviations; full break in

G2D   Amateur Auxiliary; minimizing interference; HF operations

G2E   Digital operating; procedures, procedural signals and common abbreviations

SUBELEMENT G3 — RADIO WAVE PROPAGATION
[3 Exam Questions — 3 Groups]

G3A   Sunspots and solar radiation; ionospheric disturbances; propagation forecasting and indices

G3B   Maximum Usable Frequency; Lowest Usable Frequency; propagation

G3C   Ionospheric layers; critical angle and frequency; HF scatter; Near-Vertical Incidence Skywave

SUBELEMENT G4 — AMATEUR RADIO PRACTICES
[5 Exam Questions — 5 Groups]

G4A   Station Operation and set up

G4B   Test and monitoring equipment; two-tone test

G4C   Interference with consumer electronics; grounding; DSP

G4D   Speech processors; S meters; sideband operation near band edges

G4E   HF mobile radio installations; emergency and battery powered operation

SUBELEMENT G5 — ELECTRICAL PRINCIPLES
[3 Exam Questions — 3 Groups]

G5A   Reactance; inductance; capacitance; impedance; impedance matching

G5B   The Decibel; current and voltage dividers; electrical power calculations; sine wave root-mean-square (RMS) values; PEP calculations

G5C   Resistors, capacitors, and inductors in series and parallel; transformers

SUBELEMENT G6 — CIRCUIT COMPONENTS
[2 Exam Questions — 2 Groups]

G6A   Resistors; Capacitors; Inductors; Rectifiers; solid state diodes and transistors; vacuum tubes; batteries

G6B   Analog and digital integrated circuits (ICs); microprocessors; memory; I/O devices; microwave ICs (MMICs); display devices

SUBELEMENT G7 — PRACTICAL CIRCUITS
[3 Exam Questions — 3 Groups]

G7A   Power supplies; and schematic symbols

G7B   Digital circuits; amplifiers and oscillators

G7C   Receivers and transmitters; filters, oscillators

SUBELEMENT G8 — SIGNALS AND EMISSIONS
[3 Exam Questions — 3 Groups]

G8A   Carriers and modulation; AM; FM; single sideband; modulation envelope; digital modulation; over modulation

G8B   Frequency mixing; multiplication; bandwidths of various modes; deviation

G8C   Digital emission modes

SUBELEMENT G9 — ANTENNAS AND FEEDLINES
[4 Exam Questions — 4 Groups]

G9A   Antenna feed lines; characteristic impedance, and attenuation; SWR calculation, measurement and effects; matching networks

G9B   Basic antennas

G9C   Directional antennas

G9D   Specialized antennas

SUBELEMENT G0 — ELECTRICAL AND RF SAFETY
[2 Exam Questions — 2 Groups]

G0A   RF safety principles, rules and guidelines; routine station evaluation

G0B   Safety in the ham shack; electrical shock and treatment, safety grounding, fusing, interlocks, wiring, antenna and tower safety

General Class Question Pool ♦ Effective July 1, 2015

SUBELEMENT G1 — COMMISSION'S RULES
[5 Exam Questions — 5 Groups]

G1A — General Class control operator frequency privileges; primary and secondary allocations

G1A01
On which of the following bands is a General Class license holder granted all amateur frequency privileges?
A. 60, 20, 17, and 12 meters
B. 160, 80, 40, and 10 meters
C. 160, 60, 30, 17, 12, and 10 meters
D. 160, 30, 17, 15, 12, and 10 meters

G1A01
(C)
[97.301(d)]
Page 3-8

G1A02
On which of the following bands is phone operation prohibited?
A. 160 meters
B. 30 meters
C. 17 meters
D. 12 meters

G1A02
(B)
[97.305]
Page 3-8

G1A03
On which of the following bands is image transmission prohibited?
A. 160 meters
B. 30 meters
C. 20 meters
D. 12 meters

G1A03
(B)
[97.305]
Page 3-8

G1A04
Which of the following amateur bands is restricted to communication on only specific channels, rather than frequency ranges?
A. 11 meters
B. 12 meters
C. 30 meters
D. 60 meters

G1A04
(D)
[97.303 (h)]
Page 3-8

G1A05
Which of the following frequencies is in the General Class portion of the 40-meter band?
A. 7.250 MHz
B. 7.500 MHz
C. 40.200 MHz
D. 40.500 MHz

G1A05
(A)
[97.301(d)]
Page 3-7

G1A06
(C)
[97.301(d)]
Page 3-8

G1A06
Which of the following frequencies is within the General Class portion of the 75-meter phone band?
A. 1875 kHz
B. 3750 kHz
C. 3900 kHz
D. 4005 kHz

G1A07
(C)
[97.301(d)]
Page 3-7

G1A07
Which of the following frequencies is within the General Class portion of the 20-meter phone band?
A. 14005 kHz
B. 14105 kHz
C. 14305 kHz
D. 14405 kHz

G1A08
(C)
[97.301(d)]
Page 3-7

G1A08
Which of the following frequencies is within the General Class portion of the 80-meter band?
A. 1855 kHz
B. 2560 kHz
C. 3560 kHz
D. 3650 kHz

G1A09
(C)
[97.301(d)]
Page 3-7

G1A09
Which of the following frequencies is within the General Class portion of the 15-meter band?
A. 14250 kHz
B. 18155 kHz
C. 21300 kHz
D. 24900 kHz

G1A10
(D)
[97.301(d)]
Page 3-7

G1A10
Which of the following frequencies is available to a control operator holding a General Class license?
A. 28.020 MHz
B. 28.350 MHz
C. 28.550 MHz
D. All of these choices are correct

G1A11
(B)
[97.301]
Page 3-8

G1A11
When General Class licensees are not permitted to use the entire voice portion of a particular band, which portion of the voice segment is generally available to them?
A. The lower frequency end
B. The upper frequency end
C. The lower frequency end on frequencies below 7.3 MHz and the upper end on frequencies above 14.150 MHz
D. The upper frequency end on frequencies below 7.3 MHz and the lower end on frequencies above 14.150 MHz

G1A12
(C)
[97.303]
Page 3-8

G1A12
Which of the following applies when the FCC rules designate the Amateur Service as a secondary user on a band?
A. Amateur stations must record the call sign of the primary service station before operating on a frequency assigned to that station
B. Amateur stations are allowed to use the band only during emergencies
C. Amateur stations are allowed to use the band only if they do not cause harmful interference to primary users
D. Amateur stations may only operate during specific hours of the day, while primary users are permitted 24 hour use of the band

G1A13

What is the appropriate action if, when operating on either the 30-meter or 60-meter bands, a station in the primary service interferes with your contact?

A. Notify the FCCs regional Engineer in Charge of the interference
B. Increase your transmitter's power to overcome the interference
C. Attempt to contact the station and request that it stop the interference
D. Move to a clear frequency or stop transmitting

G1A13
(D)
[97.303(h)(2)
(j)]
Page 3-8

G1A14

In what ITU region is operation in the 7.175 to 7.300 MHz band permitted for a control operator holding an FCC issued General Class license?

A. Region 1
B. Region 2
C. Region 3
D. All three regions

G1A14
(B)
[97.301(d)]
Page 3-2

G1B — Antenna structure limitations; good engineering and good amateur practice; beacon operation; prohibited transmissions; retransmitting radio signals

G1B01

What is the maximum height above ground to which an antenna structure may be erected without requiring notification to the FAA and registration with the FCC, provided it is not at or near a public use airport?

A. 50 feet
B. 100 feet
C. 200 feet
D. 300 feet

G1B01
(C)
[97.15(a)]
Page 3-2

G1B02

With which of the following conditions must beacon stations comply?

A. A beacon station may not use automatic control
B. The frequency must be coordinated with the National Beacon Organization
C. The frequency must be posted on the Internet or published in a national periodical
D. There must be no more than one beacon signal transmitting in the same band from the same station location

G1B02
(D)
[97.203(b)]
Page 3-9

G1B03

Which of the following is a purpose of a beacon station as identified in the FCC rules?

A. Observation of propagation and reception
B. Automatic identification of repeaters
C. Transmission of bulletins of general interest to Amateur Radio licensees
D. Identifying net frequencies

G1B03
(A)
[97.3(a)(9)]
Page 3-8

G1B04

Which of the following must be true before amateur stations may provide communications to broadcasters for dissemination to the public?

A. The communications must directly relate to the immediate safety of human life or protection of property and there must be no other means of communication reasonably available before or at the time of the event
B. The communications must be approved by a local emergency preparedness official and conducted on officially designated frequencies
C. The FCC must have declared a state of emergency
D. All of these choices are correct

G1B04
(A)
[97.113(b)]
Page 2-13

G1B05
(D)
[97.113(c)]
Page 3-10

G1B05
When may music be transmitted by an amateur station?
A. At any time, as long as it produces no spurious emissions
B. When it is unintentionally transmitted from the background at the transmitter
C. When it is transmitted on frequencies above 1215 MHz
D. When it is an incidental part of a manned space craft retransmission

G1B06
(B)
[97.113(a)
(4) and
97.207(f)]
Page 3-11

G1B06
When is an amateur station permitted to transmit secret codes?
A. During a declared communications emergency
B. To control a space station
C. Only when the information is of a routine, personal nature
D. Only with Special Temporary Authorization from the FCC

G1B07
(B)
[97.113(a)
(4)]
Page 3-11

G1B07
What are the restrictions on the use of abbreviations or procedural signals in the Amateur Service?
A. Only "Q" signals are permitted
B. They may be used if they do not obscure the meaning of a message
C. They are not permitted
D. Only "10 codes" are permitted

G1B08
(D)
[97.101(a)]
Page 2-3

G1B08
When choosing a transmitting frequency, what should you do to comply with good amateur practice?
A. Insure that the frequency and mode selected are within your license class privileges
B. Follow generally accepted band plans agreed to by the Amateur Radio community
C. Monitor the frequency before transmitting
D. All of these choices are correct

G1B09
(A)
[97.113(a)
(3)]
Page 3-12

G1B09
When may an amateur station transmit communications in which the licensee or control operator has a pecuniary (monetary) interest?
A. When other amateurs are being notified of the sale of apparatus normally used in an amateur station and such activity is not done on a regular basis
B. Only when there is no other means of communications readily available
C. When other amateurs are being notified of the sale of any item with a monetary value less than $200 and such activity is not done on a regular basis
D. Never

G1B10
(C)
[97.203(c)]
Page 3-9

G1B10
What is the power limit for beacon stations?
A. 10 watts PEP output
B. 20 watts PEP output
C. 100 watts PEP output
D. 200 watts PEP output

G1B11
(C)
[97.101(a)]
Page 3-13

G1B11
How does the FCC require an amateur station to be operated in all respects not specifically covered by the Part 97 rules?
A. In conformance with the rules of the IARU
B. In conformance with Amateur Radio custom
C. In conformance with good engineering and good amateur practice
D. All of these choices are correct

G1B12

Who or what determines "good engineering and good amateur practice" as applied to the operation of an amateur station in all respects not covered by the Part 97 rules?
A. The FCC
B. The Control Operator
C. The IEEE
D. The ITU

G1B12
(A)
[97.101(a)]
Page 3-13

G1C — Transmitter power regulations; data emission standards

G1C01

What is the maximum transmitting power an amateur station may use on 10.140 MHz?
A. 200 watts PEP output
B. 1000 watts PEP output
C. 1500 watts PEP output
D. 2000 watts PEP output

G1C01
(A)
[97.313(c)(1)]
Page 3-13

G1C02

What is the maximum transmitting power an amateur station may use on the 12-meter band?
A. 50 watts PEP output
B. 200 watts PEP output
C. 1500 watts PEP output
D. An effective radiated power equivalent to 100 watts from a half-wave dipole

G1C02
(C)
[97.313(a),(b)]
Page 3-13

G1C03

What is the maximum bandwidth permitted by FCC rules for Amateur Radio stations transmitting on USB frequencies in the 60-meter band?
A. 2.8 kHz
B. 5.6 kHz
C. 1.8 kHz
D. 3 kHz

G1C03
(A)
[97.303(h)(1)]
Page 3-14

G1C04

Which of the following limitations apply to transmitter power on every amateur band?
A. Only the minimum power necessary to carry out the desired communications should be used
B. Power must be limited to 200 watts when transmitting between 14.100 MHz and 14.150 MHz
C. Power should be limited as necessary to avoid interference to another radio service on the frequency
D. Effective radiated power cannot exceed 1500 watts

G1C04
(A)
[97.313(a)]
Page 3-14

G1C05

Which of the following is a limitation on transmitter power on the 28 MHz band for a General Class control operator?
A. 100 watts PEP output
B. 1000 watts PEP output
C. 1500 watts PEP output
D. 2000 watts PEP output

G1C05
(C)
[97.313(c)(2)]
Page 3-13

G1C06

Which of the following is a limitation on transmitter power on the 1.8 MHz band?
A. 200 watts PEP output
B. 1000 watts PEP output
C. 1200 watts PEP output
D. 1500 watts PEP output

G1C06
(D)
[97.313]
Page 3-13

G1C07
(D)
[97.305(c),
97.307(f)(3)]
Page 3-14

G1C07
What is the maximum symbol rate permitted for RTTY or data emission transmission on the 20-meter band?
A. 56 kilobaud
B. 19.6 kilobaud
C. 1200 baud
D. 300 baud

G1C08
(D)
[97.307(f)
(3)]
Page 3-14

G1C08
What is the maximum symbol rate permitted for RTTY or data emission transmitted at frequencies below 28 MHz?
A. 56 kilobaud
B. 19.6 kilobaud
C. 1200 baud
D. 300 baud

G1C09
(A)
[97.305(c)
and 97.307(f)
(5)]
Page 3-14

G1C09
What is the maximum symbol rate permitted for RTTY or data emission transmitted on the 1.25-meter and 70-centimeter bands?
A. 56 kilobaud
B. 19.6 kilobaud
C. 1200 baud
D. 300 baud

G1C10
(C)
[97.305(c)
and 97.307(f)
(4)]
Page 3-14

G1C10
What is the maximum symbol rate permitted for RTTY or data emission transmissions on the 10-meter band?
A. 56 kilobaud
B. 19.6 kilobaud
C. 1200 baud
D. 300 baud

G1C11
(B)
[97.305(c)
and 97.307(f)
(5)]
Page 3-14

G1C11
What is the maximum symbol rate permitted for RTTY or data emission transmissions on the 2-meter band?
A. 56 kilobaud
B. 19.6 kilobaud
C. 1200 baud
D. 300 baud

G1D — Volunteer Examiners and Volunteer Examiner Coordinators; temporary identification

G1D01
(A)
[97.501,
97.505(a)]
Page 3-3

G1D01
Who may receive credit for the elements represented by an expired amateur radio license?
A. Any person who can demonstrate that they once held an FCC issued General, Advanced, or Amateur Extra class license that was not revoked by the FCC
B. Anyone who held an FCC issued amateur radio license that has been expired for not less than 5 years and not more than 15 years
C. Any person who previously held an amateur license issued by another country, but only if that country has a current reciprocal licensing agreement with the FCC
D. Only persons who once held an FCC issued Novice, Technician, or Technician Plus license

G1D02

What license examinations may you administer when you are an accredited VE holding a General Class operator license?

A. General and Technician
B. General only
C. Technician only
D. Extra, General and Technician

G1D02
(C)
[97.509(b)(3)
(i)]
Page 3-4

G1D03

On which of the following band segments may you operate if you are a Technician Class operator and have a CSCE for General Class privileges?

A. Only the Technician band segments until your upgrade is posted in the FCC database
B. Only on the Technician band segments until your license arrives in the mail
C. On any General or Technician Class band segment
D. On any General or Technician Class band segment except 30-meters and 60-meters

G1D03
(C)
[97.9(b)]
Page 3-6

G1D04

Which of the following is a requirement for administering a Technician Class license examination?

A. At least three General Class or higher VEs must observe the examination
B. At least two General Class or higher VEs must be present
C. At least two General Class or higher VEs must be present, but only one need be Extra Class
D. At least three VEs of Technician Class or higher must observe the examination

G1D04
(A)
[97.509(a),(b)]
Page 3-4

G1D05

Which of the following must a person have before they can be an administering VE for a Technician Class license examination?

A. Notification to the FCC that you want to give an examination
B. Receipt of a CSCE for General Class
C. Possession of a properly obtained telegraphy license
D. An FCC General Class or higher license and VEC accreditation

G1D05
(D)
[97.509(b)(3)
(i)]
Page 3-3

G1D06

When must you add the special identifier "AG" after your call sign if you are a Technician Class licensee and have a CSCE for General Class operator privileges, but the FCC has not yet posted your upgrade on its website?

A. Whenever you operate using General Class frequency privileges
B. Whenever you operate on any amateur frequency
C. Whenever you operate using Technician frequency privileges
D. A special identifier is not required as long as your General Class license application has been filed with the FCC

G1D06
(A)
[97.119(f)(2)]
Page 3-6

G1D07

Volunteer Examiners are accredited by what organization?

A. The Federal Communications Commission
B. The Universal Licensing System
C. A Volunteer Examiner Coordinator
D. The Wireless Telecommunications Bureau

G1D07
(C)
[97.509(b)(1)]
Page 3-3

G1D08

Which of the following criteria must be met for a non-U.S. citizen to be an accredited Volunteer Examiner?

A. The person must be a resident of the U.S. for a minimum of 5 years
B. The person must hold an FCC granted Amateur Radio license of General Class or above
C. The person's home citizenship must be in ITU region 2
D. None of these choices is correct; a non-U.S. citizen cannot be a Volunteer Examiner

G1D08
(B)
[97.509(b)(3)]
Page 3-3

G1D09
(C)
[97.9(b)]
Page 3-4

G1D09
How long is a Certificate of Successful Completion of Examination (CSCE) valid for exam element credit?
A. 30 days
B. 180 days
C. 365 days
D. For as long as your current license is valid

G1D10
(B)
[97.509(b)
(2)]
Page 3-3

G1D10
What is the minimum age that one must be to qualify as an accredited Volunteer Examiner?
A. 12 years
B. 18 years
C. 21 years
D. There is no age limit

G1D11
(D)
Page 3-3

G1D11
If a person has an expired FCC issued amateur radio license of General Class or higher, what is required before they can receive a new license?
A. They must have a letter from the FCC showing they once held an amateur or commercial license
B. There are no requirements other than being able to show a copy of the expired license
C. The applicant must be able to produce a copy of a page from a call book published in the USA showing his or her name and address
D. The applicant must pass the current element 2 exam

G1E — Control categories; repeater regulations; harmful interference; third party rules; ITU regions; automatically controlled digital station

G1E01
(A)
[97.115(b)
(2)]
Page 3-10

G1E01
Which of the following would disqualify a third party from participating in stating a message over an amateur station?
A. The third party's amateur license has been revoked and not reinstated
B. The third party is not a U.S. citizen
C. The third party is a licensed amateur
D. The third party is speaking in a language other than English

G1E02
(D)
[97.205(a)]
Page 3-12

G1E02
When may a 10-meter repeater retransmit the 2-meter signal from a station having a Technician Class control operator?
A. Under no circumstances
B. Only if the station on 10-meters is operating under a Special Temporary Authorization allowing such retransmission
C. Only during an FCC declared general state of communications emergency
D. Only if the 10-meter repeater control operator holds at least a General Class license

G1E03
(A)
[97.221]
Page 6-12

G1E03
What is required to conduct communications with a digital station operating under automatic control outside the automatic control band segments?
A. The station initiating the contact must be under local or remote control
B. The interrogating transmission must be made by another automatically controlled station
C. No third party traffic maybe be transmitted
D. The control operator of the interrogating station must hold an Extra Class license

G1E04

Which of the following conditions require a licensed Amateur Radio operator to take specific steps to avoid harmful interference to other users or facilities?
A. When operating within one mile of an FCC Monitoring Station
B. When using a band where the Amateur Service is secondary
C. When a station is transmitting spread spectrum emissions
D. All of these choices are correct

G1E05

What types of messages for a third party in another country may be transmitted by an amateur station?
A. Any message, as long as the amateur operator is not paid
B. Only messages for other licensed amateurs
C. Only messages relating to Amateur Radio or remarks of a personal character, or messages relating to emergencies or disaster relief
D. Any messages, as long as the text of the message is recorded in the station log

G1E06

Which of the following applies in the event of interference between a coordinated repeater and an uncoordinated repeater?
A. The licensee of the uncoordinated repeater has primary responsibility to resolve the interference
B. The licensee of the coordinated repeater has primary responsibility to resolve the interference
C. Both repeater licensees share equal responsibility to resolve the interference
D. The frequency coordinator bears primary responsibility to resolve the interference

G1E07

With which foreign countries is third party traffic prohibited, except for messages directly involving emergencies or disaster relief communications?
A. Countries in ITU Region 2
B. Countries in ITU Region 1
C. Every foreign country, unless there is a third party agreement in effect with that country
D. Any country which is not a member of the International Amateur Radio Union (IARU)

G1E08

Which of the following is a requirement for a non-licensed person to communicate with a foreign Amateur Radio station from a station with an FCC-granted license at which an FCC licensed control operator is present?
A. Information must be exchanged in English
B. The foreign amateur station must be in a country with which the United States has a third party agreement
C. The control operator must have at least a General Class license
D. All of these choices are correct

G1E09

What language must be used when identifying your station if you are using a language other than English in making a contact using phone emission?
A. The language being used for the contact
B. Any language recognized by the United Nations
C. English only
D. English, Spanish, French, or German

G1E10 — This question has been withdrawn.

G1E04
(D)
[97.13(b),
97.303,
97.311(b)]
Page 3-9

G1E05
(C)
[97.115(a)
(2),97.117]
Page 3-9

G1E06
(A)
[97.205(c)]
Page 3-9

G1E07
(C)
[97.115(a)(2)]
Page 3-10

G1E08
(B)
[97.115(a)(b)]
Page 3-10

G1E09
(C)
[97.119(b)(2)]
Page 3-6

G1E10
Withdrawn

G1E11
(C)
[97.221]
Page 6-12

G1E11
Which of the following is the FCC term for an unattended digital station that transfers messages to and from the Internet?
A. Locally controlled station
B. Robotically controlled station
C. Automatically controlled digital station
D. Fail-safe digital station

G1E12
(A)
[97.115]
Page 6-12

G1E12
Under what circumstances are messages that are sent via digital modes exempt from Part 97 third party rules that apply to other modes of communication?
A. Under no circumstances
B. When messages are encrypted
C. When messages are not encrypted
D. When under automatic control

G1E13
(D)
[97.221,
97.305]
Page 6-13

G1E13
On what bands may automatically controlled stations transmitting RTTY or data emissions communicate with other automatically controlled digital stations?
A. On any band segment where digital operation is permitted
B. Anywhere in the non-phone segments of the 10-meter or shorter wavelength bands
C. Only in the non-phone Extra Class segments of the bands
D. Anywhere in the 1.25-meter or shorter wavelength bands, and in specified segments of the 80-meter through 2-meter bands

SUBELEMENT G2 — OPERATING PROCEDURES
[5 Exam Questions — 5 Groups]

G2A — Phone operating procedures; USB/LSB conventions; procedural signals; breaking into a contact; VOX operation

G2A01
Which sideband is most commonly used for voice communications on frequencies of 14 MHz or higher?
A. Upper sideband
B. Lower sideband
C. Vestigial sideband
D. Double sideband

G2A01
(A)
Page 2-8

G2A02
Which of the following modes is most commonly used for voice communications on the 160-meter, 75-meter, and 40-meter bands?
A. Upper sideband
B. Lower sideband
C. Vestigial sideband
D. Double sideband

G2A02
(B)
Page 2-8

G2A03
Which of the following is most commonly used for SSB voice communications in the VHF and UHF bands?
A. Upper sideband
B. Lower sideband
C. Vestigial sideband
D. Double sideband

G2A03
(A)
Page 2-8

G2A04
Which mode is most commonly used for voice communications on the 17-meter and 12-meter bands?
A. Upper sideband
B. Lower sideband
C. Vestigial sideband
D. Double sideband

G2A04
(A)
Page 2-8

G2A05
Which mode of voice communication is most commonly used on the HF amateur bands?
A. Frequency modulation
B. Double sideband
C. Single sideband
D. Phase modulation

G2A05
(C)
Page 2-7

G2A06
Which of the following is an advantage when using single sideband as compared to other analog voice modes on the HF amateur bands?
A. Very high fidelity voice modulation
B. Less bandwidth used and greater power efficiency
C. Ease of tuning on receive and immunity to impulse noise
D. Less subject to interference from atmospheric static crashes

G2A06
(B)
Page 2-7

G2A07
(B)
Page 2-7

G2A07
Which of the following statements is true of the single sideband voice mode?
A. Only one sideband and the carrier are transmitted; the other sideband is suppressed
B. Only one sideband is transmitted; the other sideband and carrier are suppressed
C. SSB is the only voice mode that is authorized on the 20-meter, 15-meter, and 10-meter amateur bands
D. SSB is the only voice mode that is authorized on the 160-meter, 75-meter and 40-meter amateur bands

G2A08
(B)
Page 2-2

G2A08
Which of the following is a recommended way to break into a contact when using phone?
A. Say "QRZ" several times followed by your call sign
B. Say your call sign during a break between transmissions by the other stations
C. Say "Break Break Break" and wait for a response
D. Say "CQ" followed by the call sign of either station

G2A09
(D)
Page 2-8

G2A09
Why do most amateur stations use lower sideband on the 160-meter, 75-meter and 40-meter bands?
A. Lower sideband is more efficient than upper sideband at these frequencies
B. Lower sideband is the only sideband legal on these frequency bands
C. Because it is fully compatible with an AM detector
D. Current amateur practice is to use lower sideband on these frequency bands

G2A10
(B)
Page 2-10

G2A10
Which of the following statements is true of voice VOX operation versus PTT operation?
A. The received signal is more natural sounding
B. It allows "hands free" operation
C. It occupies less bandwidth
D. It provides more power output

G2A11
(C)
Page 2-2

G2A11
What does the expression "CQ DX" usually indicate?
A. A general call for any station
B. The caller is listening for a station in Germany
C. The caller is looking for any station outside their own country
D. A distress call

G2B — Operating courtesy; band plans; emergencies, including drills and emergency communications

G2B01
(C)
Page 2-3

G2B01
Which of the following is true concerning access to frequencies in non-emergency situations?
A. Nets always have priority
B. QSOs in progress always have priority
C. Except during FCC declared emergencies, no one has priority access to frequencies
D. Contest operations must always yield to non-contest use of frequencies

G2B02
(B)
Page 2-15

G2B02
What is the first thing you should do if you are communicating with another amateur station and hear a station in distress break in?
A. Continue your communication because you were on the frequency first
B. Acknowledge the station in distress and determine what assistance may be needed
C. Change to a different frequency
D. Immediately cease all transmissions

G2B03
If propagation changes during your contact and you notice increasing interference from other activity on the same frequency, what should you do?
A.   Tell the interfering stations to change frequency
B.   Report the interference to your local Amateur Auxiliary Coordinator
C.   As a common courtesy, move your contact to another frequency
D.   Increase power to overcome interference

G2B04
When selecting a CW transmitting frequency, what minimum separation should be used to minimize interference to stations on adjacent frequencies?
A.   5 to 50 Hz
B.   150 to 500 Hz
C.   1 to 3 kHz
D.   3 to 6 kHz

G2B05
What is the customary minimum frequency separation between SSB signals under normal conditions?
A.   Between 150 and 500 Hz
B.   Approximately 3 kHz
C.   Approximately 6 kHz
D.   Approximately 10 kHz

G2B06
What is a practical way to avoid harmful interference on an apparently clear frequency before calling CQ on CW or phone?
A.   Send "QRL?" on CW, followed by your call sign; or, if using phone, ask if the frequency is in use, followed by your call sign
B.   Listen for 2 minutes before calling CQ
C.   Send the letter "V" in Morse code several times and listen for a response or say "test" several times and listen for a response
D.   Send "QSY" on CW or if using phone, announce "the frequency is in use", then give your call and listen for a response

G2B07
Which of the following complies with good amateur practice when choosing a frequency on which to initiate a call?
A.   Check to see if the channel is assigned to another station
B.   Identify your station by transmitting your call sign at least 3 times
C.   Follow the voluntary band plan for the operating mode you intend to use
D.   All of these choices are correct

G2B08
What is the "DX window" in a voluntary band plan?
A.   A portion of the band that should not be used for contacts between stations within the 48 contiguous United States
B.   An FCC rule that prohibits contacts between stations within the United States and possessions in that portion of the band
C.   An FCC rule that allows only digital contacts in that portion of the band
D.   A portion of the band that has been voluntarily set aside for digital contacts only

G2B03
(C)
Page 2-7

G2B04
(B)
Page 2-3

G2B05
(B)
Page 2-3

G2B06
(A)
Page 2-3

G2B07
(C)
Page 2-2

G2B08
(A)
Page 2-4

G2B09
(A)
[97.407(a)]
Page 2-13

G2B09
Who may be the control operator of an amateur station transmitting in RACES to assist relief operations during a disaster?
A. Only a person holding an FCC issued amateur operator license
B. Only a RACES net control operator
C. A person holding an FCC issued amateur operator license or an appropriate government official
D. Any control operator when normal communication systems are operational

G2B10
(D)
[97.407(b)]
Page 2-14

G2B10
When may the FCC restrict normal frequency operations of amateur stations participating in RACES?
A. When they declare a temporary state of communication emergency
B. When they seize your equipment for use in disaster communications
C. Only when all amateur stations are instructed to stop transmitting
D. When the President's War Emergency Powers have been invoked

G2B11
(A)
[97.405]
Page 2-16

G2B11
What frequency should be used to send a distress call?
A. Whichever frequency has the best chance of communicating the distress message
B. Only frequencies authorized for RACES or ARES stations
C. Only frequencies that are within your operating privileges
D. Only frequencies used by police, fire or emergency medical services

G2B12
(C)
[97.405(b)]
Page 2-16

G2B12
When is an amateur station allowed to use any means at its disposal to assist another station in distress?
A. Only when transmitting in RACES
B. At any time when transmitting in an organized net
C. At any time during an actual emergency
D. Only on authorized HF frequencies

G2C — CW operating procedures and procedural signals; Q signals and common abbreviations: full break in

G2C01
(D)
Page 2-12

G2C01
Which of the following describes full break-in telegraphy (QSK)?
A. Breaking stations send the Morse code prosign BK
B. Automatic keyers are used to send Morse code instead of hand keys
C. An operator must activate a manual send/receive switch before and after every transmission
D. Transmitting stations can receive between code characters and elements

G2C02
(A)
Page 2-12

G2C02
What should you do if a CW station sends "QRS"?
A. Send slower
B. Change frequency
C. Increase your power
D. Repeat everything twice

G2C03
(C)
Page 2-12

G2C03
What does it mean when a CW operator sends "KN" at the end of a transmission?
A. Listening for novice stations
B. Operating full break-in
C. Listening only for a specific station or stations
D. Closing station now

G2C04

What does the Q signal "QRL?" mean?

A. "Will you keep the frequency clear?"
B. "Are you operating full break-in" or "Can you operate full break-in?"
C. "Are you listening only for a specific station?"
D. "Are you busy?", or "Is this frequency in use?"

G2C05

What is the best speed to use when answering a CQ in Morse code?

A. The fastest speed at which you are comfortable copying
B. The speed at which the CQ was sent
C. A slow speed until contact is established
D. At the standard calling speed of 5 wpm

G2C06

What does the term "zero beat" mean in CW operation?

A. Matching the speed of the transmitting station
B. Operating split to avoid interference on frequency
C. Sending without error
D. Matching your transmit frequency to the frequency of a received signal

G2C07

When sending CW, what does a "C" mean when added to the RST report?

A. Chirpy or unstable signal
B. Report was read from an S meter rather than estimated
C. 100 percent copy
D. Key clicks

G2C08

What prosign is sent to indicate the end of a formal message when using CW?

A. SK
B. BK
C. AR
D. KN

G2C09

What does the Q signal "QSL" mean?

A. Send slower
B. We have already confirmed by card
C. I acknowledge receipt
D. We have worked before

G2C10

What does the Q signal "QRN" mean?

A. Send more slowly
B. I am troubled by static
C. Zero beat my signal
D. Stop sending

G2C11

What does the Q signal "QRV" mean?

A. You are sending too fast
B. There is interference on the frequency
C. I am quitting for the day
D. I am ready to receive messages

G2C04
(D)
Page 2-3

G2C05
(B)
Page 2-12

G2C06
(D)
Page 2-12

G2C07
(A)
Page 2-11

G2C08
(C)
Page 2-12

G2C09
(C)
Page 2-12

G2C10
(B)
Page 2-9

G2C11
(D)
Page 2-12

G2D — Amateur Auxiliary; minimizing interference; HF operations

G2D01

What is the Amateur Auxiliary to the FCC?

A. Amateur volunteers who are formally enlisted to monitor the airwaves for rules violations

B. Amateur volunteers who conduct amateur licensing examinations

C. Amateur volunteers who conduct frequency coordination for amateur VHF repeaters

D. Amateur volunteers who use their station equipment to help civil defense organizations in times of emergency

G2D02

Which of the following are objectives of the Amateur Auxiliary?

A. To conduct efficient and orderly amateur licensing examinations

B. To encourage self-regulation and compliance with the rules by radio amateur operators

C. To coordinate repeaters for efficient and orderly spectrum usage

D. To provide emergency and public safety communications

G2D03

What skills learned during hidden transmitter hunts are of help to the Amateur Auxiliary?

A. Identification of out of band operation

B. Direction finding used to locate stations violating FCC Rules

C. Identification of different call signs

D. Hunters have an opportunity to transmit on non-amateur frequencies

G2D04

Which of the following describes an azimuthal projection map?

A. A map that shows accurate land masses

B. A map that shows true bearings and distances from a particular location

C. A map that shows the angle at which an amateur satellite crosses the equator

D. A map that shows the number of degrees longitude that an amateur satellite appears to move westward at the equator with each orbit

G2D05

When is it permissible to communicate with amateur stations in countries outside the areas administered by the Federal Communications Commission?

A. Only when the foreign country has a formal third party agreement filed with the FCC

B. When the contact is with amateurs in any country except those whose administrations have notified the ITU that they object to such communications

C. When the contact is with amateurs in any country as long as the communication is conducted in English

D. Only when the foreign country is a member of the International Amateur Radio Union

G2D06

How is a directional antenna pointed when making a "long-path" contact with another station?

A. Toward the rising Sun

B. Along the gray line

C. 180 degrees from its short-path heading

D. Toward the north

G2D07

Which of the following is required by the FCC rules when operating in the 60-meter band?

A. If you are using other than a dipole antenna, you must keep a record of the gain of your antenna
B. You must keep a record of the date, time, frequency, power level and stations worked
C. You must keep a record of all third party traffic
D. You must keep a record of the manufacturer of your equipment and the antenna used

G2D07
(A)
[97.303(i)]
Page 3-12

G2D08

What is a reason why many amateurs keep a station log?

A. The ITU requires a log of all international contacts
B. The ITU requires a log of all international third party traffic
C. The log provides evidence of operation needed to renew a license without retest
D. To help with a reply if the FCC requests information

G2D08
(D)
Page 2-5

G2D09

What information is traditionally contained in a station log?

A. Date and time of contact
B. Band and/or frequency of the contact
C. Call sign of station contacted and the signal report given
D. All of these choices are correct

G2D09
(D)
Page 2-5

G2D10

What is QRP operation?

A. Remote piloted model control
B. Low power transmit operation
C. Transmission using Quick Response Protocol
D. Traffic relay procedure net operation

G2D10
(B)
Page 3-13

G2D11

Which HF antenna would be the best to use for minimizing interference?

A. A quarter-wave vertical antenna
B. An isotropic antenna
C. A directional antenna
D. An omnidirectional antenna

G2D11
(C)
Page 7-8

G2E — Digital operating: procedures, procedural signals and common abbreviations

G2E01

Which mode is normally used when sending an RTTY signal via AFSK with an SSB transmitter?

A. USB
B. DSB
C. CW
D. LSB

G2E01
(D)
Page 6-9

G2E02

How can a PACTOR modem or controller be used to determine if the channel is in use by other PACTOR stations?

A. Unplug the data connector temporarily and see if the channel-busy indication is turned off
B. Put the modem or controller in a mode which allows monitoring communications without a connection
C. Transmit UI packets several times and wait to see if there is a response from another PACTOR station
D. Send the message: "Is this frequency in use?"

G2E02
(B)
Page 6-8

G2E03
(D)
Page 6-13

G2E03
What symptoms may result from other signals interfering with a PACTOR or WINMOR transmission?
A. Frequent retries or timeouts
B. Long pauses in message transmission
C. Failure to establish a connection between stations
D. All of these choices are correct

G2E04
(B)
Page 6-1

G2E04
What segment of the 20-meter band is most often used for digital transmissions?
A. 14.000 – 14.050 MHz
B. 14.070 – 14.100 MHz
C. 14.150 – 14.225 MHz
D. 14.275 – 14.350 MHz

G2E05
(B)
Page 6-9

G2E05
What is the standard sideband used to generate a JT65 or JT9 digital signal when using AFSK in any amateur band?
A. LSB
B. USB
C. DSB
D. SSB

G2E06
(B)
Page 6-6

G2E06
What is the most common frequency shift for RTTY emissions in the amateur HF bands?
A. 85 Hz
B. 170 Hz
C. 425 Hz
D. 850 Hz

G2E07
(A)
Page 6-1

G2E07
What segment of the 80-meter band is most commonly used for digital transmissions?
A. 3570 – 3600 kHz
B. 3500 – 3525 kHz
C. 3700 – 3750 kHz
D. 3775 – 3825 kHz

G2E08
(D)
Page 6-1

G2E08
In what segment of the 20-meter band are most PSK31 operations commonly found?
A. At the bottom of the slow-scan TV segment, near 14.230 MHz
B. At the top of the SSB phone segment, near 14.325 MHz
C. In the middle of the CW segment, near 14.100 MHz
D. Below the RTTY segment, near 14.070 MHz

G2E09
(C)
Page 6-8

G2E09
How do you join a contact between two stations using the PACTOR protocol?
A. Send broadcast packets containing your call sign while in MONITOR mode
B. Transmit a steady carrier until the PACTOR protocol times out and disconnects
C. Joining an existing contact is not possible, PACTOR connections are limited to two stations
D. Send a NAK response continuously so that the sending station has to pause

G2E10

Which of the following is a way to establish contact with a digital messaging system gateway station?

A. Send an email to the system control operator
B. Send QRL in Morse code
C. Respond when the station broadcasts its SSID
D. Transmit a connect message on the station's published frequency

G2E10
(D)
Page 6-12

G2E11

What is indicated on a waterfall display by one or more vertical lines adjacent to a PSK31 signal?

A. Long Path propagation
B. Backscatter propagation
C. Insufficient modulation
D. Overmodulation

G2E11
(D)
Page 6-11

G2E12

Which of the following describes a waterfall display?

A. Frequency is horizontal, signal strength is vertical, time is intensity
B. Frequency is vertical, signal strength is intensity, time is horizontal
C. Frequency is horizontal, signal strength is intensity, time is vertical
D. Frequency is vertical, signal strength is horizontal, time is intensity

G2E12
(C)
Page 6-12

G2E13

Which communication system sometimes uses the Internet to transfer messages?

A. Winlink
B. RTTY
C. ARES
D. Skywarn

G2E13
(A)
Page 6-2

G2E14

What could be wrong if you cannot decode an RTTY or other FSK signal even though it is apparently tuned in properly?

A. The mark and space frequencies may be reversed
B. You may have selected the wrong baud rate
C. You may be listening on the wrong sideband
D. All of these choices are correct

G2E14
(D)
Page 6-9

SUBELEMENT G3 — RADIO WAVE PROPAGATION

[3 Exam Questions — 3 Groups]

G3A — Sunspots and solar radiation; ionospheric disturbances; propagation forecasting and indices

G3A01
(A)
Page 8-5

G3A01
What is the significance of the sunspot number with regard to HF propagation?
A.   Higher sunspot numbers generally indicate a greater probability of good propagation at higher frequencies
B.   Lower sunspot numbers generally indicate greater probability of sporadic E propagation
C.   A zero sunspot number indicate radio propagation is not possible on any band
D.   All of these choices are correct.

G3A02
(B)
Page 8-9

G3A02
What effect does a Sudden Ionospheric Disturbance have on the daytime ionospheric propagation of HF radio waves?
A.   It enhances propagation on all HF frequencies
B.   It disrupts signals on lower frequencies more than those on higher frequencies
C.   It disrupts communications via satellite more than direct communications
D.   None, because only areas on the night side of the Earth are affected

G3A03
(C)
Page 8-8

G3A03
Approximately how long does it take the increased ultraviolet and X-ray radiation from solar flares to affect radio propagation on the Earth?
A.   28 days
B.   1 to 2 hours
C.   8 minutes
D.   20 to 40 hours

G3A04
(D)
Page 8-6

G3A04
Which of the following are least reliable for long distance communications during periods of low solar activity?
A.   80 meters and 160 meters
B.   60 meters and 40 meters
C.   30 meters and 20 meters
D.   15 meters, 12 meters and 10 meters

G3A05
(D)
Page 8-7

G3A05
What is the solar flux index?
A.   A measure of the highest frequency that is useful for ionospheric propagation between two points on the Earth
B.   A count of sunspots which is adjusted for solar emissions
C.   Another name for the American sunspot number
D.   A measure of solar radiation at 10.7 centimeters wavelength

G3A06
(D)
Page 8-9

G3A06
What is a geomagnetic storm?
A.   A sudden drop in the solar flux index
B.   A thunderstorm which affects radio propagation
C.   Ripples in the ionosphere
D.   A temporary disturbance in the Earth's magnetosphere

G3A07
At what point in the solar cycle does the 20-meter band usually support worldwide propagation during daylight hours?
A. At the summer solstice
B. Only at the maximum point of the solar cycle
C. Only at the minimum point of the solar cycle
D. At any point in the solar cycle

G3A07
(D)
Page 8-6

G3A08
Which of the following effects can a geomagnetic storm have on radio propagation?
A. Improved high-latitude HF propagation
B. Degraded high-latitude HF propagation
C. Improved ground-wave propagation
D. Improved chances of UHF ducting

G3A08
(B)
Page 8-9

G3A09
What effect does a high sunspot number have on radio communications?
A. High-frequency radio signals become weak and distorted
B. Frequencies above 300 MHz become usable for long-distance communication
C. Long-distance communication in the upper HF and lower VHF range is enhanced
D. Microwave communications become unstable

G3A09
(C)
Page 8-6

G3A10
What causes HF propagation conditions to vary periodically in a 28 day cycle?
A. Long term oscillations in the upper atmosphere
B. Cyclic variation in the Earth's radiation belts
C. The Sun's rotation on its axis
D. The position of the Moon in its orbit

G3A10
(C)
Page 8-6

G3A11
Approximately how long is the typical sunspot cycle?
A. 8 minutes
B. 40 hours
C. 28 days
D. 11 years

G3A11
(D)
Page 8-5

G3A12
What does the K-index indicate?
A. The relative position of sunspots on the surface of the Sun
B. The short term stability of the Earth's magnetic field
C. The stability of the Sun's magnetic field
D. The solar radio flux at Boulder, Colorado

G3A12
(B)
Page 8-7

G3A13
What does the A-index indicate?
A. The relative position of sunspots on the surface of the Sun
B. The amount of polarization of the Sun's electric field
C. The long term stability of the Earth's geomagnetic field
D. The solar radio flux at Boulder, Colorado

G3A13
(C)
Page 8-7

G3A14
How are radio communications usually affected by the charged particles that reach the Earth from solar coronal holes?
A. HF communications are improved
B. HF communications are disturbed
C. VHF/UHF ducting is improved
D. VHF/UHF ducting is disturbed

G3A14
(B)
Page 8-9

G3A15
(D)
Page 8-9

G3A15
How long does it take charged particles from coronal mass ejections to affect radio propagation on the Earth?
A. 28 days
B. 14 days
C. 4 to 8 minutes
D. 20 to 40 hours

G3A16
(A)
Page 8-10

G3A16
What is a possible benefit to radio communications resulting from periods of high geomagnetic activity?
A. Auroras that can reflect VHF signals
B. Higher signal strength for HF signals passing through the polar regions
C. Improved HF long path propagation
D. Reduced long delayed echoes

G3B — Maximum Usable Frequency; Lowest Usable Frequency; propagation

G3B01
(D)
Page 8-5

G3B01
How might a sky-wave signal sound if it arrives at your receiver by both short path and long path propagation?
A. Periodic fading approximately every 10 seconds
B. Signal strength increased by 3 dB
C. The signal might be cancelled causing severe attenuation
D. A well-defined echo might be heard

G3B02
(A)
Page 8-4

G3B02
Which of the following is a good indicator of the possibility of sky-wave propagation on the 6-meter band?
A. Short skip sky-wave propagation on the 10-meter band
B. Long skip sky-wave propagation on the 10-meter band
C. Severe attenuation of signals on the 10-meter band
D. Long delayed echoes on the 10-meter band

G3B03
(A)
Page 8-8

G3B03
Which of the following applies when selecting a frequency for lowest attenuation when transmitting on HF?
A. Select a frequency just below the MUF
B. Select a frequency just above the LUF
C. Select a frequency just below the critical frequency
D. Select a frequency just above the critical frequency

G3B04
(A)
Page 8-8

G3B04
What is a reliable way to determine if the MUF is high enough to support skip propagation between your station and a distant location on frequencies between 14 and 30 MHz?
A. Listen for signals from an international beacon in the frequency range you plan to use
B. Send a series of dots on the band and listen for echoes from your signal
C. Check the strength of TV signals from Western Europe
D. Check the strength of signals in the MF AM broadcast band

G3B05
What usually happens to radio waves with frequencies below the MUF and above the LUF when they are sent into the ionosphere?
A. They are bent back to the Earth
B. They pass through the ionosphere
C. They are amplified by interaction with the ionosphere
D. They are bent and trapped in the ionosphere to circle the Earth

G3B05
(A)
Page 8-3

G3B06
What usually happens to radio waves with frequencies below the LUF?
A. They are bent back to the Earth
B. They pass through the ionosphere
C. They are completely absorbed by the ionosphere
D. They are bent and trapped in the ionosphere to circle the Earth

G3B06
(C)
Page 8-8

G3B07
What does LUF stand for?
A. The Lowest Usable Frequency for communications between two points
B. The Longest Universal Function for communications between two points
C. The Lowest Usable Frequency during a 24 hour period
D. The Longest Universal Function during a 24 hour period

G3B07
(A)
Page 8-7

G3B08
What does MUF stand for?
A. The Minimum Usable Frequency for communications between two points
B. The Maximum Usable Frequency for communications between two points
C. The Minimum Usable Frequency during a 24 hour period
D. The Maximum Usable Frequency during a 24 hour period

G3B08
(B)
Page 8-7

G3B09
What is the approximate maximum distance along the Earth's surface that is normally covered in one hop using the F2 region?
A. 180 miles
B. 1,200 miles
C. 2,500 miles
D. 12,000 miles

G3B09
(C)
Page 8-4

G3B10
What is the approximate maximum distance along the Earth's surface that is normally covered in one hop using the E region?
A. 180 miles
B. 1,200 miles
C. 2,500 miles
D. 12,000 miles

G3B10
(B)
Page 8-4

G3B11
What happens to HF propagation when the LUF exceeds the MUF?
A. No HF radio frequency will support ordinary sky-wave communications over the path
B. HF communications over the path are enhanced
C. Double hop propagation along the path is more common
D. Propagation over the path on all HF frequencies is enhanced

G3B11
(A)
Page 8-8

G3B12
What factor or factors affect the MUF?
A. Path distance and location
B. Time of day and season
C. Solar radiation and ionospheric disturbances
D. All of these choices are correct

G3C — Ionospheric layers; critical angle and frequency; HF scatter; Near Vertical Incidence Sky-wave

G3C01
Which ionospheric layer is closest to the surface of the Earth?
A. The D layer
B. The E layer
C. The F1 layer
D. The F2 layer

G3C02
Where on the Earth do ionospheric layers reach their maximum height?
A. Where the Sun is overhead
B. Where the Sun is on the opposite side of the Earth
C. Where the Sun is rising
D. Where the Sun has just set

G3C03
Why is the F2 region mainly responsible for the longest distance radio wave propagation?
A. Because it is the densest ionospheric layer
B. Because it does not absorb radio waves as much as other ionospheric regions
C. Because it is the highest ionospheric region
D. All of these choices are correct

G3C04
What does the term "critical angle" mean as used in radio wave propagation?
A. The long path azimuth of a distant station
B. The short path azimuth of a distant station
C. The lowest takeoff angle that will return a radio wave to the Earth under specific ionospheric conditions
D. The highest takeoff angle that will return a radio wave to the Earth under specific ionospheric conditions

G3C05
Why is long distance communication on the 40-meter, 60-meter, 80-meter and 160-meter bands more difficult during the day?
A. The F layer absorbs signals at these frequencies during daylight hours
B. The F layer is unstable during daylight hours
C. The D layer absorbs signals at these frequencies during daylight hours
D. The E layer is unstable during daylight hours

G3C06
What is a characteristic of HF scatter signals?
A. They have high intelligibility
B. They have a wavering sound
C. They have very large swings in signal strength
D. All of these choices are correct

G3C07
What makes HF scatter signals often sound distorted?
A. The ionospheric layer involved is unstable
B. Ground waves are absorbing much of the signal
C. The E-region is not present
D. Energy is scattered into the skip zone through several different radio wave paths

G3C08
Why are HF scatter signals in the skip zone usually weak?
A. Only a small part of the signal energy is scattered into the skip zone
B. Signals are scattered from the magnetosphere which is not a good reflector
C. Propagation is through ground waves which absorb most of the signal energy
D. Propagations is through ducts in F region which absorb most of the energy

G3C09
What type of radio wave propagation allows a signal to be detected at a distance too far for ground wave propagation but too near for normal sky-wave propagation?
A. Faraday rotation
B. Scatter
C. Sporadic-E skip
D. Short-path skip

G3C10
Which of the following might be an indication that signals heard on the HF bands are being received via scatter propagation?
A. The communication is during a sunspot maximum
B. The communication is during a sudden ionospheric disturbance
C. The signal is heard on a frequency below the Maximum Usable Frequency
D. The signal is heard on a frequency above the Maximum Usable Frequency

G3C11
Which of the following antenna types will be most effective for skip communications on 40-meters during the day?
A. A vertical antenna
B. A horizontal dipole placed between 1/8 and 1/4 wavelength above the ground
C. A left-hand circularly polarized antenna
D. A right-hand circularly polarized antenna

G3C12
Which ionospheric layer is the most absorbent of long skip signals during daylight hours on frequencies below 10 MHz?
A. The F2 layer
B. The F1 layer
C. The E layer
D. The D layer

G3C13
What is Near Vertical Incidence Sky-wave (NVIS) propagation?
A. Propagation near the MUF
B. Short distance MF or HF propagation using high elevation angles
C. Long path HF propagation at sunrise and sunset
D. Double hop propagation near the LUF

G3C07
(D)
Page 8-11

G3C08
(A)
Page 8-11

G3C09
(B)
Page 8-11

G3C10
(D)
Page 8-11

G3C11
(B)
Page 8-11

G3C12
(D)
Page 8-4

G3C13
(B)
Page 8-11

SUBELEMENT G4 — AMATEUR RADIO PRACTICES
[5 Exam Questions — 5 Groups]

G4A — Station Operation and set up

G4A01
(B)
Page 5-16

G4A01
What is the purpose of the "notch filter" found on many HF transceivers?
A.   To restrict the transmitter voice bandwidth
B.   To reduce interference from carriers in the receiver passband
C.   To eliminate receiver interference from impulse noise sources
D.   To enhance the reception of a specific frequency on a crowded band

G4A02
(C)
Page 5-16

G4A02
What is one advantage of selecting the opposite or "reverse" sideband when receiving CW signals on a typical HF transceiver?
A.   Interference from impulse noise will be eliminated
B.   More stations can be accommodated within a given signal passband
C.   It may be possible to reduce or eliminate interference from other signals
D.   Accidental out of band operation can be prevented

G4A03
(C)
Page 5-8

G4A03
What is normally meant by operating a transceiver in "split" mode?
A.   The radio is operating at half power
B.   The transceiver is operating from an external power source
C.   The transceiver is set to different transmit and receive frequencies
D.   The transmitter is emitting an SSB signal, as opposed to DSB operation

G4A04
(B)
Page 5-13

G4A04
What reading on the plate current meter of a vacuum tube RF power amplifier indicates correct adjustment of the plate tuning control?
A.   A pronounced peak
B.   A pronounced dip
C.   No change will be observed
D.   A slow, rhythmic oscillation

G4A05
(C)
Page 5-13

G4A05
What is a reason to use Automatic Level Control (ALC) with an RF power amplifier?
A.   To balance the transmitter audio frequency response
B.   To reduce harmonic radiation
C.   To reduce distortion due to excessive drive
D.   To increase overall efficiency

G4A06
(C)
Page 7-19

G4A06
What type of device is often used to match transmitter output impedance to an impedance not equal to 50 ohms?
A.   Balanced modulator
B.   SWR Bridge
C.   Antenna coupler or antenna tuner
D.   Q Multiplier

G4A07

What condition can lead to permanent damage to a solid-state RF power amplifier?

A. Insufficient drive power

B. Low input SWR

C. Shorting the input signal to ground

D. Excessive drive power

G4A07
(D)
Page5-13

G4A08

What is the correct adjustment for the load or coupling control of a vacuum tube RF power amplifier?

A. Minimum SWR on the antenna

B. Minimum plate current without exceeding maximum allowable grid current

C. Highest plate voltage while minimizing grid current

D. Maximum power output without exceeding maximum allowable plate current

G4A08
(D)
Page 5-13

G4A09

Why is a time delay sometimes included in a transmitter keying circuit?

A. To prevent stations from interfering with one another

B. To allow the transmitter power regulators to charge properly

C. To allow time for transmit-receive changeover operations to complete properly before RF output is allowed

D. To allow time for a warning signal to be sent to other stations

G4A09
(C)
Page 5-13

G4A10

What is the purpose of an electronic keyer?

A. Automatic transmit/receive switching

B. Automatic generation of strings of dots and dashes for CW operation

C. VOX operation

D. Computer interface for PSK and RTTY operation

G4A10
(B)
Page 2-11

G4A11

Which of the following is a use for the IF shift control on a receiver?

A. To avoid interference from stations very close to the receive frequency

B. To change frequency rapidly

C. To permit listening on a different frequency from that on which you are transmitting

D. To tune in stations that are slightly off frequency without changing your transmit frequency

G4A11
(A)
Page 5-16

G4A12

Which of the following is a common use for the dual VFO feature on a transceiver?

A. To allow transmitting on two frequencies at once

B. To permit full duplex operation, that is transmitting and receiving at the same time

C. To permit monitoring of two different frequencies

D. To facilitate computer interface

G4A12
(C)
Page 5-8

G4A13

What is one reason to use the attenuator function that is present on many HF transceivers?

A. To reduce signal overload due to strong incoming signals

B. To reduce the transmitter power when driving a linear amplifier

C. To reduce power consumption when operating from batteries

D. To slow down received CW signals for better copy

G4A13
(A)
Page 5-18

G4A14
(B)
Page 6-11

G4A14
What is likely to happen if a transceiver's ALC system is not set properly when transmitting AFSK signals with the radio using single sideband mode?
A. ALC will invert the modulation of the AFSK mode
B. Improper action of ALC distorts the signal and can cause spurious emissions
C. When using digital modes, too much ALC activity can cause the transmitter to overheat
D. All of these choices are correct

G4A15
(D)
Page 5-20

G4A15
Which of the following can be a symptom of transmitted RF being picked up by an audio cable carrying AFSK data signals between a computer and a transceiver?
A. The VOX circuit does not un-key the transmitter
B. The transmitter signal is distorted
C. Frequent connection timeouts
D. All of these choices are correct

G4B — Test and monitoring equipment; two-tone test

G4B01
(D)
Page 4-38

G4B01
What item of test equipment contains horizontal and vertical channel amplifiers?
A. An ohmmeter
B. A signal generator
C. An ammeter
D. An oscilloscope

G4B02
(D)
Page 4-38

G4B02
Which of the following is an advantage of an oscilloscope versus a digital voltmeter?
A. An oscilloscope uses less power
B. Complex impedances can be easily measured
C. Input impedance is much lower
D. Complex waveforms can be measured

G4B03
(A)
Page 4-38

G4B03
Which of the following is the best instrument to use when checking the keying waveform of a CW transmitter?
A. An oscilloscope
B. A field strength meter
C. A sidetone monitor
D. A wavemeter

G4B04
(D)
Page 4-38

G4B04
What signal source is connected to the vertical input of an oscilloscope when checking the RF envelope pattern of a transmitted signal?
A. The local oscillator of the transmitter
B. An external RF oscillator
C. The transmitter balanced mixer output
D. The attenuated RF output of the transmitter

G4B05
(D)
Page 4-38

G4B05
Why is high input impedance desirable for a voltmeter?
A. It improves the frequency response
B. It decreases battery consumption in the meter
C. It improves the resolution of the readings
D. It decreases the loading on circuits being measured

G4B06
What is an advantage of a digital voltmeter as compared to an analog voltmeter?
A. Better for measuring computer circuits
B. Better for RF measurements
C. Better precision for most uses
D. Faster response

G4B06
(C)
Page 4-37

G4B07
What signals are used to conduct a two-tone test?
A. Two audio signals of the same frequency shifted 90 degrees
B. Two non-harmonically related audio signals
C. Two swept frequency tones
D. Two audio frequency range square wave signals of equal amplitude

G4B07
(B)
Page 5-11

G4B08
Which of the following instruments may be used to monitor relative RF output when making antenna and transmitter adjustments?
A. A field strength meter
B. An antenna noise bridge
C. A multimeter
D. A Q meter

G4B08
(A)
Page 4-40

G4B09
Which of the following can be determined with a field strength meter?
A. The radiation resistance of an antenna
B. The radiation pattern of an antenna
C. The presence and amount of phase distortion of a transmitter
D. The presence and amount of amplitude distortion of a transmitter

G4B09
(B)
Page 4-40

G4B10
Which of the following can be determined with a directional wattmeter?
A. Standing wave ratio
B. Antenna front-to-back ratio
C. RF interference
D. Radio wave propagation

G4B10
(A)
Page 4-40

G4B11
Which of the following must be connected to an antenna analyzer when it is being used for SWR measurements?
A. Receiver
B. Transmitter
C. Antenna and feed line
D. All of these choices are correct

G4B11
(C)
Page 4-39

G4B12
What problem can occur when making measurements on an antenna system with an antenna analyzer?
A. Permanent damage to the analyzer may occur if it is operated into a high SWR
B. Strong signals from nearby transmitters can affect the accuracy of measurements
C. The analyzer can be damaged if measurements outside the ham bands are attempted
D. Connecting the analyzer to an antenna can cause it to absorb harmonics

G4B12
(B)
Page 4-39

G4B13
(C)
Page 4-39

G4B13
What is a use for an antenna analyzer other than measuring the SWR of an antenna system?
A. Measuring the front to back ratio of an antenna
B. Measuring the turns ratio of a power transformer
C. Determining the impedance of an unknown or unmarked coaxial cable
D. Determining the gain of a directional antenna

G4B14
(D)
Page 4-37

G4B14
What is an instance in which the use of an instrument with analog readout may be preferred over an instrument with a digital readout?
A. When testing logic circuits
B. When high precision is desired
C. When measuring the frequency of an oscillator
D. When adjusting tuned circuits

G4B15
(A)
Page 5-11

G4B15
What type of transmitter performance does a two-tone test analyze?
A. Linearity
B. Percentage of suppression of carrier and undesired sideband for SSB
C. Percentage of frequency modulation
D. Percentage of carrier phase shift

G4C — Interference with consumer electronics; grounding; DSP

G4C01
(B)
Page 5-22

G4C01
Which of the following might be useful in reducing RF interference to audio frequency devices?
A. Bypass inductor
B. Bypass capacitor
C. Forward-biased diode
D. Reverse-biased diode

G4C02
(C)
Page 5-22

G4C02
Which of the following could be a cause of interference covering a wide range of frequencies?
A. Not using a balun or line isolator to feed balanced antennas
B. Lack of rectification of the transmitter's signal in power conductors
C. Arcing at a poor electrical connection
D. Using a balun to feed an unbalanced antenna

G4C03
(C)
Page 5-22

G4C03
What sound is heard from an audio device or telephone if there is interference from a nearby single sideband phone transmitter?
A. A steady hum whenever the transmitter is on the air
B. On-and-off humming or clicking
C. Distorted speech
D. Clearly audible speech

G4C04
(A)
Page 5-22

G4C04
What is the effect on an audio device or telephone system if there is interference from a nearby CW transmitter?
A. On-and-off humming or clicking
B. A CW signal at a nearly pure audio frequency
C. A chirpy CW signal
D. Severely distorted audio

G4C05

What might be the problem if you receive an RF burn when touching your equipment while transmitting on an HF band, assuming the equipment is connected to a ground rod?
A. Flat braid rather than round wire has been used for the ground wire
B. Insulated wire has been used for the ground wire
C. The ground rod is resonant
D. The ground wire has high impedance on that frequency

G4C06

What effect can be caused by a resonant ground connection?
A. Overheating of ground straps
B. Corrosion of the ground rod
C. High RF voltages on the enclosures of station equipment
D. A ground loop

G4C07

What is one good way to avoid unwanted effects of stray RF energy in an amateur station?
A. Connect all equipment grounds together
B. Install an RF filter in series with the ground wire
C. Use a ground loop for best conductivity
D. Install a few ferrite beads on the ground wire where it connects to your station

G4C08

Which of the following would reduce RF interference caused by common-mode current on an audio cable?
A. Placing a ferrite choke around the cable
B. Adding series capacitors to the conductors
C. Adding shunt inductors to the conductors
D. Adding an additional insulating jacket to the cable

G4C09

How can a ground loop be avoided?
A. Connect all ground conductors in series
B. Connect the AC neutral conductor to the ground wire
C. Avoid using lock washers and star washers when making ground connections
D. Connect all ground conductors to a single point

G4C10

What could be a symptom of a ground loop somewhere in your station?
A. You receive reports of "hum" on your station's transmitted signal
B. The SWR reading for one or more antennas is suddenly very high
C. An item of station equipment starts to draw excessive amounts of current
D. You receive reports of harmonic interference from your station

G4C11

Which of the following is a function of a digital signal processor?
A. To provide adequate grounding
B. To remove noise from received signals
C. To increase antenna gain
D. To increase antenna bandwidth

G4C05
(D)
Page 5-21

G4C06
(C)
Page 5-21

G4C07
(A)
Page 5-20

G4C08
(A)
Page 5-22

G4C09
(D)
Page 5-21

G4C10
(A)
Page 5-21

G4C11
(B)
Page 5-17

G4C12

Which of the following is an advantage of a receiver DSP IF filter as compared to an analog filter?
A. A wide range of filter bandwidths and shapes can be created
B. Fewer digital components are required
C. Mixing products are greatly reduced
D. The DSP filter is much more effective at VHF frequencies

G4C13

Which of the following can perform automatic notching of interfering carriers?
A. Bandpass tuning
B. A Digital Signal Processor (DSP) filter
C. Balanced mixing
D. A noise limiter

G4D — Speech processors; S meters; sideband operation near band edges

G4D01

What is the purpose of a speech processor as used in a modern transceiver?
A. Increase the intelligibility of transmitted phone signals during poor conditions
B. Increase transmitter bass response for more natural sounding SSB signals
C. Prevent distortion of voice signals
D. Decrease high-frequency voice output to prevent out of band operation

G4D02

Which of the following describes how a speech processor affects a transmitted single sideband phone signal?
A. It increases peak power
B. It increases average power
C. It reduces harmonic distortion
D. It reduces intermodulation distortion

G4D03

Which of the following can be the result of an incorrectly adjusted speech processor?
A. Distorted speech
B. Splatter
C. Excessive background pickup
D. All of these choices are correct

G4D04

What does an S meter measure?
A. Conductance
B. Impedance
C. Received signal strength
D. Transmitter power output

G4D05

How does a signal that reads 20 dB over S9 compare to one that reads S9 on a receiver, assuming a properly calibrated S meter?
A. It is 10 times less powerful
B. It is 20 times less powerful
C. It is 20 times more powerful
D. It is 100 times more powerful

G4D06
Where is an S meter found?
A. In a receiver
B. In an SWR bridge
C. In a transmitter
D. In a conductance bridge

G4D06
(A)
Page 5-18

G4D07
How much must the power output of a transmitter be raised to change the S meter reading on a distant receiver from S8 to S9?
A. Approximately 1.5 times
B. Approximately 2 times
C. Approximately 4 times
D. Approximately 8 times

G4D07
(C)
Page 5-18

G4D08
What frequency range is occupied by a 3 kHz LSB signal when the displayed carrier frequency is set to 7.178 MHz?
A. 7.178 to 7.181 MHz
B. 7.178 to 7.184 MHz
C. 7.175 to 7.178 MHz
D. 7.1765 to 7.1795 MHz

G4D08
(C)
Page 5-5

G4D09
What frequency range is occupied by a 3 kHz USB signal with the displayed carrier frequency set to 14.347 MHz?
A. 14.347 to 14.647 MHz
B. 14.347 to 14.350 MHz
C. 14.344 to 14.347 MHz
D. 14.3455 to 14.3485 MHz

G4D09
(B)
Page 5-5

G4D10
How close to the lower edge of the 40-meter General Class phone segment should your displayed carrier frequency be when using 3 kHz wide LSB?
A. At least 3 kHz above the edge of the segment
B. At least 3 kHz below the edge of the segment
C. Your displayed carrier frequency may be set at the edge of the segment
D. At least 1 kHz above the edge of the segment

G4D10
(A)
Page 5-5

G4D11
How close to the upper edge of the 20-meter General Class band should your displayed carrier frequency be when using 3 kHz wide USB?
A. At least 3 kHz above the edge of the band
B. At least 3 kHz below the edge of the band
C. Your displayed carrier frequency may be set at the edge of the band
D. At least 1 kHz below the edge of the segment

G4D11
(B)
Page 5-5

G4E — HF mobile radio installations; emergency and battery powered operation

G4E01
(C)
Page 7-5

G4E01
What is the purpose of a capacitance hat on a mobile antenna?
A. To increase the power handling capacity of a whip antenna
B. To allow automatic band changing
C. To electrically lengthen a physically short antenna
D. To allow remote tuning

G4E02
(D)
Page 7-5

G4E02
What is the purpose of a corona ball on a HF mobile antenna?
A. To narrow the operating bandwidth of the antenna
B. To increase the "Q" of the antenna
C. To reduce the chance of damage if the antenna should strike an object
D. To reduce high voltage discharge from the tip of the antenna

G4E03
(A)
Page 5-19

G4E03
Which of the following direct, fused power connections would be the best for a 100 watt HF mobile installation?
A. To the battery using heavy gauge wire
B. To the alternator or generator using heavy gauge wire
C. To the battery using resistor wire
D. To the alternator or generator using resistor wire

G4E04
(B)
Page 5-19

G4E04
Why is it best NOT to draw the DC power for a 100 watt HF transceiver from a vehicle's auxiliary power socket?
A. The socket is not wired with an RF-shielded power cable
B. The socket's wiring may be inadequate for the current drawn by the transceiver
C. The DC polarity of the socket is reversed from the polarity of modern HF transceivers
D. Drawing more than 50 watts from this socket could cause the engine to overheat

G4E05
(C)
Page 5-19

G4E05
Which of the following most limits the effectiveness of an HF mobile transceiver operating in the 75-meter band?
A. "Picket Fencing" signal variation
B. The wire gauge of the DC power line to the transceiver
C. The antenna system
D. FCC rules limiting mobile output power on the 75-meter band

G4E06
(C)
Page 7-5

G4E06
What is one disadvantage of using a shortened mobile antenna as opposed to a full size antenna?
A. Short antennas are more likely to cause distortion of transmitted signals
B. Short antennas can only receive circularly polarized signals
C. Operating bandwidth may be very limited
D. Harmonic radiation may increase

G4E07
(D)
Page 5-20

G4E07
Which of the following may cause interference to be heard in the receiver of an HF radio installed in a recent model vehicle?
A. The battery charging system
B. The fuel delivery system
C. The vehicle control computer
D. All of these choices are correct

G4E08
What is the name of the process by which sunlight is changed directly into electricity?
A. Photovoltaic conversion
B. Photon emission
C. Photosynthesis
D. Photon decomposition

G4E08
(A)
Page 4-33

G4E09
What is the approximate open-circuit voltage from a fully illuminated silicon photovoltaic cell?
A. 0.02 VDC
B. 0.5 VDC
C. 0.2 VDC
D. 1.38 VDC

G4E09
(B)
Page 4-33

G4E10
What is the reason that a series diode is connected between a solar panel and a storage battery that is being charged by the panel?
A. The diode serves to regulate the charging voltage to prevent overcharge
B. The diode prevents self-discharge of the battery through the panel during times of low or no illumination
C. The diode limits the current flowing from the panel to a safe value
D. The diode greatly increases the efficiency during times of high illumination

G4E10
(B)
Page 4-34

G4E11
Which of the following is a disadvantage of using wind as the primary source of power for an emergency station?
A. The conversion efficiency from mechanical energy to electrical energy is less than 2 percent
B. The voltage and current ratings of such systems are not compatible with amateur equipment
C. A large energy storage system is needed to supply power when the wind is not blowing
D. All of these choices are correct

G4E11
(C)
Page 4-33

SUBELEMENT G5 — ELECTRICAL PRINCIPLES
[3 Exam Questions — 3 Groups]

G5A — Reactance; inductance; capacitance; impedance; impedance matching

G5A01
What is impedance?
A. The electric charge stored by a capacitor
B. The inverse of resistance
C. The opposition to the flow of current in an AC circuit
D. The force of repulsion between two similar electric fields

G5A01
(C)
Page 4-18

G5A02
What is reactance?
A. Opposition to the flow of direct current caused by resistance
B. Opposition to the flow of alternating current caused by capacitance or inductance
C. A property of ideal resistors in AC circuits
D. A large spark produced at switch contacts when an inductor is de-energized

G5A02
(B)
Page 4-16

G5A03
(D)
Page 4-16

G5A03
Which of the following causes opposition to the flow of alternating current in an inductor?
A. Conductance
B. Reluctance
C. Admittance
D. Reactance

G5A04
(C)
Page 4-16

G5A04
Which of the following causes opposition to the flow of alternating current in a capacitor?
A. Conductance
B. Reluctance
C. Reactance
D. Admittance

G5A05
(D)
Page 4-18

G5A05
How does an inductor react to AC?
A. As the frequency of the applied AC increases, the reactance decreases
B. As the amplitude of the applied AC increases, the reactance increases
C. As the amplitude of the applied AC increases, the reactance decreases
D. As the frequency of the applied AC increases, the reactance increases

G5A06
(A)
Page 4-17

G5A06
How does a capacitor react to AC?
A. As the frequency of the applied AC increases, the reactance decreases
B. As the frequency of the applied AC increases, the reactance increases
C. As the amplitude of the applied AC increases, the reactance increases
D. As the amplitude of the applied AC increases, the reactance decreases

G5A07
(D)
Page 4-19

G5A07
What happens when the impedance of an electrical load is equal to the output impedance of a power source, assuming both impedances are resistive?
A. The source delivers minimum power to the load
B. The electrical load is shorted
C. No current can flow through the circuit
D. The source can deliver maximum power to the load

G5A08
(A)
Page 4-19

G5A08
Why is impedance matching important?
A. So the source can deliver maximum power to the load
B. So the load will draw minimum power from the source
C. To ensure that there is less resistance than reactance in the circuit
D. To ensure that the resistance and reactance in the circuit are equal

G5A09
(B)
Page 4-16

G5A09
What unit is used to measure reactance?
A. Farad
B. Ohm
C. Ampere
D. Siemens

G5A10
(B)
Page 4-18

G5A10
What unit is used to measure impedance?
A. Volt
B. Ohm
C. Ampere
D. Watt

G5A11
Which of the following describes one method of impedance matching between two AC circuits?
A. Insert an LC network between the two circuits
B. Reduce the power output of the first circuit
C. Increase the power output of the first circuit
D. Insert a circulator between the two circuits

G5A12
What is one reason to use an impedance matching transformer?
A. To minimize transmitter power output
B. To maximize the transfer of power
C. To reduce power supply ripple
D. To minimize radiation resistance

G5A13
Which of the following devices can be used for impedance matching at radio frequencies?
A. A transformer
B. A Pi-network
C. A length of transmission line
D. All of these choices are correct

G5B — The Decibel; current and voltage dividers; electrical power calculations; sine wave root-mean-square (RMS) values; PEP calculations

G5B01
What dB change represents a two-times increase or decrease in power?
A. Approximately 2 dB
B. Approximately 3 dB
C. Approximately 6 dB
D. Approximately 12 dB

G5B02
How does the total current relate to the individual currents in each branch of a purely resistive parallel circuit?
A. It equals the average of each branch current
B. It decreases as more parallel branches are added to the circuit
C. It equals the sum of the currents through each branch
D. It is the sum of the reciprocal of each individual voltage drop

G5B03
How many watts of electrical power are used if 400 VDC is supplied to an 800 ohm load?
A. 0.5 watts
B. 200 watts
C. 400 watts
D. 3200 watts

G5B04
How many watts of electrical power are used by a 12 VDC light bulb that draws 0.2 amperes?
A. 2.4 watts
B. 24 watts
C. 6 watts
D. 60 watts

G5A11
(A)
Page 4-19

G5A12
(B)
Page 4-20

G5A13
(D)
Page 4-20

G5B01
(B)
Page 4-4

G5B02
(C)
Page 4-12

G5B03
(B)
Page 4-2

G5B04
(A)
Page 4-2

G5B05
(A)
Page 4-2

G5B05
How many watts are dissipated when a current of 7.0 milliamperes flows through 1.25 kilohms resistance?
A. Approximately 61 milliwatts
B. Approximately 61 watts
C. Approximately 11 milliwatts
D. Approximately 11 watts

G5B06
(B)
Page 4-6

G5B06
What is the output PEP from a transmitter if an oscilloscope measures 200 volts peak-to-peak across a 50 ohm dummy load connected to the transmitter output?
A. 1.4 watts
B. 100 watts
C. 353.5 watts
D. 400 watts

G5B07
(C)
Page 4-5

G5B07
What value of an AC signal produces the same power dissipation in a resistor as a DC voltage of the same value?
A. The peak-to-peak value
B. The peak value
C. The RMS value
D. The reciprocal of the RMS value

G5B08
Withdrawn

G5B08 — This question has been withdrawn.

G5B09
(B)
Page 4-6

G5B09
What is the RMS voltage of a sine wave with a value of 17 volts peak?
A. 8.5 volts
B. 12 volts
C. 24 volts
D. 34 volts

G5B10
(C)
Page 4-4

G5B10
What percentage of power loss would result from a transmission line loss of 1 dB?
A. 10.9 percent
B. 12.2 percent
C. 20.5 percent
D. 25.9 percent

G5B11
(B)
Page 4-7

G5B11
What is the ratio of peak envelope power to average power for an unmodulated carrier?
A. 0.707
B. 1.00
C. 1.414
D. 2.00

G5B12
(B)
Page 4-6

G5B12
What would be the RMS voltage across a 50 ohm dummy load dissipating 1200 watts?
A. 173 volts
B. 245 volts
C. 346 volts
D. 692 volts

G5B13

What is the output PEP of an unmodulated carrier if an average reading wattmeter connected to the transmitter output indicates 1060 watts?

A. 530 watts
B. 1060 watts
C. 1500 watts
D. 2120 watts

G5B13
(B)
Page 4-7

G5B14

What is the output PEP from a transmitter if an oscilloscope measures 500 volts peak-to-peak across a 50 ohm resistive load connected to the transmitter output?

A. 8.75 watts
B. 625 watts
C. 2500 watts
D. 5000 watts

G5B14
(B)
Page 4-6

G5C — Resistors, capacitors, and inductors in series and parallel; transformers

G5C01

What causes a voltage to appear across the secondary winding of a transformer when an AC voltage source is connected across its primary winding?

A. Capacitive coupling
B. Displacement current coupling
C. Mutual inductance
D. Mutual capacitance

G5C01
(C)
Page 4-15

G5C02

What happens if you reverse the primary and secondary windings of a 4:1 voltage step down transformer?

A. The secondary voltage becomes 4 times the primary voltage
B. The transformer no longer functions as it is a unidirectional device
C. Additional resistance must be added in series with the primary to prevent overload
D. Additional resistance must be added in parallel with the secondary to prevent overload

G5C02
(A)
Page 4-16

G5C03

Which of the following components should be added to an existing resistor to increase the resistance?

A. A resistor in parallel
B. A resistor in series
C. A capacitor in series
D. A capacitor in parallel

G5C03
(B)
Page 4-13

G5C04

What is the total resistance of three 100 ohm resistors in parallel?

A. 0.30 ohms
B. 0.33 ohms
C. 33.3 ohms
D. 300 ohms

G5C04
(C)
Page 4-14

G5C05
(C)
Page 4-15

G5C05
If three equal value resistors in series produce 450 ohms, what is the value of each resistor?
A. 1500 ohms
B. 90 ohms
C. 150 ohms
D. 175 ohms

G5C06
(C)
Page 4-16

G5C06
What is the RMS voltage across a 500-turn secondary winding in a transformer if the 2250-turn primary is connected to 120 VAC?
A. 2370 volts
B. 540 volts
C. 26.7 volts
D. 5.9 volts

G5C07
(A)
Page 4-19

G5C07
What is the turns ratio of a transformer used to match an audio amplifier having 600 ohm output impedance to a speaker having 4 ohm impedance?
A. 12.2 to 1
B. 24.4 to 1
C. 150 to 1
D. 300 to 1

G5C08
(D)
Page 4-15

G5C08
What is the equivalent capacitance of two 5.0 nanofarad capacitors and one 750 picofarad capacitor connected in parallel?
A. 576.9 nanofarads
B. 1733 picofarads
C. 3583 picofarads
D. 10.750 nanofarads

G5C09
(C)
Page 4-14

G5C09
What is the capacitance of three 100 microfarad capacitors connected in series?
A. 0.30 microfarads
B. 0.33 microfarads
C. 33.3 microfarads
D. 300 microfarads

G5C10
(C)
Page 4-14

G5C10
What is the inductance of three 10 millihenry inductors connected in parallel?
A. 0.30 henrys
B. 3.3 henrys
C. 3.3 millihenrys
D. 30 millihenrys

G5C11
(C)
Page 4-14

G5C11
What is the inductance of a 20 millihenry inductor connected in series with a 50 millihenry inductor?
A. 0.07 millihenrys
B. 14.3 millihenrys
C. 70 millihenrys
D. 1000 millihenrys

G5C12

What is the capacitance of a 20 microfarad capacitor connected in series with a 50 microfarad capacitor?

A.   0.07 microfarads
B.   14.3 microfarads
C.   70 microfarads
D.   1000 microfarads

G5C12
(B)
Page 4-14

G5C13

Which of the following components should be added to a capacitor to increase the capacitance?

A.   An inductor in series
B.   A resistor in series
C.   A capacitor in parallel
D.   A capacitor in series

G5C13
(C)
Page 4-13

G5C14

Which of the following components should be added to an inductor to increase the inductance?

A.   A capacitor in series
B.   A resistor in parallel
C.   An inductor in parallel
D.   An inductor in series

G5C14
(D)
Page 4-13

G5C15

What is the total resistance of a 10 ohm, a 20 ohm, and a 50 ohm resistor connected in parallel?

A.   5.9 ohms
B.   0.17 ohms
C.   10000 ohms
D.   80 ohms

G5C15
(A)
Page 4-14

G5C16

Why is the conductor of the primary winding of many voltage step up transformers larger in diameter than the conductor of the secondary winding?

A.   To improve the coupling between the primary and secondary
B.   To accommodate the higher current of the primary
C.   To prevent parasitic oscillations due to resistive losses in the primary
D.   To insure that the volume of the primary winding is equal to the volume of the secondary winding

G5C16
(B)
Page 4-15

G5C17

What is the value in nanofarads (nF) of a 22,000 pF capacitor?

A. 0.22 nF
B. 2.2 nF
C. 22 nF
D. 220 nF

G5C17
(C)
Page 4-7

G5C18

What is the value in microfarads of a 4700 nanofarad (nF) capacitor?

A. 47 µF
B. 0.47 µF
C. 47,000 µF
D. 4.7 µF

G5C18
(D)
Page 4-7

SUBELEMENT G6 — CIRCUIT COMPONENTS

[2 Exam Questions — 2 Groups]

G6A — Resistors; Capacitors; Inductors; Rectifiers; solid state diodes and transistors; vacuum tubes; batteries

G6A01
(C)
Page 4-32

G6A01
What is the minimum allowable discharge voltage for maximum life of a standard 12 volt lead acid battery?
A. 6 volts
B. 8.5 volts
C. 10.5 volts
D. 12 volts

G6A02
(B)
Page 4-33

G6A02
What is an advantage of the low internal resistance of nickel-cadmium batteries?
A. Long life
B. High discharge current
C. High voltage
D. Rapid recharge

G6A03
(B)
Page 4-20

G6A03
What is the approximate junction threshold voltage of a germanium diode?
A. 0.1 volt
B. 0.3 volts
C. 0.7 volts
D. 1.0 volts

G6A04
(D)
Page 4-33

G6A04
When is it acceptable to recharge a carbon-zinc primary cell?
A. As long as the voltage has not been allowed to drop below 1.0 volt
B. When the cell is kept warm during the recharging period
C. When a constant current charger is used
D. Never

G6A05
(C)
Page 4-20

G6A05
What is the approximate junction threshold voltage of a conventional silicon diode?
A. 0.1 volt
B. 0.3 volts
C. 0.7 volts
D. 1.0 volts

G6A06
(A)
Page 4-21

G6A06
Which of the following is an advantage of using a Schottky diode in an RF switching circuit rather than a standard silicon diode?
A. Lower capacitance
B. Lower inductance
C. Longer switching times
D. Higher breakdown voltage

G6A07
What are the stable operating points for a bipolar transistor used as a switch in a logic circuit?
A. Its saturation and cutoff regions
B. Its active region (between the cutoff and saturation regions)
C. Its peak and valley current points
D. Its enhancement and depletion modes

G6A07
(A)
Page 4-23

G6A08
Why must the cases of some large power transistors be insulated from ground?
A. To increase the beta of the transistor
B. To improve the power dissipation capability
C. To reduce stray capacitance
D. To avoid shorting the collector or drain voltage to ground

G6A08
(D)
Page 4-23

G6A09
Which of the following describes the construction of a MOSFET?
A. The gate is formed by a back-biased junction
B. The gate is separated from the channel with a thin insulating layer
C. The source is separated from the drain by a thin insulating layer
D. The source is formed by depositing metal on silicon

G6A09
(B)
Page 4-22

G6A10
Which element of a triode vacuum tube is used to regulate the flow of electrons between cathode and plate?
A. Control grid
B. Heater
C. Screen Grid
D. Trigger electrode

G6A10
(A)
Page 4-23

G6A11
Which of the following solid state devices is most like a vacuum tube in its general operating characteristics?
A. A bipolar transistor
B. A field effect transistor
C. A tunnel diode
D. A varistor

G6A11
(B)
Page 4-23

G6A12
What is the primary purpose of a screen grid in a vacuum tube?
A. To reduce grid-to-plate capacitance
B. To increase efficiency
C. To increase the control grid resistance
D. To decrease plate resistance

G6A12
(A)
Page 4-23

G6A13
Why is the polarity of applied voltages important for polarized capacitors?
A. Incorrect polarity can cause the capacitor to short-circuit
B. Reverse voltages can destroy the dielectric layer of an electrolytic capacitor
C. The capacitor could overheat and explode
D. All of these choices are correct

G6A13
(D)
Page 4-12

G6A14
(D)
Page 4-11

G6A14
Which of the following is an advantage of ceramic capacitors as compared to other types of capacitors?
A. Tight tolerance
B. High stability
C. High capacitance for given volume
D. Comparatively low cost

G6A15
(C)
Page 4-11

G6A15
Which of the following is an advantage of an electrolytic capacitor?
A. Tight tolerance
B. Much less leakage than any other type
C. High capacitance for a given volume
D. Inexpensive RF capacitor

G6A16
(C)
Page 4-9

G6A16
What will happen to the resistance if the temperature of a resistor is increased?
A. It will change depending on the resistor's reactance coefficient
B. It will stay the same
C. It will change depending on the resistor's temperature coefficient
D. It will become time dependent

G6A17
(B)
Page 4-9

G6A17
Which of the following is a reason not to use wire-wound resistors in an RF circuit?
A. The resistor's tolerance value would not be adequate for such a circuit
B. The resistor's inductance could make circuit performance unpredictable
C. The resistor could overheat
D. The resistor's internal capacitance would detune the circuit

G6A18
(D)
Page 4-11

G6A18
What is an advantage of using a ferrite core toroidal inductor?
A. Large values of inductance may be obtained
B. The magnetic properties of the core may be optimized for a specific range of frequencies
C. Most of the magnetic field is contained in the core
D. All of these choices are correct

G6A19
(C)
Page 4-10

G6A19
How should the winding axes of two solenoid inductors be oriented to minimize their mutual inductance?
A. In line
B. Parallel to each other
C. At right angles to each other
D. Interleaved

G6B — Analog and digital integrated circuits (ICs); microprocessors; memory; I/O devices; microwave ICs (MMICs); display devices

G6B01
Which of the following is an analog integrated circuit?
A. NAND Gate
B. Microprocessor
C. Frequency Counter
D. Linear voltage regulator

G6B01
(D)
Page 4-24

G6B02
What is meant by the term MMIC?
A. Multi Megabyte Integrated Circuit
B. Monolithic Microwave Integrated Circuit
C. Military Manufactured Integrated Circuit
D. Mode Modulated Integrated Circuit

G6B02
(B)
Page 4-26

G6B03
Which of the following is an advantage of CMOS integrated circuits compared to TTL integrated circuits?
A. Low power consumption
B. High power handling capability
C. Better suited for RF amplification
D. Better suited for power supply regulation

G6B03
(A)
Page 4-24

G6B04
What is meant by the term ROM?
A. Resistor Operated Memory
B. Read Only Memory
C. Random Operational Memory
D. Resistant to Overload Memory

G6B04
(B)
Page 4-27

G6B05
What is meant when memory is characterized as non-volatile?
A. It is resistant to radiation damage
B. It is resistant to high temperatures
C. The stored information is maintained even if power is removed
D. The stored information cannot be changed once written

G6B05
(C)
Page 4-27

G6B06
What kind of device is an integrated circuit operational amplifier?
A. Digital
B. MMIC
C. Programmable Logic
D. Analog

G6B06
(D)
Page 4-24

G6B07
Which of the following is an advantage of an LED indicator compared to an incandescent indicator?
A. Lower power consumption
B. Faster response time
C. Longer life
D. All of these choices are correct

G6B07
(D)
Page 4-28

G6B08
(D)
Page 4-28

G6B08
How is an LED biased when emitting light?
A. Beyond cutoff
B. At the Zener voltage
C. Reverse Biased
D. Forward Biased

G6B09
(A)
Page 4-28

G6B09
Which of the following is a characteristic of a liquid crystal display?
A. It requires ambient or back lighting
B. It offers a wide dynamic range
C. It has a wide viewing angle
D. All of these choices are correct

G6B10
(A)
Page 4-27

G6B10
What two devices in an Amateur Radio station might be connected using a USB interface?
A. Computer and transceiver
B. Microphone and transceiver
C. Amplifier and antenna
D. Power supply and amplifier

G6B11
(B)
Page 4-26

G6B11
What is a microprocessor?
A. A low power analog signal processor used as a microwave detector
B. A computer on a single integrated circuit
C. A microwave detector, amplifier, and local oscillator on a single integrated circuit
D. A low voltage amplifier used in a microwave transmitter modulator stage

G6B12
(D)
Page 4-36

G6B12
Which of the following connectors would be a good choice for a serial data port?
A. PL-259
B. Type N
C. Type SMA
D. DE-9

G6B13
(C)
Page 4-36

G6B13
Which of these connector types is commonly used for RF connections at frequencies up to 150 MHz?
A. Octal
B. RJ-11
C. PL-259
D. DB-25

G6B14
(C)
Page 4-35

G6B14
Which of these connector types is commonly used for audio signals in Amateur Radio stations?
A. PL-259
B. BNC
C. RCA Phono
D. Type N

G6B15
(B)
Page 4-34

G6B15
What is the main reason to use keyed connectors instead of non-keyed types?
A. Prevention of use by unauthorized persons
B. Reduced chance of incorrect mating
C. Higher current carrying capacity
D. All of these choices are correct

G6B16

Which of the following describes a type N connector?

A. A moisture-resistant RF connector useful to 10 GHz
B. A small bayonet connector used for data circuits
C. A threaded connector used for hydraulic systems
D. An audio connector used in surround-sound installations

G6B16
(A)
Page 4-36

G6B17

What is the general description of a DIN type connector?

A. A special connector for microwave interfacing
B. A DC power connector rated for currents between 30 and 50 amperes
C. A family of multiple circuit connectors suitable for audio and control signals
D. A special watertight connector for use in marine applications

G6B17
(C)
Page 4-35

G6B18

What is a type SMA connector?

A. A large bayonet connector usable at power levels in excess of 1 KW
B. A small threaded connector suitable for signals up to several GHz
C. A connector designed for serial multiple access signals
D. A type of push-on connector intended for high voltage applications

G6B18
(B)
Page 4-36

G7 — PRACTICAL CIRCUITS

[3 Exam Questions — 3 Groups]

G7A — Power supplies; and schematic symbols

G7A01

What useful feature does a power supply bleeder resistor provide?

A. It acts as a fuse for excess voltage
B. It ensures that the filter capacitors are discharged when power is removed
C. It removes shock hazards from the induction coils
D. It eliminates ground loop current

G7A01
(B)
Page 4-31

G7A02

Which of the following components are used in a power supply filter network?

A. Diodes
B. Transformers and transducers
C. Quartz crystals
D. Capacitors and inductors

G7A02
(D)
Page 4-30

G7A03

What is the peak-inverse-voltage across the rectifiers in a full-wave bridge power supply?

A. One-quarter the normal output voltage of the power supply
B. Half the normal output voltage of the power supply
C. Double the normal peak output voltage of the power supply
D. Equal to the normal peak output voltage of the power supply

G7A03
(D)
Page 4-30

G7A04
What is the peak-inverse-voltage across the rectifier in a half-wave power supply?
A. One-half the normal peak output voltage of the power supply
B. One-half the normal output voltage of the power supply
C. Equal to the normal output voltage of the power supply
D. Two times the normal peak output voltage of the power supply

G7A05
What portion of the AC cycle is converted to DC by a half-wave rectifier?
A. 90 degrees
B. 180 degrees
C. 270 degrees
D. 360 degrees

G7A06
What portion of the AC cycle is converted to DC by a full-wave rectifier?
A. 90 degrees
B. 180 degrees
C. 270 degrees
D. 360 degrees

G7A07
What is the output waveform of an unfiltered full-wave rectifier connected to a resistive load?
A. A series of DC pulses at twice the frequency of the AC input
B. A series of DC pulses at the same frequency as the AC input
C. A sine wave at half the frequency of the AC input
D. A steady DC voltage

G7A08
Which of the following is an advantage of a switchmode power supply as compared to a linear power supply?
A. Faster switching time makes higher output voltage possible
B. Fewer circuit components are required
C. High frequency operation allows the use of smaller components
D. All of these choices are correct

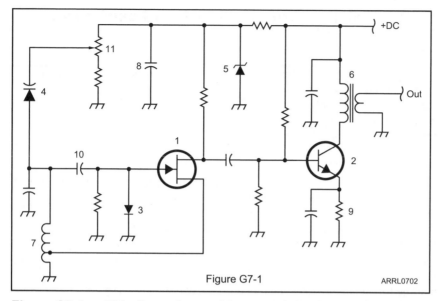

Figure G7-1

ARRL0702

Figure G7-1 — This figure is used for questions G7A09 through G7A13.

G7A09

Which symbol in figure G7-1 represents a field effect transistor?

A. Symbol 2
B. Symbol 5
C. Symbol 1
D. Symbol 4

G7A09
(C)
Page 4-7

G7A10

Which symbol in figure G7-1 represents a Zener diode?

A. Symbol 4
B. Symbol 1
C. Symbol 11
D. Symbol 5

G7A10
(D)
Page 4-7

G7A11

Which symbol in figure G7-1 represents an NPN junction transistor?

A. Symbol 1
B. Symbol 2
C. Symbol 7
D. Symbol 11

G7A11
(B)
Page 4-7

G7A12

Which symbol in Figure G7-1 represents a multiple-winding transformer?

A. Symbol 4
B. Symbol 7
C. Symbol 6
D. Symbol 1

G7A12
(C)
Page 4-7

G7A13

Which symbol in Figure G7-1 represents a tapped inductor?

A. Symbol 7
B. Symbol 11
C. Symbol 6
D. Symbol 1

G7A13
(A)
Page 4-7

G7B — Digital circuits; amplifiers and oscillators

G7B01
(A)
Page 4-26

G7B01
Complex digital circuitry can often be replaced by what type of integrated circuit?
A. Microcontroller
B. Charge-coupled device
C. Phase detector
D. Window comparator

G7B02
(A)
Page 4-24

G7B02
Which of the following is an advantage of using the binary system when processing digital signals?
A. Binary "ones" and "zeros" are easy to represent by an "on" or "off" state
B. The binary number system is most accurate
C. Binary numbers are more compatible with analog circuitry
D. All of these choices are correct

G7B03
(B)
Page 4-25

G7B03
Which of the following describes the function of a two input AND gate?
A. Output is high when either or both inputs are low
B. Output is high only when both inputs are high
C. Output is low when either or both inputs are high
D. Output is low only when both inputs are high

G7B04
(C)
Page 4-25

G7B04
Which of the following describes the function of a two input NOR gate?
A. Output is high when either or both inputs are low
B. Output is high only when both inputs are high
C. Output is low when either or both inputs are high
D. Output is low only when both inputs are high

G7B05
(C)
Page 4-26

G7B05
How many states does a 3-bit binary counter have?
A. 3
B. 6
C. 8
D. 16

G7B06
(A)
Page 4-26

G7B06
What is a shift register?
A. A clocked array of circuits that passes data in steps along the array
B. An array of operational amplifiers used for tri-state arithmetic operations
C. A digital mixer
D. An analog mixer

G7B07
(D)
Page 5-3

G7B07
What are the basic components of virtually all sine wave oscillators?
A. An amplifier and a divider
B. A frequency multiplier and a mixer
C. A circulator and a filter operating in a feed-forward loop
D. A filter and an amplifier operating in a feedback loop

G7B08
(B)
Page 5-13

G7B08
How is the efficiency of an RF power amplifier determined?
A. Divide the DC input power by the DC output power
B. Divide the RF output power by the DC input power
C. Multiply the RF input power by the reciprocal of the RF output power
D. Add the RF input power to the DC output power

G7B09

What determines the frequency of an LC oscillator?

A. The number of stages in the counter
B. The number of stages in the divider
C. The inductance and capacitance in the tank circuit
D. The time delay of the lag circuit

G7B09
(C)
Page 5-3

G7B10

Which of the following is a characteristic of a Class A amplifier?

A. Low standby power
B. High Efficiency
C. No need for bias
D. Low distortion

G7B10
(D)
Page 5-12

G7B11

For which of the following modes is a Class C power stage appropriate for amplifying a modulated signal?

A. SSB
B. CW
C. AM
D. All of these choices are correct

G7B11
(B)
Page 5-13

G7B12

Which of these classes of amplifiers has the highest efficiency?

A. Class A
B. Class B
C. Class AB
D. Class C

G7B12
(D)
Page 5-13

G7B13

What is the reason for neutralizing the final amplifier stage of a transmitter?

A. To limit the modulation index
B. To eliminate self-oscillations
C. To cut off the final amplifier during standby periods
D. To keep the carrier on frequency

G7B13
(B)
Page 5-14

G7B14

Which of the following describes a linear amplifier?

A. Any RF power amplifier used in conjunction with an amateur transceiver
B. An amplifier in which the output preserves the input waveform
C. A Class C high efficiency amplifier
D. An amplifier used as a frequency multiplier

G7B14
(B)
Page 5-12

G7C — Receivers and transmitters; filters, oscillators

G7C01

Which of the following is used to process signals from the balanced modulator then send them to the mixer in some single sideband phone transmitters?

A. Carrier oscillator
B. Filter
C. IF amplifier
D. RF amplifier

G7C01
(B)
Page 5-8

G7C02

Which circuit is used to combine signals from the carrier oscillator and speech amplifier then send the result to the filter in some single sideband phone transmitters?

A. Discriminator
B. Detector
C. IF amplifier
D. Balanced modulator

G7C03

What circuit is used to process signals from the RF amplifier and local oscillator then send the result to the IF filter in a superheterodyne receiver?

A. Balanced modulator
B. IF amplifier
C. Mixer
D. Detector

G7C04

What circuit is used to combine signals from the IF amplifier and BFO and send the result to the AF amplifier in some single sideband receivers?

A. RF oscillator
B. IF filter
C. Balanced modulator
D. Product detector

G7C05

Which of the following is an advantage of a transceiver controlled by a direct digital synthesizer (DDS)?

A. Wide tuning range and no need for band switching
B. Relatively high power output
C. Relatively low power consumption
D. Variable frequency with the stability of a crystal oscillator

G7C06

What should be the impedance of a low-pass filter as compared to the impedance of the transmission line into which it is inserted?

A. Substantially higher
B. About the same
C. Substantially lower
D. Twice the transmission line impedance

G7C07

What is the simplest combination of stages that implement a superheterodyne receiver?

A. RF amplifier, detector, audio amplifier
B. RF amplifier, mixer, IF discriminator
C. HF oscillator, mixer, detector
D. HF oscillator, prescaler, audio amplifier

G7C08

What type of circuit is used in many FM receivers to convert signals coming from the IF amplifier to audio?

A. Product detector
B. Phase inverter
C. Mixer
D. Discriminator

G7C09
Which of the following is needed for a Digital Signal Processor IF filter?
A. An analog to digital converter
B. A digital to analog converter
C. A digital processor chip
D. All of the these choices are correct

G7C09
(D)
Page 5-16

G7C10
How is Digital Signal Processor filtering accomplished?
A. By using direct signal phasing
B. By converting the signal from analog to digital and using digital processing
C. By differential spurious phasing
D. By converting the signal from digital to analog and taking the difference of mixing products

G7C10
(B)
Page 5-16

G7C11
What is meant by the term "software defined radio" (SDR)?
A. A radio in which most major signal processing functions are performed by software
B. A radio that provides computer interface for automatic logging of band and frequency
C. A radio that uses crystal filters designed using software
D. A computer model that can simulate performance of a radio to aid in the design process

G7C11
(A)
Page 5-17

SUBELEMENT G8 — SIGNALS AND EMISSIONS

[3 Exam Questions — 3 Groups]

G8A — Carriers and modulation: AM; FM; single sideband; modulation envelope; digital modulation; overmodulation

G8A01
How is an FSK signal generated?
A. By keying an FM transmitter with a sub-audible tone
B. By changing an oscillator's frequency directly with a digital control signal
C. By using a transceiver's computer data interface protocol to change frequencies
D. By reconfiguring the CW keying input to act as a tone generator

G8A01
(B)
Page 6-5

G8A02
What is the name of the process that changes the phase angle of an RF wave to convey information?
A. Phase convolution
B. Phase modulation
C. Angle convolution
D. Radian inversion

G8A02
(B)
Page 5-2

G8A03
What is the name of the process that changes the instantaneous frequency of an RF wave to convey information?
A. Frequency convolution
B. Frequency transformation
C. Frequency conversion
D. Frequency modulation

G8A03
(D)
Page 5-2

G8A04
What emission is produced by a reactance modulator connected to a transmitter RF amplifier stage?
A. Multiplex modulation
B. Phase modulation
C. Amplitude modulation
D. Pulse modulation

G8A04
(B)
Page 5-6

G8A05
(D)
Page 5-2

G8A05
What type of modulation varies the instantaneous power level of the RF signal?
A. Frequency shift keying
B. Phase modulation
C. Frequency modulation
D. Amplitude modulation

G8A06
(C)
Page 5-6

G8A06
What is one advantage of carrier suppression in a single sideband phone transmission versus full carrier amplitude modulation?
A. Audio fidelity is improved
B. Greater modulation percentage is obtainable with lower distortion
C. Available transmitter power can be used more effectively
D. Simpler receiving equipment can be used

G8A07
(A)
Page 5-2

G8A07
Which of the following phone emissions uses the narrowest bandwidth?
A. Single sideband
B. Double sideband
C. Phase modulation
D. Frequency modulation

G8A08
(D)
Page 5-12

G8A08
Which of the following is an effect of overmodulation?
A. Insufficient audio
B. Insufficient bandwidth
C. Frequency drift
D. Excessive bandwidth

G8A09
(B)
Page 5-11

G8A09
What control is typically adjusted for proper ALC setting on an amateur single sideband transceiver?
A. The RF clipping level
B. Transmit audio or microphone gain
C. Antenna inductance or capacitance
D. Attenuator level

G8A10
(C)
Page 5-11

G8A10
What is meant by the term flat-topping when referring to a single sideband phone transmission?
A. Signal distortion caused by insufficient collector current
B. The transmitter's automatic level control (ALC) is properly adjusted
C. Signal distortion caused by excessive drive
D. The transmitter's carrier is properly suppressed

G8A11
(A)
Page 5-10

G8A11
What is the modulation envelope of an AM signal?
A. The waveform created by connecting the peak values of the modulated signal
B. The carrier frequency that contains the signal
C. Spurious signals that envelop nearby frequencies
D. The bandwidth of the modulated signal

G8B — Frequency mixing; multiplication; bandwidths of various modes; deviation; duty cycle

G8B01
What receiver stage combines a 14.250 MHz input signal with a 13.795 MHz oscillator signal to produce a 455 kHz intermediate frequency (IF) signal?
A. Mixer
B. BFO
C. VFO
D. Discriminator

G8B01
(A)
Page 5-4

G8B02
If a receiver mixes a 13.800 MHz VFO with a 14.255 MHz received signal to produce a 455 kHz intermediate frequency (IF) signal, what type of interference will a 13.345 MHz signal produce in the receiver?
A. Quadrature noise
B. Image response
C. Mixer interference
D. Intermediate interference

G8B02
(B)
Page 5-16

G8B03
What is another term for the mixing of two RF signals?
A. Heterodyning
B. Synthesizing
C. Cancellation
D. Phase inverting

G8B03
(A)
Page 5-4

G8B04
What is the stage in a VHF FM transmitter that generates a harmonic of a lower frequency signal to reach the desired operating frequency?
A. Mixer
B. Reactance modulator
C. Pre-emphasis network
D. Multiplier

G8B04
(D)
Page 5-4

G8B05
What is the approximate bandwidth of a PACTOR3 signal at maximum data rate?
A. 31.5 Hz
B. 500 Hz
C. 1800 Hz
D. 2300 Hz

G8B05
(D)
Page 6-9

G8B06
What is the total bandwidth of an FM phone transmission having 5 kHz deviation and 3 kHz modulating frequency?
A. 3 kHz
B. 5 kHz
C. 8 kHz
D. 16 kHz

G8B06
(D)
Page 5-9

G8B07
What is the frequency deviation for a 12.21 MHz reactance modulated oscillator in a 5 kHz deviation, 146.52 MHz FM phone transmitter?
A. 101.75 Hz
B. 416.7 Hz
C. 5 kHz
D. 60 kHz

G8B07
(B)
Page 5-9

G8B08
(B)
Page 6-10

G8B08
Why is it important to know the duty cycle of the mode you are using when transmitting?
A. To aid in tuning your transmitter
B. Some modes have high duty cycles which could exceed the transmitter's average power rating.
C. To allow time for the other station to break in during a transmission
D. All of these choices are correct

G8B09
(D)
Page 5-16

G8B09
Why is it good to match receiver bandwidth to the bandwidth of the operating mode?
A. It is required by FCC rules
B. It minimizes power consumption in the receiver
C. It improves impedance matching of the antenna
D. It results in the best signal to noise ratio

G8B10
(B)
Page 6-9

G8B10
What is the relationship between transmitted symbol rate and bandwidth?
A. Symbol rate and bandwidth are not related
B. Higher symbol rates require wider bandwidth
C. Lower symbol rates require wider bandwidth
D. Bandwidth is always half the symbol rate

G8C — Digital emission modes

G8C01
(B)
Page 6-3

G8C01
Which of the following digital modes is designed to operate at extremely low signal strength on the HF bands?
A. FSK441 and Hellschreiber
B. JT9 and JT65
C. Clover
D. RTTY

G8C02
(A)
Page 6-7

G8C02
How many data bits are sent in a single PSK31 character?
A. The number varies
B. 5
C. 7
D. 8

G8C03
(C)
Page 6-7

G8C03
What part of a data packet contains the routing and handling information?
A. Directory
B. Preamble
C. Header
D. Footer

G8C04
(C)
Page 6-6

G8C04
Which of the following describes Baudot code?
A. A 7-bit code with start, stop and parity bits
B. A code using error detection and correction
C. A 5-bit code with additional start and stop bits
D. A code using SELCAL and LISTEN

G8C05
In the PACTOR protocol, what is meant by an NAK response to a transmitted packet?
A. The receiver is requesting the packet be retransmitted
B. The receiver is reporting the packet was received without error
C. The receiver is busy decoding the packet
D. The entire file has been received correctly

G8C05
(A)
Page 6-8

G8C06
What action results from a failure to exchange information due to excessive transmission attempts when using PACTOR or WINMOR?
A. The checksum overflows
B. The connection is dropped
C. Packets will be routed incorrectly
D. Encoding reverts to the default character set

G8C06
(B)
Page 6-13

G8C07
How does the receiving station respond to an ARQ data mode packet containing errors?
A. It terminates the contact
B. It requests the packet be retransmitted
C. It sends the packet back to the transmitting station
D. It requests a change in transmitting protocol

G8C07
(B)
Page 6-8

G8C08
Which of the following statements is true about PSK31?
A. Upper case letters make the signal stronger
B. Upper case letters use longer Varicode signals and thus slow down transmission
C. Varicode Error Correction is used to ensure accurate message reception
D. Higher power is needed as compared to RTTY for similar error rates

G8C08
(B)
Page 6-7

G8C09
What does the number 31 represent in "PSK31"?
A. The approximate transmitted symbol rate
B. The version of the PSK protocol
C. The year in which PSK31 was invented
D. The number of characters that can be represented by PSK31

G8C09
(A)
Page 6-6

G8C10
How does forward error correction (FEC) allow the receiver to correct errors in received data packets?
A. By controlling transmitter output power for optimum signal strength
B. By using the varicode character set
C. By transmitting redundant information with the data
D. By using a parity bit with each character

G8C10
(C)
Page 6-8

G8C11
How are the two separate frequencies of a Frequency Shift Keyed (FSK) signal identified?
A. Dot and Dash
B. On and Off
C. High and Low
D. Mark and Space

G8C11
(D)
Page 6-5

G8C12
Which type of code is used for sending characters in a PSK31 signal?
A. Varicode
B. Viterbi
C. Volumetric
D. Binary

G8C12
(A)
Page 6-7

SUBELEMENT G9 — ANTENNAS AND FEED LINES
[4 Exam Questions — 4 Groups]

G9A — Antenna feed lines: characteristic impedance, and attenuation; SWR calculation, measurement and effects; matching networks

G9A01
(A)
Page 7-17

G9A01
Which of the following factors determine the characteristic impedance of a parallel conductor antenna feed line?
A.   The distance between the centers of the conductors and the radius of the conductors
B.   The distance between the centers of the conductors and the length of the line
C.   The radius of the conductors and the frequency of the signal
D.   The frequency of the signal and the length of the line

G9A02
(B)
Page 7-18

G9A02
What are the typical characteristic impedances of coaxial cables used for antenna feed lines at amateur stations?
A.   25 and 30 ohms
B.   50 and 75 ohms
C.   80 and 100 ohms
D.   500 and 750 ohms

G9A03
(D)
Page 7-17

G9A03
What is the characteristic impedance of flat ribbon TV type twinlead?
A.   50 ohms
B.   75 ohms
C.   100 ohms
D.   300 ohms

G9A04
(C)
Page 7-18

G9A04
What might cause reflected power at the point where a feed line connects to an antenna?
A.   Operating an antenna at its resonant frequency
B.   Using more transmitter power than the antenna can handle
C.   A difference between feed line impedance and antenna feed point impedance
D.   Feeding the antenna with unbalanced feed line

G9A05
(B)
Page 7-20

G9A05
How does the attenuation of coaxial cable change as the frequency of the signal it is carrying increases?
A.   Attenuation is independent of frequency
B.   Attenuation increases
C.   Attenuation decreases
D.   Attenuation reaches a maximum at approximately 18 MHz

G9A06
(D)
Page 7-20

G9A06
In what units is RF feed line loss usually expressed?
A.   Ohms per 1000 feet
B.   Decibels per 1000 feet
C.   Ohms per 100 feet
D.   Decibels per 100 feet

G9A07

What must be done to prevent standing waves on an antenna feed line?

A. The antenna feed point must be at DC ground potential

B. The feed line must be cut to a length equal to an odd number of electrical quarter wavelengths

C. The feed line must be cut to a length equal to an even number of physical half wavelengths

D. The antenna feed point impedance must be matched to the characteristic impedance of the feed line

G9A07
(D)
Page 7-19

G9A08

If the SWR on an antenna feed line is 5 to 1, and a matching network at the transmitter end of the feed line is adjusted to 1 to 1 SWR, what is the resulting SWR on the feed line?

A. 1 to 1

B. 5 to 1

C. Between 1 to 1 and 5 to 1 depending on the characteristic impedance of the line

D. Between 1 to 1 and 5 to 1 depending on the reflected power at the transmitter

G9A08
(B)
Page 7-19

G9A09

What standing wave ratio will result when connecting a 50 ohm feed line to a non-reactive load having 200 ohm impedance?

A. 4:1

B. 1:4

C. 2:1

D. 1:2

G9A09
(A)
Page 7-18

G9A10

What standing wave ratio will result when connecting a 50 ohm feed line to a non-reactive load having 10 ohm impedance?

A. 2:1

B. 50:1

C. 1:5

D. 5:1

G9A10
(D)
Page 7-18

G9A11

What standing wave ratio will result when connecting a 50 ohm feed line to a non-reactive load having 50 ohm impedance?

A. 2:1

B. 1:1

C. 50:50

D. 0:0

G9A11
(B)
Page 7-18

G9A12

What standing wave ratio will result when connecting a 50 ohm feed line to a non-reactive load having 25 ohm impedance?

A. 2:1

B. 2.5:1

C. 1.25:1

D. You cannot determine SWR from impedance values

G9A12
(A)
Page 7-18

G9A13

What standing wave ratio will result when connecting a 50 ohm feed line to an antenna that has a purely resistive 300 ohm feed point impedance?

A. 1.5:1

B. 3:1

C. 6:1

D. You cannot determine SWR from impedance values

G9A13
(C)
Page 7-18

G9A14
(B)
Page 7-20

G9A14
What is the interaction between high standing wave ratio (SWR) and transmission line loss?
A. There is no interaction between transmission line loss and SWR
B. If a transmission line is lossy, high SWR will increase the loss
C. High SWR makes it difficult to measure transmission line loss
D. High SWR reduces the relative effect of transmission line loss

G9A15
(A)
Page 7-20

G9A15
What is the effect of transmission line loss on SWR measured at the input to the line?
A. The higher the transmission line loss, the more the SWR will read artificially low
B. The higher the transmission line loss, the more the SWR will read artificially high
C. The higher the transmission line loss, the more accurate the SWR measurement will be
D. Transmission line loss does not affect the SWR measurement

G9B — Basic antennas

G9B01
(B)
Page 7-5

G9B01
What is one disadvantage of a directly fed random-wire HF antenna?
A. It must be longer than 1 wavelength
B. You may experience RF burns when touching metal objects in your station
C. It produces only vertically polarized radiation
D. It is more effective on the lower HF bands than on the higher bands

G9B02
(B)
Page 7-4

G9B02
Which of the following is a common way to adjust the feed point impedance of a quarter wave ground plane vertical antenna to be approximately 50 ohms?
A. Slope the radials upward
B. Slope the radials downward
C. Lengthen the radials
D. Shorten the radials

G9B03
(B)
Page 7-4

G9B03
What happens to the feed point impedance of a ground plane antenna when its radials are changed from horizontal to sloping downward?
A. It decreases
B. It increases
C. It stays the same
D. It reaches a maximum at an angle of 45 degrees

G9B04
(A)
Page 7-2

G9B04
What is the radiation pattern of a dipole antenna in free space in the plane of the conductor?
A. It is a figure-eight at right angles to the antenna
B. It is a figure-eight off both ends of the antenna
C. It is a circle (equal radiation in all directions)
D. It has a pair of lobes on one side of the antenna and a single lobe on the other side

G9B05
(C)
Page 7-6

G9B05
How does antenna height affect the horizontal (azimuthal) radiation pattern of a horizontal dipole HF antenna?
A. If the antenna is too high, the pattern becomes unpredictable
B. Antenna height has no effect on the pattern
C. If the antenna is less than 1/2 wavelength high, the azimuthal pattern is almost omnidirectional
D. If the antenna is less than 1/2 wavelength high, radiation off the ends of the wire is eliminated

G9B06
Where should the radial wires of a ground-mounted vertical antenna system be placed?
A. As high as possible above the ground
B. Parallel to the antenna element
C. On the surface of the Earth or buried a few inches below the ground
D. At the center of the antenna

G9B07
How does the feed point impedance of a 1/2 wave dipole antenna change as the antenna is lowered below 1/4 wave above ground?
A. It steadily increases
B. It steadily decreases
C. It peaks at about 1/8 wavelength above ground
D. It is unaffected by the height above ground

G9B08
How does the feed point impedance of a 1/2 wave dipole change as the feed point is moved from the center toward the ends?
A. It steadily increases
B. It steadily decreases
C. It peaks at about 1/8 wavelength from the end
D. It is unaffected by the location of the feed point

G9B09
Which of the following is an advantage of a horizontally polarized as compared to a vertically polarized HF antenna?
A. Lower ground reflection losses
B. Lower feed point impedance
C. Shorter Radials
D. Lower radiation resistance

G9B10
What is the approximate length for a 1/2 wave dipole antenna cut for 14.250 MHz?
A. 8 feet
B. 16 feet
C. 24 feet
D. 32 feet

G9B11
What is the approximate length for a 1/2 wave dipole antenna cut for 3.550 MHz?
A. 42 feet
B. 84 feet
C. 131 feet
D. 263 feet

G9B12
What is the approximate length for a 1/4 wave vertical antenna cut for 28.5 MHz?
A. 8 feet
B. 11 feet
C. 16 feet
D. 21 feet

G9B06
(C)
Page 7-4

G9B07
(B)
Page 7-6

G9B08
(A)
Page 7-2

G9B09
(A)
Page 7-7

G9B10
(D)
Page 7-3

G9B11
(C)
Page 7-3

G9B12
(A)
Page 7-4

G9C — Directional antennas

G9C01
Which of the following would increase the bandwidth of a Yagi antenna?
A. Larger diameter elements
B. Closer element spacing
C. Loading coils in series with the element
D. Tapered-diameter elements

G9C02
What is the approximate length of the driven element of a Yagi antenna?
A. 1/4 wavelength
B. 1/2 wavelength
C. 3/4 wavelength
D. 1 wavelength

G9C03
Which statement about a three-element, single-band Yagi antenna is true?
A. The reflector is normally the shortest element
B. The director is normally the shortest element
C. The driven element is the longest element
D. Low feed point impedance increases bandwidth

G9C04
Which statement about a three-element, single-band Yagi antenna is true?
A. The reflector is normally the longest element
B. The director is normally the longest element
C. The reflector is normally the shortest element
D. All of the elements must be the same length

G9C05
How does increasing boom length and adding directors affect a Yagi antenna?
A. Gain increases
B. Beamwidth increases
C. Front to back ratio decreases
D. Front to side ratio decreases

G9C06
What configuration of the loops of a two-element quad antenna must be used for the antenna to operate as a beam antenna, assuming one of the elements is used as a reflector?
A. The driven element must be fed with a balun transformer
B. There must be an open circuit in the driven element at the point opposite the feed point
C. The reflector element must be approximately 5 percent shorter than the driven element
D. The reflector element must be approximately 5 percent longer than the driven element

G9C07
What does "front-to-back ratio" mean in reference to a Yagi antenna?
A. The number of directors versus the number of reflectors
B. The relative position of the driven element with respect to the reflectors and directors
C. The power radiated in the major radiation lobe compared to the power radiated in exactly the opposite direction
D. The ratio of forward gain to dipole gain

G9C08
What is meant by the "main lobe" of a directive antenna?
A. The magnitude of the maximum vertical angle of radiation
B. The point of maximum current in a radiating antenna element
C. The maximum voltage standing wave point on a radiating element
D. The direction of maximum radiated field strength from the antenna

G9C09
How does the gain of two 3-element horizontally polarized Yagi antennas spaced vertically 1/2 wavelength apart typically compare to the gain of a single 3-element Yagi?
A. Approximately 1.5 dB higher
B. Approximately 3 dB higher
C. Approximately 6 dB higher
D. Approximately 9 dB higher

G9C10
Which of the following is a Yagi antenna design variable that could be adjusted to optimize forward gain, front-to-back ratio, or SWR bandwidth?
A. The physical length of the boom
B. The number of elements on the boom
C. The spacing of each element along the boom
D. All of these choices are correct

G9C11
What is the purpose of a gamma match used with Yagi antennas?
A. To match the relatively low feed point impedance to 50 ohms
B. To match the relatively high feed point impedance to 50 ohms
C. To increase the front-to-back ratio
D. To increase the main lobe gain

G9C12
Which of the following is an advantage of using a gamma match for impedance matching of a Yagi antenna to 50 ohm coax feed line?
A. It does not require that the elements be insulated from the boom
B. It does not require any inductors or capacitors
C. It is useful for matching multiband antennas
D. All of these choices are correct

G9C13
Approximately how long is each side of the driven element of a quad antenna?
A. 1/4 wavelength
B. 1/2 wavelength
C. 3/4 wavelength
D. 1 wavelength

G9C14
How does the forward gain of a two-element quad antenna compare to the forward gain of a three-element Yagi antenna?
A. About 2/3 as much
B. About the same
C. About 1.5 times as much
D. About twice as much

G9C08
(D)
Page 7-9

G9C09
(B)
Page 7-14

G9C10
(D)
Page 7-10

G9C11
(A)
Page 7-10

G9C12
(A)
Page 7-11

G9C13
(A)
Page 7-12

G9C14
(B)
Page 7-12

G9C15

Approximately how long is each side of the reflector element of a quad antenna?

A. Slightly less than 1/4 wavelength
B. Slightly more than 1/4 wavelength
C. Slightly less than 1/2 wavelength
D. Slightly more than 1/2 wavelength

G9C16

How does the gain of a two-element delta-loop beam compare to the gain of a two-element quad antenna?

A. 3 dB higher
B. 3 dB lower
C. 2.54 dB higher
D. About the same

G9C17

Approximately how long is each leg of a symmetrical delta-loop antenna?

A. 1/4 wavelength
B. 1/3 wavelength
C. 1/2 wavelength
D. 2/3 wavelength

G9C18

What happens when the feed point of a quad antenna of any shape is moved from the midpoint of the top or bottom to the midpoint of either side?

A. The polarization of the radiated signal changes from horizontal to vertical
B. The polarization of the radiated signal changes from vertical to horizontal
C. There is no change in polarization
D. The radiated signal becomes circularly polarized

G9C19

How does antenna gain stated in dBi compare to gain stated in dBd for the same antenna?

A. dBi gain figures are 2.15 dB lower then dBd gain figures
B. dBi gain figures are 2.15 dB higher than dBd gain figures
C. dBi gain figures are the same as the square root of dBd gain figures multiplied by 2.15
D. dBi gain figures are the reciprocal of dBd gain figures + 2.15 dB

G9C20

What is meant by the terms dBi and dBd when referring to antenna gain?

A. dBi refers to an isotropic antenna, dBd refers to a dipole antenna
B. dBi refers to an ionospheric reflecting antenna, dBd refers to a dissipative antenna
C. dBi refers to an inverted-vee antenna, dBd refers to a downward reflecting antenna
D. dBi refers to an isometric antenna, dBd refers to a discone antenna

G9D — Specialized antennas

G9D01

What does the term NVIS mean as related to antennas?

A. Nearly Vertical Inductance System
B. Non-Varying Indicated SWR
C. Non-Varying Impedance Smoothing
D. Near Vertical Incidence sky-wave

G9D02
Which of the following is an advantage of an NVIS antenna?
A. Low vertical angle radiation for working stations out to ranges of several thousand kilometers
B. High vertical angle radiation for working stations within a radius of a few hundred kilometers
C. High forward gain
D. All of these choices are correct

G9D03
At what height above ground is an NVIS antenna typically installed?
A. As close to 1/2 wavelength as possible
B. As close to one wavelength as possible
C. Height is not critical as long as it is significantly more than 1/2 wavelength
D. Between 1/10 and 1/4 wavelength

G9D04
What is the primary purpose of antenna traps?
A. To permit multiband operation
B. To notch spurious frequencies
C. To provide balanced feed point impedance
D. To prevent out of band operation

G9D05
What is an advantage of vertical stacking of horizontally polarized Yagi antennas?
A. It allows quick selection of vertical or horizontal polarization
B. It allows simultaneous vertical and horizontal polarization
C. It narrows the main lobe in azimuth
D. It narrows the main lobe in elevation

G9D06
Which of the following is an advantage of a log periodic antenna?
A. Wide bandwidth
B. Higher gain per element than a Yagi antenna
C. Harmonic suppression
D. Polarization diversity

G9D07
Which of the following describes a log periodic antenna?
A. Length and spacing of the elements increase logarithmically from one end of the boom to the other
B. Impedance varies periodically as a function of frequency
C. Gain varies logarithmically as a function of frequency
D. SWR varies periodically as a function of boom length

G9D08
Why is a Beverage antenna not used for transmitting?
A. Its impedance is too low for effective matching
B. It has high losses compared to other types of antennas
C. It has poor directivity
D. All of these choices are correct

G9D09
Which of the following is an application for a Beverage antenna?
A. Directional transmitting for low HF bands
B. Directional receiving for low HF bands
C. Portable direction finding at higher HF frequencies
D. Portable direction finding at lower HF frequencies

G9D02
(B)
Page 7-13

G9D03
(D)
Page 7-14

G9D04
(A)
Page 7-16

G9D05
(D)
Page 7-14

G9D06
(A)
Page 7-14

G9D07
(A)
Page 7-14

G9D08
(B)
Page 7-15

G9D09
(B)
Page 7-15

G9D10
(D)
Page 7-15

G9D10
Which of the following describes a Beverage antenna?
A. A vertical antenna
B. A broad-band mobile antenna
C. A helical antenna for space reception
D. A very long and low directional receiving antenna

G9D11
(D)
Page 7-16

G9D11
Which of the following is a disadvantage of multiband antennas?
A. They present low impedance on all design frequencies
B. They must be used with an antenna tuner
C. They must be fed with open wire line
D. They have poor harmonic rejection

SUBELEMENT G0 — ELECTRICAL AND RF SAFETY
[2 Exam Questions — 2 Groups]

G0A — RF safety principles, rules and guidelines; routine station evaluation

G0A01
(A)
Page 9-8

G0A01
What is one way that RF energy can affect human body tissue?
A. It heats body tissue
B. It causes radiation poisoning
C. It causes the blood count to reach a dangerously low level
D. It cools body tissue

G0A02
(D)
Page 9-7

G0A02
Which of the following properties is important in estimating whether an RF signal exceeds the maximum permissible exposure (MPE)?
A. Its duty cycle
B. Its frequency
C. Its power density
D. All of these choices are correct

G0A03
(D)
[97.13(c)(1)]
Page 9-10

G0A03
How can you determine that your station complies with FCC RF exposure regulations?
A. By calculation based on FCC OET Bulletin 65
B. By calculation based on computer modeling
C. By measurement of field strength using calibrated equipment
D. All of these choices are correct

G0A04
(D)
Page 9-9

G0A04
What does "time averaging" mean in reference to RF radiation exposure?
A. The average amount of power developed by the transmitter over a specific 24 hour period
B. The average time it takes RF radiation to have any long-term effect on the body
C. The total time of the exposure
D. The total RF exposure averaged over a certain time

G0A05
What must you do if an evaluation of your station shows RF energy radiated from your station exceeds permissible limits?
A. Take action to prevent human exposure to the excessive RF fields
B. File an Environmental Impact Statement (EIS-97) with the FCC
C. Secure written permission from your neighbors to operate above the controlled MPE limits
D. All of these choices are correct

G0A05 (A) Page 9-11

G0A06
What precaution should be taken when installing a ground-mounted antenna?
A. It should not be installed higher than you can reach
B. It should not be installed in a wet area
C. It should limited to 10 feet in height
D. It should be installed such that it is protected against unauthorized access

G0A06 (D) Page 9-11

G0A07
What effect does transmitter duty cycle have when evaluating RF exposure?
A. A lower transmitter duty cycle permits greater short-term exposure levels
B. A higher transmitter duty cycle permits greater short-term exposure levels
C. Low duty cycle transmitters are exempt from RF exposure evaluation requirements
D. High duty cycle transmitters are exempt from RF exposure requirements

G0A07 (A) Page 9-9

G0A08
Which of the following steps must an amateur operator take to ensure compliance with RF safety regulations when transmitter power exceeds levels specified in FCC Part 97.13?
A. Post a copy of FCC Part 97.13 in the station
B. Post a copy of OET Bulletin 65 in the station
C. Perform a routine RF exposure evaluation
D. All of these choices are correct

G0A08 (C) Page 9-10

G0A09
What type of instrument can be used to accurately measure an RF field?
A. A receiver with an S meter
B. A calibrated field strength meter with a calibrated antenna
C. An SWR meter with a peak-reading function
D. An oscilloscope with a high-stability crystal marker generator

G0A09 (B) Page 9-10

G0A10
What is one thing that can be done if evaluation shows that a neighbor might receive more than the allowable limit of RF exposure from the main lobe of a directional antenna?
A. Change to a non-polarized antenna with higher gain
B. Post a warning sign that is clearly visible to the neighbor
C. Use an antenna with a higher front-to-back ratio
D. Take precautions to ensure that the antenna cannot be pointed in their direction

G0A10 (D) Page 9-11

G0A11
What precaution should you take if you install an indoor transmitting antenna?
A. Locate the antenna close to your operating position to minimize feed line radiation
B. Position the antenna along the edge of a wall to reduce parasitic radiation
C. Make sure that MPE limits are not exceeded in occupied areas
D. Make sure the antenna is properly shielded

G0A11 (C) Page 9-12

G0A12
(B)
Page 9-13

G0A12
What precaution should you take whenever you make adjustments or repairs to an antenna?
A. Ensure that you and the antenna structure are grounded
B. Turn off the transmitter and disconnect the feed line
C. Wear a radiation badge
D. All of these choices are correct

G0B — Safety in the ham shack: electrical shock and treatment, safety grounding, fusing, interlocks, wiring, antenna and tower safety

G0B01
(A)
Page 9-5

G0B01
Which wire or wires in a four-conductor connection should be attached to fuses or circuit breakers in a device operated from a 240 VAC single phase source?
A. Only the two wires carrying voltage
B. Only the neutral wire
C. Only the ground wire
D. All wires

G0B02
(C)
Page 9-4

G0B02
What is the minimum wire size that may be safely used for a circuit that draws up to 20 amperes of continuous current?
A. AWG number 20
B. AWG number 16
C. AWG number 12
D. AWG number 8

G0B03
(D)
Page 9-4

G0B03
Which size of fuse or circuit breaker would be appropriate to use with a circuit that uses AWG number 14 wiring?
A. 100 amperes
B. 60 amperes
C. 30 amperes
D. 15 amperes

G0B04
(A)
Page 9-6

G0B04
Which of the following is a primary reason for not placing a gasoline-fueled generator inside an occupied area?
A. Danger of carbon monoxide poisoning
B. Danger of engine over torque
C. Lack of oxygen for adequate combustion
D. Lack of nitrogen for adequate combustion

G0B05
(B)
Page 9-5

G0B05
Which of the following conditions will cause a Ground Fault Circuit Interrupter (GFCI) to disconnect the 120 or 240 Volt AC line power to a device?
A. Current flowing from one or more of the voltage-carrying wires to the neutral wire
B. Current flowing from one or more of the voltage-carrying wires directly to ground
C. Overvoltage on the voltage-carrying wires
D. All of these choices are correct

G0B06
Why must the metal enclosure of every item of station equipment be grounded?
A. It prevents a blown fuse in the event of an internal short circuit
B. It prevents signal overload
C. It ensures that the neutral wire is grounded
D. It ensures that hazardous voltages cannot appear on the chassis

G0B06
(D)
Page 9-4

G0B07
Which of these choices should be observed when climbing a tower using a safety belt or harness?
A. Never lean back and rely on the belt alone to support your weight
B. Confirm that the belt is rated for the weight of the climber and that it is within its allowable service life
C. Ensure that all heavy tools are securely fastened to the belt D-ring
D. All of these choices are correct

G0B07
(B)
Page 9-14

G0B08
What should be done by any person preparing to climb a tower that supports electrically powered devices?
A. Notify the electric company that a person will be working on the tower
B. Make sure all circuits that supply power to the tower are locked out and tagged
C. Unground the base of the tower
D. All of these choices are correct

G0B08
(B)
Page 9-13

G0B09
Why should soldered joints not be used with the wires that connect the base of a tower to a system of ground rods?
A. The resistance of solder is too high
B. Solder flux will prevent a low conductivity connection
C. Solder has too high a dielectric constant to provide adequate lightning protection
D. A soldered joint will likely be destroyed by the heat of a lightning strike

G0B09
(D)
Page 9-7

G0B10
Which of the following is a danger from lead-tin solder?
A. Lead can contaminate food if hands are not washed carefully after handling the solder
B. High voltages can cause lead-tin solder to disintegrate suddenly
C. Tin in the solder can "cold flow" causing shorts in the circuit
D. RF energy can convert the lead into a poisonous gas

G0B10
(A)
Page 9-2

G0B11
Which of the following is good practice for lightning protection grounds?
A. They must be bonded to all buried water and gas lines
B. Bends in ground wires must be made as close as possible to a right angle
C. Lightning grounds must be connected to all ungrounded wiring
D. They must be bonded together with all other grounds

G0B11
(D)
Page 9-7

G0B12
What is the purpose of a power supply interlock?
A. To prevent unauthorized changes to the circuit that would void the manufacturer's warranty
B. To shut down the unit if it becomes too hot
C. To ensure that dangerous voltages are removed if the cabinet is opened
D. To shut off the power supply if too much voltage is produced

G0B12
(C)
Page 9-5

G0B13
(A)
Page 9-6

G0B13
What must you do when powering your house from an emergency generator?
A. Disconnect the incoming utility power feed
B. Insure that the generator is not grounded
C. Insure that all lightning grounds are disconnected
D. All of these choices are correct

G0B14
(C)
Page 9-3

G0B14
Which of the following is covered by the National Electrical Code?
A. Acceptable bandwidth limits
B. Acceptable modulation limits
C. Electrical safety inside the ham shack
D. RF exposure limits of the human body

G0B15
(A)
Page 9-6

G0B15
Which of the following is true of an emergency generator installation?
A. The generator should be located in a well-ventilated area
B. The generator must be insulated from ground
C. Fuel should be stored near the generator for rapid refueling in case of an emergency
D. All of these choices are correct

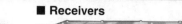

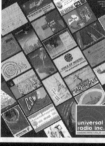

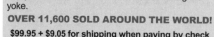
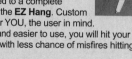

The perfect complement to this book:

HF + 6m Transceiver
IC-7200

- 100 Watt Output (25W AM)
- RX: 0.030–60.000MHz*
- Digital Twin Passband Tuning
- USB Port for CI-V Format PC Control and Audio In/Out
- Flexible Selectable Filter Width and Shape

HF/VHF/UHF Transceiver
IC-7100

- Intuitive Touch Screen Interface
- 100/100/50/35 Watt Output*
- RX: 0.03-199.999, 400-470MHz*
- 1205 Alphanumeric Memory Channels
- 32-bit IF-DSP
- Built-in Digital IF Filtering
- USB (Audio & Radio Control)
- External GPS Option
- Built-in SD Card Slot

HF + 6m Transceiver
IC-7410

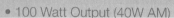

- 100 Watt Output (40W AM)
- RX: 0.030–60.000MHz*
- 32 Bit Floating Point DSP Unit
- +30 dBm 3rd Order Intercept Point (14MHz)
- Double Conversion Super-heterodyne System
- Built-in 15kHz 1st IF Filter (Optional 3kHz/6kHz)

Extend your Reach

#IcomAmateur

Information & Downloads

AMATEUR TOOL KIT | COMIC BOOKS | VIDEOS | WWW.ICOMAMERICA.COM

Electronic advertisements feature active links.

iCOM

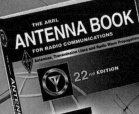

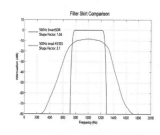
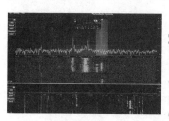

INDEX

APR -- 2016